HOLY WAR, HOLY PEACE

Holy War, Holy Peace

*How Religion Can Bring Peace
to the Middle East*

MARC GOPIN

OXFORD
UNIVERSITY PRESS

OXFORD
UNIVERSITY PRESS

Oxford University Press, Inc., publishes works that further
Oxford University's objective of excellence
in research, scholarship, and education.

Orford   New York
Auckland   Cape Town   Dar es Salaam   Hong Kong   Karachi
Kuala Lumpur   Madrid   Melbourne   Mexico City   Nairobi
New Delhi   Shanghai   Taipei   Toronto

With offices in
Argentina   Austria   Brazil   Chile   Czech Republic   France   Greece
Guatemala   Hungary   Italy   Japan   Poland   Portugal   Singapore
South Korea   Switzerland   Thailand   Turkey   Ukraine   Vietnam

First published in 2002 by Oxford University Press, Inc.
198 Madison Avenue, New York, New York 10016

First issued as an Oxford University Press paperback, 2005

www.oup.com

Oxford is a registered trademark of Oxford University Press

Library of Congress Cataloging-in-Publication Data
Gopin, Marc.
Holy war, holy peace : how religion can bring peace to the Middle East
Marc Gopin.
    p. cm.
Includes bibliographical references and index.
ISBN 978-0-19-514650-9; 978-0-19-518103-6 (pbk.)

1. Arab-Israeli conflict—1993—Peace.   2. Arab-Israeli conflict—Religious aspects.
3. Religion and politics—Middle East.   I. Title.
DS119.76 .G67 2002
956.05—dc21   2001035850

9 8 7 6 5 4 3 2

Printed in the United States of America
on acid-free paper

To Ruth Sarah Gopin, my daughter Ruthie

I write this for you to give you a spiritual path for the future,
a way to be a proud Jew, a Jew who heals, a Jew who loves, who
hates only hatred, who forgives for the sake of life,
and for the sake of the Divine Spirit that inhabits all things.
I give you a way for us to be together always.
Find me here if you should ever miss me.

Acknowledgments

I want to thank my colleagues and friends who have supported me in many ways in the course of this difficult work. Entering into the heart of the Israeli-Palestinian conflict and learning how to empathize with the lives and feelings of people on all sides of this tragedy have been wrenching experiences. Sometimes it is difficult to move from day to day, not with the writing, but with the dark knowledge of exactly who of my friends is at risk, who has been hurt, and who has died.

I thank many friends for continuing to support me in this writing, such as David Little, Aviva Bock, Julia Lieblich, Gordie Fellman, Andrea Bartoli, Arnold Resnicoff, Ted Sasson, Roger Hurwitz, Yitshak Melamed, Patrick McNamara, Robert Eisen, and Bob Carroll. In particular I want to mention Kevin Avruch for his intellectual mentoring and personal support, Joseph Montville for his unwavering friendship and devotion to our work, no matter how difficult, and Doug Johnston who has courageously marched forward in this field. I also thank Scott Appleby and Louis Kriesberg, who continue to teach me in many ways. I single out Vamik Volkan, whose psychological genius and personal compassion form the two cornerstones of what I believe the world needs most for a healthy future. I thank him for a lifetime of service, and for teaching my teachers.

With the help of Initiatives for Change (IC), for which I am deeply grateful, Bryan Hamlin and I have been partners on this long journey of Israeli and Palestinian friendships, through the exhilaration of breakthroughs and the heartbreak of witnessing the consequences of human failure. Together we have been committed to the human heart as the source of all the trouble and all future hopes. I honor with all my heart his friendship and courage. I also thank too many other members of IC to mention. Charles and Kathy Aquilina, Pierre and Fulvia Spoerri, Dick and Rande Ruffin, Christoph and Marianne

Spreng, Anne Hamlin, and many others have at times facilitated this difficult process and have been friends to me in the deepest sense.

I thank my students at the Fletcher School of Law and Diplomacy for stimulating my thinking in class. I thank colleagues at Fletcher for being supportive friends and guides, especially Eileen Babbitt, Peter Uvin, Dean Bosworth, Joel Trachtman, and Terry Knopf. I thank many friends at Temple Beth Shalom of Cambridge, an extraordinary group of people who have put up with my passions and heartbreak around Israel, and my obsessions as a writer. I thank the U.S. Institute of Peace and, in particular, David Smock and Judy Barselou for respecting my work and giving me a much-needed boost of personal encouragement at a critical time. I thank my Israeli friends, whose commitment, each in their own way, to peace and compassion bewilders me in its persistence and fills me with wonder at the surprising capabilities of the human spirit: Yehezkel Landau, Betsy Cohen-Kallus, Eliyahu Mclean, Yehuda Stolov, Rabbi Menahem Frohman. As the years pass, I find myself less and less able to convey in words my love for and solidarity with them. To my Palestinian friends, to the Abu Ghazaleh family, and to some of the most honorable men in the security forces who will remain nameless here, I thank you for everything you have taught me, for your graciousness and hospitality, and for your role model of dignity in the worst of circumstances. I wrote this book always with you in mind and with the peace and justice that we can see together before our eyes. And to Sheikh Abu Saleh, a man of unsurpassed spirituality and humanity whose courage in peacemaking is an astonishing teaching for me.

Finally, I thank my family, as always: my wonderful wife, an incredible mother to my daughters, two amazing children, astonishing creations whose gifts, whose beauty, whose laughter and love of life carry me through the most difficult days of my work.

Brookline, Massachusetts　　　　　　　　　　　　　　　　M. G.
March 2001

Contents

I

ANALYSIS

The Interaction between Religion and Culture in Peace and Conflict

The complexity of human social relationships seems to require a degree of healthy conflict, by its very nature.[1] Yet it is clear that what is a normal part of social intercourse often turns into a phenomenon that is destructive to at least one but usually all parties to a conflict over time. This is as true in the life of individuals as it is true in the life of peoples, nations, and religious communities. We all have experienced both productive disagreements as well as destructive conflicts. We all have experienced difficult moments of crisis that led inexorably to better self-knowledge, as well as better and deeper relationships, but also personal confrontations awash in resentment and anger that may have died down but were never resolved. They thus fester and become shelved in the space we leave in our souls for lifelong regrets.

The same holds true for nations and religious civilizations, except that just as some individuals remain unconscious of past mistakes that thwart their ability to flourish, so do many civilizations. Just as, by contrast, other individuals, plagued by feelings of shame over bad habits of the past, tend to forget the goodness that also resides in their souls, or the gifts that are to be found within their families, so do refugees from nations and civilizations. They reject with horror the destructive side of their community, and they tend to forget or need to suppress the gifts that they have within them. They tend to deny that all things change and evolve, depending on how we view them and treat them. They thus squander the cultural assets conducive to a full and flourishing life, as well as the skills necessary to prevent or resolve difficult confrontations.

It is a fundamental belief, call it a principle of faith, of those who practice peacemaking or conflict resolution that human beings can better resolve conflict with aid from others, as well as with the help of various processes of self-awareness and healing. The same holds true of great civilizations, cultures,

3

and historical religions. Just as individuals evolve endlessly, whether for the better or for the worse, until the day that they die, the same holds true for civilizations. What they evolve into is very much up to us, what we put into them, how we treat them, and whether we encourage their evolution along a path of peace or a path of violence, along a path of love or a path of hatred, a path of life or a path of death.

There are numerous causes of human conflicts, and they all interact in complex ways that theoreticians and practitioners sometimes overlook. In our search for some semblance of order in the chaos and nebulae of conflicts, we search often for one overriding causal factor, to find a way to solve the conflict or the damage that results. Often this is self-serving, in that individuals and institutions gravitate toward singular causes to promote singular solutions in which they specialize, thus making themselves useful. Furthermore, there is a nasty tendency to suppress evidence of certain causes of conflict that the conflict resolver may revile for one reason or another.

Some people tend to suppress evidence of economic or class issues in conflict, because they themselves have various resentments against certain classes from which they or a parent originates. Some people may suppress evidence of culture or religion as a cause of conflict because they have particularly ambivalent feelings about those phenomena in their own lives. Some may suppress all conversation about psychology and conflict because it opens up a Pandora's box of emotional vulnerability that they are not ready to cope with or share as a part of peacemaking.

Religion and culture unquestionably play a critical role in numerous conflicts, all the way from intrapersonal to global conflicts. The challenge is trying to tease out the subtle way in which religion and culture interact with conflict. The latter is an enormously complex subject, almost completely neglected by students of conflict.[2]

The basic reason that the study of culture and anthropology is such an essential challenge to theories of conflict and peacemaking is the infinite variability of human experience that anthropology revels in portraying. Certainly etic approaches make it easier to come to overall principles of causal understanding and, therefore, some general strategies of intervention. But one can never fully leave the emic approach to human life, which uniquely and truly respects the uniqueness of every culture, even the smallest of them, maybe especially the smallest of them.

More important, it is in the deep study of the peculiar individual group that we discover our humanity, and gain wisdom that could never be gained by artificial structures—material or conceptual—superimposed, sometimes violently, on the matrix of human life in question. The same is true of the study of world religions. It is so tempting to generalize. We know the violence caused by universal definitions. One could argue that universal definitions of any human phenomenon are essentially violent, when one follows the consequences or application of those definitions to the solutions to human problems—in other words, when one moves from analysis to implementation. It is in the latter phase that a moral judgment on our intervention is needed. And universalist, generalized recommendations usually come up short, betraying subtle—and often not so subtle—forms of disrespect and violence.

In this book, I try to respect the unique sources of religious traditions as irreducible markers of a civilization. They are only one set of markers. The lived reality of communities is another marker, as well as the economic and class underpinnings of cultural institutions. But religious traditions, embodied in texts, laws, rituals, myths, and metaphors, offer us a unique perspective on cultural problems and cultural possibilities. We must, as we audaciously presume that we can constructively intervene in other people's conflict, do our utmost to understand and respect the uniqueness of every encounter, as well as how it intersects with underlying larger trends of culture, religion, economics, and psychology.

The general relationship between religion and culture, independent of conflict analysis, is complex, and it is beyond this work to address this issue thoroughly. I assume, for purposes of this book, that religious texts, myths, metaphors, laws, and values are a subset of all cultural phenomena of a particular civilization. Those phenomena, cultural or more narrowly religious, are also subject to analysis by conflict theory, as well as political, psychological, and economic theory. All of these disciplines can help explain religious traditions, especially as they relate to conflict generation and peacemaking. Furthermore, despite the fact that when possible I enter deeply into single traditions, in an emic way, there is value to cross-religious study.

This is particularly true of religions that have complex common origins, such as the Abrahamic faiths. In fact, the very interrelatedness of these traditions betrays the causes of their interreligious rivalry and deadly historical conflicts. But such study also uncovers places of conflict transformation[3] and peacemaking by discovering discreet points of convergence, across the indelible but porous barriers of spiritual identity. We also can discover unique places of need and, therefore, injury, which can both clarify historical interreligious antagonisms and uncover the means to remove them.

I assume also that religious texts and traditions inform far more of a culture's presentation of its collective self, especially in moments of cross-cultural relationship, than secular members of a civilization might wish to acknowledge. This is the case even when large segments of the population are no longer rigidly subordinate to some religious form of authority. Despite this, however, a great deal of energy has been expended in the past century by some analysts of human nature in the realms of psychology, sociology, and biology to distance all human phenomena from their cultural moorings. They attempted this to see these phenomena distilled into predictable, universal patterns, bereft of all cultural or religious uniqueness. While this has produced some remarkable results in terms of our understanding of *the* human being, it has also obscured our understanding of *a* human being in a particular context of place and time.

Group conflict is constituted by a series of unique human beings who evolve, for one reason or another, into a complex interaction of adversarial relationships. To understand this we cannot suppress the roots of that human being, or group of human beings, in the historical cultures and religions from which they have emerged. Connecting the human being to her cultural moorings will help us understand why and when she fights and why and when she makes peace. It will give us tools to help the human being travel in the direction of peacemaking by reconnecting the individual to her cultural moorings. If those cultural moorings have ways of peacemaking, then they may resonate in ways that no other peace processes will. If those cultural moorings generate conflict, then we may see what needs to change for her culturally and/or psychologically in ways that normal theories of conflict may not be able to perceive. This holds true of very large political/military events that are unrelated, on the surface, to religion or culture. Often the rituals, myths, and metaphors of a community—especially in the modern context—are buried in oblique spaces that are not supposed to affect public behavior. But they do.

The task of this book is to uncover these deeper roots of conflict and apply them to the challenges as well as the possibilities for Palestinian-Israeli relations over the coming decades. There are many interlacing subsets of this conflict, including the inter-monotheistic ones, as well as the larger Arab-Israeli and Western-Arab conflicts. Furthermore, as I have delineated elsewhere, internal conflicts within both Palestinian and Israeli societies over the role of religion are also important.[4]

The role of religion in perpetuating the principal conflict hardly needs delineation: Hamas and Islamic Jihad, Jewish assassins, nationalist religious parties, aggressive seizing of land in the name of God, suicide-mass murder in the name of God, outside religious entities with vested interests in worsening the conflict, Jerusalem as an object of desire and conquest by all three religions, holy sites as burgeoning reifications of conflict. But even more lies below the surface, much more that needs to be exposed. It is essential, therefore, as an outgrowth of such analysis, to integrate the relevant cultural values of these peoples into a deepened peacemaking process. This has not been attempted until now by most scholars of conflict, conflict resolution activists, or diplomats, and as a result the peace process has barely penetrated the moral consciousness of either side. This is our task.

Family Myths and Cultural Conflict

Relatives, such as father, mother, brother, sister, and cousin, seem to be pervasive as metaphors for deep, collective human entities and their relationships. In the Middle East, in particular, the use of the metaphor of family, specifically the family of the biblical Abraham, to describe our cultural and religious origins, is remarkable. In this metaphor of Abrahamic family, identities are established. In this metaphor, old wounds are expressed. In this metaphor, ancient competitions and conflicts are given a quality of cosmic significance. In this metaphor, victory over the forces of ignorance and idolatry is celebrated, and those forces are seamlessly conflated with any enemy of the Abrahamic tribe. The Abrahamic tribe is also held to strict standards of devotion to a single God whose betrayal has harsh and violent consequences. But in this metaphor there also resides some profound possibilities of a non-violent future.

What is possibly even more remarkable is that this family of Abraham is truly mythic in the sense that there never has been and probably never will be any evidence, independent of the Bible and the Qur'an, for the existence of Abraham or his family. The Bible, even by traditional counting, was written many centuries after Abraham's existence. Centuries of scholars have doubted that the book of Genesis was written earlier than at least a thousand years after the life of Abraham.

The Abrahamic family myth lives and breathes an independent reality, nevertheless, in the lives of hundreds of millions of Jews, Christians, and Muslims. It is a critical means of organizing the world and making sense of one's history, one's origins, and even one's future. However, it is a story mediated through different lenses, depending on the religious group, with innumerable variations, based on the subgroupings and individual predilections of millions of interpreters. Yet the potentially unifying power of the metaphor is unmistakable. Its persistence becomes a metaphor, in and of it-

7

self, of an abiding connectivity that monotheistic peoples feel toward each other, even though that connectivity has often expressed itself as jealousy, competition, disappointment, and brutalizing murder. In a word, monotheists often act as relatives in an intense but troubled and murderous family.

I use "myth" in the sense of a story that contains some ultimate and enduring truth, and a way of making sense of amorphous reality, for those who believe in it. Whether the myth is believed to be literal history, approximate history, or simply didactic legend, depends on the believer.

But myth means something much deeper and more important for conflict and peacemaking. Myth that is shared has a way of bringing infinitely complex problems into a manageable cognitive structure of reality, allowing problems of dizzying proportions to be understood by the human mind and absorbed by the human heart. This, in turn, is a perfect tool for motivating large groups of people to violence.

However—and here is the central point—myth *also* can allow communication to proceed by means of its own expansion and development, or extension, into modern constructs that often elude rationalistic methods of negotiation and diplomacy, especially those intended for masses of people. This creates possibilities in the prosocial development of human relations. And mythical possibility is the midwife of cultural conflict resolution and peacemaking.[1] It provides the dramatic construct for thinking about and treating enemies in a fundamentally new way—which at the same time becomes embedded in familiar myth.

Let us outline the parameters of the Abrahamic myth by stating at the outset that the mediation of this myth by all three traditions is extremely varied and that, roughly speaking, the mediated interpretations of the myth generally serve the interests of each respective corporate religious entity. Islamic versions will confirm the centrality and importance of Arabian ancestry in Abraham and the confirmation of Abraham and Ishmael as the first believers and servants of Allah. Jewish mediations of the story will centralize the importance of Isaac and Israel as the inheritors of God's favor. Christian retellings of the story are much more rare but generally emphasize Abraham as the first man who believed in one God.[2] All will claim the special favor of God proved through their telling and retelling of the story.

Let us begin with the Hebrew biblical myth. Abraham was a man who discovered a monotheistic worldview in the midst of an idolatrous culture. In particular, he developed a relationship with a God who promised that Abraham would be the father of many peoples, *av hamon goyim*.[3] Abraham and his wife Sarah were unable to have children until a very old age, but Abraham had a child, Ishmael, with Sarah's maidservant, Hagar. God promised Abraham another son, and Sarah gave birth to Isaac.

The Hebrew biblical tradition is clearly focused on the fate of Isaac as the ancestor of the Jewish people. In fact, Sarah, resenting or suspecting the influence of Ishmael on her son, insists that the maidservant and son be thrown out of the house, which Abraham does. Thus, in addition to being willing to sacrifice his son, Isaac, Abraham is also willing to send his other son and wife to the desert, both times with the approval or command of a divine voice. This is the first in a series of subtle presentations of family tragedies in the Genesis stories, which will have consequences for intergroup relations later.

In Jewish rabbinic interpretation, Isaac is the key to Jewish lineage, Ishmael to Arab and Islamic lineage, and Esau, Jacob's brother, is the key symbol for Roman/European/Christian lineage. The separation of these three relatives— and their animosity—is the key to the rabbinic mythical account of later history and later tragedies.[4]

That Abraham expelled Hagar and Ishmael is mediated somewhat by some later rabbinic myths that Abraham went seeking after Ishmael, concerned with his welfare and whom he would marry.[5] On the whole, however, the moral problematic of this expulsion is not confronted in most rabbinic literature.[6] On the contrary, the expulsion is seen as a necessary way to protect Isaac from Ishmael and to prepare Isaac to be God's chosen, the patriarch of God's people.[7]

Sarah clearly instigates the expulsion of Hagar and Ishmael (Gen. 21:10), and it seems to be based on some actions of Ishmael involving the verb *metsahek*, a difficult word to translate. She sees Ishmael "making sport," or perhaps the verb means ridicule. We really do not know from the biblical text, which is why rabbinic literature elaborates and interprets. Rabbi Akiva claims that Sarah saw Ishmael bringing idolatry into Abraham's house. Rabbi Simeon ben Yohai is very telling. He claims that the "ridicule" was motivated by all the attention being given to Isaac as the son of Abraham who will inherit a double portion. But Ishmael says that he is, in fact, the eldest and by right (Deut. 21:17) should inherit the double portion.

We have right here in the rabbinic literature the essence of the tragic relationship of brothers—and competing monotheistic religions. They compete over who is idolatrous and who is authentic, and they compete for the love of the father, embodied in the double portion of inheritance.

Rabbinic defensiveness over the expulsion of Ishmael and Hagar betrays ambivalence over this historic relationship, and this defensiveness is further confirmed as we read some modern interpreters. Aviva Zornberg, for example, a modern Orthodox Jewish Bible interpreter who resides in Israel, sees Sarah's insistence on expulsion as a necessary response to the dangers that faced her son. She emphasizes Ishmael as a mortal danger to Isaac.[8] Furthermore, in a progressive reversal of traditionalist rabbinic gender typologies, Zornberg portrays Sarah as the embodiment of incisive analysis and calculation of danger, versus Abraham, who is "too entangled in emotions" (a characterization generally reserved in Jewish and Western culture for women) to make the tough, analytical decision for expulsion. Ironically, however, Zornberg's embrace of the Jewish Sarah as a strong model of female analytic capacity is coupled in her interpretation with an uncritical acceptance of the expulsion of a woman and her child without any protection! This is a feminist position for Jewish wives only, not for gentile maidservants.

The mortal Jewish fears of Jews from Ishmael, that is, Arabs, in the Israeli context must be seen in light of the interpretive emphases and hermeneutic choices of contemporary interpreters such as Zornberg. When she concludes that the brothers seem to be playing together but that they cannot coexist "for there is murder in the wind," this strongly echoes one contemporary attitude on Arab-Israeli coexistence that reverberates in both Jewish and Arab circles, always accompanied, of course, by partial and selective evidence.[9]

As stated, there is a tendency in ancient Jewish rabbinic culture to justify the expulsion and to paint both Isaac and Jacob as vulnerable to the wildness or simple evil of their respective brothers, Ishmael and Esau. But the Hebrew Bible has a subtle and complicated relationship to both brothers. Ishmael is, in fact, blessed. Esau is later embodied in Edom, and there is a specific prohibition against hating Edom in the Bible.[10] Furthermore, despite the tendency to see Ishmael as utterly other in rabbinic Judaism, there are some curious issues, such as the fact that Ishmael, through the voice of Rabbi Simeon ben Yohai, cited previously, does make a good biblical case for why Ishmael, not Isaac, should inherit the double portion. This is enormously telling, in terms of the dramatic and tragic tension between these two monotheistic people, concerning who is the one that is favored by God, or who has the purest faith. In the Jewish sources the emphasis is on who is favored and loved. In the Islamic case it tends to be described as who has the purest faith, the true Islam.

Another interesting point in the Hebrew Bible complicates the relationship to Ishmael. When the Bible records the death of Ishmael, it uses a classic ethnic/national metaphor of death that is usually seen as a deeply unique place of Jewish reunion. It says Ishmael was "gathered unto his people,"[11] a phrase generally reserved for the most important figures of Jewish life![12] Who could Ishmael have been gathered into other than the family of Abraham? And if so, what does it say about the nature of this family? Is there consciously or unconsciously embedded in ancient Jewish tradition, a Jewish family, a family of Adam or humanity, and then some in-between family? An Abrahamic family perhaps that includes both Jews and gentiles, or at least all Semites? If so, why has this been left undeveloped in Jewish theology? We will leave this open for now, except to point out the rich texture of hermeneutic possibility, the curious way in which this subject has been repressed or ignored, and the way in which hermeneutical observation is intimately related to the believer's horizon and psychological context.[13]

Arab culture and Islam share the belief that Abraham existed, was the founder or restorer of monotheism, and that Hagar and Ishmael are the key ancestors of the Arabian peoples. But whom God has chosen is a different matter. The biblical account of the expulsion of Hagar and Ishmael is accepted in Islam. It is elaborated upon later, however, in critical ways. According to Al-Baizawi, Abraham does expel them, because of Sarah's jealousy.[14] According to one tradition, Abraham accompanies them but then leaves them in Mecca. According to another tradition, Abraham takes them to Mecca, leaves them with a bag of dates, and then prepares to leave. Hagar beseeches him to stay and asks him if God commanded him to do this, and he says, "yes." And she says that God will cause no harm to come to her. Later Abraham prayed for them that others may be kind to them.[15]

The spring or well that God provided for Hagar's survival, according to Islamic traditions, is seen to be in Mecca. It is called Zamzam, and it sprang miraculously from beneath the foot of Ishmael. The hills that are critical to this myth are Safa and Marwah, and to run between them is a rite of pilgrimage to this day. Ishmael and Hagar are believed to be buried in *hijir ismail*, an enclosure right next to the *ka'abh*.[16]

Hagar and Ishmael are critical to the mythic interactions of every pilgrim to Mecca, now and throughout all these past centuries. Is there room here for a hermeneutic rereading of both traditions, Arabic and Jewish, in terms of mothers and sons, the pain of mothers in the threats of violence to their sons, but also the violence that mothers may encourage toward other or rival sons and mothers? Is this not a mythic backdrop for all violence and war where the sons must be sacrificed for the sake of the survival of the family? Are there not in every culture unique ways in which both mothers and fathers, in different venues, are simultaneously and paradoxically engaged in the nurturing and even exaltation of their sons, only to sacrifice them to violence and abandonment on the field of battle? Which 18 year old dying on the field of battle does not cry out for his mother? Who cannot see the essential mythos of sacrifice in the movie *Born on the Fourth of July*, where Tom Cruise, in one of his best performances to date, embodies the favored son born to be abandoned and sacrificed? This movie is a must-see for a classic contemporary rendering of the Abrahamic sacrifice stories.

We have here a historic opportunity for intercultural engagement on these fateful matters. Especially in the circumstances of the Israeli-Arab conflict, where several generations of mothers and fathers have now sacrificed their children to this battle, such discussion in familiar cultural terms may open a gateway for communication. Furthermore, there may be an opportunity for a kind of cultural/psychological process of reconciliation and mourning in which Abraham, Isaac, Ishmael, and Hagar become the central mythic actors. This family's chronological distance, which is paradoxically combined with their cosmic significance in both communities, may provide the basis for a dramatic evolution of their relationship. We will address this more in recommendations in the final chapter of the book.

Let us return to Islam's relationship to the Abraham story. Abraham is seen as the first Muslim, the one who truly accepts Allah.[17] In contrast to the biblical version, Abraham and Ishmael are seen as partners in the establishment of the worship of Allah.[18] Ishmael is seen as enjoining prayer and charity on his people.[19] His progeny, however, eventually forgot this. Forgetting Allah is the principal source of sin and rebellion according to Islamic theology. The Arabian peoples became steeped in idolatry until Muhammad converted them to Islam or reminded them of Allah.

The children of Isaac, however, went on to inherit a book of prophecy from Moses (Surah 40:53) and establish a legitimate monotheistic faith. However, they are severely criticized in many places in the Qur'an for not understanding the true and authentic faith in Allah.[20] Furthermore, they failed to accept Jesus or Muhammad as legitimate prophets when these men came to them. There are extensive portions of the Qur'an dedicated to a detailed criticism of the Jewish people and their behavior on this score.

The competition over who inherits the legacy of Abraham, who is the favored son, reaches the level of competition over martyrdom, at least as far as the way the Qur'anic story has been interpreted. As we mentioned, the Hebrew biblical Abraham's willingness to sacrifice Isaac is inverted into a permanent blessing of Abraham through Isaac as a reward for that attempted martyrdom.

The Qur'anic story of the sacrifice of Abraham's son can be found in Surah 37:100–13. The name of the son is not mentioned directly in the description of the sacrifice. But Ishmael's name is nowhere to be found, whereas Isaac is mentioned at the end of the story, "And We gave him the good news of Isaac— a prophet—one of the righteous. We blessed him and Isaac. . . ."

The commentaries of Abdullah Yusuf Ali are revealing here. It is assumed that the Qur'an means Ishmael as the sacrifice. Furthermore, it is suggested that the biblical version falsifies the facts, in that it has God say to Abraham to take his *only* son to be sacrificed. But Ishmael is much older than Isaac, even according to the biblical story. Therefore, the biblical story must be falsifying, according to this Islamic interpreter, in making the younger son the privileged one, the martyr, to privilege a "tribal religion," that is, Judaism, as opposed to the more authentic universal religion of Islam.[21] Furthermore, the biblical version is inferior, according to this interpreter, in that Isaac is not portrayed as a willing partner, and the sacrifice therefore resembles a pagan sacrifice.[22]

What is inescapable here is the competition over the father by the sons, mythically mediated by competing texts of revelation. The fight over which monotheism is more authentic is a fight over blessings by fathers for sons, but, in particular, blessings that come from God to parents and children. In Christianity the father and the son both become part of the godhead, but the conflict is the same, namely, "Who is the true son of God, Israel or Jesus; who is His true incarnated presence?"

The stage is clearly set for what I shall term "mythically based conflict," and indeed such conflict was plainly apparent in the vast apologetic literature of the monotheisms, which began in the early centuries of the Common Era.[23] There was a self-conscious separation of all three monotheistic faiths as they claimed their own place of chosenness and superiority. There is a zero-sum quality to these claims of superiority or favored love. A father can only love one son above the others; he cannot love equally several sons, and daughters are excluded from the mythic conflict altogether. The mythic view of family and the limitations of love become a cosmic war over religious authenticity. But it is the limits on love implied by these themes of superiority that intrigue me. They betray both tragedy and opportunity, seen from the perspective of the hermeneutics of myth and its impact on human cognition, as well as from the perspective of family psychodynamics.

Chosenness is the key category here, and it unquestionably involves the relationship of family metaphor and national metaphor, combined with a fixed assumption of how parents relate to children. It is assumed that there is one that is chosen to be the key inheritor of the parent. Specifically, it is a focus on the male heir inheriting from his father, with the women, such as Sarah or Rebecca, playing key roles in the promotion of their sons.

Polygamy, and its disastrous effects on love relationships between men and women, between children and parents, takes on ultimate existential signifi-cance here. It becomes a signifier of the human condition, a condition that is seen to lend itself to a dualism of love for one and hate for another, or the unchallenged axiom that love is limited in quantity. It goes to the heart of the human emotional life asking some simple questions: Is it possible for love to be shared? In the absence of love, is there only hatred? Are love and hatred our only capacities? Does love for one person or nation or idea exhaust our prosocial capacity?

There is an assumption in the hermeneutic reaction to these ancient texts that everyone can receive a birthright (even this can be forfeited), *but* that only one will be the chief heir. This has translated culturally—and militar-ily—into a vast pan-millennial monotheistic struggle as to who is the authen-tic heir of the father, be that father Abraham or God. This is the struggle over who are chosen, who is the Chosen People. And the consequences of this jealousy, both in the book of Genesis, and, eerily, mirrored so closely in Western history, have been riveting and deadly as the longest-running inter-cultural psycho-drama, a millennial tragedy rivaling any that Shakespeare could conjure.

Ultimately it has proved to be barbaric, with pretensions to chosenness and being the true Israel leading to the oppression, cultural destruction, and physi-cal slaughter of millions of people. It has been a decisive historical refutation of the highest moral aims of monotheism, such as compassion, peace, and justice for all human beings which so many prophets lived for and died de-fending. This touching and deadly drama could end no more peacefully in the life and history of nations than it does in the life of families that have a limited quantity of love for only one or some of the children.

It seems to me to be no accident that the mythic category of father and son proceed to play such a critical role in Christian mythology. The major differ-ence is that the mythic relation of father and son, kept strictly in the human realm by Islam and Judaism, becomes part of the inner dynamic of the godhead in Christianity. But the results of the mythic engagement of father and son clearly involve the same kind of exclusionary competition, with very deadly consequences. Right up until our own day, the most exclusionary and intol-erant versions of Christianity will seize endlessly on a single text that pro-nounces unequivocally that the only path to the Father, God, is through the one begotten Son, Jesus.[24] Again, the metaphor is family, but there is a highly exclusionary character to this sacred family and only one way to be privi-leged, chosen, saved, an inheritor of the true faith, reunited with the heav-enly father. This also makes the signification in Catholicism of the Pope as

Father—indeed of all priests—all the more telling (perhaps also explaining the unusually strong resistance to women as priests).

The metaphor of the sacred, primordial family persists in monotheistic history as a strangely compelling anchor, however, despite all its bizarre and brutal consequences. We are stuck with it, in other words, and, to be truthful, some of its consequences have not been completely destructive. I have found it curious, for example, that in my many encounters with Arabs and Muslims, generally with the Middle East conflict as the immediate subtext of our encounter, that talk of Abraham always comes up in some subtle way. Words such as "brother," "cousin," and "father" emerge, usually at the end of the encounter, as if they form a sacred capstone, a need for the parting encounter to embrace relationship, lost brotherhood, and a special kind of intimate peace that only family reconciliation truly embodies.

The Abrahamic family metaphor seems to evoke or embody a very special kind of craving for identity and reconciliation.[25] The words and the encounters are almost always centered on males and maleness in my Middle Eastern experience; it is always about "father," "brother," and "cousin." Usually these words, and the facial encounter and body language that accompany them, entail looks and nuances of longing, longing for something lost. And I have been told recently that Muslims and Jews in Israel who have been working confidentially on improved relations often call each other, in familiar language, "cousin."

A separate study should investigate the relationship between the myth and metaphor of family and the foundations of human ethical systems. It seems to go beyond monotheistic, biblical, and rabbinic origins, to a much more universal phenomenon, though, as stated earlier, I am very cautious about universal conclusions. Any usefulness to this possibly universal metaphor and theme as a peacemaking tool would have to be checked carefully with the people who are parties to a given conflict. The relationship of nuclear family, tribal family, and the human family as such is only useful to the degree to which it is integrated into and transformed by the cultures in conflict.

Besides the family metaphor, other cultural constructs can play a vital role in framing peacemaking and the communication constructs of adversaries. For example, I am struck by the cultural nuances described by Lederach in Latin American encounters between Christians in deadly conflict.[26] The Christian prayers before and after those difficult negotiations between enemies have been critical to creating what I call a bonding "cultural envelope" that surrounds the intractability of rational power negotiations, where lives, property, security, and dignity are at stake. This cultural envelope cements relationships in a nonrational fashion between people who hold viewpoints so essentially divergent that only it can continue to bind them. Often only this bond, this uniquely spiritual nurturer of relationship, seems to keep at the "table of negotiation" those adversaries who may have no motivation otherwise for being there.

This is the kind of interaction that we want to study and replicate for many different cultures. This is what moves intractable conflict to manageable,

constructive conflict, and to the extraordinary persistency that marks a successful long-term conflict resolution encounter. It is only the latter that provides the hope for the ultimate goal of the transformation of relationships and
peace, which moves beyond the fragility of achieving just a settlement, or a
cease fire in the case of war. This transformation cannot take place without
the persistence of relationship. And the relationship often cannot persist when
power-based impasses plague the negotiation and deepen the nonrational
injuries that lurk underneath. This is where the mythic construct of prayer or
some sacred interaction at the beginning and end of the meetings played so
crucial a role for those Latin American meetings.

I have also noticed, as a scholar and practitioner with strong roots in Judaism, that as my relationship with the Mennonite community has grown, so
many of them call to me, especially when I arrive or when I am about to leave
their world, "Hello, brother," or "See ya, brother." And I am affected profoundly by these words—spoken so nonchalantly—spoken by Christians, of
all people! I feel so powerfully the centuries of sorrow of my people. It is
embedded in the prayers I have always said, in the lives of the teachers whom
I have revered. The living memories of horrible abuse in Europe are still so
powerful in various members of my family and teachers that it is absolutely
jarring to hear a Christian call me brother.

Of course, I am used to some Christians saying such things as a ruse of
missionizing and conversion. This use of the family metaphor brings no comfort, only revulsion, fear, and, frankly, rage. But the simple, nonmanipulative,
almost unconscious gesture on the part of my Mennonite friends has given a
rare permission to my mind and my heart to mourn in a profounder and purer
way about the past, as well as to ponder a different future. It is as if we human
beings know, at an unconscious level, when it is safe, and when it is not, to
mourn purely, in a complete way, without the admixture of panic and consciousness of defense. But our inner self seems able to smell inauthenticity
in these matters from a great distance.

Finally, it is not insignificant that the Pope chose, in the first of many
speeches aimed at Jewish-Catholic reconciliation, to refer to Jews as "our elder
brothers," and for the Jewish community to sense from the Catholic Church
simultaneously that this was no deceitful tactic of proselytism but a new stage
of relationship.[27] But the church speaks in many voices, despite its acutely
hierarchical structure; and countervailing pronouncements of the church regarding its ultimate superiority as the only path to salvation leave lingering
doubts about the future in the hearts of its former victims. This results in our
inability to mourn purely and let go of the past.

Mourning is generally reserved for the end of wars, but if the war persists
then there is no appropriate time to mourn. This is a complicated matter.
Triumphalism in the church about what religion is truly salvific is not terribly different from Orthodox Jewish visions of the messianic future, embodied in classic Jewish prayers such as *Alenu*. Many religions have fantasies of
triumph in the future. It is the track record that is the problem, and bad track
records, whether they be the church's or those of Judaism and Islam in rela-

tion to certain minorities, require special reassurance and hard work to repair the distrust. Certainly, Judaism and Islam have much work to do in the immediate future to repair the damage done to their enemies by their justifications for violence and injustice in the Holy Land.

Let us return to the issue of family metaphors and peacemaking. One of my students from Africa—also my teacher—is a survivor of the Liberian genocide and now dedicates his life completely, as a Christian, to peacemaking and reconciliation in Africa. He has formed, through tireless efforts, some exciting new frameworks for pan-African work on reconciliation. Sam Doe wrote me recently concerning a project with ex-child soldiers. These are children taught to kill mercilessly by their cultural warlord fathers, and are now orphaned by real mothers and fathers who are either dead or who cannot abide by their evil. Sam wrote me the following about a workshop with them in 1998:[28]

> At the beginning of the sessions these kids generally expressed attitudes of dominance, disrespect for authority, arrogance, and intimidation. At the end they all broke down and for the first time came in contact with their hearts, with their full humanity. There were commitments made to serve as social actors for peace in their communities. One, a female heavy artillery commander, said, "I always thought of myself as a militant. I have been called to Monrovia to join the Armed Forces of Liberia, but after these six days it is clear to me that militancy is not what I desire. I will destroy my forms and work for peace in my community." Another wrote me a letter, "Dear Smiling Sam (they all called me this), having gone through the six days intensive training, I have come to gain interest in you, thus asking that you be *my father* (my emphasis) as you depart. May God bless you in your cause to foster peace for Liberians throughout the country." Tears of joy welled up in my eyes as I read this letter. Yesterday they all called Charles Taylor, George Boley, Roosevelt Johnson, and all the rebel leaders their fathers. Today I have become a father. This is a great challenge because they have all learned to do exactly as their fathers. I am challenged to be a father who honors life. A father who builds and [does] not destroy communities. Not only that, but to be a father who will work with others to also become fathers and mothers to these lost souls of Liberia.

Such is the power of the myth and metaphor of family that it can both serve as the instrument of unparalleled human evil, but also become the foundation of heroic and extraordinary devotion to peacemaking.

Returning to the Middle East, I would argue that the mythic talk of family, father Abraham, and "cousins" that insinuates itself into conversations between religious Jews and religious Arabs betrays an inspired, intuitive grasp for the unique cultural envelope that can hold together this relationship of Semites in the midst of a great deal of pain, argument, and mortal suspicion. It is the transformation of this Semitic relationship, and the mythic recovery of the "lost brother" that is at the heart of our inquiry. I am aware of the irony that I utilize the myth of the "Semite" here, despite the fact that, genetically and racially at least, Jews have roots in more than one racial group, as is evidenced by their varying features in different parts of the world. But it is also the case that, even historically speaking, there are deep connections between Jews and the Middle Eastern peoples. After all, the ten tribes of Israel who were exiled in 721 B.C.E. to Assyria no doubt eventually merged into the fabric of Middle Eastern cultures and religions. On many levels, the deep cultural and ethnic connections persist to a surprising degree, even to this day.

It seems that many human beings find it difficult to encounter the Other with whom they are in conflict, discover her humanity, and then walk away without some lasting bond. There is too much emotion and intensity invested in this unique kind of human encounter to not say something like, "You know, we are cousins," or, in a light, shared moment, say, "We have the same sense of humor and eating habits; we must be cousins." I am fascinated by these peculiar moments of relatedness. Generally, they are suppressed in formal negotiations. And yet, religious people or people who experience their culture deeply live and breathe these cultural constructs. They almost cannot help but relate mythically to the other.

The critical point is that often people feel that they must fall into one of two opposite constructs: the relationship with the distant other is conceived either as cosmic adversary, an eternally hated brother, or as a beloved long-lost relative. The cosmic construct is crucial for many people, a way of placing these relationships inside a deep structure of reality. But whether that cosmic construct is violent or nonviolent seems to be "up for grabs," depending on the social and economic structures and their influence on preconceptions of the other, as well as on the psychological and moral predilections of individual actors. But it seems clear that a mediated context of meeting that specifically allows for, or subtly sets the stage for, a nonviolent cultural lens through which to see others is called for by the methods of cultural conflict resolution.

This means that, although it is very problematic for the third party to impose or suggest mythic connections of relationship, the third party or parties should allow for a full fruition of deeper cultural/psychological interaction between the parties. Allowing extensive time periods, during breaks or at night, in the midst of negotiations, for cultural exchanges by the participants themselves is just one small example of how to operationalize this. I would argue that extensive and deep cultural interactions, in one form or another, religious or otherwise, should be an indispensable part of any high-level or grass-roots-level efforts to engage enemies in meetings. Naturally it must be done with great care and attention to detail.

Occasionally it might be possible to suggest a specific cultural envelope that would make sense to the parties and be nonthreatening. Its exact nature must vary with the parties and the situation. Furthermore, third parties, in some ways like a therapist for a deeply withdrawn patient, must have the elasticity to go with the flow of the metaphors that emerge from the group encounter. They must listen carefully to the way in which the positive and negative contours of the relationship are being expressed through cultural metaphor and then encourage a deeper look at the implications. In general, many of the deepest moments of these encounters, the greatest opportunities for transformation, are squandered by facilitators who are not trained to see the more profound dynamics at work, and the opportunities these present. Often the emotionality and outrageous statements that surround these metaphors prove too much to handle for unprepared third parties. But this is precisely where opportunity is knocking!

There is an infinite set of possibilities when it comes to the analysis of metaphor in the moment of encounter between enemies, and how this can be utilized. Let us take an example of a very violent metaphor. I have made reference elsewhere to the pervasiveness of Nazi and Holocaust metaphors in Jewish life and, in particular, the adversarial styles of Israeli relations.[29] Demonization proceeds apace with the help of the Nazi metaphor. What I neglected to mention was the pervasiveness of the Holocaust as a subject and object of the Arab-Israeli conflict. Holocaust denial has become a weapon of war. There is really no better way to injure millions of Israelis at once than belittling the Holocaust, because just about all European Israelis lost at least some family, and certainly all their geographic roots, in the Holocaust.

I was recently in a private meeting, which I was helping to moderate, concerning my work in Gaza and Israel. At the meeting was a very educated European Israeli couple and several Arabs and American Christians. A distinguished young man from Gaza, in an utterly convincing and powerful way, described his life under occupation, and brought to life the depths of the tragedy of Gaza. His description moved everyone. Following immediately on the heels of this, and really without warning, after I had given an introduction about my work, this young man felt the need to purposely and consciously persuade the group that Gaza is a "concentration camp" created to destroy the Palestinian people. And he hammered away at this repeatedly and purposefully.

So I watched this unfold, feeling the rage and hurt inside me, but also attending to the analyst inside me. Sure enough, the Israeli couple present had lost all of their extended family in the gas chambers. Their reaction was very understated but deeply adversarial in certain subtle ways. Most Jews that I grew up with would have begun screaming at this point. Not this couple. Frankly, the Gazan engaged in metaphors designed to injure Jews, whether he understood this or not. The Israelis engaged in a few metaphors of their own that had the look and feel to me of colonial condescension, and they seemed designed, consciously or unconsciously, to injure. Their retaliation was to make this young man feel that he was part of a group incapable of taking care of itself. We thus saw unfold the special way in which injured people find the weakest point of the enemy other to hurt them more.

I do not consider such an event a failure of dialogue. I consider it an opportunity *that turns into failure* when the opportunity is squandered or the encounter suppressed in some way. I have almost always seen terrible moments like this one suppressed by facilitators eager to "save the encounter," to emerge with a "positive outcome." But, rest assured, the injurious words are profound and not forgotten. Thus, metaphoric and dialogic injuries are an invariable part of enemy encounters, but usually only destructive because they are not seized upon and worked with.

I seized upon this moment and tried to share the way in which there is a competition for superior injury when two groups are at war, especially where there are great imbalances. I shared with the group that I had heard repeatedly from various Arabs, in my many encounters, a deep resentment of the Holocaust and its aftermath, particularly all of the apologies being showered upon "the Jews." They would ask, "Why is everyone apologizing to the Jews, when the Jews should be apologizing to us?" That is profound. They were effectively saying, "What about us?" "What about our pain that is happening now, not fifty years ago?" Here is the most important point. Unfortunately, when people are angry they do not say, "I am hurt and need comfort." This would be humiliating in many cultures. They say, "What about me?" with outrageous words designed to injure maximally. This is a typical part of conflict—and highly destructive.

The imbalances here include the fact that, on the one hand, the Israelis are at a distinct advantage militarily in the conflict with the Palestinians, which is perpetually humiliating to the Palestinians. On the other hand, few groups can "claim" as much destruction and victimization as Jews of the twentieth century. Thus the need of the weaker party here to belittle or deny the Holocaust. Furthermore, what weaker parties are capable of doing through terrorism and wars of attrition is to make every enemy civilian feel like a target. That the Palestinians have done very well, which further fuels the conflict.

I tried to say to the Gazan man that we all can effectively describe to third parties and even our enemies the great pain that has been inflicted on us, a unique place of injury, without this needing to belittle the unique injury of the other. Each injury is unique and different and becomes, for better or worse, a key part of identity for several generations of traumatized peoples. As we try to awaken empathy between enemies, we must narrate in detail our places of injury, but not by slicing into the wound of the enemy other's own injury, which serves only to continue the injury/counter-injury cycle of violence.

It seemed to this young Gazan that he was really trying to share with these Jews the depths of his misery by using the concentration camp metaphor. But he did the opposite in one moment of metaphoric or mythic injury. He stole their unique place of pain, and thus the sacred memory of murdered family members. I think we all learned things that night, and the American Christian observers seemed much more upset than I was by the style of encounter. I was prepared and sensed that, indeed, I needed an event like this to crystallize a strategy of dealing with the Holocaust metaphor in the Palestinian-Israeli conflict. But I would be lying to say that the interchange was not hurtful.

Further, the cultural framing of meetings between enemies is becoming more and more prevalent as a way of breaking the barriers between Israelis and Arabs. Rabbi Menahem Frohman of the West Bank settlement of Tekoa has on numerous occasions engaged in extensive dialogue with what secularists would certainly refer to as Islamic fundamentalists. He has also met with Islamic extremists in Palestine who are dedicated to the violent removal of Jews from the land. He has reported to me that his conversations can go on for hours before the difficult issues even arise. Sometimes he will first speak with them about God and about Muhammad's prophecy. They will share insights on religion and only then will the conversation proceed to the difficult matters.[30] In classic Middle Eastern fashion (but also reminiscent of the style of the Bet Midrash [traditional Jewish hall of study]), conversations weave in and out of the substantive and hard issues and are interlaced with enjoyable bantering about life, family, and shared sacred texts.

A person who wants to be a peacemaker must know and understand the dynamics of such meetings. He must come to master the need for open-ended time frames, that such banter and weaving in and out of serious issues is a way of testing each other, a way of seeing how prepared each party is to respect and understand the other. Businesslike agendas for discussion have no place here, and Rabbi Frohman knows this better than most. That is why, in the midst of all of the violence of October 2000, with gunfire audible in the distance, Rabbi Frohman could receive a phone call of greetings from Yasser Arafat through his chief of Tanzim forces in the region. What kind of surrealistic reality was this, to paraphrase Rabbi Frohman's incredulity? Because the months of culturally and religiously framed discussions with senior Palestinians, including rejectionists, had not been wasted even though the diplomatic elite were fumbling through their own failures.

In the midst of Arafat's calls for the violent conquest of Jerusalem by the children, a children's crusade effectively, he had taken the time to send greetings to a West Bank rabbi. A separate study is needed to undercover the political and psychological roots of Arafat's many paradoxes. My interests are pragmatic, however. All I want to know is how one gets dangerous leaders, at the height of battle, and in the heat of irrationality, to send a prosocial greeting? The skills of intercultural, interreligious communication and gestures, the effects of the same psychologically, are inescapable factors that distinguish Arafat's simultaneous attitude to this rabbi and to Barak at that moment in time. Rabbi Frohman reports other similar encounters with senior Islamic rejectionists far more militant than Arafat who changed after a few hours of conversation about Islam with Rabbi Frohman. The effects of this method of encounter cannot escape notice.

At the same time of the fall of 2000, and during the same terrible month of violence, in the midst of the Jewish holiday of Sukkot, the traditional outdoor tabernacle of that holiday became a meeting place for Jews and Arabs throughout Israel, just days after the terrible violence expressed by and unleashed upon Arab Israelis. Why? Because for years certain themes had been emphasized in Israeli religious culture, including the Jewish tradition that Sukkot was a time of gathering in Jerusalem of all peoples, not just Jews, that Sukkot as a holiday has a universal element to it that includes prayers that represent all the nations of the world, and that the Sukkah itself symbolizes protection, security, and peace. Add to this the years of cultural development of progressive Judaism and Zionism that sought to recreate the Sukkah, the temporary tabernacle inhabited by Jews for one week of the year, as a place to negotiate peace.

And so, when the horrible events of fall 2000 occurred, this temporary place of meeting became ideal for Arab/Jewish encounters, in that neither side at that time wanted to invite the other to their homes, and the sterile meeting places of dialogue groups would only aggravate the negative dialogic dynamics of these two very angry communities. But the external envelope of this temporary sanctuary, this tabernacle, provided a warm embrace and a symbol of hope in the midst of a very hopeless period.

It certainly accomplished this for the Jews, though the effect of these encounters on the Palestinians would require further investigation. But for at least one community it provided a necessary psychological bridge to the other at a very ambivalent time. Justifiably or not, Israelis were shocked and terrified by Israeli Arab violence. The two peoples continue to live in different realities where each is unaware of the deepest injuries that it perpetrates on the other, and thus each is unprepared for the actions of the other group.

So far, I have discussed the utilization of metaphor and cultural constructs as a frame for meetings between Israelis and Arabs. But these meetings and negotiations are highly verbal encounters that often take place between educated elites. There is another very significant place of meeting, mostly neglected by conflict theory (though not by social psychology), yet crucial for turning large populations toward peace and away from violence. That is the street encounter, the quintessential shared space of mixed cultures.

In the street, the market, or the public space, everyone in a civilization meets—rich and poor, literate and illiterate, selfish and generous, violent and peaceful, the verbally inclined and the nonverbally inclined, all colors, religions, and cultures, all throughout human history. Here most encounters actually take place, much suspicion and injury are born, and the greatest opportunities for human transformation are lost. Here much anti-Jewish violence originated in the villages of Europe, and here, to this day, in India, the stage is often set for angry encounters that foment larger riots. Anyone who frequents the streets as an end in itself, and not as a means to go from one place to another, nor as a place to make money, can tell you that the street is the true mythic center of the human encounter with the unknown Other.

Analogous to the myth of the human family, the street is the place where we encounter long-lost brothers and sisters at every moment of every day. And for those who live and breathe this myth, as I do, the modern street in large cities, with its massive assault on the senses and its strict rules of nonengagement with the stranger, is a place of intolerable alienation. It is no wonder that so many religious people around the world have run headlong back to premodern ways of constructing the universe. It is not the Enlightenment that they find so destructive. The Enlightenment is in books, in the classroom, and only the most dogmatic are enraged by and/or fear books and knowledge.

Most people who have run away from the Enlightenment have actually run away from its bureaucratic stepchild, namely, the modern materialist street of large cities as a place of unbearable loneliness, a place that turns the human being into an object of commercial engagement only, so that authentic gestures of interpersonal conduct are always suspect. Often we find that the only person on the street who has looked us in the eye or smiled was paid to do so, a clerk or someone who needs our money. This is not even the worst of what the modern street does, but we cannot go into this here.

I often wonder about the origins of the extreme violence of the twentieth century and, specifically, how so many millions of people came to support the extremely violent mass movements to uproot and destroy everything around them. I think especially of fascist movements from Nazism to the Khmer Rouge, but also of today's extremist religious movements. There are many causes, of course, but I suspect that we have neglected the damaging impact of modernity that is emblemized by modern, public space.

Perhaps only with the transformation of the modern street or public space can we heal the wound that has sent so many millions running away from the genius of modern human constructs, such as the democratic state and civil liberties. Democracy and civil liberties, perhaps among the most precious creations in human history, would not survive a return to fundamentalist constructs of the past, for example. Yet the alienating constructs of city life overwhelm so many people. So does Western suburban life. The latter seems almost designed to provide no cultural outlet for teenagers other than centers for video games (mostly violent ones) in malls as a culturally shared public space, which in turn drives many adults and teenagers headlong toward romanticized, amoral constructs of culture. One cannot escape this element of alienation in the spate of teenage mass killings in the United States that occurred in the 1990s.

Further on my concern about the street as an arena of cultural conflict, let me share some personal thoughts. I have a strong relationship to the street. The abstractness of research on international conflict resolution and overseas development leave me often with a feeling of disengagement from the real world of the majority of the inhabitants of the world. And when, in a moment of restive agitation, I question the value of my studies, my teaching of elites, or my engagement with peace work that has results only 6,000 miles away (if there), I find myself on the street.

Once there, I engage the homeless, the crazy, the cashier, the waiter, anyone I can find in the public arena, anyone who will talk to me. I seem to find myself in a deceptively quiet framework of existential uncertainty, and I long for any kind of immediacy with the unknown others who surround me. It is as if my professional concerns have no true reality, no immediacy that could challenge that gnawing modern feeling that one's life and one's work is an illusion, a phantom that could disappear in a flash and no one would notice, except the person itching to replace me.

None of the work in rigidly fixed modern settings, no matter how noble, matches a discovery of the long-lost stranger one finds on the street. True devotees of the street find themselves searching for the stranger, longing to overcome the barrier that separates us from the countless, nameless lives that inundate and encroach upon us physically in the subways and malls, or on the highway. All these encounters give no satisfaction to our inner, most rudimentary yearning as human beings to know and be known in the deepest sense, their very frequency and volume adding to their mockery of true encounter. The irony is that the more people one concentrates in small spaces, who remain strangers, the deeper the aloneness. Yet this is increasingly the state of most human existence on the planet in all the major cities. No wonder so many are turning to extreme solutions for these feelings.

In such extraordinary circumstances, which wed unprecedented human contact with unprecedented estrangement, one can either hate the stranger or seek him out, because our agitation propels us toward one or the other. Contemporary overpopulation is particularly acute, but ambivalence toward the stranger is not new. The problem of the stranger and the belief that one must seek him out as a moral/spiritual act has ancient roots in biblical cultures, although its fundamental dialogic immediacy has been papered over by the religious legalisms of later generations. In later times, the simple, pervasive, and audacious biblical command to love the stranger became hermeneutically buried inside worlds of Jewish life protected from and prejudiced against gentile neighbors, while other monotheists betrayed this principle through that dubious engagement with the stranger commonly referred to as proselytism.

It is the street and the stranger that originally lured me out of self-enclosed ethnic cocoons. The deepest roots of Jewish tradition are biblical and Abrahamic. Abraham is the quintessential stranger in both his self-perception as stranger and in his eager embrace of the unknown other.[31] And this biblical myth of stranger, housed inside the personality of Abraham and then turned into the legislative "ought" of loving the stranger,[32] is, I would argue, the axis of moral imagination in a global, cosmic context. By this I mean that the state of the stranger is the litmus test of any society's fundamental goodness or fundamental evil.[33] The street is the dramatic stage upon which the life and death of the stranger unfolds and also the place where one can diagnose a society's health or illness. The issue is not simply about who is homeless or disempowered. It is about public interactions, the inclusions and exclusions, the mix of benevolence, fear, animosity, indifference, and curiosity. The street is an essential place of diagnosis.

Every time an ambulance siren reaches my ears, and I see it pass by, I am sad not because someone is sick. Everyone gets sick and dies at some point. Rather, I am sad because I do not know this sick person and never will in this modern desert of anonymity. This offends some primordial sense of relatedness to others in close geographic proximity, and it offends my religious feeling of the unique sacredness of the person sick or dying inside that vehicle. By ignoring that ambulance, which we all try to do, I ignore a part of me. For that person is I, or will be some day, and I would not want to go to my death surrounded by plastic tubing in the midst of an anonymous traffic jam. That person deserves that I at least know who is in pain, and that I offer some help, or at least that I do my part in either helping him to recover or to pass on from this existence. The vehicle siren (always an irrational, eerie reminder to me of the indifference of "civilized populations" across Europe to the orderly removal and murder of the Jew next door) screams out the human indignation at an anonymous and muffled dance with death, with only bleating machines to utter prayers as the car careens toward an emergency room that rivals the ambulance as a prison of anonymous indignity.

Human dignity is one of the ultimate goals of many ethical systems, secular and religious, and its loss we must always regard as offensive. Many of the best insights of rabbinic approaches to sickness, death, and bereavement center upon the retrieval of human dignity from the hands of its natural enemies. What cultural elites have often misunderstood is that, in the course of their own flights toward dignity—through the acquisition of art, music, and expensive clothing—if they leave behind the stranger in the public space, then they leave behind the human being as such, and then all the dignity and majesty of the natural order is diminished.

How in a constructed world where the public space is one of studied and agreed-upon indifference, where millions pass us by in an overwhelming way, can we exercise a God-given right to feel the pain of neighbors? How can we follow the texts that so courageously declared millennia ago, "Do not stand by while the blood of your neighbor is flowing"?[34] Through indifference we become drawn to create artificial enclaves, far removed from the street and redirect all our natural caring inclinations to people who look exactly like us, and act exactly like us, a tiny band of people from our particular communities. Of course, we also write checks for the strangers in pain. In other words, we withdraw from the stranger and from the place to meet him even as we take pity.

But it is precisely in the public space that we can encounter the truly estranged other—even, maybe especially, the enemy other, and it is only from there that he can take us ultimately to his home. How can we solve any deeply embedded violence and hatred that persists in large civilizations without coming to visit the home of the stranger?

It is undoubtedly the case that many otherwise decent people withdraw from the larger world of the stranger in search of an escape from the overstimulation that is endemic to overpopulated life. I always found that after I moved from relatively small-town life to New York when I was 18, I never ceased to be amazed at the capacity of the average person to be utterly oblivious to the stream of human life passing him on all sides at every moment. My failure to acquire that "skill" hurt my ability to cope in New York. The paradoxical truth is, however, that I see no way to heal the ills of modern civilization without penetrating this wall between self and stranger in these crowded contexts.

Such a wall was precisely the most salient feature of my encounters in Israel in 1996. More than ever before, perhaps partly because of the ongoing destruction of the public space by terrorist bombs, and perhaps partly due to the steadily increasing destruction of internal Jewish cohesiveness at that time, there was an emptiness in the Israeli street, even as thousands passed each other by and jostled physically for room. I especially felt it inside the vast space on the street that lies between the faces of the Jewish other and the Palestinian other, and their separated and hostile psychologies tore me up inside. Each time I have gone to Israel over the last twenty years, fewer and fewer people on the street, even cabdrivers, can bear to greet me with the traditional Israeli greeting, "Shalom," peace. Though I first noticed this decades ago, now many cannot bear to even *return* the greeting to me, as if a reminder of that utopian phrase that suggests so much harmony and beauty is too much to bear in the present context.

One of the cardinal rules of indifferent coexistence in the modern street is the avoidance of eye contact. I remember that in one of my first street encounters with a Palestinian, in 1983, I actually was not afraid to look him in the eye. I had been to Israel several times before as a child and naturally never was allowed by elders to associate with Arabs. In the 1970s, fear dominated those who prevented me from talking to them, fear of terrorists or potential murderers, but somewhere in the 1980s this fear turned into racial or ethnic disdain, increasingly exhibited by both sides in various ways.

I went to Israel in 1983 out of pain. The siege of Beirut, the slaughter at Sabra and Shatila, had shattered much of my self-conception as a Jew and as a newly minted rabbi, and I went to Israel to do peace work with fellow religious Jews committed to Arab-Israeli peacemaking. But I had no conscious plan to meet Arabs; I had many reasons to fear them. After all, significant groups of terrorists considered me—and still do—a legitimate target of warfare simply because I was born Jewish. And yet an encounter with a Palestinian is all that I could think about.

It was a very tense situation. The ever-present threat for Jews of terrorist bombs and attacks was there as usual, but there was also the activity of Meir Kahane and his lieutenants directed against Arab Israeli civilians, as well as the persistent injustices of the entire fate of the Palestinian people.

I found myself one day in the Arab *suk*, the marketplace in the Old City, on my way to the *kotel*, the Wailing or Western Wall. The Wall is the last remnant of the ancient Jewish Temple that had been the object of many of my traditional prayers my whole life, as well as those of all of my ancestors who prayed from the same texts that I used. The *kotel* had been the holiest shrine that I had always dreamed about as a boy. I could not go to Israel without visiting. And yet each time that I go to Israel, it becomes more and more a marker, as far as I can see, of military conflict, of ultimate ethnic confrontation. I visit less and less, and when I do, I find myself weeping intensely, not for the ancient Destruction, but for the present tragedy and militarization of holiness on all sides.

I was always nervous, even terrified, around Arabs. Walking quickly down a narrow alleyway one day, I was hurriedly glancing at the olive wood statues in one shop, when the owner, eager to make a sale, greeted me. For some reason his image stopped me in my tracks. He was a simple Arab man, probably in his sixties, with poor clothing and a broad smile that made his eyes shut most of the way. He wore a traditional head covering, combined with a very old gray jacket and pants. He had only some of his teeth, and his whitish-grayish beard was a few days old.

He looked at me, and I looked hard into his smiling eyes. I saw something disarmingly familiar there, and it pained me in its gentleness. First I could not take my eyes off of him, but then I refocused them on his statues. I saw Moses. My name is Moses. I saw Abraham. And then I looked back at him intensely. I knew Kahane's men had been through that alleyway just days before, overturning carts and making terrible threats, and I could not get that picture out of my mind as I stood before this man.

The Arab man clearly could barely speak English but seemed not to value speaking very much anyway. I think he sensed that I was in pain. And then he did something that will stay with me for the rest of my life. He looked at me, just as I caressed the statue of Abraham, and he pointed up with his finger, and he said, with a heavy accent, "One father?" I nodded, feeling strangely commanded to do so, and I said quietly to him, "One father." Overcome with emotion, and unable to speak, I said good-bye and walked on. I never saw him again.

To this day I am unsure to what he was referring exactly. Was he referring to God as father of all of humanity, including Jews and Arabs? Or was he referring to Abraham as the father of the Jews and the Arabs? I have had difficulty finding texts in the Qur'an about God as father. This metaphor would seem to violate the rather strict antimaterialist, incorporeal language used about God in Islam. But at the time I did not know this, and I assumed he was referring to God, mainly because it resonated with rabbinic language of God as Merciful Father of all of humanity. Now that I teach world religions, I am less sure what he meant but suspect that he meant Abraham as father of all the Semitic peoples.

This, of course, is the genius of metaphor and symbol. Whereas rational negotiation and conflict resolution are confounded by ambivalence, myth and symbol welcome ambivalence and multilayered meaning, which in turn deepen the underlying purposiveness of symbol. In this case, the symbol was intended by this man to be a bond between us that traversed all political and religious walls. It did not matter that I may have gotten it wrong. All that mattered was that it resonated in me with my own set of emotive and sacred referents. This bonded us. If I had sat there and held a rational discourse with him, deconstructed the gesture with the aid of pretentious erudition, and even argued with him about the incorporeality or corporeality of Divine imagery (and I know some people who would have taken the opportunity to argue), I would have destroyed the symbolic gesture and the moment of reconciliation. And all we need, to begin with, to start repairing enemy relationships, are frequent moments of wordless reconciliation. They must slowly build up to a crescendo of trusted dialogue, argumentation, and cooperative solutions in the context of the new relationship. But new relationship is at the core. This Arab man, whom I will never see again, had the genius to create a bond with me, in a split second, with his gaze, with his smile, with one finger, with the backdrop of an actively engaged religious myth, and then with just two words. We shared pain, regret, and hope, all in a single moment of symbolic communication.

Something somewhat similar happened years later in a cafe in Harvard Square in Cambridge, Massachusetts, although not nearly as poignant. A pretty waitress was serving a group of us some hot drinks. She was Middle Eastern, I thought, and I noticed that she had a gold necklace with a beautiful pendant that I thought was in the shape of Israel. It made me smile because I love that unique shape, and she noticed my smile. But then I looked closer and there was a purposeful crack down the middle, and then I realized it was Palestine, rent asunder by the Occupation. She then saw me looking at it, first intently, then disconcertingly, and I imagined she realized who I was—and who she was. I look pretty Jewish, apparently. She looked me in the eyes deeply but casually, smiled, held up the pendant in one hand, and, in the other hand, put two fingers up, and asked, "Two states?" Taken aback, I paused, and I smiled back and said, "Two states." She smiled broadly and walked away.

This was a more politically charged encounter than the one in the *suk*, but the shared commitment to the land, to that pendant and what it symbolized, was an unmistakable cultural if not religious bond. And it worked the same way because of that shared cultural metaphor. Hardly a word was spoken, however, and there was certainly no dialogue workshop, yet what we accomplished should not be belittled. Thousands of such encounters in the public arena could be transformative in the long run, if we paid attention to their importance, taught their importance in our moral and cultural frameworks. Perhaps we even need moral and psychological training for how to respond well to such events, how not to squander or spoil these golden moments of new relationship.

Of course, she and I agreed politically on what must be done. Some would say that this political agreement is the entire battle and nothing was accomplished by my encounter because we already were allies, as it were, politically. I strongly disagree. If the millions of Jews, Christians, and Muslims who *are* committed in principle to coexistence and compromise actually took the time and developed the skills of reconciliation, the sheer power of their activism, the sheer strength of all their new relationships, would have overwhelmed the political and cultural milieu by now. But they have not because most lack the skills and the courage necessary to engage the stranger, the other who has been an enemy. On the contrary, these potential relationships are constantly squandered for a variety of reasons. For example, the elites who engage in peace processes have not invited most people into these processes. In fact, the vast majority of people seem to have been deliberately excluded and cannot be completely blamed for that exclusion, particularly in the Middle East. The truth is there is enough blame to go around on all sides of the conflict, and at all political levels. The most important point is that we constantly underestimate the power of human-to-human encounters to form the basis of new relationships and alliances. We also underestimate the damage done by ugly public encounters and destructive symbolic gestures, which undo the rational willingness to compromise among many people.

Such encounters represent just a few examples from my own experience of the power of symbol in the evocation of relationship between enemies, enemies who exchanged no rational discussion whatsoever, in other words, enemies who typify the vast majority of humanity. We will delve into the nature of such encounters in greater detail later on, as well as suggest practical recommendations to implement peacemaking at this level of human encounter. This is a complex subject, and almost all of us can recount from personal experience many failures as well as successes. But this kind of human interaction is rarely studied and integrated into a conscious way of relationship building with the other. Instead, we herd a few people repeatedly into dialogue sessions, usually the liberals on both sides, as if this is the only form of communication that matters. And we let the public encounter on the street to be tyrannized by crassness and brutality, at best dominated by manipulative commercialism and, at worst, terrorists and their bombs or the likes of Meir Kahane. This is painfully evident on the streets that Jews and Arabs share in the Middle East.

Even as of this writing one senses that those who are in charge of the peace process still do not understand what it means to engage and include the large masses of population on both sides in the peace process. The encounters between Israeli and Arab officials continue to deviate from the agenda of conflict resolution, with a disdain for the masses that is rather insufferable.

The mythic language and symbol that occurs often between enemies, such as the examples given above, suggest vast, untapped power of human reconciliation that peacemaking practices have yet to access. Let us be clear. They do not substitute for rational negotiation but constitute a vital ingredient of human transformation without which rational negotiation becomes its opposite, irrational warfare by means of clever verbal assault and cynical, coercive manipulation of the enemy, and even one's own population. There can be no rationality ultimately in official negotiations without addressing the inner depths of the enemy relationship. Symbol, myth, and the moral rituals of human encounter present an array of important ways to reach the depths of the enemy relationship. Then, a deeper, more authentic understanding better positions us to outline the ways to transform the enemy dynamic.

Regarding the title of this book, I want to engage in a self-reflexive process of acknowledging my use of family metaphor. My basic aim is to bring into peace processes those who identify with old cultural metaphors of family, such as the Abrahamic family. The problem is that this also can alienate, or at least challenge, those who live with and for abstract constructs of the modern period, such as democracy and civil rights, and who have consciously distanced themselves from those selfsame old metaphors. This is certainly true of many secular Israelis for whom religion and anything associated with it are oppressive and destructive. In many ways, the self-consciously secular advocates of democracy, human rights, or economic justice often function as the adolescents of the human family. It is their job to tear down the old in order to make a space for the new, or to make space for themselves and their lifestyles.

Much of the social justice agenda since the 1960s, but even in the last couple of hundred years to a degree, has been dominated by child and adolescent modes of interaction—in other words, noisy protest, the liberal use of "no" as a way of responding to the world, and the need to question authority. In a more extreme expression, we are obviously speaking about Oedipus, and the need to destroy the father to make a space for the son, for the new, in his place.

I do not say this to disparage the need to occasionally tear down the old or to protest, but to see it in perspective.

Building alternative structures that work, however, rather than destroying the old, is the challenge of constructive social change, while protest is easy and unchallenging intellectually, although it takes great emotional courage in the context of oppressive family, social, or political systems. But the child's response to the family is only one piece of the puzzle of human family. It is the parents' job, by contrast, to create and preserve structure, to create a functioning, moral reality in the most profound sense of that term. Anyone who has tried to raise children faces the choice of chaos versus constructed reality every day, with the accompanying choice of whether to construct that reality with brutality or with compassion and patience.

In the societal context, some adults gravitate heavily toward the adolescent response to the human family, while others prefer the parental model. The parent longs for the structure of metaphor, while the adolescent, though often creating alternative metaphors, really longs for the freedom of abstraction. In other words, the sense of injustice, of the unfair status quo, of the desire and need to break it apart, is essentially antimetaphoric.

The metaphor is a bond, or a prison, that connects everyone to their roles and place in reality. It is precisely these old human metaphors—whether it be the metaphorical constructs in India of caste, or class in European culture, or monarchy, or the Divine as above and humanity as below, not to mention metaphors of racial or religious superiority—that are anathema to the adolescent model of creating a better future. But I must also make the case that ancient metaphors, such as the idea of a human family, or a sacredness that resides in all beings, are crucial to humanity and to the basic decency of civilization.

Old metaphors of monotheism to which I am referring include the idea that the human being is a creature in the "image of God," or that the earth is a living organism that needs nurturing or, in non-monotheistic traditions, that the earth is our Mother. Peacemakers in many cultures and religions heavily rely on these metaphors as the foundation of all their work. The parental kind of human being who sees herself as a nurturer and protector tends to defend old metaphors but often blindly ignores their coercive accoutrements. But the adolescent reaction often destroys myths, often blindly running toward an unstructured future without any plan to truly include all people and all generations. To put it more starkly, old metaphors often prevent future changes for the better, while, on the other hand, their destruction often destroys everything that the human mind and heart have accomplished so far. But I would argue that both reactions to metaphor, the parental and the adolescent, need to work together, because there is no good human plan that does not cajole the past and the present into a birth of the future.

In this book I embrace the constructive use of metaphor to bind human beings together and to create the possibility of coexistence and community. I do not deny the coercive functions of metaphor, nor do I deny the critical role of abstractions, such as justice, in the protest against the human capacity for hatred and barbarism. Nevertheless, it seems vital at this point in human evolution to acknowledge that human beings crave metaphor and myth, and that the myth of originating families in monotheism is not worse or better than other old myths. It is the way that millions of people think and perceive. And it can be a vehicle for peace in the future, even as it has also been in the past a repository of self-perpetuating injury and anger.

The injurious side of the family metaphor must be acknowledged and analyzed, however. There is no way to constructively engage myth-infused cultures (and I believe all human life is myth-infused, be it from ancient sources or contemporary constructs[35]) without acknowledging the damaging side of their myths.

The myth of the Abrahamic family is tied inexorably to the experience of deprivation and suffering. This includes infertility, beginning with several of the matriarchs in the biblical book of Genesis. Most important, it has been founded on the fear of exile and homelessness, and the drive to land possession as an antidote. We first meet Abraham as a man who must leave his family, his home, and his land. Abraham's progeny, he is told, will repeat a journey of exile, only after which they will inherit a promised land. This theme is repeated throughout biblical literature and becomes, tragically, a terrible constant of Jewish life for over two thousand years.

It should be noted, however, that the same myth of exile is seen in a positive light as a purifying odyssey, a way of atoning for past sins and imperfections. This is true in both biblical and rabbinic literature.[36] Thus, on one level it builds in a construct of reality that ties its adherents to suffering. Furthermore, the power of myth to generate behavior that confirms its own vision of reality is self-evident. But the healthy aspect of myths involving suffering is their power to help people cope and survive through unbearable circumstances. Not everyone by any means, but billions of people throughout the world are away from the land of their origins. All of their ancestors had to suffer, and many people continue to endure the misery of persecution, migration, and lack of acceptance in new places.

Myth lends meaning and dignity to these experiences and thus provides a crucial means of coping with ultimate suffering and loss. The benefits to humanity are obvious. It may explain why those who have deeply ingrained myths of exile and return may fare much better, from the long view of history, than those indigenous peoples who have been forcibly removed from their place of origin by various empires or, in the contemporary period, by ultranationalism or corporate acquisitiveness and destruction. Indigenous peoples with no experience of migration, and no mythic structures to cope with it, may fare worse when they have no myths to help situate them in a foreign place.

In Islam, the painful exile of Hagar and Ishmael from their home with Abraham is memorialized and reenacted by anyone who performs the Haj, one of the five pillars of Islam, involving a once-in-a-lifetime odyssey to Mecca. Hagar and Ishmael's exile is seen as a part of Allah's plan, according to the story, and it does generate great faith in Allah, who has Ishmael survive and flourish. Thus, once again, whether the mythic aspects of the

Abrahamic story reinforce the experience of suffering or provide a means of coping with it depends on the hermeneutics and the interpretive orientation of the believers involved. In many ways it is a matter of emphasis.

Another key derivative of the Abrahamic myth involves the sacrifice of Isaac, the preparedness of the father to sacrifice the son. This has a direct bearing on the central mythic image of Christianity, the Crucifixion. Now one can see the Crucifixion as a myth of ultimate sacrifice for the love of others, as Jesus offers his life in expiation for the sins of humankind. Certainly, Christian pacifists, peace seekers, and humanitarians have interpreted it in this light throughout Christian history. But it is also an image of ultimate torture, embodying the essence of evil, namely, to kill a blameless prophet and messiah, the "lamb of God." That is why the words "Christ killer" have been on the lips of so many Christians in history who killed Jews, and why the Cross could become conflated with the sword in medieval armor as it evolves into the essential symbol of the violent Crusades. These actions in history, continuing right up to the Bosnian genocide, encapsulate unresolved or perpetuated wounds of Christian identity.

Muhammad's wars, recorded in the Qur'an, become the mythic foundations that justify wars to defend Islam or increase its domain, just as the biblical conquest of Canaan has become the mythic foundation for the Zionist settlement of Israel.

These are all mythic constructs directly related to the Abrahamic family stories. The stories generate at least three understandings of the Abrahamic family, the meaning of its lineage, and its significance for human history. In all three cases, the myth can also generate feelings of isolation and persecution, as personified in the suffering of Isaac as a sacrifice, as well as Jacob, Hagar and Ishmael as wanderers in fear of their lives, Joseph as a prisoner hated by his own family, among many other images of persecution. Furthermore, myths have a way of building on each other over time. In monotheism, the God of Israel is the God of history, and what happens in time must be a part of divine benevolence or divine punishment, and sometimes both, one containing the seeds of the other. Thus, in Jewish tradition, the Exile and promised return at the end of history revisit the exiles and returns of the Patriarchs and the desert-dwelling generation that received the Torah but also worshiped the Golden Calf. The desert generation becomes a permanent representative of an odyssey toward the Promised Land that is singular and unique, requiring repentance and an austere, sanctified life before God in life-threatening circumstances: a basic metaphoric and mythic model for Jewish existence. The persecution of Ali and his family becomes a repetition in Shi'a Islam of the persecution of the Prophet in Mecca that causes his exile to Medina but also paves the way for his triumphant return. Innumerable saints in Christianity suffer the same fate as did Jesus. But, in fact, they often long to do so, because martyrdom is the ultimate act of devotion to God, and, I would argue, also a powerful mythic construct of life that gives meaning to not only one's existence, but, more important, one's death.

Death is the great enemy of human meaningfulness, at least as we all instinctually fear and loathe it. But martyrdom in the footsteps of a prophet, messiah, or God Himself is the ultimate victory over meaninglessness in death. Dying on the way to the Holy Land, in a desert of godlessness or cruelty, becomes a noble victory over death in Jewish tradition, as long as one's children continue the life of Torah, which, by its nature, guarantees an ultimate return to the sacred home. The life of Torah in exile, even an exile of thousands of years, becomes the secret route through the desert to the Holy Land.

There are also at least three ways that this mythic structure can generate hatred, conflict, and violence. One is that the mythic sense of persecution and suffering becomes interpreted as a license to take revenge on enemies, rather than leaving justice to the divine author of history, a theme so often emphasized in biblical literature. The second is that the sense of persecution becomes internalized and transformed into various forms of self-hatred and mutual recrimination. The third is that the sense of family chosenness and uniqueness, combined with the mythic aspects of suffering, leads to a sense of superiority over others that gives one license to persecute in turn those who are not from the family. In various ways, this is epitomized in the Genesis stories themselves by the murderous actions of Simeon and Levi, who kill an entire town of people who just became circumcised to join the Abrahamic clan. Their own father curses their rage and punishes them in his final blessings to them.[37]

Now some have argued that these by-products are endemic, built into the very notion of family chosenness, and that all ethnic violence, especially in Abrahamic contexts, is attributable to the chosenness theme of the Abrahamic family myth.[38] I differ strongly with this position. It argues implicitly and explicitly that only universalist mythic constructs work in creating the good society, and family mythic constructs, especially of Abrahamic chosenness, cause conflict, chauvinism, and racism. But if family mythic constructs create hatred, then we must side with Plato and Marx and try to dispense with the family, which after all is an intentional construct that need not necessarily exist in reality.

There is no question that family creates boundaries of special love and privilege that often lead to chauvinism or the inculcation of chauvinism, and selfishness in the case of some parents. But intentional family also creates the most basic avenue that we have as human beings for passing on nurturing and love, which are at the heart of the good human community. Anyone who is a parent sees a directly proportional relationship between the time and energy that they put into parenting and the prosocial results with their children. I have been able to trace my daughter's good moods and prosocial tendencies directly to the days and weeks when I was able to give her exclusive attention. Of course, this assumes parents who have basic social skills and moral teachings that do not make children *more* angry and miserable by being with their parents. Even assuming parents of the best character, children require enormous amounts of time that could not possibly be given by adults to every child he/she sees on the street. On the contrary, part of what gives the child security and a meaningful identity is that her parents treat her specially and differently. In other words, the unique bonds of special treatment generate the *most* loving tendencies in children.

Can this lead to inner orientations such as "family at the center and every-one else be damned"? Of course, but that is exactly the point. It is not family or special family love that creates hatred and conflict historically. Rather, it is how that special love is negotiated in the face of competing values, norms and feelings vis à vis other human beings. The myth of family is not the prob-lem, but the way that myth either closes in on itself or, alternatively, becomes extended by adults to the application of care, justice, compassion, and friend-ship to others beyond the family.

The Abrahamic myth of a loving Patriarch and a loving God who care for a special people has created a home and a meaning system for millions of human beings, in all three Abrahamic faiths, for centuries. In addition to the notion of a special and unique relationship to God, there is also the mythic construct of the Abrahamic family as a historic phenomenon through which all the peoples of the earth would be blessed.[39] It is also a construct of family and a special people who will follow the path of the parent, the "path of YHVH," to do justice and righteousness.[40] This can, and for some does, ex-tend the myth to a universal commitment.

The hateful family teaches hatred of other children, but the family as such does not require hatred. Families can be beloved and privileged in their self-definition but care for others precisely because their own belovedness gives them the emotional strength to take care of the outsider. The real challenge is not the separation of human beings by the bonds of family, but rather how the boundaries between family and others are negotiated.

This returns us full circle to the biblical stranger myth. The key is how we negotiate the boundary with the stranger, not whether we see ourselves as a part of a special family. Here is my most important rebuttal, however, of the antifamily or antitribal position. I have never encountered a civilization or subculture whose claim to absolute universalism did not turn out to be a mask for tribal needs and boundaries. Most human systems of meaning, *whether they claim officially to be tribalistic or universalist in their orientation*, seem to fulfill a human need to feel unique, gifted, even superior in some sense. Liberal democrats in today's global society consider themselves the most universalist, but they too belong to a tribe that is convinced that their way of life and their values are superior to everyone else's. That does not make them evil, just human. But, unfortunately, claims to antitribal universalism and the denial of boundaries often lead to violence against others who do not fit this "universal," one-size-fits-all, construct of values, normality, intellectual ad-equacy, and civility.

This does not mean that we human beings need to deny our obligation to argue in the public or international arena for values we think are universally applicable. I am merely arguing for more humility and more respect for the wisdom of many meaning systems. Thus, to impute exclusively to tribal peoples and beliefs the human need to be different and special is dangerous and wrong. It has not been ethnicity and the family values of ethnicity that have created countless human wars, but rather *inadequate* family and ethnic values, family values that did not take seriously and honorably the world beyond one's family. It is not ethnicity and family that have been to blame, but ethnicity and family borne of rage and hatred for the other. But for all the wars that have been caused as a result of this, just as many wars have been prevented by people who did have a concept of family and ethnic self-definition that allowed them to live well with others. By contrast, many wars and unjust international practices have been directly related to arrogant universalist presumptions, from *pax romana* two thousand years ago, all the way to communism. It is the dynamic possibility of the family metaphor, therefore, that we must investigate here, as far as this affects the past, present and future of mythic interpretations of the Abrahamic families.

I illustrate the dynamic possibilities of family metaphors in supporting peace processes, based on encounters that I had on the West Bank in the fall of 1999. There are at least several West Bank rabbis, major players in the community of settlers, who are now openly speaking in midrashic (metaphoric) terms about re-evaluating the past relationship between Abraham and his two families, and specifically Ishmael. Midrashic thinking[41] is critical to Jewish moments of cultural change. In most religious traditions, law and ritual are very hard to change, especially in tumultuous times, precisely because for so many people ritual rigidity and legal adherence are anchors in the midst of a chaotic world. In Jewish life this is especially the case because there exists such a rich history of forced displacement. Place offers no security at all. For many religious Jews, the answer is ritual predictability. Religious Jews may not know where their grandchildren are going to live and be secure, and they may have really no memories of the place that their grandparents grew up. But it is significant to them that they can go anywhere in the world and find a few religious Jews who are engaged in the same prayers or dietary rituals. This is their one anchor.

When change needs to occur, the law is usually the last place to which it comes. But midrash, sermonic expansion upon the biblical text, and the creative interpretation of rabbinic adages comprise a path of creativity and dynamic growth. For this reason, the first signs of a profoundly new cultural matrix on the West Bank are coming from midrashic and sermonic thinking.

It must be recalled that Genesis is seen in Judaism as a set of stories demonstrating the chosen lineage of Abraham which links the Jewish people to Abraham, through Isaac, Jacob and the twelve brothers, but especially Judah. The choices of the matriarchs and patriarchs involved a favoring of some sons over others. One rabbi to whom I listened was expounding on these matters to his young students, all of them rather nationalistic settlers. As usual, he focused heavily on the holiness and centrality of the land of Israel as a special gift to the Jewish people. And, also as usual, the focus was on the special status, yes, spiritual superiority of the Jewish people who have unique gifts to offer the world.[42]

Curiously, however, and out of the ordinary, were this rabbi's many references to Ishmael, and some suggestions that perhaps Sarah had been wrong for sending him and his mother into the desert. As someone who can recite typical Jewish sermons in my sleep after a lifetime of listening, I was startled. This perspective was different and new. Furthermore, the rabbi made surprising comments about the destiny of Isaac and Ishmael to live near each other, and, indeed, for this to be part of the divine plan for the world. A new look at coexistence with Ishmael was at the heart of these complex midrashic comments that were revisited intermittently over the course of a Sabbath. An artful combination of chosenness and coexistence was afoot.

All this must be understood within the backdrop of all of rabbinic culture, which sees Ishmael as the symbol of Arab Muslim descendents of Abraham, and Esau as the Christian descendants. To say such things in sermonic reflections in Israel is a very clear way to speak indirectly about the future of Jewish/Islamic relations. But had the rabbi spoken directly about it, he may not have been heard. It might be too much for his students to accept. But they are forced, culturally speaking, to listen to his "words of Torah," that is, his interpretations of biblical texts and rabbinic commentary, on a typical Sabbath, in the study hall or synagogue. He is deftly inserting a new set of midrashic possibilities into the nationalist Orthodox imagination, ones that will surely be met with resistance but not the righteous kind of resistance that rejects the "self-hating, leftist, anti-Jewish" rhetoric of non-Orthodox, nonsettler Jews. This is yet another piece of the highly detailed puzzle of peacemaking. It is a piece that some will find exciting and innovative, while others will find it revolting. But it is a piece without which the puzzle is impossible to complete.

These metaphors penetrate deeply into the Jewish imagination. I was shocked recently when a congregant of mine confessed that he actually did not come to synagogue the week that the Torah portion focused on Abraham's expulsion of Hagar and Ishmael to the desert. It upset him so that he could not come. It was the first time in my career that I saw an act of not coming to synagogue as a deeply spiritual gesture of engagement with the sacred text. Engagement with Jewish texts by disagreement is a tradition going back to hoary antiquity—as long as one stays engaged.

I responded to my congregant with my own faith position that has evolved over many years of analysis of the biblical text, as well as many painful realizations about my own family's history. I argued to him that most of the tragedies of Genesis, the hatred, the jealousy, the family violence, are traceable to the preferences made for one child over another by both parents, and for one wife over another by the men. Indeed, if Jacob's family had not self-destructed, they may have never went down to Egypt and experienced exile. But the plain meaning of the text also indicates that this was a path of salvation as well, in that Joseph saves the family from starvation.

The Bible is a nuanced and paradoxical book. I have little doubt that the later rules that prohibit a man from prejudice against the son of the unfavored wife is a specific rebuke to the Patriarchs and the tragic mistakes of their family life.[43] The Bible specifically does not deify human beings; they all must have flaws, including the founders of a religion. This flaw of preferences for children is the central flaw of Genesis, I argue, possibly even implicating God Himself in the Cain/Abel tragedy. Furthermore, all the later moral laws of justice, equity, care for family, and the prohibitions against jealousy and revenge are designed to mollify and heal the wounds of the Abrahamic family.

To take this one step further, it implies that, in the long view of history, Ishmael and Isaac, as well as Jacob and Esau, must establish a new relationship for this family of Abraham to truly flourish, for this family to be able to fix the wrongs of the past, and then, after all the injustices have been repaired, to find the way to repent for what they have done to each other.[44]

This has broad implications for the powerful possibilities of Arab/Jewish reconciliation in general, and for Israeli/Palestinian reconciliation in particular. It means that as we pursue our analysis of the deeper aspects of the conflict, as well as pragmatic ways to move forward, we must be aware that we are tampering with primordial identities. We cannot change these easily, but when we do change them the effects are more profound than anyone can imagine. The mythic and moral imagination is allowed to freely construct a new future, and, to the degree to which the latter is wedded to a new construct of coexistence, one can create the bedrock of moral society.

3 🍃

Political and Mythic Interdependencies

It is self-evident that official processes of diplomacy and rational methods of negotiation are indispensable to the solution of any conflict involving states and/or large numbers of people who live within particular geopolitical boundaries. However, it is equally true that right beneath the surface of most human exchanges is a myriad of constructs of reality, of the collective self, and of the "other," by each and every party to a conflict, including intervenors. These constructs can only be described as mythical. The myths often express themselves in terms of some idealized self-image, together with a demonized mythic construct of the "other," both replete with centuries of evidence.

I am sorry to report that, in my experience, most intervenors carry other myths (certainly less destructive, but also problematic occasionally). Examples include the myth that everyone can win in the conflict situation if they just rationally construct a win-win scenario,[1] or that everything would be solved if everyone agrees to forgive and forget the past, or that democracy will solve all conflicts, or that accessing the rational faculties of the brain will provide all the answers to intractable arguments, or that faith in God is the answer to all conflicts, and many more constructs of reality. All of these constructs have "evidence," but, of course, only *partial* evidence—that great deceiver of the neocortex.[2]

My analysis of this is related to the nascent school of conflict resolution known as worldview theory,[3] but also the general approach of anthropology to human conflict,[4] as well as psychodynamics.[5] These approaches help to explain the persistence of conflicts over years and even centuries, the kind that defy all appeals to rational self-interest. In addition, and farther along the spectrum of mythic perception, there are, of course, the constructs of peoplehood, nationhood, and religious community, which play a critical role in many conflicts.

Myths are so pervasive in human constructs of reality that it is impossible to consider strategies of conflict resolution that do not confront them. Those who tend to minimize as far as possible the significance of myth, and try as much as they can to delimit its effects, assume that the effects of myth can be only deleterious—a prejudice in itself, namely, that we all can completely escape our myths, and an irrational response to the phenomenon of human nonrationality. It is like ignoring gene mutation theory, and fighting cancer as if genes did not exist.

Clearly, one works with the mutated gene or the cancer cell, seeking to understand how a healthy gene turns into a deadly one, but not by denying that genes are the key to life! Myths are the genes beneath much of human life, and, like genes, there are healthy myths and destructive myths, or interpretations thereof. Bad myths, like "the thousand-year Reich," kill people and destroy many things in this world. But good myths, like "inalienable human rights" or "the inherent dignity of the human being," save lives and help to construct extraordinary communities and civilizations that possess immense gifts, without which human life could not really continue.

The rational processes of political negotiation can never get very far away from the myths that undergird human life. There is a political and mythic interdependency that requires us to work with both in order to achieve political settlements that involve major shifts in human consciousness about the Self, the Other, and the Community. Peace involves a seismic shift in human worldview. It assaults our entire conception of and emotional disposition toward whom and what we are to love and hate. It transforms the most basic moral foundation of our consciousness, namely, our dispositional answer to the question of questions, "Where do good and evil lie?" How can one accomplish this without mythic transformation as a critical adjunct to rational discourse?

It is true that elites, who believe that they are acting rationally on behalf of everyone whom they lead (but who, in fact, are often acting in the interests of their class or subgroup), may be able to, and often do, impose peace on most people in a society. But, as Johann Galtung has said often, all conflicts are old conflicts, conflicts that should have been resolved deeply and fairly, but were merely papered over. Such superficial peacemaking may be all that one can achieve in certain situations. But more often than not, peacemaking is left at a superficial level, because to go deeply into a shift of paradigms for a culture is too threatening to those in leadership positions. It would involve sharing the process of change with too many people. Everyone thinks that the usurpation of power is a trademark of warfare, but it is also a characteristic of peacemaking, and it often, therefore, sets the stage for the next conflict.

Let us take a contemporary example from 1999. If, in 1999, businesspeople and other elites in Serbia, together with the Orthodox Church, had managed to conduct a bloodless coup against Milosevic and managed to remove him completely from power, the money for reconstruction of Serbia would probably have started pouring in from the rest of Europe and the United States. All the official agencies and governments who had held off from supporting

Milosevic would have jumped on the bandwagon, and rapprochement would be eagerly sought, I suspect. But would this do anything for the future of human relationships in the Balkans? It would do some good, undoubtedly, in terms of basic material needs, assuming that there was equitable distribution—a big assumption. But it would also do harm, because it would mask just how much this was a coup against a man who came to be reviled by elites in Serbia, but not for sacrificing the lives of thousands of Muslims for the sake of Greater Serbia. For too many people in the Serbian opposition in the late 1990s, it is precisely because Milosevic failed in his goal of a greater Serbia that he was criticized. Can we really say that we saw at that point overwhelming evidence of a profound, society-wide repentance over the atrocities in the Bosnian war, for example? Of course there are many courageous individuals, some secular and some clergy. And it is easy to point to and agree with Serbian outrage at the atrocities committed against them in Bosnia and now in Kosovo. It has also become clear over time, since then, that the end of Milosevic's regime has actually empowered those who wanted a new regional relationship and more acknowledgement of past wrongs.

However, a thorough acknowledgement and rejection of Serbian atrocities is not in evidence among the mainstream of this culture as of this writing. There is no widespread willingness to face their role in the tragedy. For a true transformation of Balkan relationships to come about, all the dreams, hopes, failures, and nightmares of these warring ethnic communities need to be put on the table of peace and change. And for real change to come to Serbia, there must be a profound societywide reckoning with its past and its future with neighbors. Thus, the elite solution of simply dispensing with a Milosevic, or a Karadzic in Serbska, is inadequate, obsessing over a few elite leaders while papering over the need for much more profound change. Of course, I readily admit that politically such solutions provide an important opening to a different future, but I do not share the obsession of some with a handful of high-profile war criminals.

My concern is with permanent transformation, not tokens thrown to those who cry for justice. On the punitive side of redressing the past, for example, I would have been much more impressed in Nazi Germany, and in other situations of war crimes, with a large, meticulously researched list of murderers who would be disallowed from any role in or benefits from public life, rather than the successful prosecution of a handful and the dismissal of most cases. It is astonishing to me, for example, that German SS troops still receive pensions from the same German government that has dispensed billions of Marks as compensation to victims of those same SS soldiers! What kind of message does that send to the children of the future, or even to present-day soldiers in the German army? It is vital to think in terms of transformation, not token gestures that are rooted in political calculation.

These are the kind of calculations that are required as we consider the permanent moral transformation of a community suffering the blight of war criminality. Courageous Serbian citizens today should be encouraged in their efforts to support an entirely new leadership of their moral, spiritual, and political communities, leadership that would continue to stand up for defenseless Serbians in neighboring countries, but, at the same time, utterly disown the war criminals among them. This is the only way to renew Serbian identity, one that corresponds to the highest ideals of their culture, not the lowest common denominators of a negative identity. It is wonderful that Milosevic has been removed by popular vote, but much more needs to be done to transform the damage done to Serbian culture and society.

Identities and collective goals must be reexamined by thousands of people on all sides of the Balkan wars, all in the search for new mythic paradigms of what it really means to be a Serb, a Croat, a Bosnian, or a citizen of Kosovo. A process of multilateral acknowledgment of historical wrongs, apologies, and even repentance is also necessary. All of this would have to be carefully negotiated—yes, with the aid of rational negotiation processes, which I have nothing against. But real prevention of future conflict will require a sea change in communal consciousness and mythic self-understanding, as well as an evolution of defining religious values.

Only if these changes occur will leaders like Milosevic truly come to rest in the dustbin of history. If not, then they themselves, or the specter of their presence, will come back to haunt politics and culture. Furthermore, even the most subtle shifts in elite leadership sometimes create a profound impact on large populations, who do take their cues from leaders, but who also amplify the cultural cues that they are receiving. It is this ripple effect that I am searching for. But, if the political changes of violent actors merely smack of greedy sycophantry before Western elites in search of Western business contracts, conditions would only amplify in the direction of fellow votaries of greed, not the injured *and* injuring masses who have borne the brunt of the Balkans' violent history.[6] Their families must enter into the world of peace and conflict resolution, of meeting the "other" in a new context.

Understanding and working with their mythic worldviews is the key to this door. Otherwise a sufficient number of the masses will continue the ethnic warfare underground, right underneath the noses of international peacekeeping. This is the essence of ethnically based organized crime that ravaged the former Yugoslavia in the late 1990s. It is ethnic war gone underground, and it reveals the failure of the peace process to extend itself into the hearts and minds of the people, especially at the village level.

With these cautionary recommendations in mind, let us now turn to the Israelis and Palestinians, Jews and Arabs, the main subject of this book. I want to share a peacemaking undertaking that I have been engaged in, both as a participant and as an observer, in the recent past.

I never really wanted to visit the West Bank in 1997, but I had to, to meet an extraordinary rabbi. I had not been deep inside the West Bank since 1971, four years after the capture of the Territories, and the year of my Bar Mitzvah[7]. My mother made me an offer that, instead of having a large celebration, which she knew I did not want, the whole family could go to Israel for the first time in our lives in the summer after my Bar Mitzvah. This turned out to be the highlight of my young life. When we arrived in Hebron, as part of a nation-wide tour, I sensed that the tour guide was somewhat nervous, and I certainly sensed that the local residents, the Arabs, did not seem happy that I was there. That is all I knew or understood at age 13. But I also understood that, according to the stories of my people—which held far more truth for me at the time than anything political—that I was going to the grave of the first Jew on earth, my ancestor, to a grave and a piece of land legally purchased over four thousand years ago by Abraham for his wife and himself. It was a culminating experience of my life, and to this day it has deep meaning.

When I returned, twenty-seven years later, the region had seen all the horrors of the Intifada, and I had no desire to be there, but not because I had no emotional or spiritual investment in the place. On the contrary, the emotional investment that I had—and have—in the ancient lands of Judea and Samaria made it that much harder to be there. The millennia of yearning for it, the blood spilled to take it and to keep it, and the suffering that this has caused to Palestinians in particular, but also to the Jewish people, has made me sick at heart for much of my life. I often felt, when returning to or near the disputed lands of Israel, like a player in a drama of unrequited love. I could not bear to see that which I could not have, and so I chose to stay as far away as possible from ancient Jewish lands that had to be, in the long run, the only hope for creating a state for Palestinians, a state that was the only possible key to healing the wounds of history.

I came back to the West Bank because I had to. I had to see a man, a rabbi like myself, for whom all the ancient land of Israel is so sacred that he loathes to ever leave, even on trips, a man who was one of the founders of the very settlement process that had driven me as a rabbi into the peace movement—as well as into despair. But he also happened to be one of the most interesting peacemakers in Israel, and, almost more than anyone else, he had delved deeply into the nascent Islamic-Jewish relationship.

Rabbi Menachem Frohman is the rabbi of the settlement of Tekoa. Tekoa is a name that resonated with me, but with meaning that in many ways was theologically the antithesis of a West Bank settlement, at least in my theological universe. It is the birthplace of one of the great prophets of the Bible, Amos, an older contemporary of Isaiah and perhaps the most consistently courageous and outspoken prophet of social justice in Judaism. His passion for the poor, and for anyone who suffers injustice, is pervasive in his short but revolutionary writings.

When I left Jerusalem in the early hours of the morning in a special cab to meet Rabbi Frohman, it was with a mixture of anticipation of good work to be done, combined with fear of going to the West Bank, and a certain unexplainable disdain or disgust, as if I were doing something wrong, betraying I don't know who. The truth is that I had fought for years in a certain camp of Jewish politics. I fought against the settlements and against the settlers, and waging this battle was one of the saddest experiences of my life. I did not enjoy fighting them, which went against the grain of all my moral instincts as well as my upbringing. "You don't embarrass other Jews in public or split ranks." "You don't put other Jews at risk." "We have enough problems with our enemies, and we must never add to that burden." "*Ahavas yisroel* (the love of Israel) is one of the central commandments of Judaism." These voices in my mind made me sick at heart all the time.

In recent years I had come to see and believe that pursuing social justice or radical change by way of large-scale political confrontation and demonization is not a path that I can follow anymore. It became clear to me that profound changes for the better in human political life sometimes come from combative confrontation, but that such a method often makes matters worse as well, with many hidden costs. Ironically, much of my struggle was with the style of the ancient prophets. My recent intuitions and experience had led me to believe that Talmudic *mitsvot,* or methods, of relationship building, of love, respect, compassion, patience, and various gestures of mutual aid, friendship, and kindness contained the kernels of a sophisticated method of social change. The latter brings about both peace and justice in a way that is much more effective than the old prophetic diatribes. The old diatribes were highly articulate, inspired, in the figurative and literal sense. And they set up for all time the clear rights and wrongs of societal structure. But they exuded anger most of the time, and people cannot really listen to anger directed at them for very long, if at all. Indeed, the great prophets did fail as a group to reverse Israelite failings.

Personally as well, I was tired of shouting and rage. It exhausted me and I felt increasingly that, as right as our intentions were, shouting them was simply wrong and destructive. And yet I think it is safe to say that those old prophets and their diatribes formed the bedrock of any Jewish or monotheistic conscience that has said, at one point or another: "This is not the way things ought to be. I believe and I know that life, that we as people, can be better." Thus, I continue to love those prophets as close friends, even if their methods of social change were not so successful.

When I went to the West Bank, however, I made no association with the name Tekoa because I had come to expect that, for political purposes, many ancient names were being revived on the West Bank, and I was skeptical about these revivals. So I had no reason to feel any special attachment to the place when I got there. I safely reached the settlement, breathed at least one sigh of relief, and then made my way to the rabbi's very simple home.

Rabbi Frohman is a gregarious, extremely sharp, friendly, but also rather intimidating man, at least to me. He is famous in Israel and was appointed rabbi of the Knesset under Netanyahu, despite his peacemaking efforts. He has met with many major players of the political process, numerous times, including Arafat, various prime ministers, and even Sheikh Yassin, of Hamas. His Hebrew is quite sophisticated, while mine is only adequate. As opposed to most Israelis he has no interest in Westernizing himself in the least. Therefore, he has made no real attempt to make himself understood in the English press or in the United States. In addition, as engaging as he is, he carries the burdens of Israeli life and death on the West Bank. Jewish settler deaths hit him hard because he knows all of them, but so do Palestinian deaths. Of course, with each Jewish death in the Netanyahu years, Frohman paid a higher and higher price politically, even in terms of risk to his life from fellow Jews. Thus, he was in the mood to be nice to me, but not overly tolerant of liberal platitudes.

Frohman lives with a sense of urgency because he is on a mission to bring about a better Israel, a more peaceful society, and, above all, a religious vision in which Jews and Muslims work together to create a truly Holy Land, the *Eretz HaKodesh* envisioned by the Jewish prophets. And, yes, he is deeply engaged in anticipation of a Messianic kingdom. Of course, the land is already innately holy for him, and its holiness drives much of his existence and his passion.

For me the holiness of the land of Israel was turned into an idolatry to which all other Jewish moral values were sacrificed. But these are things I did not say as a bridge builder and peacemaker. For me the land's holiness was only one theological principle or existential reality that had to be balanced with numerous others, not the least of which were the commitment to the sacredness of all human life, compassion, justice, and the inviolate nature of other people's property rights. Here I felt a chasm between us, not because he would deny those other principles, but because the overriding existential reality for him, and others, of the sacredness of land has always made me nervous in its inherent and historically proven capacity to undergird moral and political disasters. But, at the same time, I was and am humbled by Rabbi Frohman's moral courage, the kind that comes from being on the front lines of life-and-death battles.

I grew up in a self-consciously exilic spirituality, one in which time is more sacred than space, animate things, like people, were more central than inanimate things, and the relationship with the Other was more central than the transitory relationship to place. And yet I, like everyone else, long for place as well, while merely suppressing that need as part of an immigrant family that seemed to relish the opportunity to not pass on memories of our European place. But Frohman is deeply aware of displacement as well, feeling intently his essential identity as a Polish Jew. But this drives him to precisely value place, sacred place, at this juncture of Jewish history, after the Holocaust proved all the things it proved to Jews.

So here we were, two religious Jews, strict Sabbath observers, both rabbis, yet the gulf between us was palpable, without my needing to say a word of protest. Nevertheless I liked him immediately. I liked his intensity, his humor about himself in the midst of deadly serious issues, his sharpness with Jewish texts, his genius at psychopolitical calculation that betrayed a mind and heart capable of seizing the moments of history for truly redemptive change. Yes, he was the ultimate student of Rav Kook, and one of the few who took *all* of Rabbi Kook the Elder seriously, including the universally redemptive, the care expressed for all of humanity that became overshadowed by ultra-nationalism at the hands of Rabbi Kook's successor.[8]

I asked him about the name of the settlement, and he said, with that gregarious, demanding level of surprise in his voice, that, of course, I should have known that it was the birthplace of Amos. But then I urbanely expressed doubt. He replied that, on the contrary, the archeological evidence proved, in the midst of many other questionable claims to authenticity in Israel, that this claim was authentic, and that, in his tiny living room we really were sitting on top of ancient Tekoa.

And so this seized me, as if by the throat, and I instinctively sprang from my chair and went out the living room sliding door to the veranda. I touched the tree in his garden and saw a few pieces of discarded wood, but they looked to me like a treasure of diamonds. I looked over to the next hill, which was almost as bare as desert. And, after falling in love in Northern Ireland that same year with the lavish greens of Irish hills—to which these hills could hardly compare aesthetically—the "only" thing that I loved here was, stated simply, eternity and home, and a view of the hills that was the view of Amos. It arrested me and left me speechless, so that our meeting could not go on for a time, while I recovered.

We then talked for five hours straight in his living room, eye to eye, and it seemed like five minutes. And he changed me. He made me realize how deep my own prejudices go. And I came to realize on that day that anyone, no matter what his political or religious orientation, can be at the heart of peacemaking in this world. Rabbi Frohman had been engaged for many years in contacts with Islamic leaders on the West Bank, and even with some in Hamas, at the same time that he was the rabbi of a major Jewish settlement, and while continuing to promote other settlements! He was well known and respected by Arabs in many regions, for the simple reason that he displayed one characteristic that has eluded so many Jews and Westerners. He shows respect, deep respect for Arab and Islamic tradition, for culture, for the dignity of others, even for people who had killed Jews, his own beloved people. But he was also respected and admired by many Jewish settlers, because they knew by his actions and constant gestures that he loved them, that his empathy for them was beyond any doubt, something that liberal Israel has completely failed to do as they try to bring peace to the country. Yes, he is awash in paradoxicality that must resolve itself in political choices eventually. But he undermines all preconceptions, and that kind of cognitive dissonance is good for intractable conflicts.

Rabbi Frohman's commitments to peacemaking emerge out of a combination of a savvy, pragmatic view of Jewish history and Jewish-gentile relationships,[9] together with a very sophisticated reading of Jewish theology, particularly about what it will take to bring true redemption to the land of Israel. He has a vision of coexistence in which, somehow, Israel and Palestine will be part of the same Holy Land, *eretz ha-koydesh* in his Polish-Hebrew language. How this will happen he does not spell out, although some details are emerging.[10]

Here is the central axis of what I would call his mythically based peacemaking. He is not interested in boundaries and borders but relationships and visions. And he works tirelessly to transform just those things, visions and relationships, but with a keen sense of what is wise, intelligent, and safe to do. His concern with Jewish safety is paramount, and his close attention to pragmatic details removes him from the company of armchair utopians.

What plans did he have for me? This is where the interplay of political processes and cultural peacemaking, or what I call political and mythic interdependencies, becomes interesting. Rabbi Frohman, together with a number of idealistic religious people in Jerusalem, had been creating bridges between the leadership in the Islamic Palestinian world and that of the Jewish Orthodox world of Israel, some of whom might be called modern Orthodox and others who were *haredi*. On the whole, the contacts were between very conservative figures on both sides. Now these high-level contacts have been proceeding for some time, and some of the leading figures in Meimad, elected to Parliament in 1999, have played a key role in this. However, the Meimad people involved have kept most contacts secret, in consideration of the fact that the bridges that they were building were with people on the Islamic side who would be jeopardized by publicity.

Rabbi Frohman has always taken a different route on this matter. He was, until appointed rabbi of the Knesset, a non-establishment figure, who would use the media to demonstrate his messages and did not hesitate to describe his contacts in the Arab world. This is always a point of friction between peacemakers, namely, how public or secret contacts should be, and, as a corollary, how quickly or slowly to push relationships forward. Rabbi Frohman is an intense visionary, and he also felt, at least when I saw him in 1997, when settlers were dying frequently from attacks, and the peace process was almost moribund, that dramatic measures were necessary. And we both have felt that deep cultural and psychological transformations of a public nature can often stimulate breakthroughs in the political arena, especially when normal paths of negotiation are stuck.

What he and others outside of the mainstream negotiators were planning for was nothing less than revolutionary. They wanted a first-time-ever treaty or covenant between Judaism and Islam.[11] In particular, they hoped that the public events surrounding this, and the accompanying symbolism, such as the jolting effect of chief rabbis and sheikhs embracing, would create a religious-psychological breakthrough that would generate its own momentum of peacemaking.

Wisely, and in contrast with the standard Western behavior of anti-establishment progressives, he tried at every possible opportunity to coordinate and win approval for these efforts at the highest mainstream levels of political leadership on both sides. Thus, he met with prime ministers, past and present, as well as with Arafat, among others in the Palestinian leadership. In other words, he attempted to coordinate first- and second-track diplomacy.[12] According to his testimony, Arafat agreed with the idea from the beginning but was not as yet providing the crucial public support necessary for various religious leaders to come forward publicly to participate. This was the crucial linchpin in terms of Arab participation that was still missing. On the Jewish side, there were key high-level rabbinic leaders prepared to participate. Even Netanyahu had expressed support.

Through various channels it became apparent that both sides at the time were heavily dependent on the United States for leadership in peace initiatives and peace gestures, because direct relations were at such an all-time low. Even as of 2001 there still is a dearth of leadership to address this matter from both sides. For example, Frohman had hoped that the issue of religious relations would be raised at Wye Plantation, but he received indications that, although Netanyahu was ready for discussion, the Americans never raised the issue. In some ways it was a chicken-and-egg problem.

On a deeper level, it has become apparent to me that, with the exception of a few wonderful diplomats, governments are allergic to any diplomatic efforts other than official ones. Furthermore, those around the president, perhaps around any president, in the Executive Branch, dislike anything that they cannot control. Religious figures are generally considered part of the problem, but not part of creative solutions by most people in the public policy arena. Religion itself is seen as so explosive politically that to even touch upon it lays the president and high officials vulnerable to intense attack. This predisposition may or may not change, but there are a few people inside government who would like to see it change.

No one underestimates the capacity of religious bodies and leaders to be unpredictable, or to flout standard rules of diplomacy. But this is a problem with all conflicts and all actors who do not fit the precise, government-to-government mold, and yet it is religious actors who are singled out and systematically excluded from mainstream diplomacy. Why are the warlords of Africa, or former terrorists of the IRA, for example, more predictable and better partners in diplomacy? All intractable, violent conflicts entail entry into conversation with unpredictable leadership. But among various state and non-state actors, the world of religion seems particularly far off the radar screen of creative problem solving, in terms of both first-track and secular, second-track diplomacy. It is the height of absurdity that, in conflicts where religious people on both sides are playing every bit as damaging a role in undermining peace as the paramilitaries in Northern Ireland, for example, somehow these religious actors are consistently eliminated from the sphere of diplomacy. This has deep and complicated roots in the West that deserve a separate study.[13]

Rabbi Frohman and many others have worked hard to rectify this absurd situation. Based on Rabbi Frohman's constant prodding, I have used all my contacts to communicate directly and indirectly with various people in the U.S. government, to impress upon them the golden opportunity we have now for shifting the religious cultures of the region toward coexistence. All the religions of the region have been radicalized by recent Middle Eastern history and have suffered deeply in terms of the violent excesses committed in their name, due to the Arab-Israeli conflict in particular. Many on both sides, including key religious leaders, would welcome the opportunity to clear the name of religion, as it were, and to become a part of the peace process. But this development has been ignored and even suppressed repeatedly by secular leadership, even leadership of the peace process. From my own meetings in Washington, D.C., I concluded that if we were to accomplish something dramatic independently they would welcome it, but that they were not authorized to aid such processes at all. That was the best that I could elicit from the most sympathetic listeners.

The Palestinian-Israeli relationship was sufficiently bad in the fall of 1998, before One Israel's rise to power in the Knesset, that many of us felt that the possibility of peace was disappearing rapidly. Rabbi Frohman tried his best to continue relationships on all sides, including those with Likud and Netanyahu. I got the impression that he had either direct or indirect knowledge of Netanyahu's attitudes toward the Arabs and the peace process. It was apparent to many that Netanyahu was deeply ambivalent on many levels of the peace process, and that even as he moved forward he also moved backward, and not always due to crass political calculations. He had deep ambivalence about Arabs per se that explains many of his actions. Nevertheless, for the purpose of our analysis, it seems that, at a critical juncture of Netanyahu's political vulnerability, had the Americans pushed the idea of cultural and religious peacemaking in a parallel track, it is likely that he would have gone along with it. It was territory and power that he could not bring himself to share with the Palestinian leadership. But that is the beauty of psycho-cultural gestures and peacemaking. The experience of them can sometimes pave the way for profound shifts in trust regarding the more difficult issues of power sharing.

My own perception at the time was that Netanyahu was committed to undoing the peace process, especially if he could get the Palestinians to do it for him, which I think he tried hard to elicit from them. Why? Because he simply believed that no peace with no war was the best way for Jews to secure as much of the historical lands of Israel as possible. It was also the best and only way in his mind, and the minds of many Zionists in this sad century, for Jews to be relatively safe.

One old classmate of mine, a rabbi also, who was an Israeli soldier specializing in "security issues" that he would not divulge, told me this very idea, to my astonishment. No peace keeps security on everyone's mind, but with no war it is perfect because it avoids the waste and destruction of violent conflict. Thus, a condition of no peace and no war is ideal. Of course, it is a delusion in that five or six wars in fifty years is hardly no war and no peace. It is simply mutual killing, terror, and mutilation, with periodic respites.

I persisted with this project because I felt that if we convinced Netanyahu and Arafat to open a parallel track of peacemaking that focused on religion, culture, symbolic gestures, and moral commitments, that it might create a momentum of transformation in relationships at the popular level, despite the obtuseness of the leadership on this matter. The latter, in and of itself, might soften elite positions on both sides and sway more people to the peace camp. I felt that this parallel track would in the end propel the other stalled track forward, despite Netanyahu's ambivalence. There already was a large majority of American Jews committed to the peace process and privately, at least, at odds with Likud over this. Furthermore, with every passing year surveys showed that more and more Israelis were prepared for Palestinian independence. More and more people of a *pragmatic* bent were moving in the direction of peacemaking. All we needed was a little more popular support to swing both groups toward peacemaking.

Furthermore, the holdouts, on both sides, were those people who were the most deeply identified with their group culturally or religiously, usually dismissed as the ideologues and ultranationalists. But these rejectionists are not demons. Some are greedy, wanting everything for one side, while others may have a murderous or abusive bent that keeps them fighting. But the truth is that millions of these rejectionists feel deeply—perhaps too deeply—the pain of their own people, and their hatred and distrust of the enemy is therefore infinitely greater. They remember pain much longer and feel more guilty at forgetting spilled blood. They love land passionately, perhaps too much. They have more fear of the enemy, and their respective hermeneutic reading of their cultural and religious resources helps to set this anger and fear into stone. But precisely this group needs to be eased into peace, their hardness ignored, and, on the contrary, their sense of raw, identified pain with their people honored and respected. They need deep intercultural processes of change. They need far more persuasion than crass appeals to pragmatism and economic benefits. They need much more cultural and psychological evidence as to why the enemy will not seize on peace as a vehicle of slow enervation and annihilation, war and killing by other means. Standard appeals to rational diplomacy are insufficient here.

I felt that President Clinton had displayed a keen understanding of this nontraditional side of peacemaking, in terms of the style of his interactions in Northern Ireland, as well as in several other places of conflict. Rabbi Frohman argued intensively that the president needed to give his stamp of approval to this process and, in fact, take part in this, or even host its ceremonies at the White House. Rabbi Frohman even suggested that the Oval Office, as a site for the religious treaty signing, could be seen as a place of redemption by Clinton, a place to make history as a religious person himself, who, according to numerous reports of the time, was suffering serious remorse for his actions in that very Oval Office. Clinton could see the Oval Office, argued Frohman, as a place of healing for himself as well, where he, as a Christian committed to repentance and forgiveness, could bring together and reconcile Jews and Muslims of the Middle East.

This was a bold idea, but one that I did not dare to convey to the president in writing or in person. My impression was, and is, that the president deeply resented those who had used the technical veneer of impeachment to persecute him for crass political gain, and which in turn complicated his efforts to apologize for the Lewinsky affair. He, as well as many of his defenders, felt that there was something sick going on in the Right of America, something that could even jeopardize the future of democracy in its McCarthyesque zeal and paranoia. Thus, he was determined to fight removal from office by all legal means at his disposal, especially when his apologies, once elicited, were simply ignored by his attackers who had demanded them. But his fight with this group did not reflect the entire inner workings of his conscience. Many felt that he knew that he had committed gross mistakes that would permanently scar his life's legacy and his family. It was plain to those who knew him that he was aware of how badly he had behaved. It is in that context that we hoped that he might see Middle East peacemaking, especially focused on religious processes of repentance and transformation, as appealing, an opportunity to highlight the religious-mythic significance, for Abrahamic faith communities, of remorse for past wrongs, apology, forgiveness, and repentance.

When I returned to the United States, and after continuing deterioration of the peace process in Israel, I tried very hard to persuade various people to get the president to agree to participate in a religious peace treaty ceremony in Jerusalem during his trip there, or, if not, then in the Oval Office. The problem was that, once he got to Israel, events transpired that hardened his frustration with Netanyahu for various actions that either humiliated Clinton (such as when Netanyahu met with Jerry Falwell before meeting the president, at a time when Falwell was severely attacking the president) or evoked mistrust, especially after Wye. It seemed that neither the president nor the entire administration wanted to do anything dramatic that would indicate that Netanyahu was making progress on peace. The president's trip to Israel was a grim and embarrassing disappointment, precisely when he was facing impeachment at home and needed a boost politically. For this diplomatic blow he would not forgive Netanyahu.

After intense networking over a 48-hour period, while the president was in Israel, I failed to persuade him to participate in such a ceremony, the claim being that there was simply no time. This may have been true because he was under intense pressure to return to Washington to defend himself against the impeachment vote. But I did manage in December 1998 to have a letter from me directly delivered to the president on religious peacemaking in the Middle East. But I failed to get him to a treaty-signing ceremony in Jerusalem, despite the fact that senior leaders on the Jewish and Islamic side had agreed to participate if the president would.

President Clinton's failure to participate was primarily due to the intense animosity produced by the failure of the first-track processes and the personal relationship with Netanyahu, as well as the disastrous effects of impeachment. This was a lost opportunity, which deeply saddened me. I was propelled by the vision in my eyes, and Rabbi Frohman's eyes, of bringing senior, conservative Islamic and Jewish leaders together publicly, which could trigger a watershed in the relations of millions of people on all sides of this conflict. It was also critical to undermining Hamas's military wing, which, at the time, held up the banner of authentic Islam response "in the only possible way" to Israel—with terror against civilians, which Muslims called "military struggle." But we all knew that one more bomb would be all the rejectionists in Israel needed to totally destroy the peace process. I felt that fostering the opportunity to bring Muslims to the peace camp in Israel was literally a matter of life and death, and I was desperate to make this happen. So were many of us. It was the one method available to us of undermining Hamas's appeal, due to the fact that the first track was so destructive at that point, and so completely in disrepute among the Palestinians.

I did manage to get another letter to President Clinton at the end of December 1998 and received a crucial letter back from him, that would later play some modestly helpful role. I reproduce the letters here to illustrate the kind of conflict resolution practices regarding religion that I propose in this book and in previous writings. This exemplifies intervention at the most elite level, rather than with middle-range or grass-roots populations. My aim is not to point to my own successes, because, frankly, I failed for the most part. But I want to illustrate, problematize, and raise for discussion, the entire political phenomenon of intervention at elite levels in delicate matters involving religion and culture.

Here is the text of my letter:

Wednesday, December 16, 1998

Dear Mr. President,

There have been a great number of private meetings between Jewish and Islamic religious clergy and leaders in recent months, as you apparently are aware. The challenge that we face, in terms of moving these meetings into a phenomenon that will have major impact on the peace process, is that they must become public at some juncture. This is the only way that these encounters will have a broad impact on the religious public in both communities. It is these communities that have housed the rejectionists of the peace process till now, and who hold the key to realigning the political structure in such a way as to allow the peace process to move forward.

There are two ideas floating about. One is that there could be a signing of a document, already in formation, by the highest religious leaders on both sides, that would formally embrace peacemaking as the only acceptable path for Jews and Muslims in the current context. This would have a profound impact, especially in terms of the effect on the public of witnessing the embrace of sheikhs and chief rabbis. Furthermore, there are major leaders on both sides that are interested in not only this-one time event, but also an ongoing interfaith committee that would not interfere with the details of the peace process, but would parallel its successes with spiritual and cultural reinforcement.

Everything that I, and many others in conflict resolution, have studied from around the world indicates that this is the key missing ingredient in many peace negotiations. The detailed, rational negotiations are critical, but they are constantly undermined by deep cultural and spiritual roots of mistrust and rage. We have a solution, and that is for there always to be a parallel peace process between the most respected members of the culture on each side. The secular members of the respective cultures are already well represented in the peace process, but not the religious community, and everything indicates that they will continue to be obstructionist until their revered figures become a part of the process of envisioning the future, together with the other peacemakers. This is how everyone, religious and secular, can see themselves having a stake in the future.

Here is the challenge [deleted].[14] We must help them. . . . The key to helping them . . . is the prestige of your office, and especially the trust that you have engendered in the *people* on all sides of this conflict. Furthermore, it seems that Chairman Arafat's support for this effort is crucial [deleted]. . . . involving the religious leadership with the peace process and the future vision of the respective countries, will give them more faith that they have a stake in the future well-being of the state,[15] and (2) You cannot hold off for final status, and as a reward, something [i.e., religious peacemaking] that is indispensable to getting to final status talks peacefully. And here in this last point is the rub. Few statesmen today understand as well as you do that the deep cultural, spiritual, and emotional roots of a people are critical elements in the construction of lasting peace, especially after terrible trauma and war. Religion and culture are the most powerful change agents in human psychology, and either they will be part of the problem of the Middle East, or they will be part of the solution. But they will certainly not be sidelined. All the evidence is clear on this.

There are thus numerous activists here and religious leaders who would welcome your leadership on this element of peacemaking, by simply inserting this idea into the state-to-state recommendations on how to proceed in the peace process, how to incorporate this form of peacemaking now.

The timing is critical. As you know, Ramadan begins on Sunday, and in other parts of the Arab world, it has been used by extremists as a time to unleash terrorism. Furthermore, the failure of the troop withdrawal on Friday, in addition to the Iraqi bombing, may make this a perfect time for Hamas to attack, sending the two populations into a tailspin of violence. This new path could be a way to engage Islam and Judaism now, or very soon, in a way that will make them a powerful symbolic force for pursuing peace and valuing the lives of others, even as the political and land issues remain bitter for now, and divisive, with no concrete end to the negotiations in sight. I firmly believe, based on the evidence, that cultural processes, and the symbolic power of gestures by major leaders, have an extremely powerful effect on populations, one that may bring about the realignment of political forces that we need in Israel and the Territories to move forward.

Thank you very much for considering this, and I will be glad to pursue this further with you at any time.

Respectfully,

Rabbi Dr. Marc Gopin
Center for Strategic and International Studies
George Mason University

It took time, but I would eventually receive a very good response from President Clinton. I would, in the interim, become somewhat impaired in my efforts because my father was dying in Boston, and I was holding down my teaching job at the same time in Washington. I happened to meet the president accidentally the day before his State of the Union speech. He was dressed in jeans, having just participated in house building for Habitat for Humanity. He decided to pop into the Politics and Prose Bookshop in upper Washington, D.C., where I did most of my writing in their coffee shop. Foolishly, I did not mention the letter to him because I had not yet received a response, and, honestly, I did not expect such a good one. We did speak briefly about the Middle East. He was the unhappiest person that I met that day, and he plainly wore the bruises of the impeachment assault, as well as the burden of his own misdeeds. As a rabbi, I felt sorry that I was not in a position to help him. The next day I received a letter from him. Here is the text of that letter:

January 13, 1999

Dear Dr. Gopin:

Thank you for your thoughtful letter concerning the potential for a Jewish-Moslem dialogue as a complement to the peace process.

I agree fully with you that building a genuine peace between Israelis and Palestinians demands more than political agreements. It will require an understanding between religions, one that seeks to address the cultural dimensions of a conflict that has distorted perceptions and bred intolerance.

As you know, my Administration has emphasized the role of religious dialogue in peacemaking—whether in Bosnia or elsewhere around the world. While religious hostility often is an aspect of national or ethnic conflict, I am convinced that religious dialogue just as often can be one of its principal remedies.[16]

I have asked members of the National Security Council staff working on the Middle East and on human rights and on humanitarian affairs to follow up with you on your ideas. I hope we can continue to work together on this important effort.

Sincerely,

Bill Clinton

The letter was important for a number of reasons. It went further than any statements that I had seen before in official recognition by a president of the United States of the importance of religious and cultural factors in conflict and peacemaking. I felt instinctively that, if nothing else, the text of the letter would be helpful. We lost the opportunity for the president's direct participation, but perhaps the letter itself would generate some movement.

Indeed, it did. Many months later I would learn from a worker in the White House that the president wrote on my letter, "This is excellent. Let's follow up on this." And it was sent to Sandy Berger and the National Security Council. I waited for a response, but later I learned that I should have called them, letter in hand, and pursued the matter when it was "hot." Apparently the NSC rarely calls you; you have to call them. I did not, but instead passively waited, in some measure because I was commuting to Boston so frequently and never knew when I would be available for a meeting.

I did, upon request and after careful reflection, fax the letter to Israel. The letter then, through various channels, ended up in Chairman Arafat's hands. He was impressed by it enough to bring it to the attention of the Palestinian

Authority legislature the next day, and I am told, an enthusiastic commitment to inter-religious peacemaking received an official sanction. But at the time everyone was holding their breaths for the result of the Israeli elections, and thus little was pursued. As of this writing, the process of inter-religious peacemaking is still unfolding.

I want to move to the other significant document emerging from all of this. I would like to cite an early draft of the Islamic/Jewish treaty that was proposed at the time, to analyze its significance. The treaty was developed by a number of people, Jewish and Islamic. Eliyahu McLean writes:

> . . . [T]his [treaty] is what was created by a cooperative venture with Rabbi David El Harar, Sadek Shweiki from Abu Tor East Jerusalem, myself Eliyahu McLean. Rabbi David El-Harar at first got input from Rav Kadouri and some Sephardi rabbis. Rav Kadouri laughed with delight and support when the idea for this treaty and signing was suggested. Then Harar asked me for help and I got him in touch with my friend Sadek. Harar and Sadek worked on a draft in English and Arabic. With my suggestion they called Sheikh Jamal and he later said a voice from Allah told him that he should agree to be a part of this. The three of us went up to the Temple Mount to Sheikh Jamal(Siddi)'s office across from the Dome of the Rock and added the intro [sic] and changed some of the wording of the text. Sadek, Rav Harar, and I then fine tuned the wording and translation from Arabic until we arrived at this document.[17]

Here is the text of the treaty:

Introduction by the honorable Sheikh Ismail Jamal:

> Jerusalem is the city of the prophets, a city of love, compassion, and peace. The message of God came out from Jerusalem to the whole world. This message is shared by Jews, Christians, and Muslims. A Hadith said, "Jerusalem, you are My Light and you are My Garden in this world. Whosoever dwells within thee is accepted by me. Whosoever abandons thee is rejected by me. You are the place of the Gathering and the land of the Judgement."

The Jerusalem Religious Peace Agreement :

We, as representatives of the two faiths, of Islam and Judaism, agree to the following:

Both the Torah and the Qur'an are expressions of faith which speak of the divine revelation of the oneness of G-d.

Islam and Judaism both take pride in being a Divine instrument of enlightenment for the world. As such, they teach their faithful to honor every human being as the living image of G-d.

The Holy Torah revealed to Moses, peace be upon him, the prophet of the Jewish people, calls for the respect and honor of every human being regardless of race or creed. Moreover, the Torah states that special respect and feeling of brotherhood are due to all believers in the faith of the one G-d. Thus, Muslims, who worship the same G-d as the Jews, are the primary recipients of these feelings of brotherhood.

The Holy Qur'an revealed to Muhammad, peace be upon him, the prophet
of Islam, calls for the respect and honor of every human being regardless
of race or creed. Moreover, the Qur'an states that special respect and
feeling of brotherhood are due to all believers in the faith of the one G-d.
Thus, Jews, who worship the same G-d as the Muslims, are primary
recipients of these feelings of brotherhood.

Based on these eternal truths of the Holy Torah and the Holy Qur'an, we
declare that no human being shall be persecuted, physically or morally,
because of their faith or the practice of their beliefs.

We also express our wish for greater harmony and understanding between
the believers–Muslims and Jews. We the descendents of Ishmael and
Isaac, the children of Abraham, are united today to offer our prayers from
the heart to G-d. We pray for the end of all enmity and for the beginning
of an era of peace, love, and compassion.

Note that at this early stage of the treaty, it is my opinion that this portion
of it was heavily oriented toward Islam, with some substantial input by religious Jews. It is not clear to me at this time how much input or what kind of
statement was being planned by the rabbis involved, or whether, in the final
draft, this text would have reflected more rabbinic input. Clearly an introduction by a major rabbinic figure would be necessary as a balanced parallel to
the Sheikh's introduction.

The treaty, even in this early stage of its development, is a paradigm of some
basic lessons of this book. Note the way in which the authors attempt to seamlessly
juxtapose the two religious community's highest ideals. At times there are illus-
trations of values shared, and, at others, there are specific references to values
emerging out of particular texts that each community could identify with their
own religious and cultural resources. The texts are deep cultural and psychological markers of meaning and dignity for both communities.

This combination of texts or paraphrased references from both communities is crucial, because, on the one hand, there is no peacemaking between
opposed ethnic groups without some discovery of common values. Common
ground is usually found by secular constructs in the pragmatics of "win-win"
paradigms, such as how the peace will benefit everyone financially. But it is
vital that those people for whom the existential and moral aspect of the fight
has threatened their cultural existence discover common bonds of cultural,
moral, and/or religious values. This will give them a deeper faith in the future of what for them is the most threatened in the future, namely, the continued existence of their identity and the spiritual values for which they have
sacrificed so much. Furthermore, the usual secular, liberal push to integration and unity, and all other harmonizing trends of peacemaking, should not
be so overwhelming that they may seem to suffocate cultural uniqueness or
distinctive religious identity. Thus, we have here a model of simultaneous
diversity and overarching unity, as well as deeply held values that undergird
the identity and self-perception of religious people.

We also have here a rare example of what I would call intermythic conversation. Jews and Muslims share the mythic origins of their respective com-

munities in Isaac and Ishmael and wisely highlight an overarching family unity. Wisely also, they emphasize both the inherent value of caring for all human beings, and also the permission or obligation in each culture to especially love fellow believers in the Abrahamic God. This is a brilliant move.

The exclusively integrative drive of secular, progressive peacemaking often drives many religious skeptics into rejectionist camps. But peace treaties, such as the one above, contain within them both harmonizing peace overtures and ideas that retain the distinctiveness of each community's contribution. The treaty or peace process then becomes a way of affirming identity but also transforming it into a peaceful identity. It is a transformation of identity by its hermeneutic shift of emphasis toward peace and life-affirming values directed to all, but, at the same time, it is not a threatening suppression of identity.

It is true that there are extremists for whom the most aggressive part of their religious or cultural identity is their central anchor. They will react badly to such efforts by definition. Deeper work is required with them, including a careful examination of their need to incriminate the other, their guilt at surviving while other loved ones have perished in the struggle, their transference of abuse rooted in family life onto an acceptable and vulnerable external enemy, and so forth. Their inclusion in peace processes will require a concentrated process of relationship building over time through the medium of intervenors who are skilled in reconciliation and healing, knowledgeable of religious traditions, and skilled at the use of symbol and metaphor to stimulate transformation. Honestly, a number of the most deeply damaged haters in any given community will only lay down their weapons when a sizable group on both sides psychologically overwhelms the structure of the enemy system.

For this reason, those whom I call "reasonable rejectionists" on both sides, the majority usually, are so important. I speak of those rejectionists who really do see their religion and/or culture as committed to justice, peace, and life, with exceptions in certain circumstances, but who currently see the enemy as a mortal threat. Such people can be brought into the peace process by careful bilateral processes of intercultural trust building, apologies for past crimes, and restitution . Their inclusion can ultimately overwhelm the influence of the truly damaged people on both sides.

We will develop more detailed recommendations for this process in a later chapter, but for now the Jerusalem Initiative described here is a fascinating paradigm of peacemaking in the world of religion. Its orchestration has attempted to combine first-track and second-track diplomacy by means of the efforts to gain crucial support from the governmental leadership of all parties, including the United States. Unlike many secular second-track processes that interface with the first-track, however, such as the Oslo peace process and its aftermath, this Jerusalem Initiative is fundamentally rooted in an effort to bring both the elites and masses into the experience of social transformation. It is committed to the power of texts, values, and symbols to transform large populations.

Finally, it should be noted that this treaty is a good example of the ways in which cultures influence each other. Such cooperation between *Orthodox*

Jewish and Islamic leaders in the construction of a single document involving faith statements and ethical directives is perhaps unprecedented in history. It has already, by definition, created a kind of paradigm shift, a way in which these two religions are coming to affect each other in new ways.

This brings up an important point. There is not just an interdependency of politics and myth, or politics and culture, in conflict and peacemaking. There is also a highly interactive dependency of cultures on each other, *even when they are adversaries.* Cultures that live side by side are always in competition in some fashion, and always guarding their boundaries. This is inevitable for the formation of unique identity, which appears to be a near universal need among both individuals and whole groups. We all watch each other constantly, and we take our cues from others. When one culture emphasizes a belligerent approach to the outside world, then the other, neighboring culture will do the same. Deciphering which one starts this, for various internal reasons, or whether the process is simultaneous, is difficult to know and varies with each case. But one thing is certainly true, even when we see ourselves as qualitatively different and better than our lifelong adversaries, we cannot help but be influenced by and influence the adversary culture. And the worse the conflict becomes, the more it seems that enemies begin to resemble each other, to the point where the propaganda and demonizations of each group seem identical. This is the destructive side of the whole interaction.

The good news, however, is that this process works in reverse as well. Here is the crucial point. There can be competitions for goodness as well as competitions for barbarity in human experience. It is possible to set up an intercultural dynamic wherein key religious leaders, in this case sheikhs and rabbis, begin a friendly competition of proof that their tradition is the most humanitarian, the most kind, the most peaceful, the most redemptive of the world and human history. The Jerusalem Accord is a small example of what is possible according to this kind of dynamic.

In chapter 4, we will explore ways in which religions can and sometimes do move from incrimination to inclusion or from alienation to engagement and mutual honor. I will consider this treaty and critically analyze it as a paradigm of religious, interpretive transformation that is essential to the traditional peacemaking that I outline in this book. I will also raise questions about some of its language as a way of demonstrating the dilemmas that we face in pursuing conflict resolution and peacemaking between religious people and religious traditions. It should also be pointed out that not only the secular, diplomatic processes can be elitist and leave untouched the majority of human beings who suffer and hate in the course of war. Religious treaties and relationships can also suffer this fate if the substance of treaties like the Jerusalem Accord does not translate into broad-based efforts to create relationships and bonds across religious divides. Courage is required among leaders, but also tolerance by outsiders as the religious leaders struggle with how to maintain identity while building bonds with erstwhile enemies. Often the latter process of disseminating peace is resisted by leaders who fear the loss of their base of power and their exclusive hold on the group.

This process parallels, in an interesting way, the patterns of competition between heads of state and their parliaments or congresses over issues of foreign affairs. Religious leaders, just like heads of state, often perceive their one place of exclusive control as the power over "foreign relations," namely relations with other religions. But what most of us in peacemaking expect, whether it be from heads of state and their diplomatic apparatus or from religious leadership, is that they carefully move their communities away from the need to define themselves over against an enemy Other. The political reality is that no leader or ruling class, religious or secular, will do this in a way that he loses control over the constituency in question.

This presents us with a built-in moral dilemma. We need these leaders to make historic changes, but we also wince at their control or manipulation of large populations. Each peacemaker and intervener in human conflict must decide how to balance the costs and benefits of working with conservative leadership. My instinct has always been to work with a wide variety of leaders, including conservative ones, to get to the peace table. Then one proceeds to the construction of civil society when the enemy system and its infantilizing effects on, and hypnotic power over, the average person has been undermined. As one insightful Croatian diplomat said to me—and I am paraphrasing— remove fear and everything else becomes possible.

Let us proceed now to patterns of Abrahamic incrimination and its transformation.

4 🌿

Patterns of Abrahamic Incrimination

Most religions, at some point in their way of accounting for the universe (ontology), as well as in their recommendations for human behavior (ethics), will mark some things and behaviors as dangerous, taboo, forbidden, misguided, or mistaken. There is also the designation of something as unholy, sinful, inspired by or inhabited by Evil, by the Devil, Satan, the Evil Impulse, the Antichrist (in Christianity), the *sitra ahra*, the Other Side (in Jewish mysticism), and many other designations. This often has translated, at some point in the history of most religions, into a designation for certain people, not just their actions. Often in history this designation has been applied to whole sets of people who share some common origin or some uniting characteristic that sets them apart.

Such segregation has its source in the ubiquitous human psychological process of othering, the need to distinguish and exclude. It is not unique to religion. Rather, organized religion is a recipient of this human tendency, as has been all other types of human social organization, such as the tribe, the nation, and even the liberal state, which has its necessary exclusions as well.

The mistake of secular attacks on organized religion in the West in the past couple of hundred years has been the assumption that religious dogma and practice are *solely* responsible for this process of othering, as well as the resulting suppression or destruction of basic human rights. Getting rid of the dogmas, rituals and practices would eliminate this source of human violence against others, so the argument has gone.

In fact, othering and incrimination comprise a constant source of conflict generation in all of human intercourse. We have learned from the bitter lessons of modern political history that eliminated religious rituals and dogmas of exclusion are easily replaced by new, secular ones, with very religious overtones, such as those found in classical communism and fascism. This occurs when the deeper needs fulfilled by discarded rituals, or by other exclusionary processes, go unmet.[1] All forms of collective identity formation seem to fit this process.

As we study the manifestation of othering in religious traditions, we must see it for what it is, namely, one manifestation of a perpetual challenge to all human institutions. Only if we keep this in mind will we devise solutions that truly address the problem, instead of masking it—consciously or unconsciously—with attacks on religion by those who are separating from a bad experience of their own religion, or who want to eliminate the influence of religion on the lives of others. Organized religion has become an easy target in the West, an appropriate address of blame for the ills of the past. Partially it is true, but it is also a mask and a diversion from the deeper, more disturbing realizations about human nature, about our own individual natures. Furthermore, attacking the most unsavory aspects of religious intolerance can also be a liberal, elitist method of avoiding other violence-producing moral questions we face, such as "How much is enough?" the great question of greed in a capitalist culture founded upon consumerism. Insatiability is an essential cause of human violence, whether that insatiability concerns natural resources, land, or potential converts to a religion. Thus, it is true that religious intolerance is key to understanding violence, but singling it out also evades deeper questions of violence in global North/South relations, or relations between privileged and underprivileged populations.

Fundamental questions of gender and the intertwining of sex and human relations also cause major modern conflicts. These issues plague all human cultures today, in addition to being issues that have confronted global religions for millennia. Millions of people in modern civilization have made it easy for themselves to evade the discussion of these matters by a simple process of dismissing all religion as a font of intolerance. The critiques of religious exclusion and intolerance have much merit. But they also betray a scapegoating quality, a willingness to place onto organized religion what is in fact a fundamental human problem. This is foolhardy, as all scapegoating is, because the dangerous problems that lurk underneath go unexamined.

There are fundamental disagreements between religious and secular perspectives, as well as between liberal and conservative religious interpretations, that will and should continue to be debated. These include issues concerning sexual choices, personal identity, and questions of morality and interpretation of the significance of human and global existence. But these debates must be seen in the larger context of the tendency of all groupings of human beings to other, to exclude others. Religion is an easy target because what and who it has othered is historically entrenched and easily seen in texts and traditions. But othering goes on in every group that one can imagine, from complex dress, speech, and behavior codes on Wall Street, to dress and behavior codes in the Pentagon, to very complex speech and behavior codes in academia.

We need not deny the damage that has been done in history by Abrahamic religions that other and exclude or incriminate. The evidence is clear, and the danger of recurrence should be obvious to anyone familiar with the range of religious actors today. It should be said in defense of the historical role of organized religion, however, that othering is not only a function of excluding persons as such, but also a way of rejecting certain kinds of behavior, such as theft, rape, and murder. This kind of exclusion has formed the backbone of many civilizations, and it often goes unnoticed.

The entire judicial system of any culture is predicated on the assumption that certain behaviors immediately exclude the perpetrator in some fashion. How this exclusion is accomplished depends on attitudes toward the death penalty and prison, and what progressive forms of rehabilitation and re-entry into the group exist. Organized religion has played a vital role in many Abrahamic cultures of setting up standards of inclusion and exclusion and requiring basic moral behaviors without which societies could not have survived.

The separation of church and state, therefore, is not really about ceasing *all* forms of religious othering, but rather some forms of othering, in addition to taking over, with secular police power, certain traditional religious institutions of othering and exclusion.

We have depended in Western history on Abrahamic commitments to othering those who are cruel, unjust, or murderous. That religious institutions did not live up to these standards of othering, that their representatives, on the contrary, often became quintessential hypocrites with regard to matters of injustice and cruelty, is a given. But religion is no more guilty of this than the ancient city-state or the modern state, which are also predicated on high-minded ideals even as they supported various forms of bigotry.

Let us delve more into the question of religious othering in Western history. One of the greatest tensions in the Christian-Jewish relationship since the Holocaust has been the anger of so many Jews that the Christian churches of Europe failed completely to other and exclude Fascists, to make clear commitments of exclusion, even after fascism's defeat. This despite the fact that they did a fine job of othering Communists (at least in the West) at the same time and in the same era, or dis-empowering those "heretics" who were challenging church doctrines. Hitler and his henchmen were never excommunicated.

In fact, too many religious representatives deemed it religiously appropriate to help Fascists escape justice at the end of World War II. These institutions led their believers into the depths of murderous hypocrisy, while abandoning or leaving extremely vulnerable those heroic Christians across Europe who resisted and risked their lives to save the chosen victims of fascism. Later these same institutions would fight heroically against the "great evil" of communism—an ideology that, of course, directly threatened the power base of organized religion, but there was no such stomach for a great fight to save non-Christians in World War II, Jews or Roma peoples, from torture and mass murder.

But this problem is not limited to Christianity, and it must include Judaism and Islam as well, for their less well known and less grandiose abuses of power over the weak and vulnerable. One of the most profound disappointments in general with Abrahamic religions in history has been that patterns of exclusion seem to focus very lightly on issues of social justice (othering those who are unjust) and very heavily on any behaviors or ideas that threaten the power or authority of the organized religion. In other words, exclusion and othering are a crass tool of power maintenance, which is at least one reason why millions of people in the West opted in recent centuries to defang organized religion by removing its police power.

In today's open society of the West, the assumption of liberalism is that religion should not be in the business of exclusion at all, because it is assumed that the truly vital forms of exclusion which affect life and security are taken care of by the state. I dwell on this because there is a superficial set of assumptions operating behind the institutions of religion and state. On the one hand, millions of members of Abrahamic faiths are on the march, trying to fuse religion and state or to prevent their separation. Religious coercion by states is still a basic part of Middle Eastern life, including Israel. Those who want to collapse religion and state still further, as well as those Christians in the United States who want to do the same, assume that religion should re-emerge as the arbiter of inclusion and exclusion in society. And their interpretation of who and what should be included and excluded should frighten anyone concerned with preserving their personal liberty. The groups who are pushing for this most aggressively seem to have learned nothing from the last two thousand years about the barbarity that can be accomplished in the name of religious doctrine.

On the other hand, those who oppose them are not really listening or understanding why this drive to empower organized religion has captured the hearts of millions. Their reasons are very complex, but here I simply want to highlight the relevance of issues of inclusion, exclusion, and, in particular, the commitment to the categories of good and evil. The categories of inclusion and exclusion on the basis of good and evil are an indelible part of Abrahamic faith and practice. Therefore, the clarion call of pluralism, of "everyone doing as they please as long as they do not hurt the next guy," is fundamentally jarring and even loathsome to the ears and hearts of those Abrahamic faithful who are in search of the good society. This is a fundamental dilemma and cultural conflict at the deepest level.

What I propose in this chapter is that a more fruitful—and perhaps the sole—space of compromise and relational meeting across this divide relates to the patterns of inclusion and exclusion, or designations of good and evil, that evolve and change constantly in Abrahamic history, much more so than meets the eye. In fact, there are often radical reversals in patterns of incrimination and exclusion.

Most important, however, is the capacity of incrimination to move its target away from others and toward the self, or sometimes away from people and toward ideas and behaviors. Therein lies some hope for compromise and coexistence. All of these alternatives, however, are complicated and have potentially destructive consequences. But for Abrahamic religions, and perhaps for many human approaches to ethics, it is difficult to avoid the challenge of inclusion and exclusion if one wants to assert that any behavior or action in the world is good and some other set of actions is bad. Certainly there seem to be certain ethical systems and certain religious ontologies that one would think lend themselves more to destructive patterns of othering and incrimination. But the fact that people in almost every religious system that I have studied can justify, alternatively, the most barbaric or the most saintly behavior suggests to me that the content of these traditions is heavily dependent on the psychosocial processes that drive that content in one direction or another.

I am interested in knowing enough of the content of traditions as well as the psychosocial atmosphere that surrounds them, which will help the evolution of these traditions toward peacemaking with traditional "others," while, at the same time, being able to evolve and maintain standards of good and evil. At a certain level of moral reflection, it should not be our goal to completely eliminate othering from either secular political constructs or religious ones. But clearly there is a strong need to shift the balance away from radical and violent othering toward pluralism, or, at the very least, benign forms of exclusion.

There is tremendous dynamism in these evolutions, often resulting from a variety of needs and interests, and therein lies the hope of peacemaking processes. Let us now list the options of religious traditions within this evolutionary process of confrontation with the "other":

1. Continued incrimination
2. Increased incrimination
3. Denial of incrimination and apologetics as a moderation of othering
4. Hard rejection of past interpretations and an end to othering
5. Soft rejection of the past, and historical contextualization
6. Pious transformation of old cognitive constructs as an end to othering: remythification

I want to begin with the sixth category, remythification, to demonstrate where we are going. Then I will return to the other categories. But first I will return to the Islamic/Jewish treaty described in chapter 3, as a way of providing a paradigm for what we are envisioning.

The Jerusalem Treaty and Remythification

Here I analyze in detail the text of the treaty. My analysis will appear inside the brackets:

Introduction by the honorable Sheikh Ismail Jamal:
[The Jewish initiators of this process clearly intended to go out of their way to extend great honor to the Islamic participants; this functions as a vital antithesis to the current state of attitudes between Arabs and Israelis. More on the role of honor in conflict resolution in later chapters.]

Jerusalem is the city of the prophets, a city of love, compassion, and peace. The message of God came out from Jerusalem to the whole world. This message is shared by Jews, Christians, and Muslims. [This part uses language that could in principle be shared by all three faiths, but that clearly represents a certain slant that I am not sure would have been used by a typical rabbinic or *haredi* author, especially the notion of Jerusalem as a "city of love." Nevertheless the sentiments here are universally monotheistic.] A Hadith said, "Jerusalem, you are My Light and you are My Garden in this world. Whosoever dwells within thee is accepted by me. Whosoever abandons thee is rejected by me. You are the place of the Gathering and the land of the Judgement." [This is a remarkable *hadith*. Its inclusion is clearly an appeal to and a recognition of the unique expression of one faith that is involved in this treaty, Islam. This is vital, namely, that peacemaking rhetoric and symbolic language not merely fuse all parties into one but acknowledge and honor the uniqueness of each member of the treaty—necessary for the treaty not to be, or be perceived as, an effort to suppress or overwhelm any one party, but rather a vehicle through which the parties meet, in the deep dialogic and existential sense of that word. Of course, what is missing in the document as of now is a citation from rabbinic literature that would accomplish the parallel result.]

The Jerusalem Religious Peace Agreement:
[The choice of the title as *not* "the Arab-Israeli treaty" or the "Jewish/Islamic treaty" but something centered on Jerusalem is brilliant in its perception of the heart of the cultural conflict here. It is no accident that the subject of Jerusalem is the single most explosive issue for the final settlement. Jerusalem represents the heart and soul of the lost dignity and honor of each community. For Jews Jerusalem is their only holy city in the world, and the one that has been the center of their prayers for thousands of years. It is also the place of greatest sacralized pain, the place of all the horrors of murder, conquest, and theft. That another religion's major symbol and building stands on top of the ruins of Judaism's only Holy Temple is a source of humiliation that is never sufficiently acknowledged by outside observers. In effect, it comes to symbolize all the places from which Jews have been evicted in the last two thousand years. Thus, contemporary Jewish Jerusalem becomes the symbol of return to the place of original eviction and reversal of the fortunes of history, or, in theological terms, the forgiveness of God and final reward for Jewish patience and suffering. Symbolic Jerusalem is acknowledged, however, and utilized by extremists. It is a fundamental weakness of the war on extremism when one side fully utilizes the deepest cultural spaces of injury and hope that a community has, while the other side nervously attempts to ignore this.

On the Palestinian side, Jerusalem is a place of both honor and humiliation: honor that, as either Christians or Muslims, this holy city was their prime possession as a people, before, during and after all the conquests of history. That so many families have generations of roots here is a source of great honor and pride that distinguishes them within the entire Arab and Islamic worlds. (For this reason there is not a small amount of internal Arab struggle over whose Arab political authority actually reigns over Islamic affairs in Jerusalem). The humiliation, of course, is the loss of Jerusalem to Israel and the deep sense of theft and dishonor at becoming second-class citizens in their own city, and then being deprived of the resources to have an honorable presence there.

Here is a critical point. When these groups, both Jewish and Arab, suppress matters of great pain in their efforts to be rational or pragmatic, as they do in the official, elite diplomatic processes, they often, perhaps unconsciously, leave it to extremists to articulate what they dare not say or even feel. But this is a fundamental mistake of most peace processes. Rather than suppressing this and leaving its articulation to extremists, it is far better to take the places of pain and turn them into places of comfort, redemption, and moral transformation. The latter path requires great creativity and compromise, but it usually fares better than suppression of vital cultural feelings. Transforming painful cultural moments is what the authors are attempting to do here by taking the symbol and reality of Jerusalem and transforming it from a symbol of conflict and humiliation, and turning it into a new symbol of shared honor and shared love.]

We, as representatives of the two faiths, of Islam and Judaism, agree to the following:

Both the Torah and the Qur'an are expressions of faith which speak of the divine revelation of the oneness of G-d. [Divine Oneness is what Jewish and Islamic ultrareligious representatives feel most comfortable in sharing, as opposed to Christians. On one level, I approve of enemy peoples and cultures finding what they have most in common, but there is an element in the Islamic/Jewish contacts that suggests an alliance of two Abrahamic faiths that *perhaps* could be divisive in the long run toward Christians. I certainly know that many very religious Jews harbor so much anger against Christians and Christianity because of the Holocaust and other forms of oppression that it is easy for them to slip into a preference of Muslims over Christians, and I have noticed similar trends among Muslims. But there is a Christian minority in this conflict that must not become yet another scapegoat in this sad history of persecution between Abrahamic faiths. That said, I do still affirm, however, that it is good for erstwhile enemies to articulate that which they hold most in common.[2]]

Islam and Judaism both take pride in being a Divine instrument of enlightenment for the world. As such, they teach their faithful to honor every human being as the living image of G-d. [Although the language of honoring every human being is shared by both Islam and Judaism, and the idea of human being as image of God is based on a shared biblical text[3] (Gen. 1:27), it is not clear to me that an Orthodox Muslim would have come up with this language, since there is such a strong reluctance in Islam to associate any images with God. Nevertheless, if the language represents an interparty consensus, then it forms yet another successful bridge in this document.]

The Holy Torah revealed to Moses, peace be upon him, the prophet of the Jewish people, calls for the respect and honor of every human being regardless of race or creed. Moreover, the Torah states that special respect and feeling of brotherhood are due to all believers in the faith of the one G-d. Thus, Muslims, who worship the same G-d as the Jews, are the primary recipients of these feelings of brotherhood. [This is one, very complimentary reading of Jewish sources, and it points to a typical characteristic of very religious interfaith processes, namely, the focus on the holiness and perfection of the religions involved, and an avoidance of any acknowledgment of past wrongs built into the religion, or unjust or prejudiced laws, traditions, or interpretations of the past that are rooted in sacred texts or authoritative sources. This is one clear trend in religious peacemaking. I struggle constantly with the question of how beneficial it is to peacemaking. On the one hand, it is vital to create a peaceful vision of the religions involved, which is indispensable to the cultural shifts that we seek. On the other hand, it papers over past wrongs and built-in problems in the religious traditions that have been—and will in the future be—used by some to promote intolerance and conflict. It is a step in the right direction, however, and it may be all that fundamentalists in both traditions can tolerate, but it is incomplete, in my opinion. However, if I had a choice between including fundamentalists in peace treaties that are imperfect and not including them at all, I would opt for the former without hesitation. The benefits outweigh the costs without a doubt, and this is a painful truth that liberal branches of these religions must begin to accept.]

The Holy Qur'an revealed to Muhammad, peace be upon him, the prophet of Islam, calls for the respect and honor of every human being regardless of race or creed. Moreover, the Qur'an states that special respect and feeling of brotherhood are due to all believers in the faith of the one G-d. Thus, Jews, who worship the same G-d as the Muslims, are primary recipients of these feelings of brotherhood. [This statement and the previous one put a brilliantly positive spin on Jewish and Islamic attitudes toward monotheism and idolatry. Such hermeneutic and interpretive transformation is precisely the essence of option number six (remythification) listed previously. One can look at the history of attitudes and practices of these two traditions and see some horribly prejudiced and persecutorial laws and behaviors toward polytheists, whether in ancient Canaan, Arabia, or Africa. But these authors—and many other monotheists in history—emphasize that there is a special kinship and level of respect for fellow monotheists, rather than an effort to exclude or even annihilate non-monotheists. They are emphasizing the bonds of love rather than the divisions of hatred. As such, they are highlighting one eminently reasonable reading of biblical mythology and simply ignoring other readings. Once again, they have articulated in powerful terms a bridge between these two traditions.]

Based on these eternal truths of the Holy Torah and the Holy Qur'an, we declare that no human being shall be persecuted, physically or morally, because of their faith or the practice of their beliefs. [Note how they have taken the results of the two very traditional prior statements and led to a very progressive conclusion. No *human being* shall be persecuted because of their faith. It does not say "no fellow monotheist." This represents a crucial hermeneutic development that is at the heart of the argument of this book. One could look back at old traditions in both religions for plenty of precedent for persecution of non-monotheists or "heretics" of all sorts. But this treaty is a powerful departure from this history, *even though* it appears as, and truly is in many ways, a very traditional document.]

We also express our wish for greater harmony and understanding between the believers—Muslims and Jews. We the descendents of Ishmael and Isaac, the children of Abraham, are united today to offer our prayers from the heart to G-d. We pray for the end of all enmity and for the beginning of an era of peace, love, and compassion.

This beautiful conclusion acknowledges the enmity of the conflict but evokes the indispensable family metaphor as an antidote to the war, a way of reminding the parties that they are family, after all, in the deepest sense. They also evoke the shared commitment of these traditions to (1) prayer and (2) hope in the future, which are interrelated, a brilliant conclusion that once again appeals to values, religious institutions, and myths that are shared by both communities. But it transforms these phenomena from sources of competition and conflict into bonds of friendship and love.

The authors of this treaty, I suspect, are fully cognizant of what they are including by way of religious traditions and what they are ignoring, what beauty they are highlighting and what ugliness they are choosing to avoid.[4] But this is not a cynical attempt to fool each other or outsiders. It certainly expresses some effort to avoid their religion being shamed in public, or an effort to avoid bringing dishonor on their own communities. But it also expresses an authentic belief in and practice of interpretation based on faith. It is the process of expressing their deepest beliefs in their religion, their God, and humanity. Essentially, it expresses what they see as central to their faith and what they see as peripheral, what is to be taken literally and what figuratively, what requires immediate action and what should be contextualized and circumscribed.

If one were to ask the authors of this treaty about the war laws in each tradition, or laws governing vengeance and their applicability to the Arab/Israeli conflict, they would not deny the existence of those laws nor reject their efficacy as religious law. But they would circumscribe the applicability of the laws for a variety of complicated reasons that one utilizes to argue matters of law and interpretation. But the crucial point is that this kind of reinterpretation and contextualization constitutes a space of freedom in even the most fundamentalist circles. But few will admit to this because innovation and change are so essentially shunned in reactionary cultures.

We will explore shortly other ways of confronting past conflicts and violence and changing one's religious attitudes to enemy others. The problems with remythification are self-evident, namely, the deliberate decision, at least as expressed in this document, not to confront dogmas and doctrines that are conflict generating, violent, or even murderous. Perhaps admitting to violent laws is not even appropriate in attempts to create a peace treaty, or perhaps it would be impossible to bring the people in question to the table with such a process of acknowledgement. Whatever the reason, my concern about this approach is its potential to whitewash the past and not face the dangers that lie ahead. Also, acknowledging the sins of the past is something that victims often require and need, and that is not being done here.

Continued Incrimination

Let us now move on to the other interpretive options listed at the beginning of the chapter. The first category, continued incrimination, is the classic conservative response of traditional religions to the surrounding world, even when there is a dramatic change in circumstances. The othering and exclusion can take on relatively mild forms, such as the need to separate from certain people and certain places without persecution, or shunning any participation in another group's celebrations, which involves a voluntary removal by a person or group from aspects of a surrounding culture or group.

We have come to accept these choices as benign, at least in the United States, because, in classic libertarian fashion, Americans feel that these choices affect only themselves and their children. But they sometimes lead to more deadly forms of exclusion, when, for instance, the separated group gains enough power to impose themselves on other groups, or when the separatist tradition is indoctrinating seriously bigoted beliefs. Separatist othering then turns into persecutorial othering, and sometimes separate education and culture become the hotbed for political repression.

Another, more complex category, is othering in an afterlife, where othering is expressed by those condemned to hell and those admitted to heaven. It can be relatively benign in terms of its practical effects, although it certainly can dampen social relations. Often, in monotheistic history, this form of exclusion has been a critical adjunct to abuse of others, and even torture and murder. Also deadly, of course, are laws and practices designed to excommunicate or isolate members of a community where these members are heavily dependent on their religious community. Today the destructiveness is not as bad as it used to be since there is an open vigilant society witnessing the events. But the consequences are still devastating for many religious people.

Othering takes on more subtle forms as well, such as the treatment of women and children, or those less learned, or those of a lower caste, who are considered included in the religious group, but subtly demeaned and diminished based on a variety of theological presumptions and ritual practices. Children have no choice but to remain, but the complexity associated with adults who are demeaned is that, at least in an open society, they choose to stay, and then it becomes their choice to "buy into" this subculture. Then the othering becomes harder to quantify.

Examples of othering include the exclusion of those who violate sexual taboos, such as adulterers, homosexuals, or people considered idolaters by monotheism, people who flagrantly violate basic laws of each tradition, or outsiders who attack fellow believers. But it can become as subtle as very specific forms of eating, dress, or speech that indicate that you are in or out of the group. It can also involve how much one is exposed to the outside world, such as how much one studies or knows secular matters.

The remarkable thing about these markers of identity and exclusion is the inconsistency between taboos that become centralized in a particular era and the texts and traditions to which the groups of Abrahamic faithful belong. Criteria of exclusion seem to be highly selective and often evolve quickly, as if they are evolving indicators of psychological and sociological exclusion and group creation, rather than venerated beliefs from hoary antiquity.

Let us take an example. There are an infinite number of practices in Judaism, Catholicism, and Islam that are hard to observe, such as fasting, and that, in fact, many faithful do not practice. But, without a doubt, what evokes the most controversy, and actual rage, in today's society is anything associated with the status of women and their bodies, as well as the status of homosexuals. Now, there are clear traditions and laws that liberal interpreters of the Abrahamic religions want to change or do away with, but nothing evokes controversy like women and homosexuals. And this is true in millions of monotheistic centers (and also in many other religions) around the world. Is the reason that laws and traditions are being broken? But every day millions of monotheists go to work and break laws of their tradition, such as laws against charging interest, or being untruthful, and it does not evoke anything similar to the rage directed against women and homosexuals.

Clearly, the markers of inclusion and exclusion and othering are shared across many religions today by conservatives, plainly suggesting that a global reactionary response is at work, housed within religious society, to the unprecedented challenge to the basic identity of man and woman as such, who they are, what their proper role is, and what their sexual activity will be.

Increased Incrimination

This brings us to our second category, increased incrimination, where we see today the markers of inclusion and exclusion becoming more severe with regard to only certain laws and traditions. Capitalism, with all of its problematic approaches to acquisition and distribution of wealth, has completely succeeded in winning the hearts and minds of monotheistic fundamentalists around the world, despite all the pious protestations against materialism. There are pious exceptions in each community, to be sure. But, just to take a counterexample, I suspect it would strike people as funny to even think that someone today could be excluded because he failed to tithe, or used untruthful advertising to gain his wealth, or sold weapons to questionable clients, or charged exorbitant interest to the poor who could not qualify for a bank loan, despite the fact that I can point to laws in each community that this behavior violates.[5] But every day there is a story of a priest or minister who is in trouble and isolated because of his attempting to minister to homosexuals.

Most of the markers of increased religiosity in recent years around the world involve the status, visibility, and clothing of women. Undoubtedly, a great struggle is at work, be it among secular people or religious people, over what it is to be a man and what it is to be a woman. Millions of people, both men and women, are saying that they have had enough of doubts, and they want to go back to old, clear markers of sexual identity with clearly defined roles. Millions of women are voluntarily seeking to secure a place in today's world for traditional female roles and the importance of motherhood. Of course, millions of other women are being forced back into old molds as well, *against their will*, by men, such as in Afghanistan. Still others, millions of them, especially in the developing world, are on the march, financially and politically, toward new definitions of the woman. This cause is being aided by hundreds of millions of Western dollars that are earmarked for progressive women taking control of their lives and their families.

In short, a gargantuan, global battle is in progress, and the borders and boundaries of this process are remarkably elastic. Both men and women are actively disengaging and distancing themselves from other men and women who want new definitions of male and female roles. If this battle can be couched in ways that unite a conflict over gender with an othering of another ethnic or religious group that embodies all the threats to and fears about gender, then so much the better. Conflating gender wars and interethnic/religious struggles seems to add spice to the conflict. After all, gender wars can descend to the level of torture and murder in history, but never to the eliminationist stage that characterizes ethnic and religious conflicts. Men ultimately need women, and vice versa. But if all the gender stress can be embodied in some group "over there," then one can pursue this conflict with the full rage that at least one part of the human psyche seems to demand. This is why interracial, interethnic, and interreligious, gender attractions, sex, and especially prostitution and rape[6] evoke such intense rage, and rape is such an essential part of certain wars, but not others.

Such a complex dynamic is applied toward many conflicts in history. Clearly white Christians have gone through a massive struggle over the past few centuries over whether nonwhites are equal to them or not, and the story of this struggle is well known. But there are ebbs and flows to this process. The eighteenth and early nineteenth century saw a liberalization in Europe in terms of who was and was not a legitimate human being, with Jews (a nonwhite group, by European racial standards) at the center of that question in France and other countries. The effect on Christianity was dramatic and divisive. Eventually those who claimed the illegitimacy of Jews lost out in the eighteenth and early nineteenth century but won the day from about 1880 through the Holocaust.

The embarrassing horrors of fascism and its massive destructiveness led to a complete reversal of this attitude in the last fifty years of Western history, at least until the end of the Cold War. Christianity has been transformed by this descent of traditional religious anti-Judaism into genocide. Recently, there have been some signs of reversal in the Christian community. For example, for the first time since the Holocaust, hundreds of millions of dollars are being poured into conversion of Jews by a large array of Protestant fundamentalists groups, something that was impossible to imagine culturally in the Christian community just twenty years ago. Thus, we may be at the beginning of a new cycle of othering. Anti-Semitism rates are way down among the general population of the Western democracies (as opposed to East European countries, where it is as healthy as ever), but certain Christian evangelicals are moving in the opposite direction in terms of the need to delegitimate the Jew as a religious being. The resurgence of some European ethnonationalisms, especially in Russia, is coupling with the resurgence of religious bodies that hold within them a subtle combination of traditional anti-

Judaism and racism. In some ways, the othering of the Jew is the perfect barometer of Western racism, in that it indicates to us where trouble is brewing and what problems in the collective psyche of various peoples remain unresolved. Time will tell where all this leads.

In Israel the othering process in Jewish and Arab culture is almost overwhelming, as if a culture in search of identity (with so many identities in flux and so many prior immigrant identities mixing at once) is a place that craves the need to other. For example, there is great irony in the fact that the more religious many Jews have become in recent years the higher the boundaries set up by those who consider themselves religiously superior—as I have described elsewhere.[7] In general, it is misunderstood how much the othering that goes on between Arabs and Israelis is part of a complex bigger picture of two communities battered by recent history, Israeli and Palestinian, each in search of its identity.

This form of othering has a powerful effect on religious efforts to find identity by denying the legitimacy of others. On the surface it all looks quite pious but in fact betrays a superficial, exterior set of characteristics that seem more designed to eliminate the other than deepen religious experience, a process that can reach absurd proportions. I have been told by friends, for example, that in educating their children in Jerusalem, they find it necessary, for various practical reasons, to send their children to more than one Orthodox school or Yeshiva. At one, they need to don a yarmulke (skullcap) that is knit according to the design of Orthodox religious nationalists. At another school, when dropping off their children, they need to be sure to take that yarmulke off and don a black velvet one that is the mark of *haredi* (ultra-Orthodox) life. Woe to them if they forget to do this, in terms of the possible social isolation of their children, or even possible removal from the school. This is but a small example of the use of numerous markers. Of course, on a deeper level, such markers are absurd but necessary boundaries that help simplify the universe, for oneself and for one's children. They mask deeper concerns to carve out a clarified universe of values and practices in the midst of the absolutely chaotic social universe of modern civilization.

Denial and Apologetics

Let us return now to the next category that I list, denial and apologetics, an interesting middle ground for religious people who are embracing, in some fashion, modern, liberal culture around them, and who endorse many ideas and practices on a human level not necessarily related to their own tradition. Such people are not threatened by truths emerging from other religious traditions. Truth need not be exclusive to be valid for them, and thus it is perfectly possible for secularists or members of other faiths to produce important insights and discoveries of the human mind without threatening the special status of their own religious faith.

At the same time, the idea that there could be serious flaws in their own sacred texts is unacceptable, producing dilemmas of such magnitude that many if not most people cannot cope with this middle position, turning to any of the other options, liberal or conservative, that involve less dialectic stress on the human psyche. For example, if the principles of human rights appear to such a person to be a sensible and reasonable outgrowth of the lessons of human history, in addition to affirming basic religious conceptions of a good God who wants humanity to be good, this appears to be a perfectly harmonious integration of religious belief and political practice. This works right up until one has to explain the Biblical verse in which God commands the wholesale slaughter of men, women, and children, or capital punishment for adultery or homosexual practice, or physical punishment for masturbation. Then there is a blatant contradiction that creates great stress and the need for dialectic apologetics. There are those who learn to live with these contradictions, and there are many others who cannot.

Sometimes these contradictions are not faced or they are explained away in some fashion. This leads some religious people to opt for the subsequent options I've listed.

Soft Rejection and Historical Contextualization

Soft rejection and historical contextualization, the fifth category among my options, boldly integrates faith in sacred literature, the importance of interpretation, and the human capacity to make independent judgments based on reason and/or intuition. It is often accompanied by a theological construct that embraces the human being as an indispensable partner of God in creation, or endowed on purpose by God with the capacity to determine right and wrong that is based on an evolving interpretation of sacred truths.

The challenge of this position, and the reason that it has been so strongly resisted by conservatives, is that there is no clear chain of authority, something so vital for most organized religion. The standard historical pattern of monotheistic innovation of this kind is to begin with maximum independence of the individual, such as at the beginning of the Protestant Reformation, but then for this to be quickly suppressed as too dangerous.

The other alternative, and one that is typical of the branch of Judaism referred to as Conservative Judaism, is to embrace historical contextualization and occasional change, but to refer the decision making to the recognized religious leadership. Now, the question of authority is one of the major evolving issues of modernity, and to the degree to which this option is inclusive, in terms of who is a recognized leader, it will remain a powerful model. However, in the modern context of completely secular states, where individual freedom is maximal on religious issues, this middle position is hard to enforce on anyone. Thus, it often loses its credibility, or the leadership bows excessively to prevailing societal trends.

Hard Rejection of Illiberal Traditions

Hard rejection of some traditions or interpretations and sacralization of others, based on individual decision, is an attractive model for many, but it also risks losing any cultural center to the community, since everyone is free to choose what is negotiable religiously and what is not. More important, absolute freedom of choice in liberal religious communities appears to be a mythic construct that is rarely attained in reality. For example, even in the case of liberal religious communities, based on absolute freedom of choice, there are, in fact, unwritten non-negotiables, principles of inclusion and exclusion.

As an example, for many in the organized Jewish community a non-negotiable has been support for the State of Israel, which othered and excluded for decades those Jews critical of Israel's actions. Clearly, the consensus is also to embrace U.S. wealth and suburban life, which excluded socially and politically those Jews who found American wealth to be destructive of Jewish values and spirituality. It is true that one has in liberal communities an absolute freedom to violate traditional Sabbath laws, but one cannot violate the contemporary taboos and easily integrate into the established community. Thus, it is hard to get away from processes of exclusion and othering.

Conservative Remythification: The Paradigm of the Exodus

I would like to now revisit and delve more deeply into the sixth and most intriguing method of dealing with change, which is the transformation of old cognitive constructs by way of remythification. Let us say, for example, that one is a Jewish pacifist, very Orthodox, and one reads and accepts the Divine truth of biblical scripture. Scripture must not only be acceptable, it must convey some deep truths that one could only find in the word of God. Let us say further that one has derived the truth of the sacredness of all human life from numerous sources in Judaism. However, one is confronted with the story in the book of Exodus about slavery and redemption, and in that story thousands of Egyptians suffer and die violently at the hands of God, as a result of their enslavement of the Jewish people. Many of their punishments are collective, without regard to the individual guilt or innocence of any given family in which the firstborn must die. What lessons are to be learned from this story? What is the story really about? Is it a model of political/military liberation of the Jewish people from its enemies, a paradigm for future Jewish national struggle against enemies? Is it a model for human actions against enemies? One could read it this way. The question of what this story really signifies has intrigued every generation of Jewish commentators.

Just this the kind of question is asked by Aaron Samuel Tamares, a nineteenth-century Eastern European Orthodox village rabbi and prolific author, an erstwhile Zionist, and an ardent pacifist.[8] Tamares wrote extensively on the subject of redemption precisely because the questions of exile, suffering, and redemption elicited the Zionist call for Jews to "re-enter" history, to take control of their lives, from a national point of view, both politically and militarily. While Tamares was attracted to this idea, his exposure to numerous Zionist ideologues and activists eventually led him to the belief that the Zionist enterprise would have to end in great violence, especially against the inhabitants of Palestine, who were of little concern to the more right-wing Zionist thinkers of the time. He wanted no part of it. Tamares understood redemption in an entirely nonviolent way, and like other traditional interpreters before him, he believed that the lesson of the Egyptian enslavement is that *only God* engages in violence when it is necessary to punish the wicked or protect the innocent, but humans should not. Only God metes out collective punishment to corrupt civilizations; we cannot.

This neopacifist reluctance to place the power of life and death in human hands was opposed to the political philosophy of religious Zionism, which was seeking to reestablish Jewish control over its history, through the use of force when necessary, even wholeheartedly embracing, through a new hermeneutic of Jewish tradition, the possibility of Jewish military retaliation.[9] Of course, Tamares wrote before the Holocaust, before liberal and pacifist Jewish ideals were crushed in the face of genocide, and before most Western governments came to support a Zionist solution to Christian Europe's obvious "problem" with Jews. Those who named the famous ship, the Exodus, which tried to enter Palestine overloaded with European refugees, had a very different take on the significance of the Exodus story, and the naming of that ship typifies the modernization of the Exodus myth in Jewish tradition.

Rabbi Tamares, as a modernist as well as a traditionalist, had a distinctively political orientation in his writings. But his hermeneutic move to see the enslavement and the Exodus in spiritual and moral terms had many rabbinic precedents. Many other religious Jews have seen the Exodus story allegorically, even as not about political or military events at all, but rather about the struggles of the soul. Rabbi Judah Loewe (c. 1526), the Maharal of Prague, considered a central symbol of Passover, the risen bread, leaven or *hametz*, to be representative of the *yetser hara*, the part of the human being that pushes us toward sinfulness, a bad nature that is constantly at odds, according to rabbinic anthropology, with the good nature. Therefore, leaven cannot be brought to the alter in Jerusalem as a sacrifice, except on Shavuot, the Feast of Weeks, wherein the giving of the Torah protects one from the *yetser hara*. Leaven is the *yetser hara*, also identified as the "yeast in the dough" that makes human beings sin.[10] Conversely, *matsah*, the unleavened bread that is scrupulously fashioned before Passover, becomes the alternative food of Passover, and its consumption a critical *mitsvah* of the holiday. It is the classical symbol of humility in its unrisen state and its status as poor man's bread or "bread of affliction."

Rabbi Aaron of Karlin (d. 1872), the author of *Bet Aaron* (1875), a leader of the Hasidic sect and dynasty known as Stolin-Karlin, had some interesting things to say about *matsah*, unleavened bread. It is also called in the Bible either "poor man's bread" or "bread of affliction," depending on the translation of *lehem oni*. The Haggadah states: "This is poor man's bread that our forefathers ate in Egypt. Everyone who is hungry, come and eat. Everyone who is needy, let them eat the Passover (sacrifice) [with us]. Now [we are] here, next year in the Land of Israel. Now we are slaves, next year we will be free men."[11] Rabbi Aaron saw *matsah* as the symbol of everything in this world that longs to be united with the other worlds, the nonmaterial higher worlds, as they are understood by Jewish mysticism. This unification depends on human beings who are uniquely endowed with the place in the order of Creation to unite upper and lower worlds and thus achieve the mystical unity of the world that God craves. Only human beings, who are endowed with a physical familiarity with this world, and therefore have an impulse to sin, can be the ones to unite upper and lower worlds. They can sin and become lost in the physicality of this world, but they are also capable of seeing the majesty of the world, which points them to higher worlds. They thus become, through their own inner struggles, unifiers of worlds in a way that angels, for example, never could. Even God Himself waits for the human being to unify worlds. This is extraordinarily empowering to the believer, but it is not empowerment through physical strength or military might! It is actually the opposite of a political or military message for Passover.[12]

The vision of hope in this verse of the Haggadah, the vision of the future, is that the upper worlds, symbolized by the Land of Israel, will be reachable in the coming year (or era), and the freedom spoken of is the freedom achieved by that unification. The hunger is the hunger of those who know that they are incomplete without engaging in this holy activity, and those who come to eat the Passover are actually coming to speak and be in dialogue (*peh soh*, a Midrashic reworking of the Hebrew word for *Passover*, which means "mouth that speaks"), for conversation in Torah helps one unify all the worlds.

In general, one senses in Rabbi Aaron's writings a struggle between humility and elevation, and all that those traits signify ontologically in terms of the presence of God. Passover, commemorating the Exodus, is the holiday of humility; hence the centralization of a key slavery artifact, poor man's bread, *matsah*, which has no yeast that would allow the bread—or one's soul—to rise to a state of sin. It is quite simply an embrace of humility, of the kind that a slave learns. This is hardly the stuff of nationalist pride and military liberation! It is, if anything, the opposite.

This religious set of interpretations must be seen in balance, however, with Shavuot. Fifty days after Passover, after a great spiritual ascendance, comes the moment of Revelation at Sinai, commemorated by the holiday of Shavuot, with the central symbol and offering of the risen bread, the *lehem ha-panim* in the *bet ha-mikdash*, the Holy Temple in Jerusalem. This drama of movement from lowliness to elevation is an essential rabbinic teaching, whereas political and military victory is not at the heart of rabbinic teaching,[13] at least regarding these holidays. The essential teaching of the Passover and Exodus is not political and military victory over enemies.[14] This last set of rabbinic interpretations, although recent in origin, represents classical rabbinic thinking, with elements of this theme stemming back all the way to ancient Talmudic thought and all the way forward to Hasidic thought.[15]

This is just one example of hermeneutic processes that have a direct bearing on our subject of the interpretive and mythic alternatives that communities face as far as violence and peacemaking are concerned. In the plain—and nationalist meaning—of the Exodus story, the Egyptians are othered, the enemies of the Jewish people. But these rabbinic interpretations other sins: for some, the sin of enslavement, for others the sin of arrogance, or sins that divide upper and lower worlds. For Tamares, what is othered is violence itself and the brutality of oppression.

The most intriguing option for religious mythology and meaning systems, in terms of peacemaking and conflict resolution, is to take the past constructs of othering and turn them toward benign objectives and meanings—in other words, peaceful forms of othering. This would mean that peace with an enemy does not necessarily signify to the believer an emasculation of religious meaning or practice. Rather, a new layer of meaning may be discovered through peace with the enemy, which allows historical hopes of the future to emerge without damaging sacred text and tradition. The sacred text, which, as it searches for the good and shuns evil, must other something, is not threatened by gestures of peace toward a long-standing enemy because that enemy is not embedded as an eternal other. Hermeneutics thus gives the believer the freedom and opportunity to redefine what is other. Conflict prevention and resolution theory, applied to religion, must seize on this spiritual phenomenon and strengthen it.

Hermeneutic transformation, as a spiritual phenomenon, is a delicate process, and one that is zealously guarded by the faithful. Some engage in this remythification process in a way that deliberately challenges the old order, while others engage in it so subtly that even the most reactionary observers do not notice. Rereading is thus often at the forefront of revolutionary thought and practice that is housed within a conservative edifice. This is precisely how conservative religion evolves over time, and it holds great promise in terms of extending commitments to peace and conflict resolution to even the most segregated and isolated of religious communities.

Radical Remythification and the Temple Mount, Centerpiece of the Conflict

I want to give an example of more radical remythification that is directly relevant to the Arab-Israeli conflict and, in particular, the conflict over the Temple Mount. As a general rule, traditional, nonviolent reworking of biblical and ancient Jewish sources that once had violent implications has always appeared historically in the context of the radical physical disempowerment of exiles, especially in the presence of hostile competing religions. Generally speaking, pacifist or quietistic hermeneutics tends to triumph in monotheistic traditions when there is no other option. In other words, what appears to be pacifism is actually quietism. But, as I have said earlier, this does not in any way diminish the religious authenticity of these interpretations, but rather contextualizes them historically, and it also tends to make difficult the task of upholding peaceful hermeneutics in a time of strength.

For example, rabbinic tendencies to spiritualize the message of the Egyptian slavery and the Exodus did not necessarily lead to a loving embrace of the surrounding gentile world. Indeed, this is hardly surprising, given the consistent level of theological and popular hatred directed at religious Jews for so many centuries.[16] Tamares is the exception in this regard. Plenty of other rabbinic and Hasidic statements disparage gentiles.

We have, therefore, an odd combination of rabbinic reworking of violent texts to nonviolent ends, which combines awkwardly with strong animosity toward gentiles. This is common in much of European rabbinic literature. It is as if many rabbis in history were struggling to discover the nonviolent depths of Jewish spirituality, learning well from their surroundings how destructive oppression and brutality are to the integrity of the religions that were brutalizing them. But they were at the mercy of the dominant culture, which always made them into either cultural inferiors, or worse, victims of periodic horror. The effect was deeply damaging to their capacity to trust or respect the majoritarian others. It is not surprising, therefore, that in today's Israel, the *haredim*, exclusively devoted to almost two thousand years of rabbinic texts, are, on the one hand, decidedly not at the forefront of aggressive, military training of any sort, militarism having been eliminated from their theological universe by centuries of interpretation. But, on the other hand, their voting patterns are strictly oriented toward their own interests and needs, and they certainly have not demonstrated, as a community, any commitment at all to creating a new relationship with Arabs or gentiles in general. On the contrary, there sometimes remains an encrusted theological and emotional disgust with the gentile, who is at best inferior spiritually to the Jew, and at worst the instrument of most evil things in the world. The typical response to my suggestions to them about possible Palestinian and Arab encounters followed along the lines of "What would be the point?!"

Thus, we are faced with a tantalizing set of precedents for moving Jewish religious life and practice in a hermeneutic direction that is more peaceful. But they are housed within and suffer from the damage of centuries of bitter feelings toward gentiles, especially with the crowning achievement of European anti-Semitism, the Holocaust, in the immediate memory of most Jewish families and communities. It seems to me, assuming no other catastrophes in the near future, that time and the passing of generations may very well shift this attitude to gentiles within the next hundred years. But, of course, the task of conflict resolution is to speed healthy historical processes along before other political and economic forces could worsen the relationship. For example, as long as the Palestinian-Israeli relationship remains unbalanced economically and politically, it is likely that violent forms of struggle will continue, and twenty-first-century forms of struggle invariably include the targeting of civilians. Psychologically and theologically, this will guarantee the perpetuation of hostile theological constructs on the part of Jews. It is likely that Palestinian resistance will continue to include physical attacks on civilians and eliminationist rhetoric, and that Jewish right-wing responses will increasingly call for expulsion and even annihilation. Theology will support this.

Thus, on the one hand, the slow diminution of classical Christian anti-Semitism and the receding into history of the Holocaust could lead to religious Jewish healing, but not if anti-Israeli violence continues to reinforce old categories of interpretation of this worldly experience. Furthermore, these old attitudes toward gentiles have merged seamlessly with a Jewish majoritarian capacity today in Israel for ethnic prejudice that is transforming Jewish anti-gentile psychology into a destructive ethnic posture, rather than what it used to be, a pitiful reaction to impossible exilic circumstances.

Another complicating factor is that Israeli Jewish life today is bound up in a bitter struggle over religious control of secular citizens' personal lives, especially their marriages, divorces, deaths, and status as Jews. The tribalism that such conflicts invariably breed, the sense that you either are "for us or against us," has led to a situation of relatively little religious creativity in Israel, which has in turn made it difficult, if not impossible, for there to be a large group of Jews in Israel who would be interested in seeing Jewish traditions in new ways. Of course, there is a great deal of New Age experimentation with religious identity, and some effects felt from the infusion of Conservative and Reform people and funds in Israel, but these have not touched the majority of secular or Orthodox Jews. There is a resulting bitterness and hatred by the non-Orthodox, on the one side, and a siege mentality on the ultra-Orthodox side, both of which prevent middle grounds of creative interpretation.

It is not impossible in the future, however, that the Jewish penchant for creative reading and rereading of traditional texts will again jump to the fore as a way of solving intractable problems. The peace process itself, if it produces tangible changes for the better, may very well catalyze this eventuality. The problem is one of chicken and egg. We need a sizable number of people in the religious community to support peacemaking to move forward. But it also seems to me that the "evidence" of good issuing historically from peace with neighbors may be necessary for many religious people to see the hand of divine providence supporting the peace process.

As stated earlier, one of the most intractable problems is the Temple Mount, the third holiest site of Islam, sitting right on top of Judaism's most holy site, as well as the symbol of Judaism's greatest sense of mourning and loss, namely the Second Temple, destroyed in 70 c.e. and mourned for two thousand years in every Jewish prayer, every day. It is also the traditional site of Abraham's binding of Isaac and divine covenant. It is place of profound origin, identity, and loss.

Arthur Waskow is an American religious Jewish thinker who has a respectable following of Jews who consider themselves progressives. They are part of the Jewish Renewal Movement, but Waskow's ideas have had influence beyond their borders. Waskow has a habit of combining traditional methods of reading and rereading with radical breaks from Jewish tradition and the creation of new traditions. This has baffled and outraged traditional thinkers and believers, and, at the same time, his creative methods and ideas have been path-breaking, not unlike the impact of Mordecai Kaplan. Even though his ideas would never be accepted by very religious Jews whom we are trying to bring into the peace process, it is nevertheless instructive to see how creative ideas and interpretations have a compelling quality in Jewish life, and how they seep into the community.

I will shortly give an example of this from Waskow's attitude toward the Temple Mount, but let me introduce the topic of the Temple Mount with my own experience as a participant-observer of this facet of the conflict. I have suggested before that Jerusalem embodies the deepest hopes and injuries of two peoples, Jewish and Palestinian, and three major religions. This creates the kind of intractable conflict over space that conflict-resolution theory often considers insoluble, precisely because it is about basic issues of existence and identity. Therefore, most conflict resolution theorists, when faced with any conflict, run for the cover of pragmatism and appeals to "win-win" models. The latter option, however, is really based on a materialist notion of a world of scarce resources from which, if we are clever enough, we can generate enough wealth for everyone. Whether or not this is as much a myth, or a faith, as the myths of religion is a separate issue. But certainly a fight over scarce resources should, they argue, be subject to more compromise than a fight over identity.

A fight over an unqualifiedly sacred mountain appears on the surface, admittedly, to be infinitely intractable. But things are not always as they seem, and it was a purposeful overstatement on my part to declare that this Temple Mount is valued equally by all religious people on both sides. It means different things to different people, despite the official theologies or the uses of theology for political purposes. Indeed, one could easily argue that those elements of religion that are most easily utilized for political and military conflict have been at the mercy of religious members who are more motivated by ethno-nationalist and military motives than they are by religion. Certainly this explains the overattachment to Jerusalem among many otherwise nonreligious people on both sides, and the underattachment, shall we say, to other ancient ethical prohibitions, such as murder or theft, those two ethical orphans of ethnonationalist conflicts.

One can see, in general, in ethnic conflicts around the world which involve contested land, that there exists a remarkably selective process of highlighting land-based attachments that are latent in the respective traditions. For example, it is no accident that, from Bosnia and Serbia to Israel, claiming and reclaiming burial sites of saints, ancestors, or heroes becomes a heightened, central activity during periods of deadly conflict. It is a religious way of engaging in the same contest for land that secular ethnic parties and diplomats are engaged in, except it is imbued with deep mythic meaning. And yet, aggravating as it may be to secularists, these struggles are often based on some truth. The question of the relative importance of the Temple Mount for Judaism, at least, is tied to the question of how the religious future is expected to unfold, how the great Redemption, the End of Days, is to occur. Furthermore, how much the believer focuses on Redemption as an integral part of her or his religious life is variable. It is certainly a basic feature of Jewish prayers and theology, but in Judaism there are many beliefs and practices, and which ones become centralized and which marginalized signifies a fundamental way in which organized religion changes over time. Settler Judaism, for example, has been deeply influenced by over a century of religious Zionism, and in particular by the philosophy of Rabbi Kook and son, which has centralized land, sovereignty, redemption, and even monarchy, making these things so important that they are worth dying and killing for.

This attitude has not been adopted by *haredim*, however, except Habad Hasidism. The *haredi* approach to Redemption itself has been passive on the political level (unlike the religious Zionists), but active on the level of *mitsvah*, *teshuva* (repentance), and, for some, mystically redemptive actions. It is also the case, however, that *haredi* politics and *haredi* life appear to be comfortable with coercive forms of changing those who are outside the borders of their community, namely the rest of the Israeli population, in addition to keeping control by force over their own community, when it comes to issues of personal status and domestic law. There is little concern for Arab welfare or Arab rights per se, in *haredi* circles. But, in an ironic twist, *haredim*, who shun most of modern culture, tend to pragmatically utilize what they need from modern life. In addition, they continue in a conservative way the traditions of their ancestors which involve a practical set of strategies of coexistence with gentiles who are capable of hurting them. With little confidence in military superiority as the guarantor of human security, they instead are open to pragmatic ways to coexist with whichever gentiles they need to. In other words, they have no utopian, visionary zeal that drives them to bring Jewish history to a victorious conclusion. That is for God to do. Thus, their attitude toward gentiles and gentile life is, at one and the same time, more disparaging but less dangerous militarily than that of their religious Zionist competitors. Nevertheless, their popular voting patterns in Israel have increasingly swung toward right-wing politics.

Religious Zionists, by contrast, have completely modernized the classical biblical themes, embodied in the conquests and reign of King David (ancestor of the Messiah), and of Jewish military might as the hand of God himself. Redemption is so paramount that risks of major military confrontation and death do not deter them. The upshot is that both of these rejectionist camps need to be approached with different strategies to include them in a peaceful future. More deeply, they will require two different kinds of remythifications and rereadings of tradition, for the simple reason that their central texts, traditions, and myths are different. To the outsider they may appear identical, but this is false. Two completely different interventions are necessary. But let me return now to my observations as a participant-observer.

The liberal Orthodox Judaism of my youth emphasized the importance of natural processes of redemption. This involved making the world better by example. The essential role of *mitsvah*, in a larger sense of the term, was to become part of a process of teaching and doing, in a sacred way, that would direct fellow Jews, and the world, toward a redemptive framework. Although the utopian dreams were embraced religiously, there was a greater emphasis on the deed here and now, and less on expecting any moment a Messiah who would rebuild the Temple. Everyone Orthodox grows up praying, several times a day, for messianic redemption. But in some places of worship, especially among Lubavitch, one can enter and be overwhelmed with constant references to the Messiah possibly arriving today, whereas in other synagogues you will never hear such words spoken. This is a matter of emphasis and subtle linguistic changes that point to an entirely different kind of spiritual life and interaction with the world.

As one can see in other parts of the world, theology tends to shift toward a land-based theology as intergroup conflicts become more intense, bloodier and longer-lasting. This process is apparent in highly materialist civilizations within which identity is inseparable from what one owns. Moreover, theology also becomes more land-based to the degree to which possession becomes politically and militarily more feasible. This trend developed and strengthened with every passing decade of my youth. Thus, land-centered Orthodox Jewish theology has gained increasing acceptance with every decade since the establishment of the State of Israel, although it is unclear whether it has reached its zenith or not. Much will be decided by the finality or, alternatively, the indeterminacy of the peace process and the fate of the Arab-Israeli conflict.

My experience within this process points to one inescapable conclusion. If these theologies can change over time for the worse, and they are not static, then it stands to reason that standard conflict theory is wrong about the intractability of conflict over religious beliefs and practices, or religious identity issues tied up with land. Whatever is not static, whatever changes for the worse, can also change for the better. Whatever is hermeneutically reworked to centralize land can be reworked—and has been historically—to emphasize the sacredness of, for example, life, peace or justice.

Here the prejudice of scholars of religious violence is a core issue. There is a perfectly perceptive vision of religious change for the worse in their literature, but a blindness to religious change for the better. One gets the impression that whatever is bad must remain bad and is an indelible feature of a religious mentality, while whatever is good can always be turned into a vehicle of violence. But I did not have this experience. The hermeneutics tended to change with the relative degree of fear and isolation that Orthodox Jews felt about Israel's status. The more that status was threatened, the more they retreated to survivalist theology.

In the case of the Jewish community, the shifts and tides have been readily apparent, and very little can be reduced to simplistic categorization. Despite the fact that my religious life was more ethics-centered than Messianic, for example, the fact is that the Temple Mount and the Western Wall comprise a place that is a central focus of my attention, and a place of great emotions. On the recent trips to Israel in which I have worked on peace and conflict, I have tried, despite myself, to avoid a visit to "The Wall," "the *Kotel.*" The more politicized and militarized the Old City became, the sadder I was to see it. A few years back I went there late on a Saturday night and discovered a large contingent of very high level American military men, being escorted around the plaza before the wall by Israeli generals. It made me very angry, for I could not understand what "they," the military leadership of the Western world, were doing at "my" wall. I imagine that my more radical cousins would have felt emboldened by having so many generals looking on admiringly at the wall.

The *Kotel* is, thus, a place of great pain and great ownership, if you will, for Jews, even for "peaceniks" like me. Some members of my family, on the opposite end of the political spectrum, have what can only be described as a mystical attachment to the *Kotel* that propels them to go there every week. The next time, several years later, that I went to the wall, so many terrorist incidents had occurred in the Old City that the area was militarized to the hilt, soldiers and guns everywhere. And, as I surveyed this almost surreal combination of sacredness and militarization, something broke inside me. My legs weakened, I fell down, and I wept and wept that day in the middle of the plaza overlooking the wall, in the hot noonday sun, laid out flat on my side, for it seemed an eternity. The tears were so intense that the wall became a blur and my shirt was drenched, and in some odd way I felt fulfilled, because Jewish texts often speak of intense crying as the fulfillment of prayer. I was also sick, my back in desperate pain, and I had unsuccessfully participated in a teaching program for Jewish youth, at the same time that the burden of seeing a future horror occurring in Israel was overwhelming me. All of these things were interrelated.

Religious people I knew at the time, colleagues I daresay, were speaking about needing to "do something"—violent, that is—about Prime Minister Rabin, and I believe that I began mourning over his death right then, months before he was assassinated, because I am often plagued by dark dreams of possible futures. And so the waters of my life flowed that day out of my eyes and my nose and my mouth, as if they had been stored up for decades. I had never done that in any public space in my life, and several Jews approached to see what was wrong but walked away soon, upon seeing that I was not physically in danger. After all, they probably said to themselves, "people do strange things in Jerusalem." It is a city of many passions that propel you beyond social convention.

Years ago, someone in my family managed to get hold of some of the earth that archeologists had uncovered as they burrowed deep beneath the Wailing Wall to layers that had not been uncovered for 1,900 years. But what I got was not earth but black embers that were turning into earth and dust, many pieces of burned wood plainly visible inside the dirt. These were from a fire from countless centuries ago, only unearthed now, and it is quite possible that they were remnants of the mounds of wood that ancient armies used to destroy large, stone structures. They placed the wood beneath the gigantic stones and set them on fire; the stones would explode, and the building would collapse. That is how the Temple was destroyed in 70 C.E., almost two thousand years ago, and I was possibly holding in my hands the embers that destroyed the Temple, the black dust rubbing off between my fingers and onto my clothing.

As if this were not enough, there is a question posed in Jewish tradition as to how the Romans got so much wood to burn the Temple. But the Temple had its own vast store of "sacred" wood, used for the altar, the *atse ha-shittim*.[17] It is possible that I was holding in my hands the remnants of that sacred wood, which filled me with awe. I have kept those embers in a sealed, small green glass case for the past fifteen years, on the mantelpiece in all the homes where I have lived.

I remember as a boy that the pictures of Jerusalem, since 1967, contained numerous pictures of the Temple Mount, with the Western Wall prominently displayed and the Islamic Dome of the Rock right above it. Those pictures always gave me great comfort. I liked the combination of the religions, and it seemed to me, as a boy, that Israeli occupation had led to an ideal world in which all the religions are represented in the Old City, and that this was a kind of utopia, a kind of messianic dream. And it occurred to me that maybe this was the dream of Messiah come true.

But I was a boy, and I did not know yet that one person's dreams can be another's nightmares, and I did not know how difficult it is to dream truly good dreams that do not become someone else's nightmares. I still believe, as I did as a young man, that, in comparison with the rest of the Middle East, Jerusalem now is a city of unprecedented freedom for all three monotheisms, despite the obvious injustices to the Palestinian people themselves, and that Western critics underestimate the dangers that lie ahead for a Jerusalem, or an Eastern Jerusalem, that would or could become subject to fundamentalist control. There is constant fundamentalist struggle in Jerusalem, with clear bias toward Jewish fundamentalists. But at least so far an overarching political authority keeps fundamentalist intensity from destroying most basic freedoms in the city for all three religions. There is no guarantee that this will necessarily continue in the future. Somehow the delicate balance that has been achieved religiously by secular Israeli authorities must be combined with a much more profound respect for Palestinian identity, dignity, sacred places, and basic rights to property that they own now or once owned. Ultimately, there must be a place for dual sovereignty over some locations and Palestinian sovereignty in others. But the sharing of the space at an inter-religious level complicates these dreams and possibilities.

I remember that as the years of my youth passed and the bitterness of the Arab-Israeli conflict intensified, the killing of innocents piling up every year, that something extraordinary occurred in Jewish circles. I started to notice various Jewish religious portrayals of the Temple Mount with the Dome of the Rock eliminated from the picture. And I knew then that we were in trouble, and that the trouble had become embedded into the religious psyche, at least for now. The Dome had now become a hated object, whereas before it was in a certain way part of a vision that many Jews had of a multicultural Jerusalem. This deepened the psychological struggle.

What is so subtle here, and lost on outside or unsympathetic listeners, is that the standard traditional line had always been that someday the Messiah would come and rebuild the Temple. Until then, most traditionalists had even forbidden going into the Dome of the Rock, lest one tread upon the spot where the Holy of Holies once stood, a place where only the High Priest could enter once a year on Yom Kippur. It is unknown by most outside observers that those religious Jews who have repeatedly entered and attempted to pray near the Dome of the Rock have violated Jewish law as it currently is interpreted by most Jewish traditionalists.

Nevertheless, the radicalization of the traditional community can be measured by how much this behavior is increasingly tolerated, and the variety of people who are more and more planning for the arrival of the Messiah and the rebuilding of the Temple. But the dynamics of this radicalization are obscure. Today, as with everything else, it is immensely complicated by who lends financial support to such efforts. In today's political world many radical and bizarre causes gain new life with just a handful of donors, or even one wealthy donor. It has been reported to me personally, though this is too murky to confirm, that there is a large portion of Christian money behind the most radicalized Jewish religious political efforts. *Haredi* Jews would never take money from Evangelicals. But those few Jews holding out in Hebron, against masses of Muslims, are the kind of Jews who would form such an alliance, just as Netanyahu and the Likud formed an alliance with Falwell and other Evangelicals against Arab and Muslim power over the Holy Land.

It is rumored, for example, that the extremely radical institutions that are planning for the rebuilding of the Temple, even recreating the utensils to be used, are receiving substantial funds from radical American Christians. This is a strange new world of biblical radicalism that could cross religious lines. Of course, it should not surprise us too much that, just as Jewish and Christian liberals have been working together for decades on matters of social justice, that Jewish and Christian radicals would do the same. It shocks us initially because we usually associate Jewish fundamentalism with the *haredi* world, which is separatist to the core, for the most part, and certainly uncomfortable with anything Christian. But the land-based Jewish radicalism that has emerged, in addition to receiving an infusion of new blood regularly from Jewish ethnonationalists who are newcomers to Judaism, *ba'ale teshuva*, has also rewritten the rules on interfaith relationships. The enemy becomes whoever is threatening land-based sovereignty, and since Christian evangelical dreams of Armageddon and mass conversions are simply fantasy, as far as these Jews are concerned, the Christians pose no threat. Someday, if these same Christians try their hand at forcing history then they will become the enemy. But, in enemy systems and psychological structures, the "enemy of my enemy is my friend."

These radical Jews, dangerous as they are to the physical structure of the Dome of the Rock, are a tiny minority within a minority. Most religious Jews continue in a state of limbo regarding the Messianic Age, as they have for two thousand years. On the one hand, they hold fast to the dream of a rebuilt

Temple, but, on the other hand, they have no intention of forcing the hand of history, especially when at least a number of sources see the Messiah, and his harbinger, Elijah, as peaceful figures.[18] The violence that the destruction of the mosque would unleash is self-evident. This, then, is an example of religious theology that learns to live with contradictions, awaiting a redeemer who will solve them. It leaves in suspended animation the question of historical fulfillment.

But, in my opinion, this status quo of messianic interpretation is fragile because the anxiety and tension of land-based existential struggle makes the paradoxes more unbearable than ever before. This is especially true when Jews now have the power to do something about that tension, whereas they had no choice in exile but to endure the contradictions between God's comforting promises of future blessings and the unpleasant realities of their present existence.

That is why Waskow's reworking of the Temple mythology so fascinated me in recent years. Waskow is a radical in his own right, almost eager to smash old ideologies. But he is a radical for peace, justice, and universal disarmament. With regard to the Temple, he has created a story that poses as a traditional Hasidic tale but is as destructive of old mythology as it is constructive of radically new mythologies.[19]

I cannot do justice to the subtleties of the tale, which is told in classic Hasidic fashion, but I will summarize. Waskow tells the tale of a Hasid from Vitebsk who visits his Rebbe who now lives in Israel. The Hasid notices a picture on the wall of the Rebbe's synagogue that is of the future Temple, but with the Dome of the Rock at the center. He is dismayed as he wonders how this could be, since the Messiah is destined to rebuild the Temple. The Rebbe says that the Messiah is destined to build the Temple—and this is a critical and repeated phrase—in "a twinkling of an eye." This phrase is Waskow's midrashic way of saying that the construction of the Temple, especially as it signifies the long-awaited Redemption of the Jews and humankind, is a matter of perception, or our shifting our perceptions, not actual construction.

He continues the tale with the Rebbe's vision of the Messiah entering the Temple (a tale within a tale, common in Rabbi Nachman's Hasidic tales). The Messiah laughs at the traditional rabbinic sign forbidding entry to the Temple Mount and rips it up. [This part of the tale reflects Waskow's willingness and even eagerness to overturn what he views as antiquated rabbinic laws, which has alienated many traditionalists from him and his writings. But to be fair to him, it also reflects a rabbinic tradition that some Jewish laws will be abolished in the Messianic Era, such as observance of some holidays.[20]]

The Muslims take this entry as an aggressive gesture. Jews and Muslims are lined up on either side, each ready to do battle. But then Messiah points out the beauty of the dome, and then says that the dome *is* the rebuilt Temple. This, of course, evokes outrage, but it is the Messiah, after all! But it almost comes to the use of weapons anyway, with people on both sides ready to kill. Except that one Jew stops another who is about to act, without violence somehow, and he throws the weapon down. Soon all the weapons are thrown down in a pile, and then they are burned. The Rebbe is then asked by his Hasid,

"Why?" And he answers that the weapons are the burnt offering of the Temple. And he adds, "It is written, 'Choose!'[21] You [must burn]. Or the Temple [must burn (that is, today's Israel and Palestine)]. Or the things that you use to burn each other with [weapons]."[22]

Waskow recounts human and Jewish history in one fell swoop. We Jews, he is saying, have had our places of worship and study burned by hatred fairly regularly for two thousand years. Our bodies and the bodies of our children have been burnt offerings, such as in the Inquisition, the Holocaust, and countless other anonymous times. And this too is the history of humankind. But Waskow concludes that we also have the choice to burn that with which we have always burned each other, namely, the weapons. And (here I am elaborating on Waskow) when we finally realize that it is the weapons that need to be the ultimate burnt offering on the Temple Mount, then on that great and redemptive day, Waskow dreams, the Temple will be rebuilt "in a twinkling of an eye," not by destroying anything in reality or building anything in reality, but by our perception.

Waskow knows that the Temple Mount is, according to Jewish tradition, built on the site of Abraham's sacrifice of Isaac, a site, therefore, that already saw the transformation by God of human sacrifice into something else, something less barbaric. On the other hand, Waskow knows that in Jewish tradition many believe that Isaac really was sacrificed, a belief that emerges strongly in the Middle Ages, in the shadow of burning bodies of the "acts of faith" in Spain and many other places. The offering to God is essential. But history, he knows, is riddled with the travesty of Isaac being forcibly sacrificed and burned by gentiles as a whole burnt offering, rather than the offering of spiritual self, which is all that God wanted.

Undoubtedly, as a person who built his theology upon fighting nuclear omnicide, Waskow sees the awesomeness and significance of the human race preparing itself collectively as a whole burnt offering before God. And he bears witness in his midrashic/theological position here to humanity's misunderstanding of the message of the angel to Abraham, and the significance of the Temple Mount. And so Waskow constructs a new vision of burnt offering, of destruction and recreation, and of Redemption, one in which the offering of self, and the burning of hatred, and the burning of weapons, is all God ever intended or hoped for.

This is an extraordinary and profound modern midrash. But I suspect that this interpretation will evoke anger from most Orthodox Jews—at least I think so at the present time and in the present form of the midrash. The complex truth is that midrashic reworking of the future, of Jewish dreams, has occurred many times before in Jewish history—at the hands of very traditional Jews. This in itself would not cause too much outrage, or, in psychological terms, cognitive dissonance. The crucial question is the degree to which the vision challenges or deliberately flouts the rabbinic construct of Jewish tradition. The real question of mythic transformation and re-creation is a question of degree. From Maimonides to the great mystics of the Middle Ages, we have seen radically different constructs of what the idealized future of the world might be, or even what heaven might be. However, the basic constructs and contours of Jewish law are always honored. This is where some of the details of Waskow's myth might alienate the majority of halakhically observant Jews. Nevertheless, the vision is compelling and could lead to more traditional rereadings of Waskow's rereading.

As another example of remythification, Rabbi Elijah Benamozegh, an Orthodox rabbinic leader in Italy in the second half of the nineteenth century, had a very radically inclusive Jewish theology, as well as a profound view of a redemptive future that included all of humanity.[23] His was a profoundly new model of the future and of the role of other religions. But, on the other hand, he evinces a profound respect for rabbinic Judaism that would endear him to at least a number of religious Jews.

The great schism in our own day has dug into the heart of Jewish life and religious behavior. It is on that basis that liberal midrash, such as that of Waskow's, would be suspect and, let's face it, vilified.

My own conclusion has always been that Waskow provides powerful new insights into Jewish religious life, but the midrashic and halakhic models that will move traditional Jews toward a profound level of coexistence with Arabs, both Christian and Muslim, in Israel, have yet to be created. We are at the very beginning of this theological-psychological process of transformation, and perhaps Waskow represents an early harbinger of more mainstream changes to come in the future. That is often the role that he has played in recent history. It is my belief that the more traditional a theological process is the more likely it will gain acceptance in the historical consciousness of the Jewish community as a whole. On the other hand, it is also the case that often history presents communities with fundamental impasses to future growth, or to the resolution of a conflict. It is at these junctures that radically new perceptions have an important function. But the conservative and conserving character of organized religion will require that whatever the new vision, it must become housed within traditional frameworks. For many a radical this spells the end of the vision. But for our purposes of peacemaking and conflict resolution, I beg to differ.

The successful shifts in human history that have brought us a better quality of life and a more ethical society require the mainstreaming of radically new ideas. The concept of universal civil rights and human rights, for example, once a radical and absurd idea of visionaries a hundred years ago, is becoming more and more mainstreamed into global governance, despite the constant violations. The notion of equal intellectual capacities of men and women is also a radical idea in the process of becoming mainstreamed, but it was not long ago that this was universally held to be absurd, at least by men. The empirical method, the experimental method of truth seeking, once a radical threat to a medieval intellectual universe, has now opened up secrets of nature that one could not think possible just a short time ago. Almost nobody today refuses the results of that experimental method when it offers life-saving techniques of medical intervention, or astonishing bio-engineering feats, such as potable water for millions in the world's massive cities. We are so used to seeing the glaring failures in this process, and the unfairness of selective success that often favors the rich and leaves hundreds of millions in misery, that we forget how many millions of people today have a quality of life that is utterly superior to anything known to humankind previously. All of this is due to radical visions that eventually become mainstream visions. Practice will always fall short of this. But the shift in vision is what we seek here. Vision is at the core of religious motivation, and it is simultaneously an indispensable element of peacemaking.

How vision is framed, however, will determine to whom it is acceptable and to whom unacceptable. For example, the whole idea of making midrash is a phenomenon typical today of the liberal wings of Judaism. Orthodox and *haredi* people do not tend to boldly create their own midrash, although hagiographic literature about their sainted masters does abound. But mostly they only study ancient rabbinic Midrash. In fact, making midrash would be seen by authoritarian religious models today as a scandalous usurpation of a classical rabbinic form of spiritual teaching. It is true that there is a tradition, especially Hasidic, of telling tales, *myse'lakh*. Even these, however, are limited these days to tales about *tsadikim* and *gedole yisroel*, masters of halakhic Judaism recognized and accepted by the *haredi* community. But the main source of change and creativity in Orthodoxy is interpretation, and selection of which rabbinic texts, traditions, Midrash, and *myse'lakh* to highlight. Thus, there is some freedom, too small, of course, for liberals.

At the early stages of development of traditional biblical religions, there is a great deal of ferment, struggle, and creativity of different interpretations. There are so many books of the Bible, most by a single author, such as Amos, who is accepted into the canon as inspired by God. In later periods there is also great creative input. But in all three monotheistic traditions, creativity and individual interpretation become over time increasingly regulated and delimited, and, in certain traditions, actually forbidden. In fact, the greater the competition between the monotheisms, and the greater the threat from the outside to the boundaries of the tradition—such as from modern secular society—the more one will find a clamping down on creativity. Nevertheless, it bursts forth from time to time, despite many rules designed to discourage new interpretation or forbid innovation.

The challenge is how to discover, in every tradition, no matter how conservative, the opportunities for interpretations or innovations that can move a community in the direction of seeing enemy relationships in a new way. This can only be done by courageous people in each and every subcommunity of the religious groups, from the most liberal to the most reactionary. The task of intervenors is to help them, to facilitate this process, to make it easy for them to communicate with others, to fund their efforts or their research, and help them to write and teach.

Another element of this process should be pointed out. Waskow's myth is deeply Jewish, apparently. But it has Muslim actors within it. It is common in monotheisitc sources for the other religions and their adherents to occasionally play some role in the others' myths. Usually this is a negative or delegitimating role that requires the conversion of the other to escape sin or "ignorance." We are interested, however, in prosocial gestures of vision, as in Waskow's case.

Notice, however, that there is, almost of necessity, an asymmetric power structure to the vision. The deus ex machina, the grand solution to this age-old conflict over the Temple Mount and Jerusalem, is a Jewish messiah, and his way of relating and thinking, and even problem-solving, is entirely Jewish in character. When he acts in a surprising fashion, and embraces the beauty of the dome, the Muslims react with awed silence. There is no corresponding gesture, for example, that might draw upon a *hadith*, for example. In other words, this is a Jewish vision, and that is fine. But it is vital to recognize it as such. Vision, like encounters between groups, is often asymmetric, unbalanced of necessity. There are differing power relations that complicate encounter, dialogue, and even visions. The only solution is mutuality, sharing of visions, and the recognition of the boundaries and limitations of one's own vision, thus making a crucial space for the other's vision and learning that limitation. Each community of necessity creates visions that highlight its own power and legitimacy. The real difference between conflict and peace is a matter of degree in terms of the destructiveness or constructiveness of the vision and the extent to which the vision highlights the power or legitimacy of one group over another. If it is excessive and demonizing of the other, then it is destructive. If, on the other hand, it is benignly preferential to one's own faith and community, then it will have a better impact. If it happens to be very forward looking and spiritual, a vision that is truly pluralistic, then so much the better.

Asymmetry of power is an important problem in conflict-resolving processes, such as dialogue encounters. Let us dwell on this for a little while, before returning to Waskow's myth. Asymmetry is an important element of Mohammed Abu-Nimer's critique of Arab-Israeli peacemaking encounters; and correctives to this, it seems to me, are a significant element of his own training methods, as I have observed them. Simply stated, adversary groups often arise from circumstances in which one group has more military and/or economic and political power than another. The asymmetry also may express itself in the nature of the encounter, its language, structure, and cultural ethos. This skews dialogue and contact between enemy groups as a method of conflict resolution. I would argue that dialogue itself, as a method of peacemaking, is culturally charged, maybe even biased, and may not satisfy or correspond to the best cultural methods that a group may possess for peacemaking and the transformation of enemy relationships. A peacemaking method can produce asymmetry in and of itself if its execution favors the skills of one group over another, or one subcommunity of each group.

With regard to this last point, asymmetry is a problem not just between adversary groups but within them as well. If one sets up an encounter in which one adversary group is all women and the other mostly men, or one secular and one religious, or neither religious, in every case you are setting up imbalances. You are also creating mythical constructs of encounter that do not reflect the full complexity of reality. Now, this is not entirely avoidable in practice. But one can work at this and improve upon the model. Abu-Nimer creates a covenanted community when he trains by having trainees participate in the creation of principles of interaction to which everyone agrees. This, perhaps, is one way that, at least during the training, he tries to eliminate intergroup and intragroup asymmetries. But, of course, it cannot eliminate the external asymmetries that are the subject of the conflict. In this case, the only thing to do is acknowledge the reality of these imbalances of power.

My own opinion on the subject of asymmetry and its effect on peacemaking is that the *perception* of asymmetry seems to be more important for conflict processes and their unfolding, rather than its reality. In a certain sense, "asymmetry" is the subject of every conflict. There is rarely a conflict in which there is not a group on either side that sees itself in a vulnerable position of asymetric power.

Let us take some examples. Economically, politically, and militarily, Catholics in Northern Ireland see themselves as disempowered. Numerically, they are disempowered within the context of British dominance, which is Protestant. And, of course, they are. But the Protestants see themselves as outnumbered on the *island of Ireland*, and reunification with the republic is their major fear. Thus, asymmetry is the crux of the problem.

Israelis used to be seen, for decades, as the victims of asymmetry, the tiny minority of Jews in a predominantly Christian European world, many of whose members had successfully slaughtered most of their families in Europe. Statehood was an effort to restore the asymmetry of centuries of disempowerment and dehumanization. To this day, Israelis and Jews see themselves in a contest for empowerment that they *cannot* win: there are 800 million Muslims, 200 million Arabs, 2 billion Christians, and 18 million Jews in the world. They see themselves as simply carving out one small space in that sea of Muslims, Arabs, and Christians. The sense of asymmetry is overwhelming. And yet, this Jewish perception of asymmetry of power would be laughable to the average Palestinian and Arab Israeli.

There are unstated asymmetries as well that I believe also feed into the conflict. It is deep in biblical Jewish mythology that the Jewish people has a special destiny in sacred history, but it involves a demanding relationship to God, or, in secular terms, to fate. They are destined to be among the smallest of nations[24], and yet they pine for the promise to Abraham and to Isaac to be as numerous as the stars, which was already mythically fulfilled when they were prepared to enter Canaan.[25]

This relationship to the numerousness of the stars penetrates very deeply into the Jewish consciousness, and the gnawing feeling of the lack of fulfillment of this dream probably stimulates a good deal of the religious focus on fertility. Being small versus being numberless is a paradoxical set of expectations that has never been really resolved. One lesson is clear from human history: small groups suffer and often rarely survive. But the Jews have survived small numbers and homelessness, and that is seen by the group as a badge of honor. Survival becomes the supreme *mitsvah* in this case. Nevertheless, the promise to Abraham of numberless hordes of Jews seems unfulfilled. Adding insult to injury, it does seem fulfilled for Christians and Muslims, whose numbers are in the hundreds of millions and billions. Of course, there is a vast difference between Judaism and traditions that spend untold sums on conversion. Furthermore, there is unstated resentment that such a large percentage of the high number of conversions in the other monotheisms is due to many centuries of conquest and domination. Judaism allows for conversion but does not encourage it and requires a lifestyle that is intensely demanding. This is as much a cause of the small remnant after two thousand years, as is the more obvious cause of mass killings. None of this is ever spoken of by Jews, Christians and Muslims, but it should be, because it is a critical feeder to perceptions of asymmetry and historical resentment.

Furthermore, and this will be hard to swallow for left-leaning peacemakers, the power of killing civilians randomly with easily transportable weapons, which many people call terrorism, is an extremely potent force today. Obviously, the side of the conflict that has jet fighters and nuclear weapons, and extremely advanced police forces, is the side that has the greatest power. But the perception of those who become objects of terror is that *they* are the ones without power, the real "sitting ducks." And they act and talk as if the asymmetry of power is entirely on the other side. The intervention of third parties, such as the United Nations, on the Palestinian side, only strengthens the other side's sense of asymmetry of power. This is not just propaganda, but is felt deeply by millions of Jews who reject the peace process, and even by those of us who strongly advocate for peace.

On the Palestinian side, the asymmetry of power is obvious. The humiliation of losing their land and being confronted by the wealth of a Jewish state all around them makes every facet of their lives, from jobs and education to cultural identity, a living moment-to-moment hell of asymmetric power. They see themselves often as abandoned by everyone, not part of some vast sea of Arabs, Muslims, or gentiles just waiting patiently to destroy the Jews. In many ways, Palestinian self-perception as isolated and vulnerable is exactly parallel to historical Jewish self-perception. Often, one of the more bitter ironies of enemy systems is that one's enemy is in the best position to provide comfort because he knows exactly how you are feeling. For this reason, sometimes enemy systems and reconciliation systems are a hairbreadth away from each other, if only the relationships can be built. For those who speak often to both sides and know them intimately, this hairbreadth of difference becomes both a tantalizing goal, as if you can just touch it, and, at the same time, a bitter source of sadness and frustration.

No peace process can proceed without acknowledging these self-perceptions, without the Palestinians' adversaries, the Israelis, beginning to truly internalize a separation in their mind between the status and state of the Palestinians and the mass of humanity who are Arab or Muslim. It is no accident that Jewish rejectionists will always do their utmost to keep this connection clear and alive, and never distinguish between Palestinians and Arabs. Palestinians must be perceived as asymetrically powerful. Furthermore, it is very easy to keep the feelings of disempowerment alive in any group that just one generation ago suffered ultimate disempowerment, humiliation, and mass destruction. Palestinians, on the other hand, must begin to understand how their use of power, and that of the Arab and Muslim worlds, to evoke hatred and murder of Jews and Westerners through terror is a serious force in history. After September 11, 2001, every side of the Arab-Israeli conflict must face the use of its power to evoke hatred and to kill.

Asymmetric power is a complicated problem because there is an element of truth in most perceptions of asymmetry. But this must be openly worked through and talked about. Ultimately, fact must be separated from fiction in the process of relationship building between the two sides, which will allow new visions of the future to emerge. Asymmetry is a problem of justice, and justice must in turn be a fundamental part of peace. But the *perception* of asymmetry is a fundamental part of conflict generation and must be dealt with sympathetically and fairly as part of any peacemaking process.

We must now turn toward ways to move injured cultures in a new direction by confronting their injuries and disappointments in a creative honest way. It is the perception, true or manufactured, of deep injury and vulnerablity that is the cause of so much conflict. This becomes deeply embedded in culture and religion. Thus, only if we confront injuries psychologically, culturally, and religiously, can we help individuals and communities to become part of peace processes.

We can learn, however, from our investigations of this chapter, that there are profound ways to move religious traditions toward peace and away from othering that is violent. It is true that the internal reading and rereadings of a religious tradition and an ethnic group may have asymmetries built into their nature. But that is not a problem. Every group has a right to its own history and myth making that embody and strengthen their identity. The key is to enable mythic structure and future dreams to embody the erstwhile enemy other in a benign way, even in a loving embrace. Arthur Waskow has provided us with one beautiful and radical example. More, much more, traditional interpretation and rereading must be encouraged in this direction.

5 &

Conflict, Injury, and Transformation

The cultural capacity to transform old categories of exclusion or hatred is only one part of the battle to build a relationship between former enemies. The latter prepares the theological groundwork for a hermeneutic transformation inside the religious person's mindset as well as that of her community. The outer expressions of religious belief and practice need to be read inwardly or internalized in such a way that "enemy" is no longer a particular person or group that used to be the object of aggression. We have addressed this challenge in chapter 4.

The problem is that there is much more that retards peacemaking than a failure to reread tradition, formidable a challenge as the latter is. Rereading tradition is a major social challenge for a religious community whose structural integrity depends on agreed upon categories of meaning, as well as principles of inclusion and exclusion. But intertwined with this in a very complicated way is personal and collective injury, the scars of conflict and violence.

Scars endure due to things as "soft" as humiliation and dishonor as well as hard things, like torture and murder of loved ones. All involve losses that are either difficult or impossible to restore. The more one's psyche is wedded to these losses, and the more devoted one has been to objects of love and veneration, the more sickening it would be to think of trading in one's condition of "perpetuated mourning" for cheap replacements, like economic compensation or some form of economic opportunity in peacetime. In fact, this kind of principled rejectionism and refusal of "bribes" should be at least honored by observers and intervenors as a positive expression of moral principle, as destructive as it may be for peace. The more intense one's feelings for and devotion to those who have suffered or died, the more problematic, even obnoxious, will rational solutions appear to be. In fact, they will feel like insulting tricks.

What I mean by "perpetuated mourning" is the state in which human beings find one way or another to keep old wounds open, to keep attachment to the loss by perpetuating some state of affairs in which that loss is kept at the surface level of experience, in addition to the perpetuation of moral justifications for that position.[1] In this way people keep what they have lost as close to home as possible and also avoid the guilt of living well or happily as a group, which could easily be interpreted as a betrayal of those people and things that they have lost. Lost things could also include an idealized relationship with God in the distant past, or a time of glorious sovereignty in an idealized past.

Organized religion plays an important role in perpetuated mourning. A large percentage of Jewish prayer and ritual, for example, is dedicated to mourning losses of the past, beseeching God to forgive the sins that have led to the losses (understood and framed as "punishments"), as well as prayers to punish the enemies who caused these injuries. The biblical book of Psalms, shared by all three monotheisms, is replete with these kinds of prayers. For much of Jewish history, prayers such as these had very real counterparts in their everyday reality of persecution. It is no accident that, in effect, the Psalmist, traditionally King David, is the godfather, if you will, of traditional Jewish prayer. The psalms attributed to David combine an intense and creative religiosity that offers the comfort of a personal and privileged relationship to God. They also entail an honest process of self-judgment, which is combined in subtle ways with a vivid recreation of persecution at the hands of enemies. They set up an existence wherein God is the only refuge and ultimate salvation for the righteous, consistent with the Jewish penchant for strong self-criticism and drive to repentance, both of which merges in an artful way with a persecution consciousness.

The trouble with prayer, devotion, and the construction of universes of meaning that become deeply embedded is that they tend not only to explain the vicissitudes of life, and thus give comfort and reassurance, but also to *create* reality by forming the mindset of the adherent, and thus make it hard to change reality. This combination of making sense of reality by softening its blows and simultaneously creating a rigid pattern of reality is a constant in most religious meaning systems that I have studied, Eastern as well as Western. Comfort in the discovery of meaning seems always to come at the price of rigid conformity to that very meaning system which, at least sometimes, is perpetuating some form of self-imposed misery in the guise of martyrological theological and mental constructs.

There is no question, however, that, beyond the manufactured cultural character of mourning based on habit, a very real set of injuries runs very deeply in communities that have suffered terrible losses over large spans of time. It is certainly the case that formal and informal mourning processes are the only way we know of that human beings cope with these kind of losses.

Generally speaking, included in traditional mourning processes over these losses is a corresponding attribution of blame to traditional enemies. This is not always the case, and, in fact, religion does have in its cultural repertoire something unavailable in ethnonationalist thought. Often, perhaps too often, biblical religion holds the individual, as well as the religious community, accountable for its own troubles. Simple interpretations of biblical religion assume God to be both directly cognizant of and responsible for day-to-day tribulations. Thus, if God is both all-powerful and perfectly good, then human beings must be responsible for their own tragedies.

This can make people sick with internalized guilt for things that they have never done, responsible for the death of loved ones due to some ethical act or even minor ritual that they failed to do. It can be a whip turned against the psyche by the self or by a clergyman to root out "sins," especially those involving appetites and desires. It can become a brutal agent of control and psychological punishment. At the same time, however, it *can* lead to a level of self-examination for troubles that is absolutely impossible for ethnonationalist psychology. If the essence of ultimate goodness is the ethnos, then there can be no room for collective self-criticism; but if the essence of ultimate goodness is God, then it is at least conceivable that collective self-examination can occur, unless, of course, the ethnos and God are actually one and the same in the psychic reality of the group.[2] As is plainly evident, nothing is black and white in the process of discovering peaceful solutions to cultural conflict. Nothing is purely "clean" as an instrument of peacemaking, but nothing is entirely dirty either.

The capacity for or habit of self-judgment has proved a vital resource in numerous conflicts. Of the hundreds of religious students that I have had from every corner of the globe and every religion, it is the religious impetus to self-examination that they have utilized consistently and successfully in persuading fellow countrymen to turn away from violent solutions to their problems, or to negotiate in good faith, always reminding all sides that they have sinned also. But, as I said earlier, ethno-nationalism would have nothing in its psychological repertoire to allow for this perspective. The classic Abrahamic refrain, "We are all sinners," has proved to be a vital bridge across ethnic lines, something that forces a penitential mindset that should not in principle be held hostage to ethnocentrism. This notion of no man who is not a sinner combines seamlessly with a willingness culturally to admit the possibility of personal and collective errors. It also creates a common bond with the enemy, whom one certainly sees as flawed and human.[3]

Now, admittedly the very same book of Psalms that calls repeatedly for self-examination before God is also replete with comforting prayers for those who are "innocent," "righteous," "pious," "poor," who suffer before God, and whom He loves above all others. For centuries, people of all the biblical religions who, at critical junctures, needed to take a hard look at *their own* actions, have been able to retreat behind these labels of innocence and forestall self-examination. On the other hand, millions of truly innocent victims have found refuge in these prayers.

These prayers have proved a powerful antidote to despair and have provided a nonviolent outlet to justifiable feelings of great rage, which is a secondary benefit that must be acknowledged. We have to assume that, as blood-filled as Western history has been, it would be even worse if millions turned to the sword instead of King David as an outlet for their rage. If, for example, the Dalai Lama were not daily offering his people nonviolent means of resisting oppression by the Chinese leadership, there most surely would have been an even greater bloodbath, a war that his people would necessarily lose. They are no match for the Chinese military, but cultural resistance combined with consistent efforts at rapprochement might be able to sustain them long enough to witness the end of Chinese autocratic rule. It is hard to say, but my impression is that the Dalai Lama has seized on the most realistic form of resistance possible under these circumstances, in addition to conforming to his conceptualization of the Buddha's highest teachings. He thus combines realistic strategy with a culturally authentic political discourse that allows him to perpetuate his people's identity indefinitely through the most arduous geopolitical circumstances.

Now, the secular social-justice activist will be jumping out of his seat at this point and saying that those religious people in history who were taught to examine themselves as the source of their troubles were pacified, when they should have turned to active protest of injustices. But this is my critical point. I say that pacification has been only one way in which certain historical expressions of organized religion, Western or Eastern, *utilized* and manipulated the self-examination elements of religion, as well as the comfort of prayer, as a means to pacify oppressed masses. But this need not have been the case!

One cannot indict the religious gesture of self-examination in and of itself. If one were to follow this logic, then no comfort, no psychotherapy, no trauma healing, not even foreign aid, should ever be offered to the oppressed, because it would just lull them into passivity. But this is absurd because in the process of goading the oppressed to action while refusing any comfort, one would express a gross callousness to human suffering, an antithetical model of human goodness. This is just what many revolutionaries have done, and it turned them into barbarians, a living mockery of their own ideals.[4]

The political critique of comforting prayers and peacefulness of the inner life ends in contradiction. On the other hand, I do accept the criticism of politically motivated religious pacification, which offers a necessary check for the religious practitioner and theologian against allowing his or her patterns of coping with suffering to become a handmaiden of oppression, whether that oppression is rooted in secular regimes or in the privileged hierarchy of the religion itself who are invested in the status quo.

Systems of coping with ultimate loss must become a part of any conflict resolution between enemies, whether it be formal mourning or inward processes, such as prayer and self-examination. Each community involved in conflict must accomplish this separately, to maximize the indigenous authenticity of the gesture. However, peacemakers of each group should coordinate this process in a way that overlaps at key junctures. They need to bring the mourning patterns into the realm of peacemaking and reconciliation, and, at the very least, assure that the mourning does not become an opportunity to reinforce old hatreds.

In addition to the reality of deep injuries that prevent reconciliation with enemies, there is the complicating factor of the exploitation of deep injuries by both individuals and collective groups. Their motivations can be external or internal. By "internal motivations" I mean that the injury becomes a substitute for identity formation. This can be true of individuals as well as groups, which, for one reason or another, have a weak sense of self. We live in an age (but perhaps this is perennial human problem in ages of transition?) in which it is quite easy to find oneself surviving from day to day without any clear sense of who one is. Such alienation is terribly threatening to the human psyche. It is typical of periods of great transition in the social order, and rapid mobility of people and populations—in other words, periods in which the roots of identity are severed for large populations. In such periods it becomes easy to recover identity inside the actual injury to oneself or to one's group. That is why so many people today discover their identity and their raison d'être as survivors of some childhood or adult trauma, and their self-help groups become quasi-families, and, in some case, quasi-religions.

I do not mean to belittle the effects of those traumas at all. But it seems to me that in periods when identity is strong, people tend to take refuge in that identity as they cope with the trauma, rather than make the trauma their identity. Thus, it is no surprise to me that, on the whole, the most assimilated part of the Jewish community has poured hundreds of millions of dollars into Holocaust memorials and education, whereas the ultra-Orthodox community, which lost countless institutions and entire sects in the war, barely has any memorials. It is not that the Holocaust is not on their minds. Rather, their coping mechanisms are the traditional ones, and they direct themselves toward a strengthening of the identity that they already have. Anti-Semitism is a part of Jewish identity, but it becomes *the* identity for those who only discover that they are Jewish after they have been excluded in some fashion. This happened to many European Jews in the last hundred years but continues to be important for many Jews today.

The Holocaust is just one example of how traumas can become a source of identity when that identity was not clear before. Another way for this to happen is externally, by political manufacture of injury in order to mobilize a group for a specific purpose. Certainly, right-wing Serbian leaders and Hutu extremists of the recent past furnish the best examples of this. It is also the case that these same leaders can keep alive whatever misery it is that people face in order to use that misery to maintain power. Misery is the key to much political success.

Manufactured injury is the key to augmenting power, building a larger base of support. The complexity is that manufactured injury of this sort is not necessarily false injury. It seems to be the case that, whether individuals or groups search for misery in order to discover identity, or whether political leaders manufacture misery, it does not mean that this misery is not real to the people who feel it. Thus, whatever its roots, injuries must be confronted and accepted by the highest levels of diplomacy and conflict resolution practice, although it would be helpful for groups to go through an honest process of historical examination on these matters.

A clue to a realistic assessment of the injuries would be to measure the responses of actual victims versus those who react vicariously in their name. If the latter group is far more extreme than the former, then one may assume some of the artificial mechanisms at work that I have described. In this case, it would be healthy for the group, as they try to recover from past traumas and mourn over them, to defer to actual victims, to let them speak—and argue—about the past and about the future. A key conflict resolution process may be to collect actual victims on both sides and give them an authoritative voice in their community to such a degree that political leaders cannot use them for their own purposes.

At this point a careful psychodynamic study of the group in question is needed, especially in terms of the interaction of the leaders and the led. For example, there needs to be more study of leaders of genocide and an externalized process of playing out childhood traumas. Hitler's childhood is well known, whereas we are only beginning to learn about Milosevic.[5] The *actual* horrors experienced by Germans in the 1920s, for example, or the Serbians in World War II, are well known. What is more complicated is how leaders, who combine in their psyches key political and charismatic talents with a capacity to externalize internal patterns of injury and aggression, become far more extreme in their murderousness than the real victims of violence in their culture. Who successfully commits mass violence and why? Why is it often spearheaded by people other than the victims of previous horrors? We cannot know the answers to these questions completely. But I would argue that it is vital in conflict resolution processes that incorporate psychodynamic and cultural insights to demythologize trauma, to subtly wrest it from the clutches of leaders and sadists who are acting out their own, individual, internal problems. This process simultaneously empowers the actual victims, giving them a voice and authority which, in and of itself, helps the healing process, and also *disempowers* those who are manufacturing injury for political gain that is built on their own private rage. The leader of mass violence comes narcissistically to embody the injury of his people, both in his own mind and in the minds of the followers. But this nexus must be disengaged to confront real grievances and real traumas. This is the first step to peacemaking.

Two things must happen then, in disengaging a group from the need to be violent. First, manufactured injury, which is based on the political ambitions of leaders as well as the working out of the latters' own internal damage, must be separated from actual injury. The actually injured must be given numerous paths through which to speak for themselves, to express themselves to each other, to the world, and to their enemies. Second, manufactured injuries that are rooted in weak, internal self-conceptions must be replaced by a strong sense of self that does not need injury to survive. If not, then trying to remove the injury will be an attack on the existence of the group. For this reason, groups in conflict must be encouraged to strengthen their culture in numerous ways, and third parties, *as well as the enemies*, must become part of a process of honoring this culture from the outside.

This is all necessary in order to move the collective identity of this group to a new place and to make the process of grievance and conflict a constructive, demythologized process. It is decidedly not a process of naive forgiveness or unilateral forgetting of the past. But it will make the group more ready for change, more ready to hear new voices from their enemies, to conceive of a new way to live in the world, and to be prepared to compromise and to forgive when they see actual, verifiable, permanent change in their enemies. None of this will be possible when the manufactured injury reigns supreme. Actual group injury can heal over time with constructive conflict management, resolution, and transformation. Manufactured injury cannot be subject to this because its raison d'être, internally generated by weak identity or externally generated by the psychological construct of leaders and foisted onto the people, is to prevent resolution.

Regarding the conflict that is the subject of this book, the processes that I have just recommended would be as important for Jews in the context of Holocaust-related issues as it is for Palestinians relevant to the loss of their country in 1948. Furthermore, in the more recent past, if we speak about victims of terror on one side and victims of cruel police tactics and other indignities, on the other, then we should defer to the actual victims. They must become central to peace processes, not peripheral as they currently are.

Why is this so important, psychosocially speaking? Much trauma comes to groups, not through the actual experience of injury but by the *fear* of something not yet experienced. We cannot underestimate the effects of this on a population. In fact, terrorism would not be effective without this phenomenon, because, after all, just to give one example, car accidents and pollution cause far more deaths in Israel than the wars and terrorism ever will. The fear of what has not happened, furthermore, is inextricably linked with past trauma. The only way to heal these problems, then, is to help the actual victims to talk about them, with each other, with their larger community, and eventually with their enemies. We will deal with nonverbal means of coping later, which often prove to be the most important of all.

There is another kind of trauma that involves a phenomenon very closely wedded to organized religion and, in particular, to the Abrahamic faiths. A central source of comfort for traumas of the past is actual dreams of the future. Future visions, both this worldly and otherworldly, are central for hundreds of millions of adherents of Abrahamic faiths. One could argue persuasively that great violence in monotheistic history can be positively correlated with increased obsession with the future. Certainly, these future visions have been subject to the same political manipulation as past traumas have. But the reality of these hopes is powerful, and the corresponding disappointments very severe.[6] It seems that wrapped up with the biblical story is the notion of God breaking into history, through miracles or messengers or both. The anticipation of its repetition as a solution to life's problems is quite intense. When and why and for whom it intensifies is a fascinating question, which deserves a separate study, particularly in relation to violence and peace. But this capacity or drive to dream future dreams does not just create violence. It also has been a fabulous tool for building better societies. Utopianism is tied up with messianic and/or future dreaming in monotheism. It does not necessarily lead to catastrophe but, on the contrary, is a tool of social activism.

We need also to acknowledge and deal with the disappointment of messianic or utopian dreams. Sometimes these dreams are cultural and sometimes they are religious, and sometimes both. Whatever their origin, a process of peacemaking must make a space for *lost* dreams. There must be a place for both groups to mourn over lost dreams, or to deal with this mythically in some way that allows the cultural and religious vision of their world to remain intact. If not, if the political/military solution comes squarely against the mythic future vision then violence is guaranteed. However, if ways are discovered to mourn over one vision and simultaneously create a new one, or reinterpret the old one in a constructive way, then the visionaries can become a part of the peace process rather than its implacable enemies.

An unconstructive way to rework the old myth is to simply delay its full realization. It is pragmatically helpful in moving the group forward, however, but it does not address the underlying problematics of coexistence. If future dreams are reworked successfully and new visions materialize, then religious people could become an invaluable resource of peacebuilding.

It seems clear to me, for example, that a large portion of religious Zionists need to engage in a mourning process over the loss of a dream of restoring the ancient lands of Israel to exclusive Jewish sovereignty after two thousand years. Other Jews, liberal Jews, should share in or at least commiserate in this mourning process, rather than ridicule it as the Israeli left often does. It is vital then that enemies *within* each group, as well as the principal combatants of the larger conflict, develop a healthy respect for each other's *impossible* dreams. Only in this way can people be helped to let go of these dreams or rework them in some way. For example, there are two ways to deal with the loss of ancient lands. One is to delay fulfillment to some future time, and to believe that some way will be found to realize the dream. This is not the best solution but it helps move peace processes along. A second and better way is to see sovereignty and occupation in a new light. Real peace between Israel and Palestine might open borders and the opportunity for dual citizenship within the next fifty years. It may yet be possible, with a profound peace, for Jews to see, visit, and have good access to ancient lands. Thus, a Jewish return to the land would be truly utopian, fulfilling at least some prophetic visions that explicitly state that the hoped-for return will be based on peace.[7] The future vision of return to the land in peace therefore becomes fulfilled, not in opposition to peace but through peace.

The same can be said of Palestinian and Islamic future visions. There must be, on the one hand, mourning over what cannot be restored. At the same time, there can be an equally powerful notion that through deep peace Palestinians will one day be able to visit and be near all their ancient lands as well.

Islamic theocratic dreams of future political sovereignty need to be explored intensely. What is the Islamic view of the ideal future, or the ideal Islamic state? These are questions that courageous people need to address more and more. Is it a state controlled only by Islamic authorities and ruled by *shari'ah*, Islamic law? No doubt, this is the current vision for many. But what if the ideal future is a place and a state in which Islam is honored and never subject to humiliation? What if *dar al-Islam*, as opposed to *dar al-harb*, is not a place of absolute control but a place of absolute respect, or what human rights doctrines would refer to as freedom of religion? This is something that many Muslims that I know believe in, particularly because they reject, in the name of Islam, religion that is based on coercion.[8]

Mourning over lost visions and evolving new or reworked visions are fundamental parts of the process of change in monotheistic traditions. It is vital that these become a part of social peace processes that parallel the political processes. What results is a space for unfulfillable dreams that does not paralyze them either. Once the trauma of loss is creatively confronted, it becomes possible to move on to practical methods of peacemaking. Nothing in what I have outlined should interfere with normal diplomatic processes. What it should do is to lay the social-psychological groundwork for those processes to run smoothly, both because there is greater political support and the elite peacemakers themselves, at some early stage of involvement, may need and benefit from the deeper processes we are outlining here. In fact, it may help them prevent or minimize the typical interpersonal "landmines" of negotiations that often derail elite peace processes. Such "landmines" are often rooted in unconfronted deeper issues that afflict elite diplomats just as profoundly—though more subtly—as they do average citizens.

I envision a time of diplomatic history wherein whatever international body is set up to facilitate high-level initial enemy contacts makes it a requirement that negotiators participate in a kind of pre-negotiation training/encounter in which they and their enemies confront the more subtle, existential elements of their enemy system. Only subsequently would they be considered qualified to move on to hard bargaining and formal negotiations.

Now I progress from analysis to construct, out of the Abrahamic traditions in question, a series of methods of transformation of relationship from mortal enemy to—something else, whatever that may be. It could be "friend," "tolerated neighbor," or even "nonviolent adversary." The point of these methods, and what we lump together as "reconciliation," is that they move people away from extreme violence into some kind of transformation of relationships that holds promise for the future.

II

PRACTICAL APPLICATIONS

Patterns of Abrahamic Reconciliation

Act, Ritual, and Symbol as Transformation

The Challenge of Circumscribed Moral Universes

One of the central challenges facing cultural and religious peacemaking is the self-imposed wall around ethnic and religious identities, particularly in terms of the deliberate circumscription of their prosocial moral structures and meaning systems. We have discussed before the way in which the Other has been incriminated by many if not most interpretations of monotheism and even demonized, depending on the cognitive and cosmic structures in question. By contrast, the internally directed, prosocial side of a community's tradition is the vital resource for creating a viable moral structure of engagement with other human beings; it is the indispensable resource for extending the community's best values to outsiders. The few apologetic and deferential statements in the classical sources regarding outsiders (1) are simply not sufficient to counteract the antisocial statements, the latter being subtly ignored or deflected in interfaith encounters, and (2) usually lack the subtle prosocial insights and relationship strategies generally reserved for insiders. The latter have both psychological and spiritual depth, as well as great pragmatic value, a subtle combination of attributes that makes these inner-directed values such a critical tool of conflict prevention and peacemaking. Such values, usually reserved for insiders in good standing, are actually indispensable in eliciting from cultural and religious traditions an effective method of conflict resolution with enemies, or more precisely, an ethic of engaging the Other in a way that will truly result in building peaceful relationships.

A related challenge involves the secular world's view of religion. It is no accident that the average academic knows far more about the antisocial side of religions and cultures, which have been the primary focus of academic research in the secular age.[1] The myth of liberal society, at least as it has been reread in the late twentieth century, is to put it crassly, that religion was the problem, and the liberal, secular state and public institution are the answer. This has led to an impasse in the worlds of policy making, conflict resolution, and diplomacy. The general attitude is, "Let us identify the religious, ethnic, and cultural roots of the violence, eliminate them, and 'educate' those involved to the virtues of rational, democratic, problem solving."

My sympathies are with the aims of liberal, secular institutions. My personal prejudice, in the Gadamerian sense of that term, is that the liberal, secular institution does solve numerous problems of interethnic, intercultural, and inter-religious incompatibility that have plagued human history in the most destructive fashion. The problem is that (1) this is not satisfactory to millions of people, who, if pressed, will turn to violence against such impositions that threaten the viability of their cultural worldview and survival, and (2) the secular, liberal institution is eminently capable of imperialism and intolerance that tend in subtle, and not so subtle, ways to suppress the vast reservoir of cultural and religious prosocial resources. It is often guilty of an obtuse win/lose strategy to conquer alternative worldviews, which is—ironically—inherently illiberal, as well as pragmatically counterproductive in many places of the world.

But religious myth, one of those alternate worldviews, is vital for those whose cultural identity is the deepest identity that they have. It is simply intellectually dishonest and shortsighted to try to repress from memory the prosocial fabric of religion and culture. Suppression of any prosocial models of human life betrays an unquestionable insecurity, a nagging doubt inside the heart of secular, intellectual thinking that perhaps the secular model is lacking something. Rather than acknowledge what is lacking and learn from it, to strengthen modern civil society, an ironic obscurantism betrays a terror before the more blatant obscurantism and repressiveness of contemporary fundamentalist models of social and political hegemony.

This helps no one, and it falls into the most basic trap pointed out by conflict analysis, that of a win-lose psychology, namely, that secular models of diplomacy and coexistence can only be built on the ruins or emasculation of religious culture. Proponents will swear that this is not their goal. But their very methods (let alone their personal prejudices in terms of whom they do and do not work with) make it extremely difficult for them to work with religious people and institutions, or to translate their methods into religious worldviews.

Our critical task is to examine methods religious cultures use to teach enemies to fundamentally change as they confront each other. While many of the change processes outlined later are brilliant and insightful and in many ways have much to teach secular conflict resolution theorists and practitioners, they are also flawed. The major flaw by far, shared almost universally by all religions that I have studied, is the limitation of these conciliatory processes to enemies who are, in every other way, upstanding members of the religious community who conform to all community religious standards or boundaries.

However, the same insights and processes are *suppressed* vis-à-vis the chosen enemies of the particular religious system. The latter can include those who choose not to practice or believe, those who did but now reject it, those whose spiritual decisions about practice or belief differ from some human/ religious authority structure that claims divine or historic sanction, and large groups that threaten or stand in the way of the expansion or maintenance of power by the organized structure of the religion. This flaw is singly responsible for the suffering and death of countless millions of people throughout the history of religion, and certainly in the history of the Abrahamic faiths. Needless to say, despite some restrictive and even violent religious laws and dogmas, there are countless religious adherents in history who were not responsible for the latter, and who read their traditions within a mental framework of the deepest humanity. They either reread or selected the most humane paradigm of their tradition.[2] Nevertheless, the antisocial tendency in many religious texts, and the uses thereof for violence, remain a principal challenge that cannot be denied.

Therefore, as we examine the methods of interpersonal transformation, we need to negotiate and expand the moral universe of religions and culture. Of course, there is some literature in all traditions on the subject of extending moral commitments to outsiders, but it is complicated, in Islam and Christianity, by the missionary imperative, which can make prosocial commitments and extensions of values secretly or unconsciously dependent on its aspirations. This seriously compromises such prosocial expressions of care or love for the purposes of the kind of conflict resolution that we expect in free society. Thus, the key is to find the basis for prosocial commitments to outsiders who will never convert. This goal is harder, but not entirely elusive.

What is less often acknowledged and analyzed is the way that the extension of prosocial values to outsiders is often complexified and contradicted by existential fears of the group, which poses a subtle and deadly challenge. With every effort to extend moral boundaries, there is a corresponding backlash that contracts the moral universe of a religious or cultural group. One example is the dramatic increase in the liberalization, inclusivity, and tolerance of mainline American Protestantism since the Holocaust and the 1960s, coupled with the corresponding and equally dramatic backlash of conservative Protestant denominations. One senses among these dynamics more than simply a rational process of discerning religious faith and values in the contemporary age, which leads different believers to different conclusions. Rather, there is also a deep angst about our similarities to and differences from others in an extremely diverse contemporary world. As they struggle with boundaries, believers are always wondering how cultural and religious boundaries of their erstwhile homogeneous groups survive or die. The more integrated a group becomes with the world, the more some of the members shrink back in horror, concerned for the viability of the group.

As another example, it cannot be an accident that in the very period of unprecedented tolerance, prosocial relations, cooperative social justice work, even sharing of rituals and very high intermarriage rates between Jews and Christians, there is an antithetical Jewish development, a level of religious insularity, ritualistic isolationism, and ethnic chauvinism that attempts to drive out all non-Jewish influences from Jewish life in a way that is far more extensive and dramatic than anything seen in recent memory. Even in progressive Jewish circles, the more that Jews become similar to others, the more that what is defined as Jewish becomes what makes one different. Thus, distinctive Jewish rituals and commitments become the markers of who is truly committed to the people, and even the religion, and who is not.

For many people just thirty years ago, a deep mark of Jewish spirituality would be the work of universal social justice, and this is still the case for many Jews. But the very assimilationist character of the latter, and the extremely high intermarriage rates that have emerged, drive other Jews to spurn universal action—no matter how much based on Torah values or prophetic texts—as a betrayal of Jewish interests and Jewish spirituality. Now, some may conclude that those who narrow their boundaries of moral care, and therefore behave cruelly, do so because they have a diminished conscience, are hypocritical, or selfish. For example, a group might direct the greatest care toward the honor of its poorest members, while simultaneously neglecting, abusing, or even killing nonbelieving women and children.[3] But another aspect of such moral obtuseness is the existential fear of obliteration that *requires* the contraction of the moral universe.

This dilemma must be faced with more than clever hermeneutic transformation of religious tradition, although the latter is helpful and important. It requires trust building and empowerment that remove the perception and emotion of existential threat. Only empowerment removes the poison of moral contraction. We must remember that existential threats to a group often have a good basis in reality. They are not just psychological phantoms. White racists in the South of the United States really did have reason to fear that southern culture was disappearing. Germans who were pounded and destroyed by World War I, and then devastated economically by a punishing "resolution" to the war, had every good reason to believe that the world of their past culture was being destroyed. And if, in either of these cases, only the racists among them articulated this fear, found a victim to blame, and promised a protection of their identity, then it should come as no surprise why a number of people succumbed to their worst instincts in the drive for insular community.

What is the alternative? The only response to exclusivity is not absolute universality and the blurring of all boundaries, as liberals generally assumed. I would never suggest that only a cultural universe in which everyone is on the same moral plane of care is acceptable. This is manifestly not the case in the real world. There are an infinite number of cultural examples in which the special moral care and preference for loved ones, especially family, do not necessarily lead to destructive conflict. On the contrary, the cultural construct of family is the primary example of a preferential and exclusive cultural unit that does not necessarily lead to destructive communal life. It does lead to the very human but not necessarily violent struggle for scarce resources. Destructiveness only enters in when the "other" strays so outside the moral universe of the family or cultural unit that he/she becomes either not valued at all as a human being or valued only for economic usefulness. In this conclusion, I am clearly parting company with Kant's absolute universalism in terms of the construction of moral standards.

One digression is in order here. I do side with Immanuel Kant in one regard, and against the enlightened self-interest arguments of social contract theorists. From a conflict analysis point of view, the minimal standard for successful or authentic human ethical relationships involves some valuation of the Other as more than just a useful means to some end, as Kant argued. It has been my experience in conflict analysis, both historically and today, that groups and people who only see each other in pragmatic terms of usefulness may benefit from each other in the marketplace and tolerate each other in the short term. But in the long run they could engage in genocidal behavior.

For example, the economic usefulness of European Jews in the Middle Ages to princes and bishops, especially to circumvent the "inconvenient" biblical rules against charging interest, while "the Jews" were simultaneously devalued as agents of evil on a spiritual and cosmic level by the church, could only end in genocidal disasters, as it did—often. By contrast, despite Sephardic[4] resentment of what they saw as second-class citizenship in certain Arab environments, the fact is that their inherent valuation on a cosmic and spiritual level, as a People of the Book, according to the Qur'an, made murderous repression much more infrequent and genocide impossible. There were bad times to be sure, but the difference between treatment of Sephardim by Islam and treatment of Ashkenazim by Christianity is a qualitative not just a quantitative difference of prejudice, and this should be studied further, in terms of the relationship between theology and violence.[5]

Here is the most critical point of this section. Ways to value the outsider, as an ethical end in himself and not just for his usefulness to me right now, must be addressed by every contemporary religious and cultural system, and this valuation must not lead to a backlash by the group's own existentially threatened members. A much more subtle process of intracultural communication is required between progressives and conservatives within every culture and religion. It is the latter that progressives and liberals have found so difficult to face, namely, the hard work of reconciliation that they need to do with their own indigenous communities. Cultural and religious chauvinism on the part of religious conservatives may embarrass liberals, but conservative backlashes usually embody some element of understandable existential concerns of a particular group. This is the "dark" place that most progressives have a hard time facing.

Prosocial Resources

Among the ethical resources within Abrahamic traditions for peacemaking and conflict resolution, one of the most important in terms of building prosocial relationships is the way individuals and communities cope with moral failure of the individual. How does one recover from failure in basic personality dispositions as well relationships? There are many ways, including profound and extended periods of self-examination, mystical valuations of the power of action to promote good or evil, acknowledgment of wrong done, confession, changes in behavior or repentance, apology, active penance, and, ultimately, the request for, and/or receiving of unilateral or bilateral offerings of forgiveness. Understanding this is vital for intercultural work because, almost by definition, the outsider group is often the object of the failed relationship, that is, a relationship involving serious moral failure. Of course, it is the outgroup, not one's ingroup, to which failure is usually attributed. However, potentially at least, such a relationship could be examined by means of traditional processes of acknowledging sin.

A Critical Examination of Forgiveness

For the purposes of this complicated investigation, and for simplicity's sake only, I use the word "forgiveness" loosely to refer to the transformation of relationships in general that has been just described. Shortly, we will analyze the problems with defining "forgiveness" in the religious world. But I am concerned in this chapter, and in this book, with the entire panoply of the moral and emotive transformation of human relationships that results in a new and better relationship between erstwhile enemies. This transformation can include but not be limited to the psychologically difficult process of acknowledging failure or sin, acknowledging harm that we have done to another, apology, repentance, penance, and formal processes of reifying the above in ritual.

How all this takes place is extremely varied in human experience, and in many ways is another subject of this book. But many people in the West use the word "forgiveness" to refer to it, due to the central role of forgiveness in Christian, particularly Protestant, mythology and metaphysics. I am not satisfied with the overuse of the word "forgiveness," because it is my experience in conflict and its resolution that people can profoundly transform their relationships, through deed and word, without ever asking for or receiving "forgiveness" in any formal sense. Furthermore, they certainly can improve their relationships and make them nonviolent without formal processes of forgiveness or even an internal sense of forgiveness, and this would more than satisfy my dreams for war-torn countries and peoples. Nevertheless, forgiveness is an important subset of the process of transformation, especially because Christian/Western culture dominates a large swath of global culture at this point, and forgiveness is a central crux and question of Christian culture.

I also assume that these largely interpersonal methods must, with the aid of social science and conflict resolution theory, be extended to intergroup processes, a very complex endeavor, but one that is essential for the future of humanity. A further assumption of my method is that, when these processes are eventually extended to intercultural, multicultural, and interreligious moments, it is vital that there be a psychological and theological preparedness of groups to learn one from the other. They may even want to adopt and adapt the best that they see in another tradition, and to discover a hermeneutic way within their own culture or religion to give this interactive process spiritual meaning. The process cannot be dismissed as just another example of barren relativism of modernity, easily discarded by the "true believers" who suffer existential angst. It must hermeneutically attain cultural legitimacy. We will revisit this often as we examine how it is activated by religious peacemakers.

A corollary of this assumption is that an ability develops to see that, in any given conflict, an act can be deemed right by one worldview, and wrong by another, and can make sense religiously and culturally. It is vital that one has a hermeneutic of one's traditions that allows, *at least sometimes*, for both sides of a conflict to be wrong and right simultaneously. Only in this way can two rights coexist in different worldviews. There is a tendency in the Abrahamic faiths to assume that right and wrong are clear in all circumstances, and that wise judgment will lead to the justification of one party and the incrimination of the other. This is an unfortunate limitation of some conservative forgiveness processes, as well as many liberal social protest movements. It is very important that it be conceivable culturally and spiritually that, in the human realm, there is, at least sometimes, wrong and right on both sides. This, it seems to me, is a sine qua non of the psychology of conflict resolution. It has its counterpart in some religious, judicial concepts, such as, for example, the spiritual rightness of *peshara* and *bitsua*, "compromise," in Jewish jurisprudence, at least according to one school of thought, or the way in which the trinitarian nature of God in Christianity, or Jesus' nature as both fully human and fully divine, embodies, according to some Christians, the ability to live with paradox.[6]

This does not, nor should it, require the surrender of strongly held values or opinions. As human beings investigate and cope with conflict and violence that they have suffered, they do—and really must be allowed to—express outrage at injustice, to hold fast to values of right and wrong, truth and falsehood, justice and injustice, good and evil. However, the critical transition to peace allows the individual and the group to acknowledge that not all the justice, truth, right, and goodness resides only in their group or one moral perspective.

Now let us begin an investigation of the socially transformative phenomenon referred to often as "forgiveness." Forgiveness as a way of healing human relationships and solving human conflicts is an age-old practice that appears in numerous religious traditions across the globe. There are a number of problems, however, with defining what exactly this activity is or has been in these traditions, what its significance is within these meaning systems, and, finally, what usefulness, if any, these traditions have in contemporary analysis of conflict and peacemaking. In particular, forgiveness as a means of peacemaking, depending on how it is realized, brings into sharp relief the perennial challenge of balancing peace and justice in the pursuit of conflict resolution. Often, at least on the surface, forgiveness appears to be at odds with the demands of justice, at least as justice is perceived by either side of a conflict.

One would imagine that the first task of this exploration is to attempt definitions of the term "forgiveness" in a representative sampling of religious cultures. But this is not easy. The definition seems to change with the religious agent. For example, I have observed and participated in numerous gatherings associated with Moral Rearmament (MRA). This is a mostly Christian group whose founder was deeply influenced by evangelical styles of Christian religiosity. MRA in particular has utilized forgiveness as a major tool of international peacemaking.[7] For now, let me just point out that forgiveness has a very dramatic, public confessional character in several MRA centers of work, especially at its center in Caux, Switzerland.

But there is much more than this to MRA's methods of peacebuilding and relationship building, even at the Caux center. Briefly, it involves a profoundly persistent pattern of relationship building with key individuals on either side of a conflict, and the use of spiritual awakening to provoke self-examination and transformation of one's relationships. It also involves support for and evocation of a spirit of personal responsibility that recognizes primarily one's own part in the failure of one's relationships. Further, awakening to the "spirit of God" within you as well as between you and others is critical, in addition to a very strong focus on personal morality. Indeed, for many associated with this society, personal morality and the morality of one's culture are at the heart of their message and teaching, with peacemaking taking a secondary role. But I want to highlight the public confessional moments between enemies that has taken place often over the years in MRA contexts. The latter have been particularly fascinating.

I have expressed discomfort at various junctures as to what I perceived to be the limited nature of the kind of forgiveness exchanges that I have witnessed, in their unilateral, highly public character, with confession of wrong and apology being unilateral, not reciprocal. So, when I would witness dramatic, unilateral confessions of forgiveness, I would occasionally ask Christian friends skeptically, "What about repentance, what about detailed admissions of what was done, and what about the commitment to the future? How will there be a practical change in the life of the thousands or millions of victims? What about the needs of justice? Often, the answer would be, to my astonishment, "All of that is included in forgiveness."

This was not a whitewash or some apologetic gesture, as I thought initially. It simply means that forgiveness was a faith category for them that must always be included in peacemaking, even if its definition and parameters evolve. It is like hearing an ultra-Orthodox Jew claim, in the spirit of the talmudic rabbis, that the Torah has all the answers to human problems, and that the Torah creates peace. Now, outsiders or Jewish liberals, confronted with evidence of some decidedly conflict-generating statements or laws of Judaism, might find such language hard to swallow or smacking of a whitewash. But, in fact, the person involved may simply mean that he will be working with Torah principles to arrive at precisely the same place that others hope to arrive, in terms of peacemaking. But he will do this through the interpretations, the hermeneutics, or the "wisdom" of Torah, with "Torah" meant as a dynamic phenomenon that, as the font of all truth, must be able to respond to the conflict peacefully.

It started to occur to me in Caux, among my MRA friends, that in the lived religion of many—certainly not all—Christians the reality of forgiveness is so important a faith principle that its exact moral parameters and interpersonal characteristics can change, as long as the living reality of forgiveness is acknowledged. They may agree with me upon reflection or meditation and argue that a true presence of forgiveness may ultimately have to result in much more just social arrangements, for example. But, in any case, believing in forgiveness is a sine qua non of believing in the living reality of God for them.

Here is a critical point. Forgiveness processes may take on an entirely different meaning than for those people—religious or otherwise—who, as non-Christians, see forgiveness as just one possible element in human relationship building that involves many other elements of equal or greater importance. This distinction in spiritual reaction to forgiveness clearly seems to have much to do with the metaphysical meaning of forgiveness for some Christians, that is, its centrality to the life, death, message, and "living presence" of Jesus. Forgiveness's role as a conflict resolution device thus becomes hard to distinguish from its role as a dogma or means of teaching or spreading the faith. For some Christians, analyzing or breaking down forgiveness into its constituent parts, or, put another way, critically examining and separating out forgiveness as a means of reconciliation from its role in the affirmation of the work of the Holy Spirit may be unnecessary and even jarring. But for those Christians, and certainly non-Christians, for whom forgiveness is an independent moral act that must be seen in balance with many other moral acts when it comes to conflict resolution, critical analysis of forgiveness must be pursued.

It becomes vital, therefore, in evaluating the benefits of forgiveness to conflict resolution, to carefully study the highly varied cultural uses of the concept in the conflict situation. This is not to suggest any criticism of the use of forgiveness in one particular cultural way. It simply requires that we put all of these different styles of forgiveness into their proper context. It may be that if we do this carefully and respectfully we might arrive at different definitions of forgiveness for different religious and sectarian traditions, with perhaps differing nuances of ritual and style. At the same time, we may also discover parallel conflict-resolution processes between many cultural traditions that will form the basis of cooperation and intergroup reconciliation.

The Lived Characterizations of Forgiveness

The many contradictory characterizations of "forgiveness" include, for various people, (1) a strictly internal process of forgiveness of another that is considered inauthentic unless it is internal and unilateral; (2) unilateral expressions of forgiveness; (3) "forgiving and forgetting"; (4) bilateral expressions; (5) external verbal acts and formal gestures, including confession, apology, repentance, and acknowledgment of the past; (6) ritualized bilateral exchanges that give efficacy to forgiveness but only within a prescribed set of interactions; (7) this-worldly punishment as part of a spiritual or otherworldly forgiveness for someone's soul; and (8) forgiveness only in the context of legal compensation, justice, restoration, or the righting of past wrongs. All of these approaches have some roots in individual texts and traditions of the Abrahamic faiths.

Another variation in practice involves the tendency to negotiate forgiveness and guilt by proxy. In other words, people in forgiveness contexts, especially in group situations with many historic wrongs, will take it upon themselves to hold their group, or another group, collectively responsible for some wrong and, consequently, will forgive a whole group at once or ask forgiveness *in the name of their own group*.

Unilateral forgiveness raises the highly problematic moral issue of collective responsibility, and the dangers of playing into one of the most conflict-generating of human tendencies, namely, the tendency to hold whole groups or even one individual responsible for the actions of large groups. Often in public gatherings involving forgiveness in the West, there is a tendency for the peacemakers to take on themselves the sins of their own group, whether or not they personally committed those sins. More important, there is a dangerous tendency to forgive a whole group, implying that all are collectively responsible for crimes committed.

What an irony that this is the precise foundation of the first stages of most ethnic violence, where victims are guilty because of their ethnicity and are held responsible as if they have committed all the offenses of a group! Indeed, there can be no mob psychology without this cognitive and emotive construct of the world! The problem is serious in terms of the usefulness of forgiveness for effective conflict resolution. Such collective statements may be well-intentioned but are flawed from the start and betray embedded stereotypical thinking.

On the other hand, it is an indisputable fact that accountability for an entire group is a foundational religious notion in numerous cultures. Religious leaders and functionaries, such as priests, often take on this role, in essence the Christian notion of Jesus taking on the sins of the world, suffering for it, and providing forgiveness for those who believe in him by dying for their sins.[8] This may be a profound religious reality for many people, but, in terms of intergroup relations, we must at least raise the question of the wisdom of collective patterns of apology and forgiveness, when they tend to hold responsible the innocent, or at least the less guilty, for the high crimes of others.

There is also a tendency for members of victim groups to offer forgiveness in the name of those who have not consented to such a process, while the latter are simultaneously demanding a closer attention to justice, restitution, and even large-scale punishment. Here is the crucial critique. This engagement may satisfy the emotional and spiritual needs of those present but actually enrage those who are not present, something that has certainly characterized many Arab/Jewish encounters. Perhaps this step is productive as a model. But perhaps it is also counter-productive. If it acquired greater cultural nuance, and could be more carefully honed to include the voices of those not present, it might appeal to a much broader group of people in need of reconciliation.

Other understandings of "forgiveness" seem to include restitution, punishment, justice, and others seem to suggest unilateral absolution. No one suggested that Pope John Paul's forgiveness of his would-be assassin should or would lead to parole, at least until recently. In some Christian contexts, one must be careful to distinguish between this-worldly absolution and other-worldly absolution, as one evaluates the intended character of the gesture. It gets very complicated to understand, quite honestly, because it depends sometimes on the power position of the forgiver, to inflict this-worldly judgment and punishment. Forgiveness is a very emotional issue, and it provokes differences within and between religious groups which are both profound and confusing.

Let us now list, for purposes of clarity, the different styles of forgiveness that can be observed in the lived human experience:

1. Unilateral forgiveness—internal
2. Forgiveness with forgetting
3. Unilateral forgiveness—external, by words or by deeds:
   a. Toward individuals who have injured you personally
   b. Toward groups who have injured you personally
   c. Toward groups or individuals who have injured people you love or your group but not you
4. Delimitation of guilt to only those who have actually perpetrated crimes, no group responsibility, or, alternatively, group forgiveness with individual exceptions
5. Forgiveness for some crimes but not others
6. Bilateral forgiveness—internal, or external and formal
7. Unilateral apology, which may include contrition, acknowledgement of guilt, detailed confession of crimes
8. Bilateral apology leading to mutual forgiveness
9. Forgiveness only in the context of restoration of what was lost, if possible; that is, payment for sins
10. Forgiveness only after a series of symbolic, ritual acts that express or reify (6) and (7)
11. Forgiveness but no forgetting
12. Forgiveness with repentance that includes formal moral acts, moral changes in behavior as evidence of profound human transformation, as if a new person were born, especially when the person or group is confronted by

the same potential for crime again but now resists or reacts in an opposite fashion

13. Forgiveness as birth of a new person: either victim, perpetrator, or both
14. Acts of embrace of the other in response to apology, though not specifically using the language of forgiveness
15. Unilateral symbolic acts that never acknowledge forgiveness, but symbolically signal a return to the previous relationship, or a new and better relationship
16. Forgiveness as a part of "reconciliation" and "restoration" of relationship (in the Mennonite sense of these terms)

The Prejudices of Forgiveness Formulations

I will shortly investigate the uses of forgiveness in religious contexts but first briefly critique its uses in current trends of psychotherapy. It should be stated that there have been arguments recently, which I submit stem from a particular Western/Christian cultural context, that forgiveness is good for your mental and physical health, and that this is, therefore, a good reason, in and of itself, to engage in this activity.[9] The definition of forgiveness used by some of these researchers includes the following:

> Genuine forgiveness is *voluntary* [my italics] and *unconditional.* Thus it is not motivated by pressure from a third party, nor is it dependent on the apology or recognition of wrongdoing on the part of the offender. Genuine forgiveness constitutes an *internal* process that transforms the forgiver and also may transform the one forgiven, if he or she is able to receive the *gift* of forgiveness.[10]

This definition would eliminate most of the models of forgiveness, described later, that I have seen in Judaism and Islam, in addition to what I suspect would be the result of researching Buddhist and indigenous peoples' styles of reconciliation or resolution of conflict. This "scientific" definition does, however, fit perfectly one particular reading of the Protestant ethos. The trademark phraseology of forgiveness as a "gift" cannot be discerned except in the context of the "gift of grace" that is so vital to Protestant theology. In fact, in one of the scientific studies cited on religious uses of forgiveness, people were divided into "extrinsics" versus "intrinsics," the latter described as having "religiousness that is motivated by the conviction that one's religious *faith* (my italics) is the "master motive" for one's life."[11] Needless to say, the study concludes that the "intrinsics" demonstrate a deeper level of both guilt and forgiveness and are therefore more "successful" at this enterprise. In fact, the study even resorted to using blatantly Christian language of "grace" and "no-grace" as a means of categorizing the recipients of the forgiveness. The emphasis on interior faith and grace, and the lesser emphasis on, and even disparagement of, "extrinsic," external symbols and rituals, are classic markers of Protestant culture, but on a deeper level, a rebuke of ritual-based modes of human interaction—and reconciliation—that dominate the Hebrew Bible, rabbinic Judaism,

Islam, and Catholicism, not to mention all indigenous people's traditions of reconciliation around the world. This "extrinsic" character of religion is what Paul, as interpreted by many, opposed or felt to be inadequate in the Judaism of his day. It is no surprise that emphasis on internal forgiveness and disparagement of "extrinsic" expressions thereof should still characterize some trends in neo-Protestant cultures of the United States.

The prevailing American context of discussions on forgiveness involves a religious cultural orientation that values internal faith and internal processes rather than external, formal transformations. It assumes that the latter are more mechanical and less authentic. Now it may be the case for many human beings globally that "extrinsic" religion can become less authentic in terms of human transformation, and that internal processes are ultimately critical in truly changing the dynamics of conflict. But many other people, from every culture that I have studied, including Christian culture, find that, on the contrary, the extrinsic, formalistic, symbolic moments of bilateral reconciliation, apology, or repentance are the *only* way to transform a relationship with an estranged other, especially when that estrangement is decades or centuries old. It is as if the encrustation of violent history can only be broken by symbol and external action, not pious words or claims of internal transformation. The latter are rarely trusted by enemies when the damage is old and deep.

The problem with the conclusions of these analyses is not that they are invalid by definition, especially for certain populations, but that they have not been subjected to cross-cultural examination, especially in non-American and non-Christian environments. When applied to humanity as a whole, they smack of cultural/religious imperialism, even when this may not have been intended. We are just at the beginning of understanding the full range of humanity's processes of interpersonal and intergroup transformation. We must be aware of the cultural constructs of what we recommend for peacemaking if we do not want to do even more damage as intervenors in violent or deeply conflictual situations.

I should emphasize that many Christian contexts that emphasize unilateral, internal transformation also engage in symbolic or action-oriented processes of reconciliation. This is true, for example, of many of MRA's activities over the years. Thus, these categories are more fluid in reality.

This critique of American psychological approaches to forgiveness should be distinguished from the work of Volkan, Montville, and others. The latter should be properly referred to as psychodynamic approaches to reconciliation.[12] The latters' research, and the projects that have emerged from it, have adopted a much more subtle approach to the subject of human patterns—internal and external, formal and informal, symbolic and verbal—of injury, rage, mourning, and reconciliation. Their approach allows for a very wide degree of cultural diversity and latitude. Psychodynamic conflict resolution also requires cross-cultural scrutiny, as all global investigations do, but so far those engaged in this work have been keen to incorporate multiple religious and cultural perspectives into the processes of recovery from historic injuries.[13]

Forgiveness and Human Transformation

I now turn to human moral transformation and forgiveness in the monotheisms, which are so essential to the life and culture of the Middle East, and, therefore, the character of the Arab/Israeli conflict. Understanding of this is critical, not only to create more effective methods of intercultural reconciliation, but even more important—and a central point of this book—to *know what human beings expect in times of reconciliation, which is the key to understanding why their enemies' behavior is so injurious to them*; why, in other words, they find their enemies' behavior so repulsive. What people expect and hope for in reconciliation will answer the questions when and why they hate their enemies so much: because their enemies epitomize the *opposite* of what they have hoped for in human relationship and in reconciliation. For this reason, understanding cultural and religious variations is critical, and inattention to them leads to perpetual insults, even at the hands of official and unofficial peacemakers. Religion and culture hold within them the deepest human responses to injury and recovery, alienation and trust, despair and hope. Only by attuning ourselves to these subtleties can we build new relationships between enemies of different cultures.

To understand the use of forgiveness as an explicitly religious means of transforming relationships and peacemaking, it is necessary to see it in the context of its other theological uses, specifically in terms of the God-human and God-tribal community relationship. Furthermore, in its pristine religious form, we need to divide it into the uses of receiving versus offering forgiveness.

Divine Engagement with Forgiveness

Receiving forgiveness from God is a key to being in the good graces of God, to avoiding punishment, receiving rewards, in addition to regaining a close relationship to God. The forgiveness may be necessary because specific sins were committed, or, in the case of Christianity, because the human being by nature, due to Original Sin, requires forgiveness from God that can then lead to a rebirth in grace without that burden.

The latter is only accomplished through acceptance of God's only-begotten Son, Jesus. Thus, forgiveness is a key to the restoration of relationship to God, and, in the conservative Christian case, it is the key to becoming legitimate as a Christian and as a human being. Furthermore, that legitimacy is wrapped around an exclusive characteristic of forgiveness, namely, that it can only be accomplished through faith in Jesus, as well as God. Needless to say, many more liberal Christians today may dispute this exclusivity, though not necessarily the central myth of the sinful human being in need of a forgiving God.

Offering forgiveness, in the Christian case, is also an opportunity to be close to God, in that one emulates this central divine characteristic. It should be noted that this has old Hebrew biblical roots, in terms of a God who, according to the myths, repeatedly first forgave humanity before the flood, and then the Israelites for their various trespasses, until God could no longer avoid exacting punishment.

Patience with human failing, however, infinite compassion, and forgiveness, are seen as basic characteristics of God in the Hebrew Bible, the New Testament, and the Qur'an. This somehow exists side by side with the image of the punishing God. God is not seen as exclusively forgiving, and He is seen to punish for several generations, as mentioned earlier. However, the forgiveness element of the divine character lasts infinitely, or in biblical phraseology, for a thousand generations.[14] God is presented as infinitely compassionate, as well as forgiving.[15] Needless to say, divine wrath and punishment are also liberally expressed in all these Abrahamic sources, and the paradoxes thus persist permanently inside the sacred consciousness of all three religions.

To what degree God's compassion or forgiveness requires human emulation of that divine characteristic is an interesting question. Let us first address this issue in Judaism. There is no question that divine emulation, *imitatio dei*, is critical in Judaism. Emulation in terms of compassion has clear sources,[16] but emulation specifically in terms of forgiveness is not as universally known. The standard emphasis of rabbinic Judaism rests squarely on forgiveness as embedded in a process of change that is initiated by the person who did something wrong. In this sense, crime, personal change, and forgiveness are embedded in the much larger practice and metaphysical reality of *teshuva*, repentance.

Forgiveness and Repentance in the Sources of Judaism

Teshuva, the capacity to transform oneself or a community, is considered to be one of the most sublime elements of faith in a good, forgiving God. The fact that repentance can change a guilty verdict, and even sin itself, is a great blessing. Resh Lakish exclaimed, "Great is repentance, for it transforms intentional sins (*zedonot*) into sins of negligence or forgetting (*shegagot*)." And in another version, "Great is repentance for it turns intentional crimes into testimonies for a person's goodness."[17] The last quote presumably means that the degree of evil in the crime is now matched by the heroic effort it took on the part of the sinner to change his character, which turns the previous crime into a testimony for the person's present goodness. The discrepancy between the two versions of Resh Lakish's aphorism is solved talmudically with the suggestion that the latter refers to someone who repents out of love, while the former is someone who repents out of fear.[18]

There is also an important rabbinic idea, which is critical for Jewish consciousness, that true repentance comes when the person stands again in the same place, with the same opportunity to do the crime, and then resists it.[19] This will be important later, in terms of strategies of building trust between enemies, but for now it suggests some concern with the authenticity of processes of repentance, confessions of wrongdoing, unless they have some external reality. In fact, the rabbis suggest limits to the legitimacy of repentance; for instance, if someone sins and repents three times, the fourth is not believed and he is not forgiven. But this last conclusion may reflect the legal/spiritual court system of the rabbis and how to handle repeat offenders. On a God-human plane, numerous sources, both biblical and rabbinic, suggest that the patience of God and the willingness to forgive repenters are infinite, an eternal feature of the world.[20]

Several interacting themes of forgiveness are at work in these sources. There is, as stated, the idea of *teshuva*, "repentance." There is *mehila*, which is the standard word for "forgiveness," but there is also *seliha*, which is sometimes translated as "pardon" and sometimes as "forgiveness." An interesting translation of *seliha* in Psalms 130:4 is "the power to forgive."[21] There is also the metaphor of wiping away or blotting out sin.[22] There is, of course, the concept of atonement, *kapparah*, but it is the wiping away, the pardoning, and forgiving that is stressed in many prayers, both biblical and rabbinic, and often accompanied by the hope that this process is not accompanied by suffering. Suffering is considered an atonement for sin, but the praying person expresses hope for those paths of atonement that do not entail suffering. The prayers, both daily and for special occasions, stress that divine forgiveness is a perpetual activity, and that this is an ongoing process between God and human being that literally requires permanent patience on God's part.[23]

Another crucial phrase is *over al pesha*, literally, "passing over or overlooking sin," and *noseh avon*, literally, "carrying the burden of the sin."[24] All of these divine qualities entail forgiveness, forbearance, patience, a resistance to anger, in addition to the obvious quality of mercy in overlooking someone's guilt. God, in these texts, is the ultimate knower of sin. He knows just how guilty everyone is, in ways that are far more expansive than the sins that the public occasionally witnesses. Thus, God's continuing to sustain human beings, to nurture their bodies from moment to moment, knowing full well the extent of their failings, is seen as an exquisite paradigm of perpetual commitment to mercy, forgiveness, and patience. God loves and sustains every living human body even as the same God is conscious at every moment of the failings of the occupant of that body. This willingness to nurture while cognizant of another's failure is the quintessential quality of a forgiving being.

Such a theological foundation is critical to understanding what is hoped for in the personality of the human being who is called upon to forgive those who have hurt her. The rabbis characterize forgiveness as something that should come immediately to a person if it is clear that the offender is embarrassed by what he has done or if he feels guilty about it.[25] In fact, there is a notion of a person having a right to forgiveness when he has clearly repented and is now living a decent life. He may even insist upon it![26] The right to forgiveness is another concept that should be explored further.

In all of the these cases, forgiveness is seen as a kind of quid pro quo for the moral transformation of the person. In interpersonal terms, it involves a bilateral, formal process that also has internal elements. But it seems that the rabbis saw something in forgiveness that goes beyond a bilateral process. They stated, for example, that anyone who cries at the death of a good person is forgiven for all his sins,[27] that if someone is a good, kind man but he buries a child, then all his sins are forgiven,[28] that if even one person does authentic *teshuva*, "repentance", it is enough to forgive the entire world (!).[29]

This last point is particularly astonishing, suggesting that there is an independent power that forgiveness has on a metaphysical level that extends well beyond a simple tit for tat of "one sin, one repentance and one forgiveness for that sin." But it is also clear that most of the emphasis of this literature is on the responsibility of individuals who have hurt someone else or sinned against God, to initiate the process of change themselves and only then receive a response from the injured other.

There is, however, an accompanying body of literature that suggests a unilateral process whereby the pious individual who forbears the hurts of others, who is patient with them, and who surrenders his own principles or at least overlooks his indignation and sense of right and wrong, is acting in a patient fashion, as God does. This is seen as classic *imitatio dei*. Patience seems to be the key idea here. Vengeance, even if it is justified, is seen as the opposite of this divine quality. This is where the ideas of *over al pesha* and *noseh avon* come into play.[30]

There is an important interplay of several related concepts here. Arrogance or "hardness of the face" (*azut panim*), which is considered the opposite of humility, characterizes someone who never surrenders or wipes away his own principles. He always stands in a "hard" way before people. He is vengeful. The hard person never forgives his friends who have injured him. This, in turn, causes conflict and hatred. The person who is perpetually angry is also the one who cannot surrender his own positions, and this too leads to endless conflict and revenge.

I conclude that forgiveness as a means of peacemaking must be preceded by the cultivation of the kind of person who has humility, who has an extraordinary level of patience over a period of a lifetime, who avoids a "hard face" in his presentation of self to others, who learns to control his anger, and who is willing to surrender his positions sometimes, even if he is in the right.[31] Patience is critical here, and we should, therefore, deconstruct this characteristic. First, emulation of divine infinite patience would suggest a lifetime of patience for the individual, whose "infinity," as it were, is his or her lifetime. Furthermore, patience intimates a kind of self-sacrifice, and a characteristic that is particularly hard to persuade injured parties to embrace in conflict interactions. On a deeper level, however, religious patience, especially as emulation of a divine being, suggests an expansion of one's perception of reality, a perspective of reality in terms of the future even more than the present or past. Only a divine being could do this perfectly, and yet the religious imagination here wisely perceives that a very long view of a human being or group almost requires patience from the point of view of common sense, or, in theological terms, wisdom.

Wisdom and experience prove that this individual or group of people will repudiate the worst of their behavior someday, when confronted with the evidence. Without even requiring compassion for an enemy or self-sacrifice, the wisdom of long views of time suggests that violent actions of enemies are at least as destructive to themselves as they are to others. The long view of time, or patience, knows that those who act so horrifically as to be indistinguishable from monsters will someday have grandchildren who will recoil in horror when confronted with the evidence and will repudiate those actions, just as we have seen in a new generation of Germany. In so doing, the very permanence that so many enemies seek in eliminating others, such as "a thousand-year Reich" will be drowned in the shame and wish to forget of their descendants. This long view of change requires enormous patience, but Judaism suggests it is essential to processes of reconciliation. It requires building a relationship with future persons and a confidence, which history corroborates time and again, that those new persons will emerge and are emerging even as one expresses patience with their failures.

Jewish mystical tradition recommends a profound process of reconciliation involving forgiveness. A person should emulate God as one who actively wipes away another's sin. A person should take it upon himself to wipe away the sin of his fellow human being, and this personal involvement in improving the life of the other, helping him with his failings, makes him too ashamed to then revert to his old behaviors in front of the one who has generously helped him. This aid includes engaging the other even to the point of absorbing insults. Similarly, a human being, like God, should forbear the sin of his fellow. With an enormous investment of patience, he should actually nurture the other, as God does, even as the other fails, suffering through this with him. In so doing, he stays with the other person until the person is "repaired" and the sin is wiped out.[32]

This process has profound implications in terms of conflict resolution. The standard conflict resolution method of engaging the other involves bilateral communication and negotiation. The latter involves, on a moral level, a subtle combination of two values, peace and justice, in which, for the sake of peace, you agree to the first stages of engaging the enemy in a nonviolent meeting. But, for the sake of justice, that engagement will not involve self-sacrifice to the point of self-abuse. And yet part of the process of helping someone to change in a *religious* sense, at least in the sources cited earlier, involves the acceptance of some humiliation. This is only possible because there is an implicit calculation of ethical values, namely, that it is worth occasionally absorbing insults to reach a deeper level of relationship with the estranged other.

We all are familiar with the ways in which we have done this with the people that we truly love, a father, a mother, a child, or a lover. In the context of conflict dynamics, we yield to occasionally awful treatment (especially when we know that someone is going through a particularly traumatic time) that we would never accept from others. Why? Because we know that there is a higher goal and a deeper relationship at stake which is too precious to sacrifice. We suffer occasional insults, as long as they are not violent, and see them as worth it, as we help someone whom we love to change. Classic conflict resolution theory and psychology might suggest that none of these insults, large or small, should be tolerated. They certainly should not be buried or left unaddressed. But we know that we all do this, often, to preserve our most cherished relationships.

We never allow for this kind of sacrifice, however, for the sake of enemies whom we do not know, and this may help explain a very important feature of conflict analysis. There are critical differences between the members of a particular, badly victimized group who try to make peace, and those in the same group who see these same peacemakers as traitors. The latter cannot comprehend the motivations of the peacemakers, such as the simple wastefulness and mutual destruction that warfare often entails. Or peacemakers may argue that much of the craved security that justifies so much mass violence could actually be achieved through careful, verifiable cooperation. But such arguments for peace do not really anger the rejectionists, who in this context find them naive.

Many peacemakers, however, especially religious ones, often have some unmistakable sense of a love connection with the enemy other. They apply to the enemy other, due to a perceived sense of common humanity or common origin in God, a level of tolerance for evils that others usually reserve for family loved ones,[33] as I just described. How many of us have so often looked into the eyes of an enemy's little children and recoiled in horror at the prospect of injuring them? The peacemakers see abusive behavior of some in a group in the context of the overall humanity of that flawed group, which, in turn, is deserving of some kind of caring relationship. In fact, the flaws of the "other" evoke much of the empathy, because they suggest a common humanity, and also—that great generator of human bonds—they evoke a need in the "other" for aid and understanding. All of this makes perfect sense in normal bonds that develop between lovers. But extending this to the larger, injuring world is sensible to some and horrifying to others—in fact, an act of ultimate betrayal. The act of truly caring for an enemy group is enormously difficult, which explains why many in the enemy group often reject even the peacemakers from the other group who engage them. They sense that the enemy peacemakers treat them with compassion, even pity, rather than authentic, equal engagement. This is a serious problem that I have witnessed repeatedly in Arab-Jewish encounters. But many peacemakers ask themselves, "How else can I embrace those who have killed members of my community other than through pity and patience for sinners? Can I simply overlook their crimes and injuries against my community?" This would require either superhuman love or callousness for the suffering of one's own community.

I would agree with this less-than-perfect basis for relationship at the initial stages of reconciliation between enemies, but not as an endpoint or ultimate goal. Ultimately good human relationships require the kind of dialogic egalitarianism that is at the heart of Martin Buber's conception of relationship. However, as we conceive of ways to encourage the *initial* breakthrough in treating the enemy other as "other than enemy," we must allow one group to objectify the other in some way, to see them as sinners or, in secular terms, as criminals, but criminals who one believes one can change by engagement. This is crucial in that when one makes peace with an enemy it is insufficient to simply transform your own relationship to that enemy person or group. Often progressive peacemakers end their efforts with this transformation. But everyone pays a terrible price. The progressives are dismissed—or killed— as traitors by their own group, and so the peace process does not seep into the cultural consciousness of the majority.

The better way is for the peacemaker to always act as if she is the *bridge* between her community and the enemy community. As such, she must discover a prosocial relationship with the enemy other but also maintain a caring relationship with her own group. Otherwise, she is no longer a bridge, and therefore no longer an effective peacemaker. It is hence difficult to avoid judging the enemy as morally evil in some way, because if a person's group identity means anything then it must mean some sympathy with their pain and, therefore, moral outrage at their inflicted injuries. That having been said, the values of compassion, patience, and friendship are at the heart of these biblical means of reaching out to the enemy, even as one judges him unfavorably.[34]

Further into my investigation of Abrahamic approaches to reconciliation, I want to provide a more detailed understanding of Jewish repentance and personal change before moving on to Islam. Historically there has been an effort on the part of numerous legal codifiers to collect and unify classical Jewish sources on any number of subjects, including repentance. In addition, various Jewish thinkers collected Jewish traditions on repentance and developed a philosophy of repentance.[35] One of the greatest Jewish legal minds and codifiers of all time was Maimonides (d. 1204). His codification of the procedure and basic elements of repentance contains significant insights into the process of change in relationships that we will develop further later on.[36] Maimonides' codification by no means represents the final word on the subject, but he was brilliant at eliciting all of the various strands of thought from the classical sources, and it is this variety that interests us in the case of damaged human relationships. It provides us with many tools for changing relationships.

Most prominent in the rabbinic notion of repentance is confession (*viduiy*), which contains the elements of specifying the wrong done, regret (*haratah*), and the commitment to a completely different future (*kabalah le-habah*).[37] This element of change is over and above—but never a substitute for—restitution, where restitution is called for by the law, such as in injury or theft. A "complete" repentance is one in which the opportunity to commit the crime presents itself again, and it is at that point that the person resists. This proves that the repentance is not due to some external fear or loss of physical strength, but rather an authentic change of heart.[38]

Other elements of repentance, not as fundamental, enhance the process. These include crying, giving charity, public confession, in addition to privately expressing sorrow. There is also the notion of changing one's name to express the idea that one is an utterly new human being now. Additionally, there is the concept of voluntary exile from one's home as a kind of penance for what one has done. Exile is considered so powerful a trauma that it becomes an additional atonement for the sins in question.

To engage in appeasement or a process of gentleness in approaching one's victim, in addition to restitution and repentance, one can also apologize until the victim forgives the offender (*piyyus*). If this does not work, there was apparently a tradition of bringing three friends and apologizing before them and the victim, and repeating this up to three times with three different sets of people. Maimonides suggested this as a last resort. But Rabbi Hisda, in the talmudic period, recommended this as a formal requirement of repentance, replete with a ceremony of successive rows of three colleagues, to be repeated on three separate occasions.[39]

Finally, the Talmud, as well as Maimonides, as a later codifier, recommended a procedure for the most tragic—and most common—circumstance among human injuries, when the victims are already dead. The perpetrator goes to the grave of the victim with ten people, confesses, and asks forgiveness there. If restitution is due, it is given then to the heirs, and if there are no heirs, then it is given to the court, who presumably would distribute it to the community in as just a way as they could conceive. One of the great dangers of this particular variety of *piyyus* is how heavily it focuses on words that may or may not reflect the inner life of the perpetrator. Thus, the Talmud warns against those who do not mean what they say. This danger encompasses any process based on words, and we will discuss it further later. It does intimate that, although Jewish repentance has many elements that go beyond word to deed, the victim must at some point be willing to trust the words of a perpetrator, perhaps the most difficult step of all.

The Day of Atonement, the holiest day of the Jewish year, is completely devoted to repentance, in the form of repeated and detailed confessions. It is also a day characterized by great physical deprivation, in the form of fasting, among other things. Fasting is an offering of one's body and one's self to God. It is a kind of human sacrifice without the bloodshed. This would fit nicely with the theme of a new person in the making through repentance and forgiveness. The metaphor of the death and sacrifice of the old and the creation of the new has powerful implications in the context of the psychology of enemy reconciliation. The notion or feeling of new relationship and a new "other" may be much easier to internalize for erstwhile enemies, where much damage has been done. Of course, in an enemy system, it would require a kind of mutual rebirth. This has many implications for the kind of rhetorical language that should be used by cultural leaders in pivotal ceremonies and moments of transition.

Some remarkable qualities of this process suggest that *teshuva* can be a profoundly healing element of social change. Indeed, some of the rabbis speak of repentance as something that brings healing to the world.[40] That injury must be followed by confession, regret, and commitment to the future is a powerful antidote to the damage done to victims. It speaks directly to the need of victims for their story to be acknowledged as true. Thus, it speaks to memory, to one's basic sense of identity, to one's sense of justice, and, perhaps most important, to one's trust in a completely new future. A detailed confession is the hardest to elicit from perpetrators, especially when the crimes have gone in both directions, as is so often the case. It is the most difficult of all to confess for two reasons: 1) It exposes the perpetrator to criminal prosecution and restitution, and 2) It often feels wrong to a perpetrator to do this in circumstances where crimes have been mutual.

In circumstances of mutual injury, it is best to "take what you can get" in terms of reconciliation processes, which may be more than enough to create peace and reverse destructive cycles of violence if one can elicit from the parties a general regret about past action and a commitment to a different future. Detailed confession may prove more rare and elusive. On the other hand, detailed confession has a powerful impact on healing rage and allowing victims, and perhaps even perpetrators or their community, to move on. Denials have a way of festering for as long as people pass on the memory of the crime, which could be forever.

"Complete repentance" (teshuva gemurah), mentioned earlier, involves the opportunity to repeat the crime but resisting it when it presents itself. This speaks to the distrust that victims justifiably have for the words of perpetrators. Teshuva gemurah is often an elusive circumstance of peace processes wherein security measures have been taken to ensure that the violence is not repeated. Or, equally often, there is total defeat of one side, and the opportunity to commit the same crime is gone, such as we have seen in the case of Nazi Germany. Everything is gained in guaranteeing security for former victims, but something is also lost. Without a repetition of the circumstances, it is doubtful that real trust can ever develop again, a price worth paying in circumstances of deadly violence, but we should still acknowledge the power of teshuva gemurah as a tool of conflict resolution and perhaps creatively conceive of ways that, at least symbolically, we may be able to capture the force of this experience.

The power of venting the deep emotions involved in injury through crying is self-evident. Not so evident is the importance for people who have injured or been injured to witness each others' tears. Of course, the cultural variation regarding public display of emotion is self-evident, but the Jewish sources here speak to the power of tears in reconciliation, in the search for authenticity and trust, and this should not be taken lightly.

How often have communities that have been involved in terrible crimes concealed the tears of countless members who cry in private over the crimes committed by members of their own group? But they never shared that sadness with the victims or survivors! How can the victims know the inner life of these people, if the sadness is not shared? I often have sensed this tragic missing element in Jewish-German encounters, for example. Of course, there is also a subtext here of differing cultural expectations in terms of expressions of regret. It is therefore the paramount task of the peacemakers to understand and communicate the expectations and needs of enemy groups, particularly when it comes to the subtleties of deep reconciliation.

There is a short video whose subject is the encounters between the families of Jewish victims of Palestinian terror and Palestinian families of victims of Jewish violence. It features ongoing meetings between these two groups in Gaza and elsewhere that have been spearheaded by the wonderful work of Yitshak Frankenthal and Yehuda Wachsman, both of whom lost children. The video is the most simple and wrenching witness to transformation of relationships and shared mourning that I have ever seen. Tears are at its core, though in a subtle and honorable way. It captures at least a glimpse of the profound relationships being built, and it deserves as much support as the world can give it.

Charity and acts of kindness as a kind of penance are yet another way that Judaism recommends going beyond verbal repentance to the deed. Just recently I received a detailed report concerning a Friday night community prayer service at a synagogue, to which the public of Sacramento, California, was invited.[41] The invitation followed an unprecedented burning of three synagogues in that city, which evoked a powerful governmental and private communal response. The event was packed with people of every religion in Sacramento, including a large contingent from a national Methodist convention taking place at the time.

At one point a woman who represented the local region of the Methodist church went up to the podium and donated $4,000 toward the rebuilding of the synagogue library. This evoked a gasp, two minutes of applause, and much crying from the Jews present. The donation represented to at least one Jewish witness a complete reversal of history, a move beyond pious words of apology to an unprecedented Christian effort to help Jews rebuild their *religious* lives. This hit him the hardest in terms of healing the legacy of injury and suspicion that he had grown used to as a Jew.

The literal demonstration of a change in one's identity is another powerful form of repentance that occurs in various expressions of the Abrahamic traditions. In Judaism, the tradition of changing one's name begins with the founding patriarch himself, whose name is changed by God from Abram to Abraham, according to the Genesis story.[42] The change in name and identity opens the door to a radical departure in terms of one's ethical interaction with the world. How we could translate this notion into qualitatively altering interpersonal and intergroup relationships, and even their identity or presentation of self to other, is an interesting challenge that we will address later.

Voluntary exile as repentance brings up some interesting issues, especially where conflict and violence have focused on land dispute. Place and identity are integrally related for most people on the planet. But exile has a way of bringing the issue of identity into a different light. Exile in Jewish tradition represents punishment, but it also is a means of purification, a way of teaching humility, and a way of avoiding the idolatry associated with land or the abuse of land that led to the original exile of the whole people in 586 B.C.E. It is not an exaggeration to say, along these lines, that massive abuse of a majority by a minority takes place only in disputes over absolute ownership of a piece of land. Refugees are capable of many crimes, but not organized, massive abuse. The biblical prophets speak clearly on the relationship between organized crime and land ownership, and the resulting removal of the privilege of land ownership.[43]

Voluntary exile, a well-known way of experiencing life in an utterly new way, was practiced by saints in Jewish history. In particular, communal leaders or rabbis who may have been used to special, honorable treatment would voluntarily exile themselves for a time and thus acquire a new and anonymous identity. In this way, they discovered humility, and detached themselves from their own egos, which are, after all, intimately related to, and falsely exaggerated by, attachment or overattachment to place and social position, which is a derivative of permanent place. In Buddhism, as in some rabbinic approaches to Judaism, this overattachment to place, position, and ego is the basis of all misery (*dukkah*[44]), as Buddhism expresses it, or sin (*he'et*), or the "other (wrong) side" (*sitrah ahrah*), as Judaism would phrase it. Exile heals this in providing a new perspective on ego and human attachments.

Extending of this understanding of sin and its consequences to conflictual relationships in the context of land is a further challenge. Ways to operationalize this value as a conflict resolution measure will be considered in the next chapter. Here we are getting into methods of peacemaking that should be characterized as conflict transformation or even character transformation. Character transformation as a path of reconciliation is a clear principle in Abrahamic traditions, and we must think creatively in the future about how to translate this into workable practices of intergroup and interreligious conflict transformation.

I will expand on this later, but for now let me just acknowledge that if terrible crimes have been committed over land disputes then the surrender of at least some cherished land, and the subsequent abandonment of it, comprise a powerful way to transform relationships. But first it must be acknowledged just how cherished that land is. For example, it has been tragic that as Israel has given up land that was part of the historical Holy Land, the secular, peace-oriented Jews who acquiesced to this to make peace expressed little concern for this lost property, at least publicly. But religious Jews, on the whole, who deeply felt the loss of the ancient, sacred land, had no interest in giving it up. They have therefore had a harder time facing and admitting the injustices perpetrated on Palestinians. Rather, the focus is exclusively on what Palestinians, Arabs, and gentiles in general have done to them. The actions and emotions of these religious Jews, at least in part express passionate love for a land. They have resorted, as they must, to any and all arguments to avoid losing it.

This is a traumatic loss, just as the loss of Palestine was such a traumatic loss for hundreds of thousands of Palestinians. It would be better for all actors on all sides to acknowledge how difficult it is to sacrifice land, and not dismiss it in such a cavalier fashion. Some will always act as if they are in a schoolyard, and, as they surrender something that they cannot have, will mock it as worthless: "Who wants Gaza anyway?" But this also mocks deep sentiments on both sides and helps no one.

When land is given up, or when the rights to land are surrendered, as the Jews must surrender the West Bank, and as the Palestinians surrendered Haifa and pre-1948 Israel, the sacrifice must be acknowledged and honored in a fundamental way. The real heroes of this process of transformation from war to peace will be those who deeply cherish the land, who feel that they own it and that God gave it to them but are willing to give up part of it, out of a sense of justice and a commitment to peace. The best gestures of peacemaking do not involve a begrudging surrender of what one does not really want anyway, but an act of sacrifice. Often the other side will have to make supreme sacrifices as well, and they must see their opponents doing the same thing.

Let us move on to other methods. Repentance expressed through *piyyus*, a unilateral process of approaching the person or group that you have injured with words of kindness and reconciliation, has obvious benefits, and the power of the rituals and acts recommended by Rabbi Hisda, mentioned above, is also self-evident. Formal ceremonies concretize emotions and moments of transformation in a way that rational dialogues can rarely accomplish. We must be more creative about how to apply them to the scenario of complex conflicts. They certainly cannot replace the negotiations over the future relationship, security arrangements and distribution of power and resources that must take place. But they are an indispensable tool of transformation.

Rational negotiations and dialogue can do nothing for the dead, the murdered on all sides. And the murdered weigh on survivors as a burden of indescribable pressure. In nonrational terms, ghosts of the dead wield tremendous power in so many global traditions. Survivor guilt, in my experience, is a principal goad that motivates those who perpetuate conflict. Conflict keeps the memory of the dead alive and the guilt of survival assuaged. Death also poses an inherent moral problem to peacemaking, even the kind that seriously engages issues of justice and reparations. Nothing is so valuable to human beings as their lives and the lives of their loved ones. In deadly conflicts, this loss *cannot* be replaced. Therefore, we tend in rational and even emotion-based peace processes to ignore the dead. Monetary compensation for their deaths is rarely brought up and feels obscene anyway. And yet it seems to me that the religious traditions cited here suggest that we have to try to address this anyway. The formal methods of address at burial sites seem worthy of serious consideration as part of a complete process of peacemaking in deadly conflicts. I can certainly affirm their importance in conflicts involving Jews, who have this relationship to the dead embedded in either their current religious experience, or at least in their cultural consciousness. It is not only something they expected as victims, but also, potentially, something they may be willing to do for victims of their own actions. What power this could have in conflict resolution is difficult to predict, but experimentation is definitely worthwhile. Based on experience, as well awareness that something is painfully missing, I argue that, if done well, formal burial rituals could be the decisive factor in moving reconciliation work to a new scale of global success.

Limitations of Jewish Methods of Reconciliation

Clearly there are paths of repentance and reconciliation with enemies within biblical tradition and monotheistic religions, as demonstrated in numerous sources, and encouraged as a part of one's general commitment to emulate God's ways or to fulfill sacred traditions. The sources also reveal, however, one of the fundamental and unfortunate weaknesses of religious traditions with regard to enemies, which is the following. The same sources suggest that when it comes to dealing with those who are designated as "wicked," who are against the Torah, it is permissible to be tough and display all the negative qualities disparaged earlier in this chapter to "fight them" and their influence successfully.[45] There are thus two dilemmas with this and many other sources: 1) Who decides when the prosocial side of these texts are operationalized, and when the antisocial side is operationalized? Who decides who is wicked? 2) In the contemporary pluralistic age, most people could be classified as "wicked" or "against God," and does this thus not neutralize these sources as useful building blocks today of forgiveness and conflict resolution?

This issue is at the heart of the problem of the hermeneutic variability of historical religions, and our fundamental ambivalence in approaching them as resources for conflict resolution. In general, religious authorities, often connected with reigning structures of economic and police power, decide who is wicked and who is righteous, and to whom prosocial values must and must not be directed. The marriage of religious authority, embedded in larger power structures, as well as the selective application of religious values, has generally been a prescription for disaster in human history. The cause is not only the removal of large groups of people from the purview of ethical responsibility, but also the *selective* and politically useful application of typical monotheistic moral values of submission, passivity, and humility, as tools to pacify the faithful. Thus, forgiveness can be selectively withdrawn from the enemy groups who need most to be engaged, while it can also be applied and enforced more narrowly to keep religious people from expressing anger at unjust situations. This becomes a poison inside the heart of monotheistic ethics, particularly the ethics of forgiveness, and renders it ineffectual in processes of peacemaking between enemies, or between majority and minority groupings in a single culture.

Clearly this problem must also be confronted. It lies at the core of the question whether forgiveness will become an authentic, carefully crafted component of a mature system of conflict resolution that honestly confronts injustice and issues of distribution of power. It could also become a pious tool of pacification, selectively applied by authorities, or public opinion, to conflicts that disturb the harmony of the acceptable order of religious society. For example, forgiveness might be applied—and I have witnessed this—to fellow Christians, all involved in furthering the mission of the Christian faithful, but not to, say, communists, who are the "sworn enemies of the church."

The examples proliferate. Peacemaking values may apply to members of another religion, such as to Muslims by Orthodox Jews, but not, "God forbid," to Conservative or Reform Jews who would be dismissed as dangerous heretics; I have witnessed this also. As another example, an unfaithful husband may encourage and insist on his wife's forgiveness, but a distant "infidel," whom one may be slaughtering with perfectly righteous indignation, would not even be considered. Thus, in this context, from the perspective of today's concepts of conflict resolution, forgiveness could become an unfortunate adjunct to brutality or an enforcer of injustice.

Furthermore, religious patterns of forgiveness are only as good as the moral system that they serve. For example, if a religious system condones slavery or the death penalty for adultery, as all the biblical religions did at one time or another, would the issue of apology, confession of guilt, and forgiveness even arise? Did it arise historically when religious traditions embraced slavery? Was it possible, in a society and a religion that accepted slavery, for example, to strongly encourage a master to apologize for his act of slavery in a moral structure that did not condone it to begin with?! Of course, this question strikes us as laughable, historically speaking, although it should not. As another example, if a man was caught not standing before his elders, would not contrition and apology be the first order of business, even as everyone involved happen to be on or near a battlefield fighting some religious enemy? Is this an impossible scenario? In other words, religious forgiveness, in terms of conflict resolution and justice, is only as helpful as the moral values that it accompanies, and only as inclusive or expansive as the moral and social system that it buttresses.

Islam, Forgiveness, and Peacemaking

I turn now to Islam, to texts of forgiveness and compassion as they may relate to peacemaking. Here we find some hermeneutic dynamics remarkably similar to those of Judaism. Forgiveness is mentioned a number of times in the Qur'an. As in Judaism, much of its usage refers to Allah's kindness. Allah is referred to as "oft-forgiving," which, in this sense, is parallel to divine mercy (Surah 39:53). One commentator suggests that there are three applications in the Qur'an: (1). Forgiveness as forgetting, (2) forgiveness as ignoring or a turning away from another, as a defensive maneuver if someone insults you, and (3) divine forgiveness (*ghafara*), which refers to Allah's willingness to cover up sins.[46] Allah's forgiveness extends especially to minor sins that should not be dwelled upon (53:32), but he does not forgive for joining other gods to Allah (4:48), the primary betrayal of Allah. Furthermore, repentance after a life of sin only when facing death is considered inauthentic, and forgiveness is not offered (4:17–18). Throughout, both implicitly and explicitly, it is clear that divine forgiveness is contingent on human repentance. As in Judaism for the most part, the emphasis is on a bilateral process of change involving initiative from the sinner, and forgiveness as inextricable from that bilateral process.

There is evidence of forgiveness even of idol worship, presumably with the requisite human repentance. Allah is seen as forgiving "the Jews" for the golden calf episode (4:153), and at least being patient with Abraham's slow search for God that involves initial belief in other deities (4:76–78), as seen through the lens of Islam. Furthermore, the general character of God is portrayed as forgiving. In fact, the angels are seen as praying for the forgiveness of all beings on earth (42:5). Now this text, at least, takes this bold position apparently knowing full well that a large portion of humanity not only commits sin, but also joins other gods to Allah, in other words, commits idolatry.[47]

Needless to say, all of this language of forgiveness occurs in contexts that very explicitly approve and ordain this-worldly, violent encounters with nonbelievers, when this is legitimate and appropriate, according to Islamic law, just as we see in the historical sources of Judaism and Christianity. I will not go into here the justifications of *jihad* in Islam. There are limits to the brutality of *jihad*, according to the beliefs of many Muslims, and no compulsion is allowed in terms of conversion, at least according to the widely believed interpretation of Shari'ah today. But every collection of *hadith*, reports on the Prophet, has a special section dedicated to *jihad*, which recounts the exploits against "heathens," those who would not become Muslim, who would not accept Allah. Judaism has an extensive and subtle moral interpersonal system that is highly instructive in terms of conflict prevention and resolution, but also an extensive legitimation of violence against a variety of people and groups, especially idolaters. Here too, this Islamic literature must be seen in the context of other forms of aggression against those who are out of favor with Allah.

Hermeneutic Tension and Peaceful Interpretation

For those trying to build an Islamic philosophy of peacemaking, there is therefore a clear hermeneutic tension that they, as believers, perceive.[48] They often remedy it by reading and rereading their tradition in ways that nonbelievers, as well as Muslims who have a stronger commitment to violence in Islam, would find apologetic. We will come back to this later. But for now, my aim is not to present a one-dimensional picture of a complex religion, but rather to present the hermeneutic possibilities of a tradition in relation to forgiveness and peacemaking, and then to critically evaluate its possibilities.

Rabia Harris's interpretations of these matters in Islam are among the more sophisticated and honest arguments that I have seen for nonviolence in Islam. Of course, she bases her nonviolence on models from Islamic life, such as her reading of the life of al-Husayn ibn 'Ali, revered by Shi'ites; al-Hallaj; and the more recent leader of the Pathans, Badshah Khan. There are also Sufi masters on whom she relies, such as Bawa Muhaiyadeen, who has stated, "It is compassion that conquers. It is unity that conquers. It is Allah's good qualities, behavior, and actions that conquer others. It is this state that is called Islam. The sword doesn't conquer; love is sharper than the sword. Love is an exalted, gentle sword."[49]

Let us study this text for a moment. Notice the hermeneutic of religious symbols common in Qur'anic literature that, in the hands of others, are tools of violence: "conquest," "unity," "the sword," even "the state." All these crucial terms are reinterpreted in terms of what the nonviolent believer sees as the essence of the Divine truth, namely, compassion, love, and human transformation.

Apologetics, Sincerity, and Strategies of Intervention in Fundamentalist Contexts

Nevertheless, Bawa Muhaiyadeen is a nonviolent Sufi master, and a nonviolent believer, by definition, has to argue that the peaceful texts and traditions in which she or he believes truly reflect divine truth, to be taken literally. The texts or traditions that support violence, however, must be "explained," placed in context, delimited, but not extended ubiquitously or be allowed to impose themselves on the "deeper," divine essence of the tradition. This crucial distinction, common to all prosocial monotheistic hermeneutics of sacred texts, appears to others as apologetics. But, on a certain level, it is not. It is rather the essential act of faith, a worldview that must be seen as primal, the ultimate religious gesture. And, after all, who decides what in a tradition is to be taken literally and what figuratively, what is "deeper" and what is not? Why do we assume in the modern period that the deeper essence is violent? Is that not the essential prejudice of our own horizons? Ironically, violence is the place where contemporary religious extremists and the secular left meet in their interpretations of religion.

Let us examine the term "apologetics," which is important for the questions that I have raised here. "Apologetics" carries the implication, as a pejorative term, of dishonesty. It is assumed that apologetic statements are meant to dissemble, to steer the outsider—or the naïve believer—away from uncomfortable facts about a text or tradition that would be better concealed. This does occur in religious literature all the time. But when someone rereads their tradition and honestly believes that their interpretation is the *only* possible way to account for their deepest beliefs about the sacred, and they conclude that the deeper meaning of the tradition is for peacemaking and love, then the term "apologetics" is no longer applicable. Such a religious approach, in its very essence, is or becomes a religious worldview as legitimate as any other.[50]

In that light we must interpret many—not all, to be sure—religious statements in the Abrahamic faiths that express an unqualified commitment to peace and peacemaking. It is also the case, however, that politically oriented texts and leaders in history, as well as today, may publicly say, "Our religion stands only for peace," to deflect negative public opinion, while simultaneously holding no such view. But we as outsiders cannot blithely conflate all such statements and assume that all is falsehood when it comes to describing religious traditions in positive terms. Nothing could be farther from the truth empirically.

Just like Jews and Christians, millions of Muslims live and die by their faith that their religion is committed to peace, despite the highly publicized character of well-known militant groups. To dispute this would resemble a conclusion that Lutherans are comfortable with the elimination of the Jewish people from public life, because of the actions of the Lutheran church in Germany during the Nazi period or the anti-Jewish ravings of Luther himself in his later years. Furthermore, strategically, nothing could be more destructive in the process of peacemaking than dismissing statements about peace as apologetics. Rather, we build on these statements but then press for concrete affirmations in the lived practices of the community.

The question addressed here, on the validity of peaceful interpretations of a historical religion that has justified or utilized violence in the past, is essential to religious peacebuilding. It emphasizes the difference between two groups: one, of those who are willing to dissect, with modern historicist methods, their historical religion: extract in a liberal fashion the peaceful, prosocial elements; and then *consciously decide* to reject and eliminate the rest; and the second, of those—the majority globally, I believe—who find it difficult to believe in the results of such an exercise. The latter seem to need a deeply religious hermeneutic—apologetics to others, scandalous reading to historians—that justifies all of their religious tradition in a deep way, even as they move the religion interpretively toward peace—rejecting none of the sacred traditions, but reading and reinterpreting many.

This touches on the problem (and the opportunity?) of the relative ignorance among the vast majority of believers across the world of the texts of their own tradition. It is in the nature of lived religion, and perhaps always has been, that the vast majority of people, even those who are knowledgeable, live within the historical or psychological horizon of a relatively small number of chosen texts, laws, symbols, rituals or dogmas that dominate their inner lives. How to confront this phenomenon in terms of training and intervention remains a perpetual dilemma of conflict resolution that I have faced with very conservative, religious people. Does one simply "burst the bubble" of religious peacemakers who do not know or refuse to acknowledge violent sources in their tradition, to get them to confront their society more effectively, and also become more honest about their religion? Or, alternatively, does one simply help religious peacemakers to build the best synthesis of conflict resolution measures and their chosen religious traditions, without challenging their knowledge of the totality of their tradition and its history? I have struggled with this many times in my trainings and have come to the conclusion that it depends on the student, his or her capacities, and how subtle their faith may be.

Ideally, the best results come from those who know well the arguments for violence, understand and acknowledge past wrongs of their community and traditions, and try to move forward. But this ideal type could not be fundamentalist, in the general meaning of the term. If I simply reject the latter as interlocutors or students, however, then I eliminate all fundamentalists from working toward peace with outsiders. But this alternative is indefensible as well as morally irresponsible, because it consigns the most isolated segment of the religious population to those who would only interpret the tradition violently. It would also be intellectually dishonest, because, however they may come to their positions and activities, there is evidence the world over, in fact among most students that I have trained, that some people cannot in principle see certain deeply violent aspects of their religion but, at the same time, manage to be successful and creative peacemakers. In fact, they are often better at peacemaking and far more committed to it than some secular peace institutions with which I am acquainted. How can we have the arrogance to dismiss this vital resource for peacemaking as an aberrant group of fundamentalists? Training and conflict resolution must, in one form or another, and at different times, address *all* people in a conflict, even if we have to modify our methods occasionally for the varying shades and styles of religious commitment within a single group. Otherwise, we surrender the right to consider ourselves true peacemakers who have the capacity to make peace with all people.

At the same time, all of the potentially violent elements of a religious tradition often emerge anyway in an encounter between religious enemies. The other side is usually keenly aware of the deadlier side of the enemy culture. All sides, including fundamentalists, will have to confront this possibility in such encounters. A good intervenor will seize the opportunity to help both groups face their own problems. His or her task in these circumstances is to avoid paradigms of encounter and reading of secular and religious traditions that, by definition, exclude one group, unless one is planning a multitiered intervention that engages radically different segments of the community at different times. Admittedly, the work is very imprecise and difficult, requiring a great deal of skill and experience by trial and error in each situation. But I am arguing in favor of the effort to develop multiple, finely tuned methods of intervention for the various constituencies of a religious community, including the most extreme elements of that community.

It would be wrong, on the other hand, to conflate all methods of intervention into those that appeal only to fundamentalists. On the contrary, the greatest allies, in the long run, of civil society are those moderates who have a theological conception of coexistence between religious institutions and public institutions that are shared by many faiths, including agnostics or atheists. But it is foolhardy to conceive of conflict resolution methods that can never be adjusted to include highly conservative or extreme expressions of religion. On the contrary, intervention geared toward the latter group is the most important in undermining religious violence.[51]

Interpersonal Models of Forgiveness in Islam

Continuing the focus on Islam, I turn now from divine forgiveness, to its human analogue. The Qur'an records that one of the instructions to Muhammad is, "Hold to forgiveness," even as he resists evil (7:199). It is expected that people have the right to repay evil for evil. However, it is also stated that those have the highest reward who, even when they are justifiably angry, can forgive

(42:37). Ideally, the Qur'an suggests that people deal with their differences by a process of "consultation," a method that is not further described, at least in the Qur'an. This reference could and should become the basis for religiously sanctioned processes of conflict management.

There is no blame for those who cannot forgive. However, forgiveness combined with reconciliation yields a reward from Allah (42:40). Forgiveness combined with compensation for injury appears to be a preferable path to retaliation, even if retaliation is permitted (*Hadith Sahih Bukhari* 3.49.866). This interesting position recognizes that the strictly just recompense for injury is injury, following along the lines of Exodus 21:24, the *lex talionis*, eye for an eye, legal principle. Judaism never accepted the literal reading of this legal principle, and Islam, too, sees forgiveness as the preferable act, despite the fact that one may have a moral right of demanding injury for injury. Most important, forgiveness is seen as the act of a "courageous will" (42:43). "A strong person is not the person who throws his adversaries to the ground. A strong person is one who contains himself when he is angry (*Malik's Muwatta* (47.3.12)." This responds to some troubling questions that a conflict resolver would have with forgiveness, namely, what it accomplishes and does not accomplish in terms of empowering of both sides.[52] In addition to the achievement of justice in authentic conflict resolution, the sense of powerlessness often felt by victims of violence must also be addressed.

If forgiveness is merely a religious requirement but is not seen or felt as some form of empowerment, then its effectiveness in truly resolving and transforming conflicts may be limited. The religious act, in repressing hidden anger, may turn into a formalistic act that does not address the person's deeper needs. It is vital that forgiveness, if it occurs, be seen and felt as an empowering act. Qu'ran 42:43 would affirm this inner process, as does the rabbinic dictum, "Who is the greatest hero among the heroes? He who turns an enemy into a friend."[53] Once again, classical Judaism and Islam share a strategy of how to influence a person, especially the male, to become a peacemaker as well as a classic hero. This is particularly vital to both, the biblical and the Qur'anic traditions, with their having religious prophets and heroes who were male warriors, such as Abraham, Moses, Joshua, David, and Muhammad.[54]

In terms of the relationship to those who are not believers in good standing, there is some evidence for the willingness to forgive unbelievers in Islam. "Tell those who believe to forgive those who do not look forward to the Days of Allah: It is for Allah to recompense (45:14)." The notion of suspending judgment of others and leaving it to God to judge is a crucial middle position for ethical systems containing a great many moral absolutes. It is not the classical progressive position of "each to his own" and it does allow the believer to continue on his or her path of moral absolutes. But by elevating judgment to the divine realm, the moral system provides the space for coexistence on the earthly plane. The precedents for this position should be studied and compared in all three Abrahamic traditions, because they should form the basis for a pragmatic, if not theoretical, pluralism for a functional, diverse civil society.[55]

The *hadith* literature yields some more interesting ideas on forgiveness and conflict resolution. *Malik's Muwatta* states: "Every Muslim forgives, except a man who has enmity between him and his brother. Leave these two until they have made reconciliation (47.4.17)," and the following text adds, "Leave these two until they turn in *tawba*." Now it seems to me, and I could be wrong, that this text refers to reconciliation with a fellow Muslim. But whether, under what circumstances, and according to whose interpretation it could be extended to Muslim–non-Muslim relations is an important hermeneutic challenge for Islamic peacemakers. Clearly, however, the forgiveness is not simply an internal act, but rather an external act of reconciliation that parallels an inner process.

The proactive element is important to highlight here, as we did in the case of Judaism. Just as there must be an active interaction of human repentance with Divine forgiveness, here too, human forgiveness is inextricably related to a process that has both internal and external, formal aspects. On the internal level, the *hadith* stress anger as a key impediment to forgiveness and reconciliation.[56] For example, it is not considered *hallal*[57] to shun one's brother for more than three days. The shunning is attributed variously to envy, anger, suspicion, spying, and competition (*Malik's Muwatta* 47.4.13-16). The better of the two enemies greets his fellow first. Shaking of hands is considered an important act that cures the rancor. Thus, specific symbolic/ethical acts provide important clues to this deep, cultural process of reconciliation and forgiveness that stem from the oldest strata of Arab culture and Islamic religion.

Charity, as a critical, even primary, element of Islam, is another key method of conflict resolution. Often the most elemental moral impulses of religious systems are interrelated. It is thus not surprising that peacemaking, compassion, and justice would interact in Islam. This dynamic includes charitableness. Even when justice may demand retaliation or in a particular case compensation for loans, charitableness is seen as key to conflict resolution. Specifically, generosity in debt disputes that were arbitrated by Muhammad, was seen as a central way to bring about peace (*Hadith Sahih Bukhari* 3.49.868–70). The basic ethical impulse evoked through the model of Muhammad is that even if someone is in the right in a dispute, the generous person has compassion on his or her adversary and therefore finds a way to forgive or compromise.

Sulh as an Indigenous Paradigm of Islamic Conflict Resolution

The proactive element in forgiveness and reconciliation that we have seen in Islam has old monotheistic roots, as we have demonstrated in the case of Judaism. But it is also rooted in the old Arab method of reconciliation referred to as *sulh*. George Irani refers to several Arab methods of dealing with conflicts, including *wasta* (patronage-mediation) and *tahkeem* (arbitration).[58]

Sulh, which Irani translates as "settlement" and *muslaha*, which Irani translates as "reconciliation" are rituals that are formally institutionalized in past as well as present Arab cultural institutions, to some degree. The details vary from region to region in the Middle East, but some roughly similar elements are held in common.

Sulh, understood to be conducted between believers, is a form of contract, legally binding on both sides. According to some authorities, *salaam* carries the connotation of permanent peace, whereas *sulh* may be temporary but could lead to permanent peace. In any case, it is action- and ritual-oriented.[59] Public *sulh* is often conducted between large groups, such as tribes, whether or not the original parties to the conflict are known or are still present, historically speaking. Permanent peace among them requires compensation for those who have suffered the most, and a pledge from all the parties to forget everything and create a new relationship. Private *sulh* takes place between known parties, and the purpose is to avoid the cycle of revenge. If, for example, a murder is committed, the families go to *muslihs* or *jaha* (those who have esteem in the community). A *hodna* (truce) is declared.[60]

The task of the *sulh* is not to judge, according to Irani, but to preserve the good name of both families and reaffirm the ongoing relationships of the community. Mennonite peacemakers refer to this as a restorative quality, which suggests that the process is much more than a judgment of who is right and wrong. Nevertheless, this judgment does occur in *sulh*, and the process is arbitrated. If one party is guilty of something as serious as murder, for example, *diya* (blood money) may be required to avoid bloodshed.[61] There is, moreover, a formal process of *muslaha*, a very public event in the village center. The families line up, the parties shake hands (*musafaha*), the family of the perpetrator may visit the family of the injured or murdered, and they drink bitter coffee (in some traditions it is *mumalaha* [partaking of salt and bread]). Finally, the family of the offender hosts a meal. There are many important elements in this process. The use of symbolism is critical. The ritual use of food and the body for the handshake are key, involving all the senses, and especially touch between the parties. The bilateral way in which the parties relate, each with its own assigned symbolic role, is critical, the role that all ritual plays in critical turning points of life and death. *It restores to the parties an ordered universe of peace, predictability, fairness, and security, when this is precisely what the violence or offense stole from them.* The contractual element of this process is critical to the culture. Treaties of an oral or custom-based nature are important to Middle Eastern cultures. They could and should play a role in any intercultural process of Middle Eastern peacemaking.[62]

I have heard from Palestinian friends that there is also a version of *sulh* in which the offending party goes to the house of the offended, removes his shirt, places a dagger on his folded shirt, and bowes his head, symbolically offering or forfeiting his life. My breath was taken away by this, due to its sheer psychological import. This is an extraordinary act of apology and surrender that pales dialogue, and words themselves, in comparison. It is the kind of apology for injury that reverses actively, with one's body, in absolute terms, the circumstances of the injury. It places the offender in mortal vulnerability before the victim, and its psychological power is brilliant. It empowers the victim, or restores his sense of self, placing him now as the holder in his hands of life and death. It is demonstrated publicly in an absolute and dramatically symbolic fashion that leaves no room for ambivalence. This is vital to the healing of victims who have been thoroughly destroyed psychologically as well as fundamentally humiliated publicly.

Such a process, carried out in the West, would be akin to postwar Germans choosing a representative body of German Jews—of those who were left—to function as the leadership of Germany's national police force. It would have been more effective for everyone on both sides, in my estimation, than abstract gestures like financial payments to Israel. Or it would be like the U.S. Congress deciding, as an act of repentance for decades of murderous abuses and theft, to appoint a commission of Native American tribal elders to oversee the management of federal lands and oversee land-based disputes. In sum, we have only begun to investigate the power of indigenous methods of conflict resolution in the Middle East, in addition to critically evaluating the limitation, applications, and replicability on larger scales.[63]

Returning to our subject, *sulh*, let us critically analyze some of its limitations. *Sulh* generally assumes that there is one offending party. Of course, in complex group conflicts there is usually a large amount of injury to innocents and crimes on both sides, and usually these are lopsided in ways that the combatants can never acknowledge or agree upon. But combatants can agree on specific crimes on both sides that are regrettable and/or subject to restitution and processes of reconciliation and apology.

How *sulh* could be applied to complex conflicts is an interesting question. Applying *sulh* to intercultural and interreligious conflicts is a further challenge. There is the obvious problem of religious authorities, on both sides in fact, questioning the orthodoxy of extending the process in this way. But there is also a deeper question of how and whether the symbolic process can be meaningful when it has primordial roots for only one side. A syncretistic process, typical of modern interfaith experimentation, would only be appealing to some, and probably appalling to the most religiously conservative or ethnically partisan on both sides, who probably need the process of reconciliation more than most. Thus, the problems of application are clear. One group that is creatively applying *sulh* to contemporary situations, at least among Palestinians, is the Christian-based Wi'am Palestinian Conflict Resolution Center in Bethlehem.[64]

I have also been involved with a West Bank rabbi who is in close contact with Islamic leaders, even among Hamas, and at least one element of *sulh*, namely *hodna*, has come up as a possible first step in improving Jewish-Islamic relations, as noted earlier. Furthermore, various quiet discussions are taking place between religious Jews and Muslims on this subject and have been proliferating dramatically in 1999 and 2000. In fact, it was reported that a young Jewish man, who accidentally hit an Arab in the West Bank with his car, was so distraught that he came back repeatedly to the village to take part in a process of *sulh*, this despite the warnings he received from fellow Jews about the danger of returning. But I have been unable to find the source for this story.

There are intracultural anecdotes about *sulh*, even in battle-torn Hebron. One young Arab man who had attacked another Arab young man came to the house of the victim, apologized, and kissed him on both cheeks. The alternative offered by the police was two nights in jail, and thus the forgiveness process was hardly unilateral, or "freely given", but it was authentic in this culture. After the apology, they served tea. If it had been a more serious crime, according to reports, they would have served bitter coffee![65]

Now there is a coercive quality here, in that engaging in this ceremonial process is an alternative to more serious punishment. Does this disqualify it as conflict resolution, or is *sulh* actually a quasi-legal phenomenon, a form of arbitration that is perhaps less effective than freely entered processes of conflict resolution, but more personal and effective than the Western court model of justice? Furthermore, is the whole question of "effectiveness" culturally determined? Or do human needs theory and conflict transformation's insistence on filling the need for empowerment make quasi-coercive strategies of arbitration like *sulh* less desirable than freely entered conflict resolution processes? This issue we must continue to debate, and the answers seem to vary situationally, from case to case, at least in my judgment.

If there were no police structure backing up the procedure, it has been argued that the incentive to compliance would exist anyway in old Arab culture, to avoid the cycle of revenge; on the other hand, if people were that rational, we would never have violence! This invites serious reflection on the interaction of apology/forgiveness processes, issues of justice, enforcement of the law, and the balance of justice and peacemaking. Clearly, many of these matters devolve into situational and cultural calculations of what is right and appropriate, and what *can* be done realistically, as opposed to what could be done in an ideal universe.

Let us take the next step, however. Situations of massive wrongdoing and injury to large groups of people, even over generations, are more complex. Most descriptions of *sulh* that I have seen presume, in classic court style, that there is one guilty party, although the written literature on this may not reflect the subtle variations of its lived reality at the hands of elders and arbitrators. But one-sided wrong does not reflect the nature of long-standing, inter-ethnic conflict, where there is usually extensive and unjust injury on both sides. In fact, recognizing this is half the battle of conflict resolution.

Certainly, these village-based methods could not be automatically applied to highly complex conflicts facing the Middle East, with their numerous subconflicts. However, they may prove to be, in altered form, a crucial adjunct or parallel process to formal negotiations over matters of justice, war, and peace. Furthermore, the published literature on *sulh* is only beginning to emerge, and we probably have underestimated the hermeneutic elasticity and great potential of this venerated tradition. *Sulh* and its Jewish counterpart, *teshuva*, may speak to peoples' hearts and deeper needs in a way that virtually nothing currently proposed by diplomacy is accomplishing for the majority of people affected and injured by the Arab-Israeli conflict that has lasted several generations now. This disconnect between the deeper needs of the people and elite diplomacy is exactly what has undermined the Oslo peace process so many times.

I have been involved in recent months in a concerted effort to elicit the beginnings of a reconciliation process between Jewish and Islamic clerical leadership, as I outlined in earlier chapters. It is certainly leading to statements of reconciliation or peacefulness that may or may not see the light of day, depending on the security of the parties and the political/military state of enemy relations. Forgiveness ceremonies, apologies, and *sulh* and *teshuva*-type ceremonies, at an intercultural level remain only a theoretical possibility at this point, but we are closer than ever before to preparing the political/religious ground for such a possibility as of this writing.

The symbolic and transformative power of leading sheikhs and rabbis embracing in such a ceremony is an image that drives all of us forward in this difficult work, because we believe that this is the missing ingredient of the peace process.[66] This image has been at the heart of Rabbi Froman's efforts, which we examined earlier. It is the mythic, symbolic trigger that is needed to transform this bitter, merciless, haggling struggle, which has characterized the peace process till now, into a deeper process of trust-building, honest bilateral conversations about justice and even reconciliation. This deeper level of rapprochement will be necessary for many years to come, well after the political negotiations have finished. It behooves us to work strenuously to provide possible models of how this could occur. We want especially to formulate this process to truly respond to the human needs expressed on all sides.

One of the key elements in this endeavor is for the peace process to be maximally inclusive. In one way or another, every subgroup within the conflict needs to become a part of the solution, now or even after the political settlements have been reached. There is a tendency in peace processes to be satisfied with bringing majority groups on both sides to the table. But "the table" of peace is often overturned, in the long view of history (which is the most important one), by precisely those groups who have not been invited to that table. Often a group considered a minority, such as Sephardim in Israel, are deliberately left out of important social change, precisely because they are a feared group whose power is growing. But such cases reflect simple cultural prejudice.

In inter-religious peacemaking in Israel, there is a tendency for some Jews and Muslims to deal exclusively with Christians and others to precisely exclude Christians! The Christian presence in the Arab/Israeli conflict is complex. On the one hand, Western culture, and specifically modes of peacemaking, are dominated by Christian and especially Protestant styles of interaction. Thus, I have critiqued earlier the easy conflation of certain Christian notions of reconciliation with Western efforts at intervention in the Middle East, and, in general, methods of conflict resolution. On the other hand, there is an important minority of Israeli Christian Arabs and Palestinians who must form a vital element of any conflict resolution in the Middle East. Viewed as extensions of the dominant Western order, which brutalized Jews and Muslims at various times, Christian Arabs are seen as part of a dominant order. But the reality is that *they* are the minority. As with Jews in Europe, the minority makes up for their vulnerability by emphasizing education, financial stability, and political power where possible. Thus, they become even more suspect to the majority. This explains much about the disastrous struggles occurring in Nazereth and Bethlehem between Muslims and Christians.

There are reasons on both sides, Jewish and Muslim, to exclude Christians from consciousness. In both cases hidden subconflicts make this tempting psychologically. But anytime one group is singled out for irrelevance in the process of relationship building, the peacemaking process deteriorates and the peacemakers displace conflict rather than resolve it. Clearly, there are historical reasons that both Jews and Muslims would like to wish away the presence of Christians. But this will solve nothing in the long run, despite the fact that the majority of the combatants in this case are Jewish and Muslim.

What we have here is a spectacular effort to sidestep difficult encounters and the hard realities of power sharing between the Abrahamic families. It is not easy to convene all three faiths in a single room in Israel, for a variety of reasons, despite the best of efforts by some broadminded people. It is much easier to make alliances one over against the other. The most obvious alliance is an Arab-Muslim and Arab-Christian one against the Jewish community, in that the ethnic Arab-Israeli conflict over land and power overshadows the religious conflict. But it does not end there. There is also a subtle tendency of some Jews to be more comfortable with Christians while others actually distance themselves as much as possible from them, wanting nothing to do with Christianity or Christians. It is conceivable that there could be a Muslim/Jewish alliance over against Christians and the West, and I have seen some evidence of this. It is vital, therefore, to think about what every community has to offer to the peace process, but also what injuries and memories they bring to the table. Only in this way can we move forward without displacing hatreds onto third parties rather than healing those hatreds.

Every Abrahamic community has vital contributions to make to our understanding and practice of conflict resolution. Despite my critique earlier of Protestant notions of unilateral forgiveness gestures, for example, it is clear that there are some parallels to sources in the other Abrahamic traditions. There is no question that there is great power to the unilateral offer of forgiveness, certainly in Christian cultures, but possibly in others as well. We simply do not know enough to dismiss it out of hand in non-Christian contexts, or contexts that are mixed. We do not know how it would affect relationships in a non-Christian context, but that does not mean it should not be considered as a possible path of intercultural conflict resolution.

The Christian idea of love of enemy does not have exact counterparts in the other traditions, but we have noted the importance of care for enemy and gestures toward the enemy that have clear biblical roots (Exodus 23, for example) as well as later elaborations in the other Abrahamic traditions. Aid for an enemy and love of an enemy are very closely related, and could at the very least form a bridge of shared practices, which could in turn, be useful in building pan-Abrahamic methods of peacebuilding, as long as the nuanced differences are respected.

To take one example, the religiously inspired suspension of judgment of others, referred to earlier, found in many Abrahamic sources, is an important tool of conflict resolution that could strengthen a cross-religious encounter, if it is framed in terms of shared religious values. This could become, in the hands of good trainers, an important skill to impart to in all Abrahamic communities. In some sense the commitment to that skill is already sanctioned, the comfort with it as a fulfillment of one's spiritual life has already been embedded. It merely needs to be elicited as well as consciously and skillfully integrated into the relationship-building process of erstwhile enemies.

The Christian notion of being reborn in Christ and thus attaining grace certainly has no parallel in Judaism and Islam, by definition of the identities. However, we would be remiss not to note the importance of new self-identity and character transformation as a path of reconciliation, and the striking parallel that we can see between this Christian notion of rebirth and old rabbinic paths of *teshuva* that we outlined earlier. Of course, the metaphysical frame in which Christian transformation is characterized is obviously completely different and in opposition. But the psychological substrata of the metaphysical constructs are remarkably similar. In other words, the notion that a newness of identity and self-understanding is critical to repentance, along with a qualitatively new relationship with others, is very similar within the Abrahamic faiths. This has clear ramifications for the construction of inter-religious peace processes, or general, public peace processes whose character and framing must appeal to a broad spectrum of Abrahamic communities.

For example, Shimon Peres and others may be onto something in talking repeatedly about "a new Middle East." He is trying to shift the self-image of a region, to create new possibilities and a new Middle East identity in which war and weapons are not at the core of the national ethos of the countries of the region. On the other hand, his exclusive focus on a new identity in terms of economic prosperity could make his vision suspect. He could be suspected of offering a thinly veiled effort to create a Middle East identity dominated economically by Israel, with the Arab cultural identity of the region wiped out. There is no question that the most frightening aspect of new identities is the possibility of obliterating the old identity, and the suspicion of the agenda of those who want you to take on a new identity. Furthermore, the replacement of military might with economic might is a tempting shift, but one that favors small elites and more developed countries. It is not surprising therefore that some may suspect Peres' motives.

New national identities bereft of war must be able to appeal to the widest possible community, not just the economically ambitious, and here I would argue that Peres' vision is actually too limited and, therefore, more suspect. It needs to be more explicitly inclusive of all peoples of the region, as well as a fulfillment of more than just economic human needs. The language of new identity is also very threatening to many people for good reason. Utilizing religious language of new identity as a peacemaking gesture would make many nonreligious citizens suspicious. "Who benefits from all these efforts to create new identities?" they would and should ask. The Jewish repentance (*ba'al teshuva*) movement is one such example. Viewed by Orthodox Jews as a renaissance, but by secular Israelis as a cynical rabbinic effort to gain control of Israel, it easily becomes a political football. Confronting basic questions of identity is necessary in deeper methods of conflict resolution. But the question of new identity must be broached in the widest possible venue, so that it does not become yet another method of oppression, which is the last thing the Middle East needs.

This relates closely to the question of the identity of the Abrahamic family (families), the central metaphor of the book. Clearly, the hope of this book is that this identity and this family are still evolving. They will have to evolve in a way that respects the individual identities of constituent members and yet still aspires to larger senses of shared values, unity and higher purpose. As an extension of this argument, it is undoubtedly true that there can and really must be differences in methods of peacemaking and conflict resolution between the Abrahamic religions and the cultures that they inform. However, there clearly are many values and practices that they do share and that can form the basis of common methods of trust building. Furthermore, greater awareness of their different sensibilities, through cross-religious study and communication, will yield a greater sensitivity to the scenarios where the differences are likely to arise. It is likely, for example, that certain Protestant traditions may emphasize the grace of God or spirit of God entering their lives and only then embarking on the road of peacemaking, while Jewish and Islamic peacemakers will be more likely to emphasize shared moral values and laws, with greater suspicion of "God talk."

Recently I heard just such a review of an encounter in Jerusalem. A non–Middle Eastern Christian group came to Jerusalem and set up a meeting in which they "bore witness" as to how God personally entered their lives and changed them, and only by this change do they now have the strength to be peacemakers. This struck some Jewish listeners as odd, not really appealing to their inner lives at all. The "God talk," the need to use peacemaking as evidence of God's role in the world, does not speak to them nor frame the entire experience for them. It is not even clear that the average Arab Christian in Israel would approach the experience of peacemaking from this perspective, based on my own interviews. Nevertheless, this represents one piece of the puzzle of global inter-religious peacemaking, and it should not be disparaged but rather circumscribed.

Just because the Jews listening to the Christian group were uncomfortable with the "witnessing," having very bad historical memories of how that missionary style was used so many times historically to humiliate Jews publicly,[67] it is not that they have never experienced similar feelings of God's guidance leading them to lives dedicated to peace. In other words, sharing ways of peacemaking between the Abrahamic faiths often evokes strong memories of injury, in addition to reflecting conflicting styles of interaction. However, if we were to talk about this openly, we might discover more in common than we think. But it requires very honest communication about what we like in the other, as well as what offends us.

The key seems to be that each tradition, and many individuals within each tradition, should be allowed to express reconciliation in their own cultural/religious patterns but should open themselves to the possibility of parallel efforts in the other traditions. Each community will be looking, however, for authenticity in the adversary's efforts at peacemaking, real change, trust building, new relationships, and righting wrongs of the past. All sides, whatever their methods, must face detailed acknowledgment of past and present realities, as well as a commitment to the future each side envisions. Time (past, present, and future) encompasses our identity, and no method of reconciliation can avoid any of its constituent parts.

In sum, we have explored the various parameters and uses of reconciliation in the traditions of Judaism, Islam, and Christianity. It is clear that there is potential in all three religions for this phenomenon to prove important in processes of conflict resolution. In chapter 7, we will address the problem and challenge of concrete implementation in the context of the Arab/Israeli conflict and official peace processes and final settlements.

The Use of the Word and Its Limits

Dialogue as Peacemaking

As we move more deeply into practical methods of conflict resolution in the Arab/Israeli context, a word is in order about "words," the use of language as a means of conflict resolution. The use of the word as the principal means of peacemaking is ubiquitous in Western culture, at least among those who consider themselves peacemakers and diplomats. But this is a fundamentally flawed method in that it does not provide an accurate picture of ways in which, in fact, human beings reconcile and make peace, when they manage to do so.

Neither in practice nor in principle do words open us up to the vast range of possibilities of internal change in us, nor to how words transform our relationships with adversaries. Western cultures, and in parallel form, Abrahamic religions, are excessively wordy and textual. We must analyze what we have done till now and then make recommendations for the future. This should not be misunderstood as a broadside against any use of the word. Nothing is categorical here but rather inclusive, an argument for what is missing, not an either/or formula. Furthermore, the use of the word is indispensable in all peacemaking when we come to the stage of negotiations, that is, once people find themselves willing and ready to come to "the table" to outline their differences and to agree on future arrangements.

There are subsets of the use of the word that include, for example, its use for written treaty, and in the context of dialogue, and for study and training in conflict resolution. Dialogue is considered often to be the main or only means of conflict resolution. Many people use "dialogue" as the equivalent of peacemaking and conflict resolution. But that is a mistake.

Even as I write this, I am reminded that whenever we have a dispute with my very verbal 4 year old we remind her to use her words, especially when she is very upset and starts to throw things or hit or whine and cry. The truth is that, to the degree that one can get either enemies—or 4 year olds—to use their words, one will move closer to peace and away from confrontation. But one cannot always rely on this. Most 4 year olds happen to be less articulate than my daughter at this stage and even she has many moods that go well beyond what she is capable of articulating. Most of us do. Most enemies cannot or will not articulate their true feelings. Either it is beyond their present capacity, or they feel it is really too shameful, like deep envy, or shame at the collective humiliation of one's group. Conducting a war is far more virile and honorable than articulating in words one's envy for an enemy group.

In the final stages of conflict processes, many progressive people in the West envision reconciliation and apology. Here again the parallels with children's behavior are instructive. What comes naturally to my daughter after she has hurt us in some way is to saddle up next to us, looking for physical affection, or, alternatively, to explicitly act as if nothing is wrong, hoping to go back to the old and good engagement. But we are the ones who train her in such situations, several times a day it seems, to use the word "sorry" before resuming good relations. She, naturally uses emotional acts, however, like affection, to reconcile, or symbolic actions, like a return to normal play. These symbolic acts embody her way of saying "I'm sorry." Which alternative is better? Are we training her for something superior, the use of the word for reconciliation, or are we ignoring her natural capacities in this regard and failing to work with her natural means of ending a state of anger?

These questions are critical. On one level, whatever comes naturally to a child, or to a culture, might be preferred, but this is impossible to know once we reach the infinite complexity of human diversity, especially in multicultural contexts. Then the question of which method is better becomes unanswerable due to the infinite diversity of reactions, and what becomes paramount, perhaps, is access to as wide a range of means of reconciliation as possible. The maximum range is necessary, because the infinite complexity of human encounter across genders, religions, races, and countries requires great elasticity of engagement.

Even with my 4 year old, elasticity of method is preferable. We should listen as carefully to the way she reconciles as we expect her to listen to us. Of course, we are the adults/teachers/models. But, without deferring completely to Rousseau's prejudice against natural states, an accurate view of life acknowledges that children are our teachers also, because we have often become flawed as adults in our ability to truly listen to the other.

Missing the cues that the adversary, the alienated other, is trying to send us is a profoundly understudied phenomenon. It cuts to the heart of the persistence of many family and international conflicts. For example, if one party expects words and the other expects emotions, one expects symbols and the other deeds, one expects rational negotiation and the other expects apology, then we have the makings of conflict perpetuation, and even escalation, with the intervention of verbally obsessed peacemakers who do not understand this problem. If the peacemakers do not train themselves to watch all nonverbal cues, to see the depths and the power of human symbolism, sometimes conscious and sometimes unconscious, then they will miss the most important opportunities for transforming relationships.

Let us turn to the example of Falkland Islands War. Why was there so much miscommunication between Argentina and Great Britain during that war? Great Britain made unilateral gestures that were ignored or distrusted by the Argentinians, while the Argentinians engaged in what they saw as healthy negotiations but that insulted the British in the process.[1] Some have argued that these processes failed due to timing conflicts, which I agree are very important. What stage the conflict is in is crucial, although either side may find itself experiencing the stages of the conflict differently. But I would argue that a hidden cause here is the expectations of each side, the way in which positive actions are symbols rooted in the combatants' culture, and the forms of reconciliation that they prefer or require, either consciously or unconsciously.

In the case of the Falklands war, a predominantly Protestant society, from a cultural point of view, was at war with a predominantly Catholic one. The Catholic side considered hard bargaining and detailed bilateral offers to be a good sign, while the Protestants saw it as a bad sign, a symptom of untrustworthiness. The Protestant side saw unilateral gestures of good will, acts of unconditional grace, if you will, as a good sign, while the Catholic side viewed them with suspicion. We have only one adversary here for whom hard negotiations and the use of the word are good and useful in and of themselves.

Could this be related to old differences within Christianity about attitudes to law and to unilateral gestures of grace? Could the Protestants be offended when their gestures of good will, their acts of grace, are rebuffed, but they find hard, legalistic bargaining and contractual dispute to be in bad faith? Catholicism, closer to Islam and Judaism, has depended heavily, historically speaking, on law and complex treaty negotiation. Law, canon law, is an extension of the inherent value of the Holy Spirit as it is expressed through the church. Furthermore, hard bargaining was a time-honored means of negotiating realms of temporal power in which the church was a key player. But Protestantism, in protest against the "legalism," ceremony, and ritual of the church, not to mention its corruptions by temporal power, found redemption not in law and its casuistic debates, nor in hard bargaining over power (which was properly left to the princes of Europe, not the church), but in acts or words of grace.

What emerges from Chris Mitchell's analysis of the Falklands war are some universal lessons about gestures that may be suspect in conflict situations. For example, suspicion of the motives for conciliatory gestures is a fairly universal reaction in situations of intense conflict. However, the definition of what constitutes and what does not constitute a conciliatory gesture is much more culture-specific.

There is no indication—in my experience of cultures at least—that a "tit-for-tat" offer of de-escalation or confidence-building is, by definition, less conciliatory than a unilateral gesture. On the contrary, in some hard-bargaining cultures a good tit-for-tat offer ("if you do X, I will do Y") resonates as more honorable, more tangible, and more trustworthy. On the other hand, in every culture and every situation of conflict, everyone is worried about mixed motivations. I am not convinced that the strategy of the "Grand Gesture" is universally efficacious. More research needs to go into the reactions of a broad range of people and cultures to grand, unilateral gestures.

Let me make one thing very clear about my audacious generalizations here about Protestant and Catholic culture. And it is the case that unfair generalization is the great danger of cultural conflict analysis. I want to emphasize that in practice plenty of Catholics think in terms of grace, and plenty of Protestant denominations became heavily committed over time to biblical law and other laws of their own making. Furthermore, the differences here may originate in British culture and Argentinian culture, not necessarily their Protestant and Catholic origins.

My major point, however, relates not to the actual, objective cultural reality, but to the particular evil we *expect* from the enemy other, and the good we expect from them in moments of peacemaking, and what we offer them in return. We are particularly prone to generate conflict by our stereotypical expectations of and sensitivity to what *we think* are the worst qualities of our enemy. Conversely, when reconciling with an enemy—an extremely difficult moment for the human pscyhe—we offer what we consider to be our best qualities of prosocial engagement, our ideal selves, and utterly reject the methods and character of what we perceive to be our enemies' worst traits. Most important, we expect our enemies to do exactly the same thing. But here is the catch! We expect them to engage in peaceful gestures that reflect *our own* highest selves, not theirs. And here the tragic failings in communication occur.

Let us take an example. In repeated interviews and social engagements between Arabs and Jews, some at very high levels of government, I have noticed a single pattern. Arabs tend to offer honor and *expect* honor as a conciliatory gesture in initial meetings, and Jews see the same honoring as far less important, or something that would be part of the culmination of the relationship instead. In fact, the Jewish members often miss the honoring cues altogether. Conversely, the Jews repeatedly expect that issues of security and life are the cornerstone, even assumption, of the discussion, including the oft-repeated "right of Israel to exist." They consider this basic to any initial contact with enemies who they expect will minimally agree not to kill. Then they are shocked and hurt when in fact that assumption is not shared. The right of Israel to exist is considered part of the endgame by the Arabs in these encounters, not the initial gesture. Thus the Jews miss the precious nonverbal gestures involving honor and dignity as they receive them improperly and do not reciprocate, while the Arabs miss the critically important existential needs expressed by Jews. There are old cultural reasons for both of these tendencies and prioritizations of values.

This two-way failure is also related in complex—and non-cultural—ways to the fact that Israelis represent the "haves" in the standard conflict formula, while Palestinians embody the "have-nots." The "haves" always play the role of prioritizing the sacredness of life, civility, and peace, acting rather condescendingly to their adversaries who do not live up to such values. The "have-nots" always play the role of the justified fighters to attain what has been taken from them. Thus, cultural differentiations mentioned earlier interact in complex ways with the role-playing inherent in conflict asymmetry. Both of these elements yield inherent miscommunication and disappointment at the moments of encounter.

Another kind of Arab-Jewish interaction went on for years before the PLO changed its stated position toward Israel. That involved Israelis eager to speak, interact, and argue with Arabs and Palestinians, while the latter in principle would refuse, even at international gatherings devoted to the subject, to look the Israelis in the eye and speak to them directly. This was taken by rejectionist Jews, and even by peacemakers, as proof positive that Jewish existence in the Middle East would never be accepted under any terms. Without a basic commitment to the value of their lives, to their existence, there was nothing to talk about. Palestinians saw their refusal to directly engage as a response to the fundamental denial of Palestinian national existence by the State of Israel. In the case of Syrian-Israeli negotiations of 1999–2000, the fundamental divide over cultural needs continued. In general, the Arab side is fixated completely on land and all the honor and dishonor that is implied by its gain or loss in war. They want the land.

The Israeli side centralizes the question of security and normalization of relations, which for them are subsets of the existential question, the question of the life and death of the new nation—or of the old Jewish nation that has repeatedly experienced genocide. The latter concern really is at the heart of their warfare and peacemaking. They want normal relations that they can trust, something that has eluded Jews as a minority in hostile majoritarian environments for thousands of years.

What so many Palestinians need and demand of Israelis is dignity, and what so many Israelis crave and need is a long-term feeling of safety, of a safe haven. Both sides cognitively and emotionally seem to misunderstand the others' needs and are bitter about the deprivation of their own needs. Both adversaries (maybe all adversaries?) are seeking a secure home. The Arabs' overriding concern with home concerns what they have missed the most, the dignity of home and the actual ownership of ancestral lands, while the Jewish side craves what they have most missed, multigenerational safety from murder. Both adversaries thus misunderstand actions, symbols, gestures, and guarantees that the other needs the most from them. The conflict appears on the surface to center mostly on contested land, which can only be subject to arduous compromise and division—there is only a limited quantity of this scarce resource. But it is much worse than this, and also, at the same time, filled with potential solutions that go beyond negotiated compromises.

Herein lies the tragic essence of intercultural conflict, but also its supreme potential. Dignity, honor, compassion, the experience of safety, a sense of a safe home or an honorable home—the fulfillment of these needs is potentially in infinite supply. Is there any limit to how much honor I can give you if I want to? What does it really cost me? Is there any necessary limit on how many actions I can take to make you feel safe with me? How much do gestures of compassion cost? Not much in terms of tangible, scarce resources. And yet, these free resources, of infinite supply, are the hardest of all for these two peoples to offer each other. It is far easier to fight. It is far easier to negotiate in a hard way over the very limited amount of land than it is psychologically to offer the enemy dignity, safety, or a feeling of home. But this, I argue, is the more profound task, and the one that clears the way for verbal, rationalistic bargaining to actually yield results that are truly lasting.

The conclusions are clear: (1) Words and dialogue must not be the only path of reconciliation that we explore or that we train enemies to heed and; (2) we must be open to a variety of possible paths of reconciliation, and open to the injuries sustained by either side when their gestures are ignored and not reciprocated. Yes, clarification of these missed opportunities can and must go on through the use of language. But correctives can also occur when enemies, made aware of these processes, make up for the failures by reciprocating nonverbal gestures, even when these do not come naturally to their own culture. In other words, in addition to training diplomats and peacemakers in dialogue and negotiation, they must be trained to detect other gestures of reconciliation—actions and deeds that mean much more, and are trusted much more, than words. They must train themselves to detect deleterious processes of engagement that result from missed symbolic and nonverbal opportunities, and to invent strategies to consciously align or engage the culturally and religiously familiar conciliatory paths of adversary groups.

Religion is a fabulous resource that, if studied carefully, turns out to house many of these cultural peculiarities of peacemaking and reconciliation. It helps us see what we missed and why our best efforts are failing. It houses deep instincts of a culture, *even* when that culture is mostly nonreligious. It is a chronicle of the past cultural instincts of a people and thus provides us with a blueprint to pass beyond alienation, even in the most bitter conflicts.

That there are many dialogue groups in Israel and Palestine today is an exciting and growing phenomenon that has had a steady and increasing impact on Israeli attitudes. The increased commitment, decade after decade, of an ever-increasing portion of the Israeli public to Palestinian independence is evidence of this, even if a tragic disconnection remains between this growing commitment and an actual engagement with the conditions of both Arab-Israeli life and Palestinian living conditions.

On the whole, many more relationships are developing between Arab Israelis and Jewish Israelis than between Jews and those Palestinians beyond the Green Line. There are reasons on both sides for this, and I personally would like to see a proliferation of encounter groups across the Green Line that would be extended to every subgroup of the cultures, including groups explicitly for health professionals, psychologists, businesspeople, religious leaders, women professionals, women who are primarily caretakers of children, the children themselves, and many other groups.

As I have stated, however, dialogue is only one subset of the potential of human reconciliation, favoring those who are verbal and aggressive in group encounters. It favors the better educated, and in my training experience, fixation on the exchange of words frustrates and disempowers those who engage in reconciliation through gestures, symbols, emotions, and shared work. But it can and does contribute to strategic work toward a more just and comprehensive peace. Much of this dialogue work becomes overshadowed and even thwarted globally when the "official" dialogues take over. The latter, while necessary at some point, are deeply disempowering to the vast majority who have no say in the process. We should expect this counterproductive disempowerment as an element in any progress toward official peace but learn to help people counteract the deleterious effects. Whatever the value of dialogue, official or otherwise, it is only one part of peacemaking. Furthermore, the ups and downs of the official dialogue process tend to hold everyone captive, imprisoned really.

Imagine yourself, for example, in a dialogue group. Around you are conditions of absolute misery. On top of this, others are negotiating for you in "more important" venues of dialogue, whether you asked them to or not, bargaining with their interests in mind, without your input. How much value can you bring yourself to place on your own efforts to dialogue? How much of a price are you paying for this in your community?

But what if what you are doing is helping people, for example? What if you are doing something concrete to improve the situation? And let us say your adversaries are partners with you in this. Do you pay a price with your rejectionists for this cooperation also? Yes. Do you feel insignificant and a sense of futility in the face of the more powerful who are negotiating? Not really, because you are actually doing something where they may not be, engaging in gestures and concrete actions that every day improve someone's life. And when you do it with your enemies, you are also creating some reconciliation where there was none. You are not only not disempowered by the official dialogue, you are doing better work than they are, making more progress, and the ups and downs of their negotiation affect you far less. You are culturally in a much deeper place, and much more independent of the vagaries of power relations.

It must also be stated here that in my years of experience with training people from every religion and every region the basic sociological reality remains constant in terms of the dynamics of dialogic encounter. The same is true of the many workshops between enemies that I have witnessed. The more people in a room around a table, the more lies are spoken, and the more distorted the presentation of self, the more tribalistic the psychology of adversaries. With every decrease in the number of participants, more truth is revealed, more emotional honesty, trust, risks taken, and depictions of the past become more frank, visions of the future more creative, and people represent themselves rather than some artificial construct of their group. The best of all seem to be one-on-one encounters, and relationships that develop between adversaries in informal settings.

One simply cannot escape notice of the progressive way in which larger and larger groups of human beings tend to behave in ways that they themselves cannot control. And the less individual control, the more aggression. The far end of the spectrum here is a state in which aggression and enemy psychology reach a level of mass hypnosis and a hysteria of other-directed rage. One can see this occasionally played out in European soccer events. But the meeting of warriors on the battlefield is the most ancient and perennial example. And I have seen this progressive level of aggression play itself out in many an Arab-Jewish encounter. The greater the number of people, the worse the encounter, particularly because the mediators were totally unprepared for the mob psychology occasioned by large groups. Conversely, the smaller the encounter, the fewer the skills required by the mediators, and the more chance of success.[2] This too militates in the direction of seeking alternatives to dialogue in peacemaking.

Education for peace and justice is also based on the use of the word, but not in a dialogic encounter. Thus, the power of words and verbal exchange is central to education, but as a peacemaking tool education has a different set of advantages and strengths. A good example is the fabulous work of the Open House in Ramle, founded by Yehezkel Landau, one of the most important Israeli religious peacemakers. A co-director is Michael Fanous, a very talented and courageous Israeli Palestinian. Yehezkel Landau has articulated in many writings a creative theology of Jewish peacemaking. The school, founded by Yehezkel and his wife Dalia, is a fascinating experiment in many ways, serving the Palestinian population as well as Jewish families. Most important, it serves as a bridge through education, programming, and the shared concern for children. Yehezkel himself is among those Israelis finding themselves in a middle no-man's land. He is religious and thus in tension with the majority of religious Jews who have opposed peace, and he has not received sufficient support from the secular peacemakers who have never found it useful or comfortable to accept the fact that a Jew can be religious and a peacemaker.

Secular education and peacemaking is the work of the Adam Institute, which focuses on education for democracy, although they too have become more interested in aligning democratic values with indigenous, religious values. In general, the Abraham Fund and the New Israel Fund have supported numerous efforts to use education as a peacemaking device. But, as I have stated numerous times, religious efforts in this regard have had a harder time being accepted, due to the cognitive dissonance that many liberal Jews feel at the possibility of religion contributing constructively to peacemaking. They thus fulfill their own prophecies by making it so hard for religious projects to get funded. Thus, the religious and secular subconflict interacts with and deepens the interethnic conflict between Israelis and Arabs.

Education uses words for peacemaking but not through dialogue around a circle or at "the table." Another example of this has been the interesting work of those who have pioneered intensive textual study and in-depth understanding of religious experience between Jewish and Christian intellectuals. This exchange is also being extended to Islam, aimed not specifically at the Arab/ Israeli conflict, but pioneering in the depths of understanding it creates.

Several Israeli interfaith organizations have moved in this direction as well, sharing numerous study sessions on each others' religions, and Yehuda Stolov has worked brilliantly and tirelessly on these meetings with great success. Study appears to be a natural activity for Jews and Arabs trying to get to know each other and may, in fact, create much deeper bonds than do Western styles of dialogue. The text-centered reverence in Judaism and Islam is a likely cause of this successful mode of interaction, as well as the power and wonder of discovering shared values and traditions *before* one engages in difficult exchanges with adversaries about inflicted injuries. In fact, one could envision an indigenous Jewish-Islamic method of conflict resolution that engages in public joint study and appreciation, while the difficult exchanges on the conflict are reserved for intentional meetings in a very private space. This maximizes the possibility of honesty but minimizes the possibility of dishonor and shame for the respective religious traditions, a formula that may work best for conservative traditions in the region.

The deep resentments and competing mythologies of the Abrahamic families are an important underlying cause of the persistence of the Arab/Israeli conflict, as we have seen earlier, as well as the historical Western confrontation with Islam and the Middle East. The patterns of study just discussed sidestep, if only for a time, those ancient resentments and competitions. They create a temporary but sacred time of reconciliation, and temporary suspension of judgment. The theme of oasis is crucial here, as it has always been as a first stage of peace, and it may resonate with the geography and psychology of desert peoples. As a result, there are people participating in these exchanges who start mulling over a new understanding of these ancient jealousies, and possibly new ways to envision monotheism, the Abrahamic family, and the possibilities of coexistence.[3]

Such exchanges, at least in their public face, often veer away from the most controversial subjects. But there is a unique way in which this is unfolding and yielding great benefits for peace and justice. It was surprising to me that in the winter of 2000 when so many Palestinian/Israeli dialogues fell apart that Stolov's inter-religious seminars inside Israel not only continued but seemed to become more intense a place of meeting with prominent people from both sides in attendance. Why was it not boycotted? Perhaps because from the beginning it was a place of honor and equality rather than one of pain and humiliation. They avoided politics but seemed to be building something deeper.

I have also been informed of more study on the sacredness of land, or the importance of Jerusalem that is evolving. In this vital and unique way religious people are beginning the process of valuating the enemy other's attachment to and care for the same sacred space. We must pay close attention here to these developments. Very religious people do not—and perhaps cannot—approach the enemy other in the same way that, say, a military general might, or a seasoned diplomat, or an attorney. Religious people may be, and are in their public lives, also generals and attorneys and diplomats. But in their religious personalities, in their deepest space of religious authenticity, a different mode of interaction may very well be necessary with the enemy other, or the competing Abrahamic monotheist. An inter-religious textual study on the sacredness of Jerusalem, a study of all the texts, traditions, metaphors and symbols of all peoples, in a respectful, nonbelligerent atmosphere, may be accomplishing what no dialogue or rational bargaining session ever could.

This may very well be setting the stage for future coexistence in Jerusalem in a way that no rational bargaining can accomplish right now. Furthermore, even if there are rational breakthroughs on these matters, the latter may only impact a limited elite, whereas the religious revisioning of sacred spaces can impact the existential orientation of millions of citizens. For this reason, while I sympathize with those pragmatists who worry that such interfaith exchanges are a smokescreen for inactivity, I disagree with them. Something extraordinary is happening here, and we could magnify this significantly if more people of influence on all sides will have the courage to support this engagement for the masses.

The discovery of study as a path of interfaith meeting and conflict resolution is an extraordinary development in conflict resolution practice, although it is still at an early stage of development, to be sure. This never would have come about in the United States or Europe, for example, despite the fact that the progressive cultures of the latter too often consider themselves the sole font of wisdom on peacemaking. It is true that in the Middle East all three Abrahamic faiths are evolving some very dangerous patterns of antimodernist fundamentalism. But new possibilities are emerging at the same time! It turns out, for example, that for legal and ritual reasons, interfaith prayer is a very problematic gesture for Islamic, Jewish, and Christian traditionalists, despite its revered status in Western circles of peacemaking. Shared prayer involves direct violations of old laws designed to maintain certain boundaries.

At the same time, study is a particularly sanctified practice in Judaism but has old roots in Islam and Christianity as well. There are those who prohibit study of Torah with non-Jews, however, for a variety of historical reasons, involving very bad experiences of use of information gained in shared study to attack the Jewish community or to infiltrate, misinterpret, and missionize forcibly—yet another disastrous injury.[4] Thus, this path will not be suitable for all religious Jews, although reassurances from the Christian community that the past will not be repeated could bring more people in. Those who do participate will accomplish important results in terms of inter-religious understanding. Of course, they will not do much to solve the questions of national boundaries or refugees, but that is not their purpose. All contact is good if it leads to informal relationships that expand the circles of those who come to know and understand the enemy beyond the destructive mythification of the other. Destructive mythification is only born in spaces of noncontact, adversarial contact, or ignorance. Such shared study, therefore, should be ongoing, and lead to or become a part of ongoing contact and relationship building at a deeper level. It really must yield new intimacies, such as mutual invitations to homes and meetings with families.

This kind of shared study, *not for the purposes of debate or conversion*, is an innovation in the history of monotheism that will engender a certain kind of healing and reconciliation for many deeply religious people. What I have observed in Israel is dependent upon an informal network of religious actors in Jerusalem, and other cities, who are quietly but courageously dedicating their lives to path-breaking and lonely innovations.

Those people who purposely situate themselves in a space where they can communicate with and display respect for the widest variety of religious actors are becoming themselves symbols of cultural and intercultural transformation. This is a unique kind of creation of space for peace, a subject I will address shortly. In this way singular people, or small bands of people, become an oasis of peace by their very nature and character, and by the way in which they interact with the broadest range of people in an utterly unique way, defying all enemy system boundaries.

One such person is Betsy or Batya Cohen-Kallus, her husband Menachem, as well as many of their friends. Betsy has spent much of her spiritual life on the Jewish Left in America, working for numerous progressive causes in Judaism's name. When she moved to Israel, she became more religiously observant. But contrary to those whose religious practice collapses into a tribal affiliation and a politically reactionary cocoon, Betsy has refused tribal affiliation. She manages to live a devoted religious life, together with her profoundly talented husband, also a peacemaker and a scholar of mysticism. Together they naturally traverse more religious and political worlds in a single week—within Judaism, and between other religions of Jerusalem—than most people attempt to traverse in a lifetime.

On the Arab side, Sufis such as Sheikh Abu Salah and his followers, both Jewish and Muslim, are pursuing an extraordinary range of relationships between enemy groups, all in the context of a variety of shared spiritual activities.

The Kalluses, the Landaus, several sheikhs and rabbis, and many other hidden people in Jerusalem and the land of Israel, from several religious traditions, have become, in their very style of social existence, metaphors of religious peacemaking in the midst of a deeply fragmented society and divided city. They embody in their own meetings, activities, and relationships a kind of peacemaking that goes beyond spoken or written words, and certainly beyond dialogue groups. Theirs is a kind of relationship building and maintenance of contacts that becomes, as far as I can see, a form of religious worship and devotion that is postmodern and ancient at the same time, an offering of supreme sacrifice as they risk every day their own religious status. In many ways, they are returning to many ancient prophetic visions of peace and simultaneously charting an unprecedented course for the monotheistic traditions. Many of them can meet in a single week with a Haredi rabbi and the leading Islamic authority in Jerusalem, with exclusively male groups and exclusively female groups, with both Palestinians and Israeli settlers on the West Bank, with feminists, and with ultra-Orthodox people.

This unique kind of peacemaking is not centered on dialogue processes, but relationships, even though dialogue is obviously an element in every encounter. It is a deeply religious model of love or care for the human being as such, but not in some abstract fashion of valuing humanity through policy choices. Rather, it is through the arduous discipline of perpetual personal contact with a wide variety of people with whom you may have serious differences.

Make no mistake, this spiritual discipline is immensely demanding. It is a way of creating space inside one's soul that makes one's personal interaction and one's daily lifestyle a kind of offering or sacrifice of peace. One's character, and the daily internal struggles with anger against others who are different or adversaries, becomes the blueprint of a world that is lived out every day in and through one's struggle to be a bond, to be the glue that bonds the world together. Sacred inner space and sacred outer space merge especially in Jerusalem and the Holy Land for these people, where every day raises the dramatic question of whether this space is a nightmare of religious disappointment or a dream come true.

One's inner and outer life become the battleground of those choices, and every day that one makes these bonds with the alienated other, one has created through one's own person, a taste of a future world of peace, justice, respect, and love. That world may only exist, in the interim, inside one's person. But that in itself becomes, and must be recognized as, a unique form of peacemaking that far surpasses dialogue and official programming in terms of spiritual depth. It is a compelling religious model in which one's life and character become an offering to peace, and therefore to God. And it can be contagious, depending on the valuation or ridicule from the rest of us. Needless to say, as the number of people committing themselves in this way increases arithmetically, their impact increases geometrically, due to the nature of their wide-ranging contacts.

Also emerging in Jerusalem is a shared spiritual journey between Jewish people with an intense spiritual orientation and devotees in the Islamic world of Sufism and Sufi masters. This has old roots as an Islamic-Jewish bridge. In general, there needs to be more study of the Islamic-Jewish relationship historically. Much of this has been buried by the deep antagonism set into stone of the Arab-Israeli conflict and its accompanying hagiography. In truth, there have been remarkable connections on a deep historical level that would be unthinkable in the Jewish-Christian relationship. The latter, whenever it was good, was buried so deeply by both sides that we have very little concrete admission of this historically. But we have elaborate demonizations embedded in venerated texts of Judaism and Christianity.

In as ultra-Orthodox a book as *Sefer Ta'ame ha-Minhagim*, for example, there is an extraordinary story reported, emerging out of Sephardic rabbinic literature, about an intense spiritual encounter between a sheikh and rabbi, and *not* on shared ethical values, but on the discovery of the deepest spiritual truths.[5] Of course, it is a friendly competition over who has the greatest font of truth. But the story resonates with mutual respect, if also a competitive spirit. Such a report, based on myth or reality, would be unthinkable in *haredi* literature, if framed as a story between a Christian priest and a rabbi. Yet the sheikh-rabbi encounter can make its way into a *haredi* Ashkenazi work that in many other places has unpleasant things to say about gentiles, presumably Christians.[6] One is tempted to conclude that the difference involves a straightforward rabbinic theological revulsion with the deification of Jesus, versus an approval of the absolute monotheism of Islam. But I suspect that it is deeply contextual as well, embedded and conditioned by lived experience and misery.

Spiritual spaces of meeting and understanding have less to do with theology and more to do with deep emotional reactions to the other that are often absorbed into religious mythical constructs. For various reasons, from the Gospel of John to Shylock to Fagin, the Jew was destined to be regarded as the antithesis of goodness in European Christian cultural mythology, and consequently, or correspondingly, the Christian becomes the hated and feared other in many a European rabbinic source. It is notoriously difficult to reverse such designations in deeply textual cultures—but not impossible.

I was educated at Columbia University, and I remember that many of my fellow Orthodox Jewish students were studying the same canon of liberal European authors. I marvel at how many of them went from the inherent liberalism of that course of study straight to the West Bank. Why? I often ask myself. I remember during those college years how often I was bitterly disappointed when a European author I had admired for years, canonized by the West as a font of wisdom, turned out to be an anti-Semite, casually dismissing the value and existence of my entire people. It drove me back to Yeshiva at one point. Maybe it drove them to the West Bank? Texts matter. The embedded messages we give to each other, culture to culture, often determine the fateful choices of our lives, and the tribal affiliations that we all choose.

As another example of subtle but profound differences even within conflicting groups on these matters, I would like to share a conversation with a Sephardi rabbi. Apparently, there is much to be unearthed about extensive cooperation between sheikhs and rabbis over many centuries in Syria. In fact, it has been reported to me by a Syrian rabbi that Jewish people used to consult Islamic authorities, and vice versa, on various issues of shared law! This would be unthinkable in the European context. Therefore, there are other, more profound but subtle emotive differences between the Jewish-Islamic and Jewish-Christian experience. For example, this same rabbi told me that many people in his community—and he is a seventh-generation rabbi—would use the Arabic-Islamic phrase that praises God, *allahu akbar*, "God is great." This shocked me, because I was familiar with that phrase, until I studied and taught world religions professionally, as the words that suicide terrorists would shout before they killed Jews. This is the only resonance that the phrase has for European Jews and most Westerners. How shocking and jarring it was for me to discover that a group of religious Jews, for *centuries*, were comfortable with these words as not only a benign phrase, but something that they would use themselves as a religious devotional phrase! In other words, the very words that strike fear and loathing inside the heart of European Jews are, or were, actually a classic interfaith bridge, a Jewish-Islamic bridge, in much the same way that talk of peace and justice are inter-faith bridges in liberal religions of the United States.

Such bridging suggests that the healing that we seek between cultures lie hidden from view, waiting for the skilled listener to elicit the language and modes of relationship that once existed. And the more authentic and older the bridge, the more that traditionalists, as well as liberals, can cross it to discover the alien other, without feeling that they are betraying the venerated past.

As we continue on the political level to press for peace and justice in the Israeli-Palestinian conflict, one option that many will take, perhaps in desperation, is a kind of cultural merging of religious traditions. There are some small but fascinating examples of people in Jerusalem who are now freely mixing the metaphors of Judaism and Islam, through the precedent of Sufism. In the months of the Al Aqsa Intifada in 2000 up to the present, this group was busy chanting near the Temple Mount, every Friday, alternating between chants of Shalom and Salaam. They were often joined by passersby, never assaulted, even by the ultra-Orthodox, and usually averaged about thirty people a week.

This kind of new interaction presents some interesting opportunities and challenges. On the one hand, many will be fascinated by what is discovered in the process of learning so much from a culture that was considered the enemy just a short time before. Some will discover a home in a kind of religious syncretism, for Israel is filled with people experimenting religiously. But it will also send monotheistic traditionalists of Judaism and Islam running for cover, and there could be significant backlash. The latter could hurt the interests of long-term peace and coexistence. Just as an example, when I recounted to a rather moderate Islamic scholar in the United States—committed to Arab-Israeli peace, by the way—that I was aware of a number of Israeli Jews and Muslims who were dancing the Sufi dances together, she quickly retorted, with a look of alarm, "That is very dangerous!".

As I have stated before, boundaries of identity are crucial to most human beings, and comprise a major cause of conflict. Therefore, it is logical to assume that for most people the dissolution of boundaries is not a way to defuse their conflict-generating behavior and psychological disposition. It is far better to help them find ways to make their boundaries less severe, less based on psychological barbed wire and more rooted in benign greenery, more subject to bridges and visits and less oriented to demonizing what is beyond one's borders. There are innumerable historical precedents, whereas the utopian dreams of a unified society where everyone shares the same beliefs and practices have virtually no precedent. But there is also a demonic cousin, in the many genocides inflicted while someone attempted to create such utopias.

While I celebrate those spiritual seekers who find wisdom in numerous religious traditions—and I am one of them—we must devise for the majority a way to cope with boundaries and religious identity. Thus, in Jerusalem, and in Israel and Palestine in general, we will have to work on multiple tracks at once to create the bridges between traditional cultures. First of all, the informal, secret talks between ultrareligious leadership on both sides should be continued, but formalized. The participants should arrange not to act as if everything is normal and fine, which it is not. This would undermine their credibility with their communities. Rather, they should engage in peace negotiations and treaty creation following the methods used by the national political structures. Of course, each will have to subnegotiate with their national government in such a way that their efforts augment the national processes, rather than undermine them.

In the late 1990s through 2002, it seems to me that these informal contacts between Jewish and Arab leadership have played a vital if secret role, especially by preventing deterioration of relations during difficult crises. Whatever the role, however, the contacts have been limited in two ways. First, they have been limited to religious leadership and have left unaffected the hostility of the religious communities as a whole. Second, these contacts have been dominated by the ultrareligious on both sides. It is true that a number of dialogue groups have many religious Jewish members who should be described as modern or liberal Orthodox. But this still limits the potential of this relationship building process, because most Israelis and many Palestinians should not be considered fervently religious, and many are certainly anticlerical. Thus, if clerics dominate or exclusively control inter-religious work, then they will live in peace, not the rest of the population. Worse, a great danger that many secular Israelis and Palestinians fear, justifiably, is that once they have eliminated war and occupation, the two states may become dominated by clerical authorities who neither represent them nor respect their lifestyle. Some of those people are antireligious and will therefore have to be engaged in peacemaking through the numerous secular efforts. But others, though religious, are more liberal or anticlerical, and they, as well as the secularists, should not be confronted with a religious peacemaking process that threatens them with a disenfranchised future. It is vital for the health of both states that there be more than one track of religious peacemaking. I doubt whether clerics on either side will sit with the liberals in their community, or with the women's groups.

It may be that ultrareligious interfaith peacemaking processes should move ahead in one track, and everyone else on another. The desire to merge all of this under one roof will hurt peacemaking, creating hidden tyrannies in the cause of peace. Better to let many bridges be extended simultaneously, as inefficient as this appears. Furthermore, it is vital that secularists inside and outside the governments do not benightedly abet a tyrannization of inter-religious peacemaking to pigeonhole religious culture. Certain secularists would like only ultrareligious figures to dominate certain peace processes precisely to discredit religion as such! This is an old tactic in Israel, from the earliest days, of making religion an irrelevant antiquity for most Israelis by placing all authority in the hands of religious leadership that would alienate most of the population, a sad collusion of left and right that has impoverished Israeli culture. This is a problem in general in the Middle East, though with different parameters in each country. An authentic peace process that truly transforms the cultural and religious foundations of conflict cannot be hijacked by such parochial political tactics. It must be as broad-based and inclusive as possible.

I feel compelled to conclude with a pessimistic assessment of dialogue based on words, certainly when it comes to the most fundamentalist representatives in the Abrahamic communities. Much good is being accomplished by many representatives of the communities as we speak, but for the most conservative or militant members of each Abrahamic community, it is not clear to me that dialogue through words, in the problem-solving workshop scenario in particular, has any potential. But I would be glad to be proved wrong over time.

There is some evidence, as I have shown, that private, confidential meetings, especially very small ones—maybe even one-on-one—that are governed by a spirit of intensive respect for the religious world of the other have some potential. They might, if accompanied by profound levels of personal honor, be able to transform relationships and discourage religious violence, even among the most militant. We should support and facilitate this. I do argue, however, that the careful use of symbol and deeds deemed to be righteous can have a powerful healing and peacemaking effect even among the most conservative and least educated members of any religious community. More important, it can affect large numbers of people relatively quickly. The latter is a crucial crux and challenge of crisis politics and conflict prevention. It is also particularly relevant to the unusual level of popular volatility in the Middle East situation. Let us turn now to this discussion.

8

Ritual Civility, Moral Practices of Interpersonal Exchange, and Symbolic Communication

There is one fundamental advantage to cultural processes of human social change, and one fundamental advantage to Abrahamic processes of change. The former expresses itself in an unabashed embrace of and dependence upon nonrational ritual and formalism as a way of transforming outer behavior as well as internal states of being. The latter expresses itself in an unabashed commitment to and dependence upon ethics and morality as a motivation of human behavior that has specific sanction by the highest sacred authorities, both human and divine. Cultures affected by the Palestinian-Israeli conflict share both of these characterizations.

The Abrahamic and cultural processes of change have, however, been completely neglected by elite diplomacy and conflict resolution efforts in the Palestinian/Israeli conflict, but only on a conscious level, I would argue. I have no doubt that one can find ritualistic and symbolic processes at work in both the successes and failures of secular, high-level negotiations. But they are rarely acknowledged and thus lose their usefulness in terms of replicability and expansion to larger populations. While I applaud high-level processes, they are always vulnerable to rejectionist terrorism precisely because they disempower rather than empower, exclude rather than include. Thus, the terrorist knows that he has to do relatively little to overwhelm the public consciousness with fear of and revulsion at peace with the enemy other.

Our goal is to encourage peacemaking as broadly and as deeply as possible. Here is where culture and religion can be so helpful, and where elite processes must develop more humility. A major effort is necessary to mine the ethical depths of each monotheistic tradition and elicit specific principles that will sanction the various conflict resolution practices, as well as express those practices in new ways that specifically reflect the cultures involved. But in monotheistic traditions (perhaps in all traditions), the religious/ethical prescriptions are inextricably tied to cultural habits and interpersonal expectations that elicit feelings of warmth and devotion, when adhered to, and feelings of alienation and anger when violated.

Now, these religious and cultural habits express themselves in two distinct kinds of human engagements: (1) informal and (2) formal or ritualistic. Both are vital for the future of conflict resolution. Various religious actors globally place different emphases on these two human engagements. For example, high-level relationship building between religious leadership, conducted by the World Conference on Religion and Peace, or by the Vatican, emphasizes formal contacts and conversations between key leaders, although this does not exhaust the range of their work. The origins of Moral Rearmament in a Protestant, evangelical style, by contrast, has emphasized the slow growth of interpersonal relationships over time between key figures of enemy groups, as well as some very direct appeals to emotions. MRA members also have formal gatherings and interactions, but one of their great strengths has been the model of informal networking and relationship building, which has important theological roots for them, for it is in the "surprises" of human connections and chance meetings that they see the Divine Hand guiding human beings toward reconciliation with others and with God. In this context, they have filled a void in many conflicts wherein fruitless, formal negotiations are endlessly engaged and disengaged, but deep human connection between enemies is missing entirely, off the radar screen of "pragmatic" priorities. The failures of so many formal negotiations due to the utter incapacity to bring populations along in peace processes makes one question who in this debate of methods is more devoted to pragmatism. Religious peace actors may sometimes be accused of an excessive faith in the transformative power of emotions to the point of impracticality, but elite representatives may be accused of excessive fear of emotions to the point of impracticality.

It has become clear to me over time that many of the same actors who stand for peace and peacemaking, and who commit themselves to difficult compromises, against the wishes of their own community, have little or no contact with enemies and sometimes do not want any. In fact, they often have little contact with their own community, let alone that of the enemy, confining themselves to their own group of fellow believers. The latter group, while well-intentioned, has not been challenged by peace processes to really know the enemy other in a deep way, the enemies on all sides. But without this emotional ability and/or ethical directive, negotiations cannot address or overcome the deepest impasses.

It is time for the world to learn that the nonrational interaction is a necessary catalyst of "rational" negotiations. For some, like those in MRA, there is a theological-teleological function of informal relationship building, bringing God into people's lives, by bringing about reconciliation. For others, such as Jewish religious peacemakers in Jerusalem, the relationship building acts are simple *mitsvot*, good deeds that represent an end in themselves, very difficult to fulfill, a courageous offering to God. Of course, these Jews too have a teleological agenda of religious vision. But their actions are felt to be deontological, to borrow from Kantian thought, a religious end in itself that fulfills a religious mandate that binds them to (and creates?) the Torah's path of peace, something they believe in and create by their way of life. In either case, we must trace the vital role of both formalistic and ritualistic actions, on the one hand, and, on the other, subtle, informal, nonrational processes of interaction whose value to peacemaking is insufficiently appreciated, in fact, the hidden cornerstone upon which all courageous social change depends, secular or religious.

I now turn to the specific significance of the inter-religious encounter, and the power of symbol and metaphor. I will first investigate the most elemental level of this encounter, the human face, a rich topic for social psychology, phenomenology, cultural studies, and, less well known, for monotheistic ethics.

One cannot overestimate the importance of the human face to the success or failure of human encounters. This has not been studied sufficiently in terms of conflict resolution, because the interaction between communications theory, social psychology, and conflict resolution theory, is spotty, dependent on the scholarly background of various theoreticians. Obviously, those with a background in communications and social psychology have the "permission" professionally, in terms of their home departments, to highlight the importance of these phenomena. No one in the academic study of conflict, however, has the permission or the background to examine the effect of religious and ethical sanctions on the experience of interhuman and face-to-face encounter. At best, we study this in terms of taboo, but the power of religious ethics relevant to the use of the face goes unrecognized and unappreciated.

In terms of monotheism, the face and the eyes become a crucial test of love or hate, the beginning or end of relationship. Charisma, a critical characteristic of the Biblical figure Joseph, and the evidence of his chosenness by God, is expressed through those who "find favor [*hen*] (charisma, sweetness, compassion) in his eyes." Many other examples abound.[1] The point is that the prosocial relations begin with the eyes and with the look. Clearly there are powerful effects of eyes on human behavior in the social/psychological orientation of the Bible, a material, not abstract concreteness of love or care. The face embodies one's emotions and one's ethics. The nightmarish converse of peacemaking in this regard is the strange way in which murderous people in any number of circumstances can go berserk when looked in the eye, which is regarded as a dangerous challenge, among various primates as well.[2] If this is the negative impact of the eyes and face, it stands to reason that this is an untapped resource for the emotions and ethics of prosocial engagement.

Monotheism understood this well. Thus, facial imagery, in addition to its descriptive contexts in the narrative biblical portions, like the Joseph stories, also naturally occurs in the prescriptive, legal portions of the Bible. One is commanded to honor or beautify the face of the elder in one's community,[3] but not to honor faces with partiality in terms of legal judgments, in other words, to let justice take its course, without allowing charisma or anything else to sway a judge toward one person's face.

There is also the notion of a hardness to the face, that we alluded to earlier, which, in rabbinic Judaism is one of the quintessential sins.[4] The alternatives of a kind face, based on *hen*, or a hard, murderous face, are rooted in the alternative presentations of divine imagery in the Bible.[5] There are biblical precedents for withholding the kind divine face from certain groups of people.[6] Here I will build on the constructive bridges within and between religious traditions, the most important point.

The foundations and sanctions in all three monotheisms for the compassionate use of the face should be understood as basic to the peacemaking meeting, to training in peacemaking, to the evocation of peacemaking as a religiously sanctioned discipline. No cross-religious, cross-cultural training in the Middle East should neglect to problematize the ways to greet and engage the face of the other. This has immense potential to enhance the engagement of enemies in formal and especially informal encounters, and to detract from those same encounters in which this vital cultural phenomenon is neglected. In Judaism, there are specific commandments to prohibit the whitening of the face, in other words humiliation which, in rabbinic metaphor, leads to loss from the face. They seize on this as akin to murder, the shedding of blood, which leads to another key cultural/religious realm, that of honor and shame, which are pivotal in Middle Eastern conflicts.

Honor and shame are central moral and spiritual categories in monotheistic ethics, particularly in Judaism and Islam. The bestowal of honor and dignity are critical to any listing of classic moral categories of Islam.[7] The same is true in Judaism.[8] It is something so fundamental to proper human relations, and to adhering to the personality paradigm of either the Prophet, in Islam, or God, in Judaism, that it seeps into the style and character of countless classical texts.

Honor and the prevention of shame are not only ethical precepts. They embody a way of being, a critical component of a metaphysical intentionality to the universe that has placed the human being in an exalted and responsible role of a caretaker. Therefore, the violation of human dignity is felt to be not only an ethical failure and an immense personal injury, it is also an affront to God and the divine plan. Furthermore, because these traditions have such deep communal roots in the biblical corpus, a personal affront to one human being is often seen as an affront to the Umma, in Islam, or Islam itself. In Judaism, an assault on the dignity of a Jew is an assault on a member of God's own people, and on the image of God that every human being reflects.

My impression is that one of the subtle differences in the lived tradition and experience of these people is that, at least for European Jewry, the interpretation of "assault" as a generalized assault on God and goodness seems to be particularly activated when Jews suffer actual physical injury from gentiles, especially when they are singled out as Jews. This is what seems to activate for Jews the metaphorical drama of the victimized righteous of God, which was etched in stone millennia ago by the exquisitely sensitive writing of the Psalmist, the essential book of Jewish prayer.

It is with injury and death, particularly of women and children, that so many religious Jews retreat to the safe space of historical prayers, where the righteous will survive, and enemies of God will be subdued and crushed by God someday. At this point feelings of honor, shame, and betrayed dignity seem to reach fever pitch, with the Holocaust as the ultimate magnification of this dramatic tragedy and permanent (?) fixture of God's strange and inscrutable, but ultimately just universe. Much of this metaphorical drama is also played out in Christian literature, only now applied to the truly chosen lambs of God, the True Israel, the followers of Jesus. This is not quite the same in the fusion of Arab culture and Islamic religion. In the lived experience of this culture and religion, particularly when it applies to this century of Palestinian/Arab/Israeli conflict, the dynamics of honor, dignity, and shame work themselves through this conflict in ways that are *sui generis*. This is a sensitive, difficult subject and, in a certain way, the only proper response is to listen carefully to those involved and let them determine and describe what has happened and how it has affected them.

What all this means is that, as Jews and Arabs gather and begin to attempt peacemaking in a more lasting way than mere political negotiation, they had better expect that their response to issues of honor and shame are different but equally sensitive. But they should also anticipate that the active effort to make the recovery of honor a central axis of peacemaking will yield some powerful results, if they do this carefully, listening to each other and accepting the humble processes of trial and error. What will it take to restore lost dignity? What will it take for rejectionists in the Jewish camp to feel that it is not only by the gun that the value and dignity of a Jewish life can be restored in this world? What will it take for a Palestinian family and clan to recover dignity in the wake of the humiliations and hardships of forced displacement, persecution, and merciless poverty? What about those who have good resources and education now but incessant memories of lost property and a lost sense of place that will never be recovered? And I speak here of both Palestinians and Jews, the latter having lost everything, time and again, in different locations. What will it take for those who have nothing and are forced to live in refugee camps, and how much will the latter depend on the honest integration of cultural dignity and economic rights? What will restore honor?

How do you factor into this the complex way in which the deepest and most destructive humiliations of Jews, in many cases utterly indescribable in their horror, are embedded into most family memories from events that occurred elsewhere, in Europe? Yes, at the hands of non-Jews, gentiles who wanted them dead, but not the Palestinians. But now, in the Palestinian/Israeli war, how do these Jews distinguish between a non-Jew who wanted them dead fifty years ago for one set of reasons and a Palestinian who might want to kill them now for a very different set of reasons? Some can make the rational distinction, but can they distinguish the emotional response when the images of mangled, destroyed bodies are the same? How does one cope with this triangulation of humiliation and living nightmares? There is only one answer that I know of to emotional damage, and that is the intentional reversal of that damage, healing humiliation with sorrow and mourning, but ultimately, and more constructively, with honor.

That is the short answer. The long answer, and the humble one, is that these questions should be posed to all people on both sides about themselves *and* about the other. Of course, in the actual dialogic moment, it would be obscene to tell the other side what it needs and does not need for dignity. That is not my intention. Rather, it is the empathetic psychology that I want to stimulate. The exercise, I suggest, of anticipating the other's dignity and shame is not an effort to supplant the moment of encounter, but rather an act of preparation for it. The most important point is that conversations about honor and shame may have some beneficial results, but nothing can compare to carefully crafted gestures and symbols of honor, ways in which enemies convey honor to the humiliated other. These are at the heart of peacemaking and often completely overlooked by formal processes of peacemaking, except for the perfunctory requirements of diplomacy. Rarely have I seen a conflict in which both sides, no matter how many security or economic imbalances there may be, do not need and indeed crave gestures of honor from the other side.

Let us return now to our original theme, the actual face-to-face encounter, which leads to the next categories, humility and silence, as key ingredients of empathetic psychology. Silence and humility are rather strange gestures and phenomena to bring up in the same sentence as the Arab-Israeli conflict. If there were two ingredients missing from human relations in this region that I had to choose, they would be these. Perhaps it is for this reason that so many young Israelis have turned to Eastern religions and have welcomed the likes of the Dalai Lama and Thich Nhat Han to Israel.[9] A possible explanation of young Israeli interest in these religious leaders is that, on one level, one cannot imagine anyone who would irk the religious establishments of monotheism more than these Buddhist teachers. Most monotheistic leaders—both Jewish, Muslim, and conservative Christian, by the way—would consider these men idolaters in the classical biblical sense. And the opportunity to do something just to spite a religious establishment that controls key parts of their lives is never lost in the dangerous Israeli culture wars.

On a deeper level, however, young people always help us perceive what is missing in a culture, what its great weaknesses are. A young person has not yet had to buy into his or her culture and socio-economic prison and therefore becomes an important barometer of tragic flaws. It is no surprise to me that these Buddhist teachers, who practice silence, laugh at themselves in ways unthinkable to monotheistic hierarchies and speak, above all and repeatedly, about humility and *compassion to all living things*, are the leaders that would attract young disaffected Israelis in search of spiritual solace. This is what is missing in life for many people of this region. They are happy to respect and accept the more unfamiliar and strange aspects of Eastern spirituality because, I argue, the underlying gentleness, humanity, and anti-argumentation are things that they most lack in an environment that has made a tension-ridden state of no-war and no-peace into a cultural centerpiece.

I do not blame the inhabitants of Israel and the Palestinian lands for evolving a culture of stress and argumentation. No one can pass judgment on how others cope with interminable violence. But I can diagnose what is wrong on a cultural, psychological, and spiritual level, note how many are rebelling against this, and recommend future alternatives. It seems clear to me that, from a religious point of view, humility, silence, and the wisdom of listening that emerges from compassion have ample precedent in monotheistic literature, both as recommended moral behavior and as religious experience.[10] This is not to disparage in any way Eastern resources on these matters, but rather to indicate a path of cultural regeneration for the Middle East that will appeal to a broad population.

Throughout biblical and Qura'nic literature humility is a sine qua non of the human being's position before God. It is a quintessential act of faith.[11] In Judaism it is even portrayed as a divine attribute to be emulated,[12] and for both traditions the great prophet of the Bible, Moses, is described as the humblest of all men.[13] As far as silence is concerned, Judaism and Islam are loquacious, in comparison to Buddhism, for example. Prayer is communal and loud; study is the same. But, in truth, Tibetan Buddhism has some lively and loud elements that struck a number of Jewish observers as strikingly similar to old Jewish forms of study and debate. It is the balance of silence and speech, of talking and listening that is intriguing. It is also the case that the biblical prophetic tradition is characterized by as much silent listening as it is by long speeches. After all, where do the monotheistic prophets receive their wisdom if not in silent listening in desert locations?

The monotheistic cultural tendencies of recent times would benefit from (1) conflict resolution theory and practice and (2) global religious traditions about humility, silence, and listening. In this case, at least, there is a happy coalescence of at least some religious traditions and the most avant garde conflict resolution practice. The best peacemakers whom I have observed— the best social change makers in general—understand silence and value the "power" of orchestrating the evolution of human relationships *without* dominating those relationships or encounters. Such peacemakers do not fear but rather welcome open discussion, and they do not relish argumentation for its own sake. They do not see every conversation as a win/lose phenomenon, and they do not mistake overall progress and success in their endeavors with the need to "win" in every encounter and conversation, even in their peace efforts. This requires great personal discipline, a very long view of time and "outcomes," and a strong degree of personal inner peace. It also requires patience, a basic trust in humanity and the world, and a deep-seated love of human beings.

Many people I know who love peace have not internalized these values sufficiently and thus become ineffective peacemakers despite their best intentions. The task of evoking and inculcating these values and worldviews requires a fusion of spiritual values and training in conflict resolution. The character of the peacemaker is a major concern in religious literature, and it should be the same for conflict resolution theory and practice.

So far, too much of the emphasis of conflict resolution has been on process, replicable processes for use in all contexts, as if peacemaking were a General Motors car to be disassembled and assembled in all parts of the world and all circumstances. But this becomes impossible and even barbaric, culturally speaking. It is far better, I argue, to offer ways to evoke the peacemaker herself from each culture and religion, as I have learned from my Mennonite peacemaker friends and teachers.[14] Furthermore, eliciting the peacemaker is important and vital, but more emphasis should be placed on her moral character. A peacemaking personality has been the goal of many religious traditions. It is also an elastic phenomenon. If you can trust in the personality of a peacemaker, you can trust her to adjust herself with humility to new and different situations, particularly involving alien or enemy others.

Further to the necessary characteristics of encounter, the Compassionate Listening Project, founded by Leah Green, represents a conscious institutionalization of listening as peacemaking, together with another crucial psychological/ethical capacity, compassion. Compassion is a basic divine attribute in all monotheistic traditions, and there is much to build upon in terms of merging this value with techniques of peacemaking. Leah, and many others, such as Paula Green, have combined the capacity of "active listening" with compassion. Active listening distinguishes itself as a proactive, subtle process of probing questions that signal to the other much more than respectful silence.

The *complete* silence of strangers, even the respectful kind, is often viewed with suspicion: "Do they really hold me in disdain?" "Are they really seething with hatred behind the urbane smile and false courtesies?" But compassionate, active listening leaves no doubts about the position of the listener. The listener may not agree with everything she hears, but she has demonstrated that she has not just been silent before the suffering—or the joy—of the other, but that she has heard, understood, and indeed felt it. This interlaces—as do many emotive/ethical gestures—with the bestowal of dignity and honor, mentioned earlier. Because more than anything, human beings, particularly those who have suffered indignity and injury, need to be heard and understood, almost as much as they need air to breathe and water to drink. In our rush to economic and geographic negotiations of conflict, we constantly forget this basic need. Leah's group has specialized in bringing groups to Israel to listen compassionately to the *entire* spectrum of Jewish and Palestinian political and religious life. This has proved to be transformative for many participants and should be studied further.[15]

Such encounters have been characterized by "spontaneous" outbursts of powerful reconciliation that seem to appear out of nowhere. In general, I have been witness in religious circles to many of these "sudden" outbursts of reconciliation, truth-telling, and forgiveness. Some religious people, such as those in Moral Rearmament, might characterize these moments as "evidence of God's grace" or "the hand of God". One's religious position does not matter. The fact is that humble and compassionate listening has a profound impact on both the injured and the listeners often evoking very powerful emotions, bursts of honesty. We all see the ways in which human beings are given to sudden bursts of rage, pent-up feelings of anger, that are triggered by external stimuli. But many of those caught up in conflict are tortured by *prosocial* feelings toward enemies that they suppress in conflict because of their sharp contrast to anger.

We certainly all know this from experience with family conflict. Often it is our love for others that makes us most angry and tortured by conflict. It is easy to dismiss and be emotionally cool toward those toward whom we have no prosocial emotions at all. But when those whom we like or toward whom we feel kinship have hurt us deeply, we feel compelled to criticize or punish. And yet our very love is what makes us so angry, because we do not really want to pursue this path of hatred. Certainly many parents feel this way toward children, and vice versa.

This analogy extends back to enemies who are close to us in ways too threatening to openly acknowledge. Certainly one cannot help but notice the startling similarities of Israeli and Palestinian mythic self-definitions, national dreams, and interpersonal styles. Two peoples, born in adversity, priding themselves on intelligence and ingenuity, but also viciously self-critical at times, are glued often to self-defeating ways of coping, though both are attached to land as the only sure basis of pride and survival.

Leah Green tells the story of a religious Arab community leader on the West Bank who was angry with her after their group encounter. He said that before she came to his village it was easy to hate the enemy. But now he cannot, because he has seen the human face of the other, a face that showed honor and empathy. But I submit that such a man, with such a clearly manifest conscience, must have been conflicted from early on about his hatred, and the process of being listened to with compassion put a new face on the enemy and transformed his relationship. And that is when his old feelings burst forth in a moment of transformative honesty.

This is the kind of transformation that we seek, because it builds on the basic human goodness of many actors caught up in conflict, tortured by paradoxical values and moral intuitions. These actors, at least, will form a critical mass of people who will react very quickly to the bestowal of honor, empathy, acknowledgment, and the inimitable and exalted experience of being listened to after a lifetime of being silenced by violence, in all its many forms. Many of us have been silenced by violence at one time or another, and it would seem that listening is an indispensable antidote that must accompany the more obvious restorations and compromises of rational dispute resolution and resource redistribution or compensation. The latter are indispensable but always imperfect and incomplete, leaving some unjustly treated. In fact, there is no rational justice for many injuries that are not subject to compensation. Thus, we must supplement compensation and rational justice with the restoration of dignity and the restoration of listening to the voices on all sides that have been silenced by violence. This must be as broad-based a process as possible. The more wide-ranging, the more profound the social transformation that will take place, and the more that the fragile, elite peace processes will become etched into the hard canvas of cultural consciousness.

Listening that is compassionate favors dialogue and the use of the word to engage in peacemaking. I have stated earlier my reservations against this being the *sole* form of communication. Compassionate action *as a form of communication* is, however, a critically important element of peacemaking that has ample foundation in the region's religious traditions. Compassionate gestures offered to those who are sick or weak or needy in some way, form the basis of much of the social legislation in Judaism and Islam, as well as the modeling of God's ways (or the Prophet's ways in Islam) in the monotheistic literature in general. It was the signal characteristic of religious figures ranging from Muhammad to Jesus and Jewish religious figures such as Hillel.

What could this mean for and how could this be operationalized intelligently in the Arab/Israeli conflict? The answer to this challenge requires great care and creativity on the part of the erstwhile combatants themselves. Only they will truly sense what will work and not work. Only they can engage in the requisite process of imaginative innovation coupled with the humility of trial, error, learning, and further innovation. Let me offer a few modest guidelines.

Often compassionate action is the glue that holds together communities in which some are in a state of distress. Addressing their needs involves a delicate balancing act between dignity, dependency, and aid. Communities around the world fail at this challenge regularly, in that material aid often is coupled with personal indignity, which, in turn, undoes the benefits. It also creates as much conflict as it purports to heal. This would be doubly complicated if the aid came from the enemy other going to those suffering in the other group. I merely want to problematize this, not reject the efforts, to anticipate problems.

Let us examine some symbolic and moral gestures. The sharing of vital organs has been a powerful and surprising gesture of compassion in this conflict. (I will address the importance of surprise later.) What I refer to is the occasional report in recent years of Palestinian families offering the organs of loved ones who had died to Jewish patients in desperate need of a transplant.[16] The compassionate gesture is self-evident. The symbolic merging of the Jewish and Arab physical survival, the very bodies of these two peoples intertwined and interdependent, is readily apparent and startling in a certain way. One is awestruck by the image of simple, grieving parents who, in a single moment of giving and sacrifice, can create a literal, physical symbol, in the bodies of their loved ones, of how neighboring peoples can live together. It also is a deeply antiracist gesture at the most profound level, but one that few can really oppose, because few people, no matter how damaged by the wars, stand unsympathetically before the need of loved ones to save the lives of those who are dying in the hospital. No wonder this compassionate-symbolic gesture entered into the Jewish media so many times. It was jarring and powerful.

A deeper level of consciousness is reached by the human witness to the horrors of war. The graphic character of perpetual stories of horror appeals to a place of imagination and emotion that is comparable to very few human experiences. We need to effectively counteract the damage done by of this ingrained war/trauma consciousness and imagination in ways that dialogue and rational negotiation cannot. In my experience, for example, and as I struggle as a Jew with my own feelings of fear and rage in this conflict, I try hard to memorize the image of that Palestinian bereaved family and their gesture of generosity. Yes, rejectionists will argue that such gestures are rare, and as I write this in January 2001 there are celebrations of the Intifadah in the streets of Ramallah with calls for more killing of Jews. There are celebrations throughout the West Bank and Gaza.

More damaging to my consciousness and to my very soul, however, are the images that haunt and linger from the lynching and mutilation of the two Jewish soldiers. And I myself think and ponder and try to imagine the mind of the man who butchered one of the soldiers, then answered the soldier's cell phone, and told his wife (who was searching for her husband) that he was the man who just killed her husband. I am haunted in ways that are hard to describe, and filled with self-doubt about the path of peace and trust. I honestly feel that I am back in the death camps. And that is why my consciousness needs other images, so that the war for my soul can proceed on an even keel. Otherwise, my imagination overwhelms my rational knowledge of the situation. And if I feel this way, after almost twenty years of commitment to peace work, I can only imagine the war inside the Hamas members or settlers. They struggle between their natural drive to humanitarianism and their natural drive to fear and loathing of enemies who want them dead. And yes, there are wars of conscience inside such people, and the fate of their souls and consciences should be a major subject of our efforts. This is a war not easily won. Such is the damage of violence. But one must fight this damage with the same weapons, imagination and symbolic/mythic action.

I now address a very different kind of human action and gesture, relevant to poverty and joblessness, among the most humiliating of human experiences. Aid from a hated enemy might be doubly humiliating. I honestly cannot predict the effects of such efforts with any certainty. I merely raise the possibility, and also caution that acts of compassion be conditioned by intelligent guesses as to the probable response, case by case, need by need, culture, and subculture individually. Furthermore, this should ideally be a bilateral process to preserve the dignity of everyone. In the Palestinian/Israeli case, it must proceed carefully and jointly. Furthermore, there should be an outlet, as part of a bilateral program, for the Arab community to help poor Jews, as surprising as this may sound, for the sake of everyone's dignity, and so that no party is always on the receiving or giving end of aid relationships.

Permanent receiving ingrains humiliation and self-defeating behavior, while permanent giving ingrains arrogance and a kind of willful ignorance of the less privileged.

Furthermore, there are injured poor on both sides whose effect on the conflict goes unrecognized. Everyone points to the Islamic suicide bombers who come from situations of multigenerational humiliation. But one should not underestimate the considerable number of Israelis who have voted against peace, or who have been violent from with inside army structures, such as some members of Mishmar ha-Gevul, the Border Guard ;, because they come from miserable circumstances and memories of lost family glory and forcible eviction from Arab lands. If we do not want to perpetuate this dance of death between competing miseries, between suicide bombers and dysfunctional border guards, then we had better pay attention to alleviating the circumstances that create such psychologies. And the asymmetry does not matter, the far greater number of Palestinians in absolute poverty around the Middle East. Of course there is asymmetry! And justice demands greater attention to the latter's needs. But conflict resolution and simple compassion demand care for all of those people born in misery who contribute actively to violence. Self-help opportunities, low interest loans, anything that will maximize the dignity of recipients should be preferred. Anything restorative should be given special attention, any aid gesture that also involves the restoration of lost housing, land, agricultural produce. Thus, the help in improving the quality of life becomes combined with a gesture of restoration and even apology that directly addresses the injuries of the conflict.

Another nonverbal form of relationship building is what I call symbolic communication. A classic instance of symbolic communication as peacemaking is the decision of Dahlia Landau to dedicate her house to Palestinian-Jewish reconciliation, which has now become the Open House in Ramle. Dahlia discovered the identity of the original Arab owners of her Jewish parents' house. This was one of thousands of houses occupied after 1948. She describes in detail how the old Arab father, blind already, came back to the house from exile and looked for the lemon tree he had planted decades ago. He smelled the lemons and tears came to his eyes. This made a transformative impression. Dahlia decided to open a school, in the house, together with her husband Yehezkel. The school's purpose was reconciliation of Jews and Arabs.[17] Yehezkel is a deeply religious Jew, well-known in Israel for his peace activity, his writings and engagement in dialogue, as we have described earlier. But this house became a nonverbal communication, a symbol of reconciliation in Ramle, and continues in this capacity to this day. Of course, it is one of numerous courageous efforts of symbolic and substantive peacemaking that receives insufficient funding from any of the affected communities.

Dahlia's story and the house merge as symbolic communication. This story is made more poignant by the fact that a child of that Arab family ended up in jail for terrorism against Jews. This made it harder for Dahlia to engage in reconciliation with this family, risking the accusation of sympathy for terrorists. Indeed, this reaction was unavoidable from some Israelis. Dahlia wrote an open letter to this man in jail, and it was plainly apparent that she did not accept the legitimacy of his acts. But in a deeply symbolic way the house and her gesture stood out as a recognition of the unfair damage done to families by war, and the way in which most of us, directly or indirectly, become victims and aggressors in the morass of warfare.

Symbolic communication, whether it be intentional or unintentional, can be a part of reconciliation. I recall this with nostalgia and pain from the time I visited Neve Shalom, an intentional community of Jews and Arabs on the border of Israel and the West Bank, purposely placed on the Green Line. I went there in 1983, a novice to peacemaking, having come from a family and community environment in which no one had ever communicated with Arabs. I was afraid, having been warned by Israelis to not even get off the bus near this unrecognized settlement to which the government refused to provide even a road. I was in a dangerous area according to them. I have no doubt that getting off alone in an isolated area involved some risk, when kidnapping and murder was, in fact, and still is, a weapon of war against Jews and Israelis. But I was undeterred—and frightened. I found my way there with some difficulty.

I walked up to the settlement without an appointment. No one knew I was an American Jew or a rabbi, and I did not advertise this. The Jews, interestingly, ignored me. I never met a single Jew there in 1983. I was given over to an Arab man who showed me around and by whom I immediately became intrigued. I will call him Ibrahim. Ibrahim, who wrote a great deal, late at night, had a beautiful wife who welcomed me warmly and spoke in a soft Arabic that I had never before heard through the media. They had a dirt floor, the first one I had ever stood on in my privileged little life. The brown dirt, the soil, touched me profoundly. It was both an emblem of poverty and a symbol of belonging all at once. We went for a walk toward evening, just I and this mysterious Arab husband and writer. He took me onto a ridge, from which one could see the vast green valley, and as we walked, he picked up, smelled, and tasted several of the naturally growing herbs and flowers, which appeared to me as weeds. He said that he knew all the different flowers and greens by name. And, in the instant that he nonchalantly picked up and tasted the leaves, I knew why the Arabs hated us so.

I looked down at the valley, and I saw the highly developed Jewish kibbutz, with its angular fields, perfectly planted and maximally utilized. I could see why someone could come here and see the opportunity for fruitful cultivation of good soil, and I could also see why natives who knew the earth like the back of their hands and loved the soil, just as it was and had been for centuries, would hate this intrusion, would hate this high octane agricultural cultivation that made them look primitive, they who had been so attached for so long to this earth. And then, of course, in the background, between us as a white cloud, were the facts of the wars and the way they darkened everyone's memories.

I had no doubts that Ibrahim was—just Ibrahim, and I did not peg him as a representative of every Palestinian. And I did not romanticize all of them because of this special man. No, it was just he, but that was enough for me to see what I had not seen. His unintentional symbols gave something to me, without even knowing how it would set me on a different life-path, how it would solve gnawing questions that had tortured me for several years. But he also created new problems for me. His gestures of love for the earth, and belonging, changed me.

I felt the fundamental and symbolic clash of cultures, not unlike that which goes on around the world between settlers and natives. But I also knew that in conveying his love for the earth, knowingly or not, through symbol, Ibrahim had humanized the enemy for me, despite the fact that he expressed some pretty violent solutions to conflicts. Later that evening he would gather ten of his men friends from the settlement, ten Arab men—and me, terrified before them, never before in a room alone with Arabs, feeling awfully "surrounded."

This too was a symbol for me, a moment of trust thrust upon me, as absurd or irrational as my fears may have been. I was grateful to feel the fear, to be surrounded by Arab men in a small room, quizzed and grilled by them, the object of their curiosity, and ultimately to feel safe with them. The construct of the scene, the small room, ten Arabs and me, was conciliatory in and of itself, in that it transformed me. I had to trust them. There were no phones. I would feel the same way seventeen years later, in Gaza, escorted from place to place by Palestinian policemen. But that is a separate story.

Of course, fear was an interesting shared experience for me and those Arab men at Neve Shalom in 1983. I tried to convey to them how afraid Israelis were of them. I described a wonderful Israeli mother, whom I had just had the pleasure of meeting with her family in their Jerusalem home. She conveyed to me that she could not redo her kitchen for fear of being alone with an Arab in the house and being knifed to death. (Notice the difference in fears based on class, her fears based on Arab workers, and theirs based on the police). They laughed and asked rhetorically who had all the guns. And I countered by asking what would happen to the Jews if the Arabs suddenly had all the guns. And they were silent. I described the fear around the terrorist bombs that Israeli Jews endure, and they countered with even greater fear, needing to run away as soon as there was a bomb, for fear of being rounded up and "interviewed" by the police, maybe for months. That they were afraid of me, and that I was afraid of them, in this tiny little room with a dirt floor was itself a powerful symbol. And the silences between us were more important than the words.

I never saw them again, but I will always remember their faces, particularly the wife of Ibrahim, her beautiful, warm eyes, and his intelligent, anguished eyes that looked far away, as if he were nurturing a stoic dream every night that kept him sleepless—and writing—beside the small lamp slightly above his home's dirt floor. I think of him when I write alone in the dead of night.

Years later it was I who took the initiative in symbol making, unconscious and spontaneous as it was. I remember being engaged with a series of Arab students at Caux, Switzerland, whom I mentioned earlier. They powerfully affected me when they asked me specifically to join their work team at Moral Rearmament's convention center, called Mountain House.[18] I was touched by their effort to include me, as I did not yet feel exactly comfortable in this European Christian environment. Once again, as in Neve Shalom, I was alone with a large group of Arab men. Europe is always difficult for me because of the Holocaust. Ironically the very difficulty with the environment brought us together, because they, too, were uncomfortable, for different reasons. I remember that on the last day of the convention one of the young men got up before the general assembly of this unusual religious, peacemaking retreat center and described how moved he was by his encounters with me. Spontaneously, without thinking, I rose and went to the podium and embraced him. It felt very good. The audience gasped and several people were moved to tears. For them I had created a symbol in that moment. But, I had just done what moved me at the moment. For them, however, as Christian European onlookers, it may have been the first time that they could see visibly that, yes, maybe Jews and Arabs can reconcile someday. As small as this experience was in the long history of the conflict, it did shift a few more people toward believing in and working for peace. And it was the wordless symbolism that moved them, not just the words. Perhaps it was necessarily both.

Speaking of that environment, I will slightly digress to mention an encounter over time with an elderly European Christian couple. And it is relevant because European Christian-Jewish conflict is at the heart of the Arab-Israeli conflict and Jewish consciousness. It may be unfair to Palestinians, but nothing is ever perfectly symmetric in war and violence. And yet all asymmetries must be addressed to arrive at solutions. The Holocaust and European history stand front and center, in this regard, before the Palestinian-Israeli conflict. It is especially difficult for me to feel comfortable with elderly Europeans, always wondering "where they were" back then, what they thought, and endless other unanswerable mysteries. Well, sure enough, my worst fears were realized as I ventured into European Christian relationships. I had many conversations with the husband, a good, highly intelligent man, intensely religious, of strong opinions, who struggles with European history, though he is proud at the same time of that history, very proud. His wife's family suffered, not during the war, but at its end. Why? Because her father had been involved in propaganda for the fascist regimes—the Nazis, that is. There I was, face to face with her, my worst terror, feeling the war right at my throat and my own capacity for rage.

I remembered and realized that she would rarely speak to me but always looked at me longingly, with moist eyes, and I never knew why. She had suffered, a lot, but that was not on her mind. I ultimately stayed in their home and I felt an unreality about sleeping there. It was a very simple but classically elegant space in the world that only middle-class Europeans seem to know how to create. I remember them telling me, in passing, that her family had lost all their precious old possessions due to a robbery. At the end of the trip they wanted to give a gift to me, and particularly to my wife who was back in the United States. My wife had become a bit of a "cause," shall we say, in this community to which they belonged, in that she had been ill-treated by some conservative Christians in the group the one time she had come to Switzerland; she had not been back since then. And they all knew it. The gift was two small, beautifully engraved silver spoons. But they were not new. They were very old, the wife's mother's, and, I realized later, one of her last possessions from her mother. She gave me, the Jew, in the 1990s, one of her last family possessions. They were of delicate and decorated silver. They reminded me, for some strange reason, as I looked upon them week after week, of all those thousands of classically silver Shabbos (Sabbath) candlesticks, looted from Jews across Europe and melted down into private Nazi fortunes or to serve the Führer's war effort: each candlestick a memory of countless Sabbath nights, graced with children, blessings, chicken soup, and the fleeting visit of a sometimes present and loving ancestral God. All of the memories and visions, ashes now, for over fifty years, and the silver—God knows where. Each candlestick like the ones I see bathed in light every Friday night at my table, with each candle in Jewish tradition representing my precious children, my wife, and even me. And here now were these two beautifully engraved German family heirlooms.

I have no immediate losses from that unspeakable time of history—except the ability to dream without seeing all the faces, and all the bodies, whenever I try to trust the world. And I, now in possession of two silver spoons, a German family heirloom, a gift from a German elderly woman with blue eyes, but also from a German teenage girl in 1945, who lost something precious in that insane war, perhaps the essence of her family's goodness, something that I cannot begin to comprehend or describe. I thought about this for years, and I see before my eyes this elderly woman's silence and her moist, blue eyes. I am unable still to convey my feelings to this woman. This gift was given in the backdrop and context of the intense debates over Swiss reparations to the Jewish community. I, as the "representative" Jew, was directly involved with this couple's friends in trying to think through this painful subject. And I realized years later that, knowingly or unknowingly, consciously or unconsciously, this woman had given me reparations, but not in the form of some impersonal transfer of cash that may be justified but hardly transformative of human relationships. No, she gave me what was most dear to her, and something that was tied up with her own losses. But this was no loss due to theft or a court case, it was a communication, a gift and an act of repentance for what pained her most deeply inside, a gift from a teenager from 1945 whose father, her only father in the world, did something stupid and vile, a girl who, through no fault of her own, suffered humiliation and the imprisonment of her family.

Often I have wished in my inner fantasy life that it was 1940 and I could go back, to Berlin perhaps, and do away with someone central, do away with many people, do something dramatic—yes, violent—that could have stopped the unspeakable event. But now I go back in my mind's eye and see this teenage girl, a victim of her father's stupidity, a father she no doubt loved. I have been given some other way to return to that horrible decade that God should have never created. I go back and see someone German, not Jewish, whom I can pity, and I see Europe differently, not naïvely, just differently, with the paradoxicality of a novelist's eye, not the endless rage of a vengeful relative. And I cannot hate, at least not as much. Or now I must hate and I must love, at the same time. And therein lies hope.

One of the underlying processes that characterizes these and many other encounters that I have observed and/or participated in is the power of surprising and sudden gestures. Their effects cannot really be quantified, nor replicated, nor prepackaged and sold as an unbeatable method of conflict resolution that will cure the ills of a country or a corporation in five weeks or less. That is why they have been so neglected, and yet I believe they form the heart of many of the key moments of human transformation. We need to make room for these moments, to hope for them, to expect them, to utilize them, to highlight and honor them, in all of the major conflicts of the world. I believe, in particular, that such moments can play a critical role in a deeper transformation of Palestinian-Israeli relations. Arab-Israeli relations need transformation as well, but nothing compares to the damage wrought in Palestinian-Israeli relations. And these two groups will be tied together in many ways for many decades to come. They will either be an unending source of misery for each other, or they will discover deep ways to apologize, to empathize, to share sorrow and joy, to find a way to right the wrongs of the past, as much as this can be humanly achieved. It is not achievable in a complete way, but approximations can be reached.

Key members and leaders of these communities must decide to be at the forefront of this kind of ethical/symbolic peacemaking, discovering intuitively the right time and the right way to express themselves. And those of us outside the conflict must be there to support, enable, and provide comfortable contexts in which this can occur. This is precisely the work in which I am engaged right now. It is thankless work, with outcomes that are impossible to predict. But it is extraordinary to me, despite the role of the religious communities in conflict generation, how much religious people in particular seem to understand this way of communication and human change. It fits into the style and lifeblood of religious psychology and religious morality at its best, whereas promoting this form of peacemaking has been notoriously difficult within more "rational" support systems of peacemaking, such as the world of progressive foundations. I hope this situation will improve over time; there is no reason why it should not. The religious individuals who have courage and vision have a powerful role to play, and there needs to be a complete paradigm shift in terms of the mechanisms of support for and intervention on behalf of such people and communities.

Another symbolic gesture of civility is deeply related to basic categories of religious sensibility, the expression and experience of profound gratitude, which is embedded in Buddhist traditional engagement with the other, such as in Tibet. In monotheism, as with all ethical gestures, it is tied to a basic positioning of self, and collective self, vis-à-vis God as Creator and Sustainer of the world. The sense of gratitude permeates all prayer in all three Abrahamic traditions. Jewish prayer structure, in its earliest manifestation in Psalms, and in later rabbinic formal constructs, always couches the expression of human needs in the context of and surrounded by gratitude to God for what He has granted. Even what we have lost, such as the life of someone we love, we view as something given originally as a gift to us. "God has given, God has taken away, may the Name of God be blessed" is the classic and profound response to death, expressing commitment to gratitude before the gifts of life.[19]

There is nothing more powerful than tapping into cultural/religious responses to the basic existential questions. Gratitude is something that is also easily forgotten in the midst of collective experiences of anguish. And yet religious teachers know that it is a basic and non-negotiable aspect of tradition. Sometimes gratitude can be taken to extreme levels that do not allow people to mourn, that cover up sorrow to "protect" God, to protect the theology of the organized religion from the possibility of doubt. Mature religious leaders, in periods when they are not under attack, tend to be not as defensive in this regard. The goal in our work is to discover ways in which warring religious communities can find ways to express gratitude *together* for the things that they hold dear, or whatever it is in their communities that is life-sustaining, such as children, medicine and healing, or different elements of nature and scarce resources. This would include the symbolic expression of gratitude in the context of the ending of hostilities and killing, a time that is ripe for collective appreciation of life that binds people together. Every small step along the way to peace should be formally commemorated jointly by shared moments of gratitude. This is the glue that would hold tenuous diplomatic and intercommunal processes on course in the face of difficult challenges. Diplomats and negotiators must now face just how tenuous their methods of engagement are, and how much help they need from other methods of human interaction that buttress peace.

The moments of gratitude that are based on a win/lose mentality cannot be shared. For example, the loss of land by one side and gain by another really has to be a celebration by one side and a mournful moment for the other. The release of "freedom fighters" of one side will be commemorated by the other as the release of "killers" and the violation of a basic sense of justice. But other scenarios of gratitude are not win/lose, but fundamental to human life. Everyone can celebrate the arrival of badly needed rains and find it as an opportunity to be grateful together. Everyone can celebrate agreements on cooperation in medicine, or the discovery of ways to jointly protect and enhance the life and happiness of children. Some on both sides can commemorate and be grateful for key moments of peacemaking. A joint program of concentrating on the environment in some way, such as creatively protecting the water supply, might be an opportunity to share cultural resources that celebrate with gratitude the divine gift of life-sustaining water.

Those of a spiritual and cultural bent should search together for "spaces" of gratitude, moments in time or actual physical locations, that can be shared jointly. In addition, and I know this may sound strange to some, there are people on both sides who, right now, have had the courage to perceive and acknowledge the ways in which each community has things for which it needs to be grateful to the other side. Let me give a personal example. I will never forget my shock when Prince Hassan of Jordan, in a televised message to a conference on religion and conflict at the University of Notre Dame, cited the medieval Jewish philosopher Maimonides as he, the prince, expressed hope in the future of Arab-Jewish relations. I was in shock, and as I expressed this, I was in even greater shock when an Arab intellectual came up to me, in surprise at my surprise, claiming Maimonides as a thinker dear to her community. This moved me and confused me in ways that I cannot describe. After centuries of European culture burying Jewish influences, taking the best of my culture, embedded in many texts of the New Testament, and then denying our importance or existence, I could not comprehend this gesture. After generations of Western writers, from Dante to Voltaire and Dickens, always finding a Jew to portray that which is most vile, I have grown used to the anonymity of my own value. And then to have this Arab prince honor and express gratitude to "my" Maimonides? I was stunned, exposed in some way, the veil of anonymity uncovered. I went to a school called "Maimonides" for all of my childhood, a school whose name no one in my American gentile context could even pronounce. The prince's gesture was so natural, so effortless. It simply was gratitude by a distinguished Arab and Muslim to a great Jewish mind.

The emotional irony was double. I had spent the previous years combating Meir Kahane's religious arguments for exclusion of non-Jews from Israel that were based on the very same writings of Maimonides! I was ashamed of this. Maimonides' influence on my life was overwhelming, especially on my self-esteem, for better or worse. But this Arab prince gave me great pride that day, by implicitly expressing gratitude to my philosopher. Strange turns of life indeed. The power of gratitude is immeasurable and, yes, unpredictable. It can lead to vigorous arguments and possessive remonstrations. But it opens up layers of feelings and discussions where little else can. It takes one to the heart of the matter very quickly, whereas dialogue can go around in circles for years.

The feeling of gratitude to another is in direct conflict with the need to be superior. The unfortunate tendency of human beings, particularly in Middle Eastern cultures, to either feel inferior or feel superior, to need to establish and clarify who is on top and who is not, is a particularly damaging ingredient of conflict generation. It has become very embedded in various religious traditions, laws, and myths. To the degree to which enemy communities need to build their own self-esteem on the ruins of the other's self-esteem, they will find gratitude a difficult task. But the beauty of peacemaking is the power of individuals, or subcultures, of great courage and vision. They set the way for the rest of us, and they make us see what we have not been able to see. So too this Arab prince—or his speech writer—and this professor, made me see something about old Arab and Jewish culture that I could not see with my European, or post-European eyes. My enemies made me take pride in Maimonides in a new way, not a way of inferiority or superiority, but in a way of simple cultural sharing of appreciation for a great mind.

Perhaps, after so much agonizing over war, I have trouble seeing the good in my own community. Perhaps my eyes are somewhat dimmed, like the eyes of my ancestor Isaac, who could not see his sons clearly after the one seminal event of his life, his sacrifice at the hands of his father.[20] This may sound strange, but let me explain. There is a legend (*midrash*) that when Isaac was on the altar, placed there by his father, at the command, he thought, of God, Isaac was about to be sacrificed when the angel stopped Abraham, and tears from the observing angels dropped into Isaac's eyes. That is when Isaac lost good vision.[21] The deep message of the legend is that the experience of being sacrificed, or almost sacrificed, can blur vision. And so we all need help recovering vision after such experience. Who could see straight after feeling like a sacrifice? But victim groups often feel like a sacrifice, making it difficult to see the world with clarity, for what it is and what it could be.

By contrast, the honor and the surprise of gratitude have a way of making us see things in a new way, or shocking us out of impaired vision. I have practiced this many times, in small ways, in my encounters with erstwhile enemies, always with great effect. Often I am not with my enemies at all, but simply victims of war, my students from around the world, who are always slightly damaged and humiliated by the descent of their own cultures into the depths of war-induced depravity. And so when I tell them, as I have told my African students, for example, that someday the world will learn from and marvel at the wisdom of their African cultures, and that we have much to be grateful for from Africa, they express an interesting kind of shock at my words, as if Westerners are expected to at best pity them, but never honor them or need their wisdom in some way. But this way of relating transforms our joint search for solutions to their wars into a much more noble enterprise for all of us, a shared experience of discovery. Permanent receiving leads to humiliation, and permanent giving leads to arrogance, no matter how much you may try to avoid this. Shared work with others in peacemaking, or even in training for peacemaking, requires that everyone both give and receive, especially enemies.

It is time for Israelis and Palestinians, Jews, Christians, and Muslims of the region, to acknowledge, in detail, what they owe each other, not just in the sense of reparations or land or apologies, but in the deep sense of gratitude, cultural and spiritual debt. Perhaps that is what Prince Hassan taught me that day. This kind of acknowledgment will make profound changes that can buttress the negotiated settlements. It will also resonate in the cultural and religious inner experience of gratitude that lurks in the consciousness of Abrahamic communities, stirring things that need to be stirred, as we seek real change. Enemies owe each other things in odd ways, even as they have injured each other profoundly, similar to the dynamics of family systems. The Dalai Lama has understood this about enemies and believes in acknowledging how enemies actually help us to learn, such as learning patience, a critical characteristic of the Bodhisattva.[22] The Chinese have not seen his philosophy and ethics as conciliatory, however. Furthermore, the power asymmetry between his people and the Chinese government is enormous, and thus intercultural gestures are outweighed by the incredibly powerful space that China occupies in the geopolitical security constructs of the present and future. Thus, as powerful a model as the Dalai Lama has provided of a different approach to enemies, it has not been enough to overwhelm the other geopolitical factors militating against peace. But, on the other hand, the odds against the Dalai Lama's success have been enormous, and he, at the very least, has kept a lid on the destructive potential of the situation.

While the asymmetry between the power of Israelis and Palestinians is clear, it is tied to a larger Arab-Israeli power struggle that is more symmetrical. This is probably at least one reason that a negotiated solution is more possible at present. It is in this context that intercultural gestures can deepen and solidify negotiated processes which, while rationally necessary and inescapable, are constantly at the mercy of understandably nervous and angry populations on both sides. This is where cultural gestures can be the glue that holds together peace processes that are so tenuous. Furthermore, the cultural gestures, by definition, address the deeper needs of populations for justice, fairness, and a recognition of their frustrated basic needs. They lead people away from artificial agreements and toward interpersonal and intercommunal experiences of recognition that almost force the hand of justice and fairness. Of course, they could be used by elites as a cover for unfairness. But all acts of peacemaking can be used this way, and there is no way to prevent some from abusing cultural gestures.

My argument is that, assuming that issues of justice and fairness are in fact being negotiated in good faith, it is still possible for large populations to believe in a short-sighted fashion. They are driven to violence, which hurts them as well as their enemies, precisely because they have not experienced the peace process at a cultural level. There is, therefore, no trust and no familiarity, despite the inherent logic of coexistence and peace. For this reason, positive cultural gestures are indispensable. Despite their best pretensions, enemies at all levels of education and power need this extra glue to build a new future with their erstwhile enemies.

Gestures engage both suffering and joy, two opposite emotions that are nevertheless bound together through the cycle of human experience. Hardly a year of anyone's normal life does not contain both of these experiences. Religious traditions, therefore, embody this cycle and formalize it. In other words, one of the functions or characteristics of religious ritual is to take the unpredictable cycle of human joy and suffering and transform it into a formal, predictable cycle. We all know that we will experience tragedy, but we are terrified by its unpredictable character. Accompanying these events are human connections to experiences such as eating and sleeping. In bad times we will lose our appetites and lose our ability to sleep peacefully, for example, or we may eat and sleep excessively.

One of the most powerful aspects of religious ritual, from a psychological point of view, is to ritualize the tragic and thus make it less terrifying. Religious traditions are characterized by predictable times of *kenosis* and *plerosis*, "deprivation or emptying" and "filling up," fasting and feasting, mourning and joy, suffering and exultation. Only these experiences are ritualized and thus, in some way, empowering, under our control. They may be imposed by religion, that is, God, but it is better than it coming in a random way. Feasting and fasting are fundamentally characteristic of Judaism, Islam, and Catholicism, for example. They play an important role in the biblical literature shared by all Abrahamic traditions.

When people suffer ritually for their religion, as when fasting, it is often a profound time of reflection, of emotional and physical vulnerability. Attacking them in this time, such as Muslims during Ramaddan, or Jews on Yom Kippur, is a particularly destructive act. It stands to reason, that aiding people in this time could be a particularly powerful symbol, and an act of human and spiritual engagement, an act of trust-building when people are at their most vulnerable time of the spiritual life-cycle. There is such a vast difference between suffering in isolation and, what I call interascetic communication, which would involve, for instance, extending Gandhi's *ashram* experiments of helping Muslims fast during Ramadan, to a more elaborate intercommunal conflict resolution gesture.[23] We dare not prescribe this in too much detail, since it would impose a prescribed program on parties to the conflict. But this is an issue relevant to many religious conflicts. It is the process of finding ways to aid a community when they fast, mourn, or deprive themselves in some fashion. It not only creates a powerful bridge of trust but also prevents the suffering, or *kenosis* part of the cycle, from becoming yet another space of alienation between enemies. It prevents the suffering part of the religious cycle from becoming, or continuing to be, a hermeneutic script upon which to write an ultranationalist political agenda.

Times of *kenosis*, such as Ramadan for Muslims, or Tisha B'Av for Jews, are powerful times emotionally, and they can become times of either aggression or healing, depending upon who fills the "dramatic script" of that time. In the absence of bold efforts by peacemakers, others have used these and other times to push the dramatic script in destructive directions. But we can do better. We can, with deeper understanding of the dynamics at work, see these times as great opportunities.

The same holds true for *plerosis*, feasting, times of joy. Often progressive peacemakers are particularly unskilled at seeing and experiencing joy. They have repeatedly reveled in the opportunity to bemoan so many human problems, expressing cynicism about this or that in the status quo. But they have failed to capture and captivate the human need for joy, as if to acknowledge success and joy is to abandon the interminable "struggle" of social change. But this is to stoically ignore or suppress the basic human need for joy, gratitude, and celebration.

Religion, however, understands all of these needs very well. And the joys of religion, and the joyous cycle of human religious life, can be a great time of peacemaking. Customs of generosity in joyous times are typical of Arab and Jewish culture and their religions. It would be easy to make weddings and births, for example, a time when traditional gestures of generosity or friendship are extended to those beyond the borders of one's traditional community, to the strangers in one's midst. The same could be done regarding religious holy days. In fact, in ancient times this was practiced in the Jewish community on Sukkot, the Feast of Booths. It was a time when people of other faiths and traditions came to Jerusalem to celebrate as well. In fact, in the earliest strata of the Bible—despite the countervailing tradition of intolerance for the Canaanite nations—there is a clear tradition of including "the stranger" in every joyous celebration of the yearly holiday cycle.[24] Who could these non-Jewish strangers been other than polytheistic indigenous people of the land? But this principle evolves into something different in rabbinic Judaism, a much more insular model perhaps. Nevertheless the biblical precedent is there and can be built upon by forward-thinking monotheists who seek to find a bridge of joy or celebration.

For obvious reasons each community must guard the boundaries of its ritual existence. Just as Muslims guard Mecca's integrity as a Muslim center, it is understandable that there will be and must be borders and boundaries. Indeed, I do not want to overlook or dismiss the importance of cultural intimacy in times of distress and times of joy. Nevertheless, there is always room for creative compromise on these matters, always looking for and finding spaces—in the largest sense—to share. The details must be imagined and experimented with by the actors themselves.

My argument begins and ends with the power of ritual suffering and ritual joy as fundamental entry points into the heart of human beings. Those entry points can set up either implacable borders of hatred for what is outside or healing borders of cultural intimacy that combine seamlessly with benevolence beyond one's boundaries. It takes only creativity and courage. And there is more than enough of both of these embedded inside the cultures affected by the Arab-Israeli conflict. Thus, what I seek is the kind of peacemaking that becomes embedded in the entire cycle of human experience, and not, therefore, exposed to dissolution when life turns either from joy to suffering, or vice versa. In all permutations, peacemaking becomes as natural as the cycle of life itself. This is the goal.

The final interaction between symbolism, civility, and religious ritual that has impact on the inner life, is the issue of patterns of Abrahamic reconciliation, analyzed earlier. Here I want to frame the earlier analysis in terms of the stages of human change as a cultural and religious experience. Ritualistic patterns of reconciliation are powerful motivators of change in that they provide a blueprint for the hardest, most chaotic and anarchistic demand of peace, namely, profound change in the predictable and comfortable patterns of hateful relationships. This is by far one of the toughest impasses in intractable conflict and habituated violence. At the conclusion of my study, I will offer a very concrete set of recommendations concerning patterns of reconciliation and forgiveness, in the context of a larger pragmatic program. For now, my purpose is to refer the results of my earlier studies into the concrete questions of the day.

The power of traditional Arab *sulh*, on the one side, and Jewish *teshuva*, on the other, is in their ability to reverse harm done in a stage-by-stage formal and symbolic process with profound psychological effects. That is the most common denominator between *sulh* and *teshuva*, although there are many others. The damage done by many intractable conflicts, especially those involving physical injury and death, seems to have a permanent, fixed quality. It feels to victims and, yes, aggressors as well, like a defining moment of existence that nothing can wipe away. For this reason, it is so easy to build political programs of hatred on the back of these defining moments.

The power of ritualistic reversal is that it is not a "pie in the sky," radically alternate vision of a beautiful future. The latter cannot possibly resonate with those who have been damaged by violence or tainted by its commission. Rather, it is the recognition of failure in relations that is followed by acknowledgment, and a formal way to get back into relationship with others. It does not say, pedantically, to combatants and victims that "love is the only answer" or "forgiveness is the way" or "live by the golden rule." It locates the moment of human conflict, injury, and destroyed relationships elsewhere than in the realm of pedagogy, didacticism, or pedantry: in the realm of high drama, uncertainty, and dynamic movement forward or backward. For that is the profound reality and the real truth. And nothing is more anathema to the injured than an inattention to reality, for that is what they have felt and breathed, and what defines their consciousness as witnesses. One dares not deny the witness his moment of truth. Of course, when there is injury on both sides, as there so often is, a moment of surrender will be required in which one's own hardened truth shares space with an alternative truth that must be acknowledged. But both truths, from both sides, are denied when we enter as intervenors with naïve visions that do not do justice to these living witnesses of often unspeakable crimes.

No, *teshuva* and *sulha* do no such thing. They place into high drama the process of acknowledgment and the uncertainty of just outcome or forgiveness. They highlight crime in all its details. Yet, paradoxically, they also move everyone along a *fixed journey* that does not necessarily require a denouement but certainly propels everyone in that direction. And therein lies its strength.

At least as important, is the strength in both processes of much more than symbol. They contain within them the indispensable procedures of justice. Thus, they marry within their cycle and ritualistic process the needs of peace and justice, the needs of victims but also those of perpetrators or their relatives. More important than anything, these traditions resonate culturally with all communities. The Palestinian community is clearly more traditional, relatively speaking, than the Israeli community. But I argue that it does not matter. What is important is the cultural impact that always lasts historically much longer than does adherence to the exact rituals of organized religion. Most Israelis may be not religious or anti-Orthodox, but they will respond instinctively, in Jewish ways, to most emotional issues of guilt, apology, and repentance. For example, there is an old Jewish tradition, alluded to earlier, of asking forgiveness at a grave before witnesses, if one has failed to do so in the victim's lifetime. It does not matter that this has old mystical roots in which the majority of the Jewish population today may not believe. The gesture still resonates powerfully as an old cultural gesture.

I have no doubt that had the European community of nations, implicated in the Holocaust, been more vigilant about repentance and more honest about their sordid past, and had they organized, in the last fifty years, extensive processes of helping their people to visit concentration camps together with Jews and ask forgiveness from the dead, that this would have had a profound impact on the Jewish people. It would have been far better than the war over reparations, given and taken grudgingly. Here is an example where reparations respond to the demands of justice much more than apologies over graves, and yet reparations have been emotionally satisfying to only some Jews, while utterly inadequate to others.

Such a European engagement might have helped in an indirect way to resolve much faster the Palestinian-Israeli conflict, in my opinion. Instead, the taxis in Israel were all Mercedes for so many decades, by way of German reparations. But I never once felt any kind of comfort or closure or resolution by entering one of those taxis. I doubt whether anyone in Israel ever has. In fact—and probably unrelatedly—a taxi drive is often one of the more horrendous, tension-ridden and contentious moments of Israeli life. Yet it curiously binds everyone together.[25] This seems like a silly aspect of the conflictual state of affairs, but it is not. What happens on the streets of a country is indicative of more profound processes. The point is that the last fifty years did not see enough voluntary efforts by European nations East and West to actively and symbolically repent of their barbaric behavior toward minorities, and specifically their behavior during the Holocaust.

To return to the subject of *sulh* and *teshuva*, the challenge is how to apply these (by contrast) extraordinary frameworks of transformation to justice and compassion in the contemporary context. A further challenge is how to do this when these processes have been in the hands of traditional—some say reactionary—systems of justice and adjudication until now. How will these systems adjust to a multicultural, multireligious, and secular context in which the Palestinian-Israeli conflict is taking place? What about the regional international setting? Can it speak to the needs of the entire Middle East conflict with Israel, in which the Palestinian conflict is embedded?

These are great challenges that creative religious people on all sides are capable of meeting. They will require some time, experimentation, and intelligent support from third parties, and also secular leadership that is willing to integrate or at least encourage parallel processes of peacemaking and intercultural transformation. The greater the animosity between secular authorities and religious communities, the harder it will be for these communities to become creative and bold. When attacked and threatened, they will tend to become backward looking and less creative.

Certainly it must be admitted that secular citizens of the Middle East have much to fear from organized religion. But to the degree to which they can focus narrowly their war against religious control of their lives and not let this turn into a general cultural war, they will permit both sides to focus on the issues in disagreement and the possible compromises, thus avoiding a deeper "winner take all" fight of an existential nature. The latter catastrophically diminishes creative resourcefulness among religious leadership to confront new challenges. There will always be many religious individuals—as there are currently—who will demonstrate great creativity even as they are buffeted by antireligious forces on one side and ultrareligious ones on the other. But we need the leadership of the organized religions to find a way to move forward in peacemaking as well. And this requires some cooperation and joint work with the secular communities involved in the Israeli-Palestinian conflict. We also need third parties who have the wisdom to find and support the courageous actors who are charting a new course of spiritual and cultural life. This will make them stronger agents of change and encourage religious and secular establishments to merely inch forward, which would be a profound asset to peacebuilding.

Ultimately, however, the power of symbol in reconciliation goes beyond the province of organized religion and into the consciousness of millions of people who constitute a culture. Therefore, symbolic transformation and old cultural methods of reconciliation should not be monopolized by any one community or religious authority. They exist as a natural resource waiting for any creative people in a culture to utilize them. Now this may raise eyebrows and voices among protectionist clerics. Let them raise their voices and competitively develop "more authentic" peace methods from the resources of their religion. Let there be a competition for interpretations and amplifications of *sulh* and *teshuva*, *seliha*, and *kapparah*. Let accusations of inauthenticity fly. As long as this leads to a broad-based cultural shift toward peace and reconciliation, the ultimate goal.

9

De-escalation Plans and General Steps toward a New Relationship

It is difficult as of this writing to offer conclusions and recommendations and, at the same time, ignore the tragedies of 2000 and 2001 in terms of the escalating violence between Arabs and Jews in the Middle East and elsewhere. This has been an extremely painful development for everyone involved. But it has not been a shock to me. In fact, I was plagued by this eventuality in my imagination many years ago. Of course, I hoped, like everyone else, that high-level negotiations would succeed, but I also unfortunately was vindicated in my consistent position that there is no peace without people. High-level work can often become delusional, its representatives not wanting to face the power of average people in democracies—and nondemocracies—to create either war or peace. They provide the political space for leaders to promote violence or peace. Thus, any process in which a significant group of people on both sides hate peace is by definition a failure. Peacemaking is only as strong as the number of people who support it. And whenever they are not there, everyone who wants peace and justice must do serious self-examination to understand why the people are not ready for peace, and in particular, what each and every party's role is in preventing peace, including the role of all the third parties. In this last class, we must include well-intentioned Israelis and Palestinians, Arabs and Jews, Muslims, Arab Christians, Western Christians, the governments of the West, and the Arab countries. We all have a part in what has gone right and what has gone very wrong. And until we come to the capacity for self-examination and understanding, what is called in my tradition *teshuva,* "repentance," nothing will change at a deep level.

One can also be deluded by unending analyses of the motivations of key leaders, why and when they pull back from peace, make deals with the devil, or actually move boldly toward peace. In fact, sometimes they may be doing both at the same time. While the details of this analysis are alluring and fascinating, they are ultimately a distraction. In fact, they become a regressive obsession of those who wish to pin all their fears and hopes on one or two people, which is far less frightening than facing reality.

In point of fact, 90 percent of what leaders do is what they *can* do politically and still stay in power or stay alive, 5 percent of what they do is attributable to personal peculiarities and 5 percent more may be traced to what their conscience tells them to do. The overwhelming, unrecognized, and actually feared power here rests with the moods and instincts of the majority of the people embroiled in conflict. If most want an end to it, they make the space politically for leaders to move in that direction. If most have bloodshed in their mind's eye, then that is what they will allow for politically. The obsession with the mind and personality of key leaders in conflict is a deflection from the real work of conflict prevention and resolution, which is why official peace processes disempower peacemaking, robbing peacemakers of the support they need to continue their work.

What Went Wrong with Arafat and Barak: Lessons Learned in the Psychodynamics of Leaders

I maintain my earlier claim that the power of leadership is overemphasized analytically, and most of my recommendations to come, as well as in chapter 10, focus on cultural shifts in the populations that are key to determining possible elite concessions, compromises, and creative problem solving. Nevertheless, I feel compelled to clarify some misunderstandings about Arafat, Barak, and the fateful mistakes of the summer of 2000.

From my meeting with Arafat, and meetings and interviews with his immediate subordinates and colleagues, as well as interviews with those who were close to Barak (as much as anyone was), I can say that much has been misunderstood about the downward spiral of violence. Let me suggest the following observations:

1. The final status deal offered to Arafat, no matter how far-reaching for Israelis, was life-threatening to him, as many others have observed.

2. Barak's relationship to Arafat from the beginning was less than satisfactory, and there is a great deal of evidence from many sources that Barak's lack of interpersonal skills, which increased his political isolation, was aggravated even more by the fact that he (Barak) and Arafat were adversaries in negotiation. In other words, the difficulty that Barak had in general was magnified by the intercultural and intergroup conflicts that he and Arafat were negotiating. Furthermore, it seems that each man's weak points were precisely those that would most offend the other. Arafat would be most alienated by offenses to dignity in interpersonal relations. Barak, as a result of his need for order and rationality of discourse, would be most offended by Arafat's incessantly changing positions.

3. Arafat, of all the three leaders at Camp David, was by far the best at personal political survival, even though as a Palestinian he has led his people many times on self-destructive paths. He is a man who checks with everyone conceivable as he makes any move. Most important, he had decided long ago to operate on two simultaneous tracks, using one as leverage against the other. He would go along the peace and democracy track and would simultaneously keep alive a guerilla warfare and terrorism option as leverage. Furthermore, the latter would keep him in good standing with large sections of his population, which was and is a tool of discontent and rage, to be uncorked when necessary.

4. Information filtering out from various Palestinian Authority ministers suggests that there was a plan for an Intifada by the summer of 2000, when it was clear that Arafat could not accept the Camp David deal. This Intifada was meant to evoke sympathy from the world. Thus, Sharon's entry into the Temple Mount was just a needed provocation.[1]

5. What has been completely misunderstood about Arafat, especially by his major adversaries, and most especially by the average Israeli who understandably fears and suspects him, is that these tracks really were taken seriously by Arafat *simultaneously*.

When he sat with some of us and authentically supported and took steps to create a religious reconciliation between Jewish culture and Islamic culture, he was not putting on a show. If it were just a show, then why did he televise such meetings with Jews in Palestine, which cost him politically? Many other gestures cost him politically. Why would he do that? He pursued two sets of plans at the same time and constantly checked politically with everyone as to which one of those plans would eventually dominate. This is strange and outrageous to diplomatic elites around the world, including Arab elites who are often embarrassed by this man's actions and presentation of the Arab cause. Nevertheless, this is who Arafat is, and he represented the Palestinian people in that fateful summer. Furthermore, this ambivalent practice is not that different from major powers who possess extremely deadly military forces at the same time that they have such a genteel corps of diplomatic representatives. In some ways, all of this is embodied in one person for the Palestinians, for they lack the true elements of statehood. Arafat represents a people without a recognized state, and he is the nexus around which all the contradictions of violence and diplomacy coalesce.

That he could suppress terrorist impulses during the Oslo period but always keep it alive as a possibility may seem repulsive to Israelis. But in Arafat's mind this was no different than Israel's "Masada options," such as a cache of nuclear missiles, or the continuing Israeli support for much of the Border Police corps, who, during the Oslo years, were no more clued into new ways of treating adversaries than was Slobadan Milosevic.

6. A major opportunity was lost due to underestimation of the power of gestures and stage-by-stage processes of cultural reconciliation that would have impressed Arafat more and more to move farther on one of his two tracks,

that of democracy and coexistence. The Israeli approach, especially in the hands of Barak, was too rationalistic, too outcome-focused rather than process-sensitive. Barak offered far more than his people were prepared to handle. They had no evidence yet that they could safely share Jerusalem, while the Arab world clearly did not trust Israelis enough to share the Temple Mount. Trust, slow and steady markers of trust, should have been the subject and object of negotiation.

Arafat was far more willing than the Israeli liberal elite to try cultural confidence-building measures. The Israeli elite were too rationalistic, too disconnected from the needs of their own people, not to mention the needs of average Palestinians.

It is true that the Palestinians were the ones who would not tolerate any more interim agreements. But it is the cross-cultural and ethical processes of relationship building that could have been tried, relatively cost-free, which would not have interfered with any final status negotiation. The official third parties utterly failed to see the dynamic possibilities of such measures and thus squandered the only opportunity to break the impasses.

7. It is understandable that Israelis felt complete distrust, as the Intifada developed, of a Palestinian leader who could willfully unleash the kind of murderous hatred of Jews that has been unleashed. It is understandable that the average Israeli now has good evidence of just how many Palestinians across the Green Line want him dead. But it is also true that the Israeli military reaction has shocked the average Palestinian and Arab who had favored peace into severe doubt about the humanity of the average Israeli. This is the social-psychological dynamic that has been unleashed in both communities, as of 2001.

8. What we can learn from this, in terms of the psychodynamics of leadership and war, is that (a) leaders need more political space than elites admit to make difficult decisions, (b) they often are unaware or too undemocratic to admit that they need more of their people on board to make concessions, (c) the third party is responsible for helping them make that space possible by creative suggestions on moving more people in the populations toward trusting relationships and, (d) the third parties must utilize the peculiarities of leadership styles to the benefit of conflict resolution, so that if a leader is open to new forms of peacemaking, even if he is lacking in other areas, one should pursue this path.

There were those who pleaded with Barak to treat Arafat, behind closed doors, more diplomatically, and I believe there is evidence that Barak tried at Camp David. On the other hand, I got the impression from many public comments during those fateful months that Barak kept competing in public with Arafat, showing how he, Barak, was so pro-peace and goading Arafat to catch up, trying to embarrass him into a deal in some ways. This could not work. It just fed the tendency of the Israeli-Palestinian relationship to end up in some form of Palestinian humiliation, goading Palestinians into violence. And this is exactly what happened.

Arafat embodies everything that is true and tragic about Palestinian life, and Barak has embodied everything that is true and tragic in Israel. There is a common tendency toward self-destructiveness in a deeper, collective sense, a tendency to violence, and, therefore, a tendency to miss what the enemy needs most to accomplish that leap into the peaceful realm. This is where third parties need to step into the breach and be as creative and flexible as they possibly can. They must guard first and second parties against their own worst instincts and help them find the cultural resources to bring out the best, not the worst, in their respective peoples.

There are ways in which all three leaders, Arafat, Barak, and Clinton, showed tremendous courage in 1999 and 2000. But the pressures of not really having their people on board brought out the worst in their tactics, personal styles, and decision making. Thus, the violent actions and reactions were born in the summer of 2000. But there is no avoiding the fact that these leaders could have been the heroes of the century had third-party peacemakers and theoreticians of conflict resolution consistently insisted in the last ten years that, step by step, every month, the peace process must concretely benefit average people and slowly transform the cultures in question.

Let us move on then from this postmortem to what we might be able to do in the future in terms of a plan for cultural conflict resolution.

Cultural Conflict De-escalation Plan for Israel and Palestine

I want first to make some very specific recommendations now for de-escalation of the violent confrontations as of the winter of 2002, with specific attention to culture and religion. The changing political constellations on both sides interest me less than the need for people on both sides to realize the power that they have to move their peoples toward unending violence and hatred, or toward a constructive process of relationship building between wounded people. The latter will eventually yield the kind of healing and vision necessary for creative political change, problem solving, and peace that entails as much justice as possible.

This plan is directed equally to Israelis and Palestinians. These recommendations would have to be implemented with the approval of either mid- or high-level authorities on both sides. Some of the work could be done without them, but at some risk to participants, especially those who are afraid of the Palestinian Authority or the violent Muslim groups.

There will be no success to a strategic political plan at this point in time, no matter how rational it may be, unless there is a parallel effort to de-escalate the rage and fear that is propelling popular rejectionism and hardened positions in this conflict. One can speculate endlessly and argue about which side deserves greater blame for the current sequence of tragic events. A constructive approach, however, is to initiate strategically a bilateral set of actions affecting the general population that would allow the leadership on each side to achieve the necessary political space and communal consensus to move back to negotiations and toward a final settlement. The methodology is completely focused on process, on means rather than ends, and is thus the logical opposite of prevailing official methods of Middle East diplomacy.

Holy Places

Gestures of regret, honor, and rededication should be made in every religious space that has been violated in Israel and Palestine. This includes the Dome of the Rock, Joseph's tomb, Hebron, Jericho, in addition to various synagogues, mosques, and gravesites. Such gestures should be bilateral, organized by a variety of existing interfaith organizations, but endorsed publicly by leading political figures on both sides, in addition to reasonably important (not necessarily at the top) religious leaders on both sides. Third parties, such as the United States and international religious bodies, need to make clear to both sides that this is a priority.

Loss of Human Life

Loss of life is not only a human tragedy but is also a desecration of basic cultural and religious sensibilities. As such, mourning and joint expression of regrets can reverse the cultural damage done by the infliction of harm in the last month. We will discuss this in detail in chapter 10.

The Injured

Efforts should be made to offer support to injured members of each community from the enemy community. There is evidence that this is taking place already in limited form, but, as with the other courses of action, it is given little support by the political leadership on all sides of this conflict except when it is politically beneficial to do so. The effect, however, of authentic endorsement by major leaders would be dramatic.

Fear

There is an overwhelming sense of fear among a majority of citizens in both communities about the future. Fear is a basic building block of hatred and political intransigence. Efforts must be made to build trust concerning the wishes and intentions of the majority in each community. The majority who have not participated in the violence and who do not condone excessive use of force are generally silenced by the political leadership. Ways must be found to foster greater communication between these majorities. Once again, there has never been any pressure on the political leaderships by third parties to consider this as an indispensable part of strategic peacemaking. The endorsement of political leaderships will generate the needed energy to renew and strengthen efforts already in progress in this regard. The Israeli public needs to hear the voices of average occupants of Palestinian towns on their fears, and Palestinians must hear Israeli fears, either directly, or through a major media campaign. Each needs to understand the life situation of the other. If this is not done, then the fear translates into the bravado of dark and exclusivist visions of the future. This perpetuates a downward spiral of both rhetoric and violence.

Justice and Inquiries into What Happened

It is hard to overestimate the importance of perceptions of injustice in conflict. Whatever the composition of governmental or nongovernmental inquiries, it is crucial to pursue a just and fair evaluation of what went wrong and who committed what excesses. If any international body manages this in a truly unprejudiced fashion, it will help the process of recovery. The problem is that most inquiring bodies are prejudiced by their preconceptions about the parties to the conflict, rather than capable of an honest evaluation of the moral behavior of conflicting parties. The latter, however, would be a productive contribution to creating a cultural foundation for a peace process based on justice.

Most important, the justice claims, and the rage emerging from a sense of injustice by average Palestinians must become a part of the acknowledgments that will accompany the peace process. We cannot move forward without a better venue for the channeling of this rage over injustice. A great number of people on the Israeli side also feel and claim a deep posture of injury due to injustice and cruelty from Palestinians and, more generally, the Arab world. We may need to think about the establishment of some ongoing justice and reconciliation commission through which many of these issues can be addressed.

High Level Religious Meetings, Statements, and Gestures

Meetings are already under way in very small ways, at least inside of Israel and in various settings globally, but not between Israel and Palestine. Furthermore, the efforts already made have not been endorsed, promoted, or even permitted by some of the latter. It is vital that the political leaderships be pressured to consider this vital to the peace process. This effort should include not only statements about a common monotheistic commitment to peace, justice, and the value of human life, for example, but also a concerted effort to make religious gestures that demonstrate these values to the enemy. The key missing ingredient has been the permission by political and military authorities to pursue this avenue seriously. And the latter have not received the proper international signals that this is vital. The third parties are deeply implicated in this failure.

The Shift from the Culture Of Military Force to Morally Trained and Restrained Policing

That there is a very large amount of guns available on either side of this conflict in less than responsible hands is a given. Clearly, the Israelis can escalate to much larger weapons such as gunships and have an extensive capacity for self-protection which has led to relatively few casualties on their side, in proportion to the large amount of firepower directed at them. The critical need of the hour, however, is to re-establish a culture of policing, with all the responsibilities and sensitivities that this would require. Furthermore, it is vital that we do not return to the status quo ante, as if this were an acceptable situation. Clearly, it was not acceptable to the majority on the Palestinian side who have been moved to such massive violence. The status quo ante involved a great deal of bad policing by Israeli authorities, and utter insensitivity to basic issues of cultural and human dignity. The status quo ante also involved, from the Israeli point of view, a tremendously large, blind eye to irregular Palestinian forces with guns who were and are prepared to kill Jews whenever possible. I have promoted and lobbied for an extensive training process that will be mandated for both sides of the conflict as to policing methods, the proper and proportional use of force, and methods of conflict prevention that emphasize cultural sensitivity and the utilization of cultural assets in the maintenance of peace or its restoration in the postconflict setting. The details of this book provide some of those requisite cultural sensibilities and assets. Nothing will occur in this regard unless the leaderships on both sides are pressured by the international community of negotiators to consider this a vital step of peacebuilding.

The Poor

Abject misery drives this conflict, as it does many others. Cultural and religious sensibilities around the world are really at the mercy of the damage that human misery wreaks on individual and collective identities. The disappointment with the peace process is substantially attributable to this. The poor have been pawns of one side of the conflict, the Arab world, and been mostly ignored by the other side, the Israelis. It is vital to understand how much of the rejectionist politics on both sides receives its impetus from the relative deprivation of poor communities. No peace process should move forward at a high level in the future without a parallel process of antipoverty activism that is high-profile and leads to immediate, stage-by-stage results in the lives of people who are being asked to agree to the peace process. The current antipoverty methodology associated with the peace process has been far too abstract, focused on infrastructure, and subject to high levels of corruption that further alienated the majority from the peace process. I suggest, just as an example, small business loans to large numbers of decent people, for example, rather than large loans to the few. I suggest that job training be made available on some level to every young person. I suggest this on both sides of the Green Line, to poor Jewish immigrants as well, adjusted to the relative amounts of poverty on either side, for this part of peacemaking is about the *sense* of injustice, not some outside judgment on which side is more aggrieved. I suggest bringing people with very real senses of injury and injustice into a new vision of the future, proved by actual changes for the better in their lives that comes with peacemaking. It is crucial that ongoing efforts be directed toward and publicly associated with the peace process, and if this proves impossible, then the third parties should have the courage to suspend negotiations until they do. There is ample international experience with grass roots, popular antipoverty and development work, which needs, however, the endorsement of the highest levels of leadership for both financial and cultural reasons. This is an important way to make the peace process also a justice process. Mechanisms to include in some way the poorest refugee families in the Palestinian Diaspora would not only extend the justice process but be a powerful indicator of the direction of the final status negotiations. Too many of the benefits of peace are being postponed to the very end, and it has become clear that there is no longer any patience with this. Unnecessary delay was never a good idea nor a just path. Ways must be found now to create a kind of progress in the human and cultural realm parallel to the relative political and military gains.

Honor

The valuation of human dignity and human life has been the greatest victim in this century of Israeli-Palestinian conflict, continuing in this direction in the twenty-first century. The majority on both sides feel intuitively that their enemies and even the rest of the world do not particularly value their existence. As a later stage of this de-escalation, it is crucial that the political leaderships on both sides be pressured to find symbolic ways to honor the culture and identity of the other side. They must encourage their communities to do the same. In so doing, they will put in motion the opposite of a spiral of violence. Just as there are powerful spirals of violence that spin out of control, there are often spirals of reconciliation that can take place with the proper encouragement from leaders.

None of these recommendations require leaders to surrender any ground on the remaining issues of political conflict, principally boundaries, refugees, and holy places. Thus, it would be relatively easy for third parties, such as the Europeans or the Americans, to make the case for the importance of the above measures as a psychologically difficult but materially cost-free way of breaking the cycle of hate and conflict. The real problem lies in the limitations of the culture of high-level third-party intervention at the present time. They are the ones who need to take fearful and regressed enemies to a new stage of relationship. But this is a culture that lacks sufficient imagination and courage, and, in particular, it is a culture that is crippled by a fear of and sometimes disdain for the masses of people in conflict whom it purports to reconcile.

General Recommendations for the Future

I want now to move beyond the present stage of violence and immediate issues of de-escalation to some long-range visioning in terms that directly address the cultures of the Abrahamic traditions. Specifically, I want to envision the possible uses of Abrahamic traditions of reconciliation. Several major conditions must prevail for this to occur successfully in the context of the Arab-Israeli peace process:

1. Religious reconciliation must be seen in the context of a range of other religious moral values, such as justice, for it to coordinate well with our basic understanding today of what truly resolves conflicts and stops deadly violence in the long term.

2. Assuming the first condition, we can still say that there are times when an act that involves apology, remorse, forgiveness should stand on its own as a powerful symbol at a certain stage of relationship building. Reconciliation need not *at every moment* be tied to justice, because its powerful psychological—spiritual, if you like—impact often subsequently drives the process forward toward rational negotiations about justice, powersharing, and fair solutions.

3. Timing in reconciliation-type activities (apology, remorse, symbolic reconciliation, gestures of repentance and restitution, unilateral forgiving, expressions of care) is crucial, and it varies from culture to culture. Generally speaking, most people are prepared for acts of reconciliation in the context of some progress on justice issues, as a kind of glue that binds rational processes to the methodology. Conversely, forgiveness too early is offensive to many injured parties. On the other hand, in some cultures and in some intractable situations, it seems that reconciliation-type activities are actually the first, not the last, activity, in that they break the psychological impasse that is preventing rational negotiation. This is particularly true regarding unilateral and very public apologies for past wrongs, expressions of sorrow and proof of shared sorrow, that often break an impasse in a way that little else does. Individual peacemakers must make careful judgments about timing in these matters, always learning from and building upon contextual experience.

4. Religious reconciliation must be understood and honored in its indigenous cultural/religious formulations. Of course, an honest look at the latter will lead to some internal debate, a hermeneutic debate that will be laden with a psychological substratum of struggle over how much to forgive an enemy. The cultural space of each group in a conflict has its own character, but it is not unitary, because culture is a process, not a static entity.[2] As long as the basic character of the recommendations for reconciliation resonates in the culture, it will provoke a good debate, in that it will affirm and empower the cultures in question rather than stifle them. It will honor their own modes of moral debate, justice, and relationship building. The last thing that we want to do with cultural representatives who embrace violence is give them a reason for more violence when they see their own cultural approaches to problems being suppressed. On the contrary, honoring their culture is a key ingredient of undermining the warrants for violence and an important tool of effective conflict resolution.

5. Once all sides are reasonably comfortable with their own cultural expressions, they have several choices as peacemaking proceeds. They could

(a) limit contact with the enemy group to formal negotiations without any cultural content, (b) invite their enemy group into their own cultural expressions of rapprochement or restoration of relationship, (c) agree to be a part of their enemy's cultural expressions of the same, or (d) negotiate how to alternate cultural/religious expressions of reconciliation.[3] I do not recommend synthesis but rather alternation, unless a cultural symbol is so shared by both groups that a shared ceremony or symbol would not threaten identities on either side. Threat to and confusion of enemy identities is one of the main things to avoid.

6. Religious reconciliation should never be exclusively verbal, unless it is within a culture in which words are the sole determinants of authentic relationship. But I have never encountered such a culture, at least beyond the minority of the cultural elite. Actions, symbolic actions, surprising gestures, ceremonies, and rituals are vital for most people on the planet who feel deep injury or who are trying to construct a livable world for themselves. For many, if not most, it is the *only* kind of reconciliation that they seem able to handle, especially in the setting of the family. Thus, while in some ideal universe of psychological healing it would be better if everyone could verbalize what their adversaries need most to hear, we should not consequently eliminate from conflict resolution the vast majority of humanity who cannot, for example, bring themselves to say the words "I am sorry" to an enemy. But there are many ways that people say "I am sorry" with their deeds and symbols without uttering the words. Thus, there are many other modes of peacemaking that will lessen violence, restore everyone to a dignified life based on just solutions, and even create reconciliation, our sole aim.

7. From the perspective of conflict resolution theory, it is vital that the deep needs met by traditional rituals of reconciliation not rule out the fulfillment of other needs. It would be a travesty of conflict resolution if a suffering group were desperately poor, hoping for some relief from their situation, and then only received a heartfelt apology from an enemy group that caused their poverty, with no acknowledgment of what is owed them in terms of justice. It is for this reason that one sees such division within a group at the beginning stages of reconciliation. It often is along class lines, with poorer members dissatisfied that their physical deprivation and its rootedness, as they perceive it, in the conflict is not acknowledged and incorporated into the terms of the negotiated peace. Thus issues of power, material wealth and justice must not be muted or muffled by forgiveness gestures. Such gestures and processes need to be parallel, and perceived widely and clearly to be parallel, to movements toward the fulfillment of the basic human needs of the most deprived members of each society.

8. Formal ceremonies should be a nonverbal, nonrational glue that improves upon the rational communication model, not a barrier to it. Even though many people are only able to engage in ritual processes, not highly verbal, rational negotiations, where possible, the paths of Abrahamic reconciliation, such as forgiveness, apology and repentance, should parallel other processes of communication.

9. Reconciliation must be a crucial adjunct to rational negotiations and justice seeking, because in virtually every long-standing conflict that I have ever witnessed, from families all the way to genocides, there is never complete justice, no way to recover the lost lives, the lost time, and the emotional scars of torture and murder. And there is rarely the possibility of achieving *everything* each group envisioned at the height of struggle and battle. Thus, in the context of mourning what cannot be restored, reconciliation and the creation of new bonds with those whom one fought is a vital form of comfort for such losses. It offers the possibility of a new matrix, a new cognitive and emotive structure of reality that cannot replace the losses but does create a surprisingly new reason to live nonviolently and believe that such a life can be worth living. People recovering from genocide and guilty over their survival, people who have been forfeiting their sons' lives for generations, often need a jolt, an unexpected reason to go on living normally. They need a reason to believe that a new way of life is not only possible but will actually be better than continuing endlessly to suffer, to mourn their losses and punish those who inflicted those losses. Reconciliation processes can be the soul that animates this new vision of reality in the heart of those who have suffered for so long.

Specific Steps toward a
New Relationship

Before I offer specific recommendations toward a new relationship, I want to contextualize this by summarizing our insights from the previous chapters. In a word, myth matters. Careful ethnographic analysis of this conflict reveals some basic ways in which mythic constructs and competing stories and rituals frame this conflict in very profound ways. There is, furthermore, an inseparability of religion and culture in this conflict that presents both challenges and opportunities. Just as culture is not static, but a dynamic and lived entity that is filled with paradoxes that express themselves in secular communities as social, ideological and ritualized struggles,[1] the same can be said for the religious communities. In fact, one is a function of the other. There are profound and ancient family myths at work here, competition for most favored status, and an interdependence between politics and myth that makes rational solutions to conflict elusive. Old patterns of Abrahamic demonization of the other become operative here as the struggle ensues for life, security, and the space that represents home and belonging.

But this same mythic pattern of Abrahamic interaction that is destructive can also become part of processes of reconciliation and provide the best antidote to cultural intractability. Such processes may be able to reach the deeper places of existential and cultural conflict where elite, secular peace processes have utterly failed. Furthermore, the mythic pattern of reconciliation, as opposed to the elite models, may succeed in confronting in a very pragmatic way the lived frustrations and anger of the very people who have obstructed the peace processes. It would thus address outstanding issues of justice that have always provided the pretext for derailment of the peace process.

What matters most in mythic and cultural approaches to peacemaking is that one's means address the profound human need for meaning and for cultural resonance which combines seamlessly with other basic human needs, such as safety, security, liberty, and the necessities of sustaining health. Culturally successful peacemaking should contribute to or restore a greater ordering of the world and lead to healing from conflict in a way that is consistent with one's worldview. In today's world most people are actually members of many cultures at once. To complicate matters, most people are often alienated from the traditional cultures with which their family has been identified. They also may be consciously attempting to buy into very modern constructs of culture, such as the structured worlds of business, academics, and the accompanying foundational myths of rationality. At the end of the day, and in the context of bloodshed, the lure of primitive cultural response to terror and assault is overwhelming to many. And it is my argument that the only way out of that conundrum of fear and violence is a constructive engagement with myth, with culture, and with its principal emissaries, ritual and sacred deed. Ironically, this is the best path back to rational constructs of conflict resolution and negotiation that are so crucial for the final stages of intergroup negotiation.

That is why I advocate a turning of conflict prevention and resolution methodologies toward a synergistic and humble engagement with the lived uses of ritual already in place in peacemaking in this region. In addition, I seek a creative investigation and experimentation with the vast reservoir of Abrahamic uses of ritual to heal, to establish basic patterns of civility, to transform broken relationships, to mourn, to repent, to end war, and to make peace. We must bring the issues of peace and conflict into innovative spaces of human engagement, such as the street, the public space, an area that has been engaged historically by cultural and religious traditions but is utterly neglected by the abstractions of contemporary approaches to coexistence. The public space matters. The human face in the public space matters. Basic civil exchange is near the heart of many failed relationships here, not at the periphery, even though the more obvious contest is over scarce land.

Retraining ourselves to pursue conflict resolution in this way will be a hard task, a dynamic and creative enterprise that sometimes resonates deeply with interlocutors from both enemy camps and at other times is jarring. It will take experimentation, humility, and the courage to advance and retreat with the vagaries of timing. But the chances are good that such an undertaking has already and will continue to respond to the one, most important failure of the Oslo peace process, a formula for multireligious, cross-cultural, broad-based, popular commitment to peace, justice and coexistence.

As John Paul Lederach has said on many occasions about other regions in conflict, we must try to envision the next one hundred years of Arab-Jewish relations, of Israeli-Palestinian relations, as a direct response to the first one hundred years, and we need to think in terms of three generations of memory. The first one hundred years were characterized by basic patterns of interaction that were and are narcissistic, framed only in terms of each group's own needs. This led to disaster. The next one hundred must be thought of in terms of anticipating the other's needs and interests due to the inextricable partnering that must occur in the region to avoid a miserable existence of unending fear and violence.

The irony is that when human beings in conflict begin to take a longer view they often set in motion a catalyzed process of peacemaking, a speeding up of healing processes that could dramatically reduce violence and hatred. It is the short-term land grab that is the most destructive to the existence of each community in its entirety and that has lead to very dangerous military spirals of action/reaction in the entire region. The deep irony is that the short-term, short-sighted, land grab in all international conflicts, such as in Bosnia, poses the greatest existential threat to each community, jeopardizing survival. Internalizing a long view of the conflict, however, triggers a relationship-building process that opens up the possibilities of coexistence and safety, sometimes quickly.

Before getting into detailed recommendations, I want to mention a couple of other summary points. The solutions that I am proposing must be nuanced for different parties to this conflict. There are different agendas and sensibilities at work in the Arab-Israeli relationship to Jews, versus the Palestinian relationship to Israelis. For example, equality in citizenship and a vision of Israel as more welcoming to non-Jewish citizens are central issues in the former, whereas basic issues of territory and nationalist claims are operative in the larger Palestinian/Israeli relationship. There are major fissures between religious and secular on both sides of this conflict. All of these subconflicts will imply somewhat different variations of the recommendations that follow, depending upon the target groups.

Further, many of the recommendations discussed in this book attempt to deal with conflict at an internal as well as external level. In other words, cultural analysis often limits itself to external human relations, deferring psychogenic issues.[2] I argue that they are inseparable. The search for a deeper and more transformative process of conflict resolution between Israelis and Palestinians cannot simply ignore the psychological misery that overwhelms so many of the people in both these communities. The internal damage done by this long conflict is extraordinary. The good news is that many people, especially young people, are looking for ways out of this misery. It behooves conflict resolution theory and practice to consider ways of cultural conflict resolution that at least attempt to speak to internal needs as well as external relations.

Education and Training

Education and training must begin to occur in a coordinated, bilateral way, between significant portions of both populations, and not just children. To have both immediate and long-term effects, these programs of training and education should be tailored to a variety of subgroups. Needless to say, the kind of training and education in values of conflict resolution that would resonate culturally may work better with some populations more than others.

But the construction of trainings that demonstrate great respect for and incorporation of the cultures in question will expand the boundaries of those committed to coexistence in a way that has not be done till now by liberal institutions.

The focus of the educational work will be on the bilateral or multilateral inculcation of values that are shared by all communities. Values education, education in civility, and character education will be the goals, though the means and the process of engagement may include conflict resolution training. The latter will be specifically tailored to embrace or incorporate cultural values. These trainings will sometimes be internal to the combating communities, engaged in separately but simultaneously. Where appropriate and politically possible, these trainings will be intercommunal.

One of the best frames for cross-cultural character education in the Abrahamic communities is the emulation of God or the prophets. This is a basic ethical and legal desideratum, if not an outright commandment. Most important, it can become a shared value, and a shared way of framing what needs to be right about society and what is currently wrong with the relationships in question. Among the many values to be emulated are care and compassion for the poor, which could transform this conflict resolution exercise into a shared commitment to social justice, one of the key missing ingredients of the peace process.

Patience with sinners, mercy for those who are imperfect, generosity with those who, in principal, one could rightfully engage in a hostile way or with vengeance, are other key ingredients. Patience, in particular, could be framed as a basic ingredient of conflict resolution. Patience would not be understood as passivity, but rather as a way of framing long-term commitment to a process. The long view of history is in general a great strength of monotheistic tradition, modeling a better vision of the future that is capable of adjusting itself to the realities of the present. A crucial ingredient in the character of the best diplomats and conflict resolvers, it has been completely neglected in the context of popular support for peace and justice. We have here the opportunity to augment that skill with a strong cultural and religious overlay.

Furthermore, training in patience becomes an end in itself in religious traditions rather than just a means toward a goal. This is important in pursuing large communal transformations wherein many individuals or subgroups may be violently subverting the peace process. In this sense, patience is framed and taught as persistence and equanimity in the face of setbacks and terrible tragedies. Thus, these values help instill in both communities a more positive cultural identity, and also help take the pressure off of day-to-day outcomes that can be so disappointing as to undermine the entire peace process.

Funding should be made available for a culturally informed set of trainings in civility, particularly in the street with strangers, and especially with members of different groups. But these trainings must be informed by the cultural values of several groups, honoring these values and not suppressing cultural identities.

There should be a marked increase in support for new forms of cultural and civic training in coping with anger and, more generally, the art of constructive argumentation. The latter is a major challenge to these cultures. Such trainings can reach a much wider range of people in each culture in that they can be depoliticized. By this, I mean that they can be framed as a path of sociocultural improvement for Israel and Palestine without necessarily having to address the core political problems. Nevertheless, third parties and funders can and should see this as part of a strategy of international conflict resolution, due to the overall benefits of such training to the transformation of culture. They should be funded for and directed to businesspeople, health care providers, police, cab drivers, and many others, both white collar and blue collar, who largely determine the interpersonal character of the public space.

These efforts must be seen in an utterly new way by third parties, as well as the peacemakers on both sides, as an integral part of peace processes, but now redefined in a far broader frame. *Peace processes will now be seen as a society-wide transformation in which the formal peace processes and negotiations become the last and crowning achievement of social and intergroup transformation*, rather than a vain attempt to impose peace where it is not wanted.

It is very important to understand that my intent here is for bilateral processes to take place, particularly among certain sections of the cultural communities who are ready for this kind of transformation when both sides engage in it. I am thinking in particular of a select group of spiritual activists on both sides, as well as women and young people. The aim would be to set in motion some basic transformations in the culture that would be spearheaded not by a financial elite but by a spiritual elite who will set the tone culturally for others. There is no doubt that there will be great resistance by some, but much less than would be incited by changes in borders, boundaries, and security arrangements, which often are insisted upon too quickly, from a sociocultural point of view.

Let me just give one example of cross-cultural character education and training. The reader should assume my complete deference to local creativity on these matters. I merely give an example here for the sake of clarity. As mentioned earlier, there is an old Islamic notion of not "shunning one's brother" for more than three days. It is not *hallal*, or proper, to shun for too long, as mentioned earlier in our study. Failure to stop the enmity is attributed to a variety of moral character flaws that reveal many things. They include envy, anger, suspicion, lack of trust, spying, and competition (*Malik's Muwatta* 47.4.13–16). The implication is that these negative values, and their positive antonyms, are taken seriously by Islam and Arabic culture as they are indicators of character.

It would be easy to locate similar texts concerning envy, anger, and the violation of trust in Jewish and Christian traditions. The corollary to competition would be harder to find, and it reveals an interesting source of possible miscommunication between Jews and Arabs. What we can find in both traditions is revealing. What we *cannot* find easily in all Abrahamic traditions often reveals the sources of basic miscommunication. Furthermore, the focus on envy and competition—in fact all of these flaws—is particularly poignant, enhancing all the problems that led to the destruction of relationship between brothers in the Abrahamic families, as recorded in the book of Genesis. This in turn harkens back to the first chapters of this book. It suggests that a training, or even simple education, in the cultural/religious uses of these issues to solve conflicts would beautifully integrate two benefits: (1) basic respect for indigenous cultural and religious values, and (2) a subtle repair of the primal Abrahamic family relationships, and the most ancient competition over favored sons of the father, or favored religions before God. A good analyst and trainer would use these wisely and carefully to maximize the effects of the suggested education and training on local populations.

There needs to be a series of principled and agreed-upon guidelines for face-to-face encounters that occur in informal and public settings. The guidelines should apply to the highest level political meetings, security encounters, as well as the most basic interactions on the street. I am speaking of a return to the elaborate premodern principles of social engagement, but applied in particular to enemies. They include habits of honor and prevention of shame, basic issues of civility, deference and display of care for someone else's family or the dignity of another's home and sacred spaces. The bases of these guidelines should resonate with the cultures in question wherever possible. The frame should not be "conflict resolution" but a moral or spiritual treaty that would become well known between the communities. The guidelines would then become a yardstick of accountability but also a confidence builder when and where they work.

In Jewish tradition, for example, they could build off of many ethical guidelines that encourage a certain benevolence in face-to-face encounters (*sever panim yafot*) and discourage hardness of the face (*azut panim*). This implies or embodies a series of ethical precepts, such as humility, benevolence, and the shunning of cruelty. At their worst, however, such precepts can become the subject of competition, debate, and mutual recrimination, rather than the basic status or existence of the enemy other. An important element of this approach to the anthropology of conflict is to see the human face in dynamic terms. A face can change from the embodiment of cruelty to a reflection of respect and honor. This runs counter to the racist trends of the modern study of physiognomy, which one often finds echoed in literature, such as the writings of Dickens and Conrad. These modern physiognomists also consider the face to be a crucial indicator of worldviews and ethical dispositions. But they view it in static, sometimes racist terms. The key is to take the face-to-face encounter seriously as a critical cause of hostility but not to allow either party to make this encounter into a cemented image of the other. Faces change, just as people do. The key is helping groups understand the importance of the encounter with the other to highlight its current pathological or antisocial character, as well as its prosocial possibilities in the future.

There should be encouragement of this new trend in civility through advertisements, youth group activities, clinics, and training for businesspeople and government workers, university research, and government legislation to earmark funds toward this purpose. This alternative is particularly usable in the Arab-Israeli relationship inside the Green Line. Such legislation could be successful in that it addresses a need and a flaw in society that cuts across class, political, and cultural boundaries. What it encourages could be framed in a variety of ways to address a broad spectrum of Israeli and Arab society.

Myth, Ritual, and Ceremony

Mourning

As mentioned in earlier chapters, the dead are critical to the genesis and perpetuation of conflict. They are a critical element in rejectionist politics of war. Their hold on the conscience of the living must be addressed by peace-building processes. The cultural rituals around mourning, apologies, and repentance could prove crucial here.

There needs to be a simultaneous encouragement of commemorative services, with mourning rites, and with markings, everywhere that Jews killed Arabs, for whatever reason, and everywhere that Arabs killed Jews, for whatever reason, on purpose or even by accident. I am thinking of Deir Yassin, for example, on the Arab side, and Ma'a lot, for example, on the Jewish side. Hebron could be a site for both sides, if there is a cease fire and some degree of decrease in hostilities across the Green Line. The focus will be on mourning lost life with rituals that are meaningful to the community whose dead are being memorialized at that particular place. In the Jewish sphere, obvious inclusions would be *kaddish* and *el moleh rahamim*, said by Jews and witnessed respectfully by the other community. Corresponding Arab ceremonies for their dead would be equally powerful. The parallels between the two traditions in terms of washing, burial, procession, eulogies, and condolences, are quite strong. Demonstrated mutual respect would be quite powerful.

At first these services can be accomplished by spiritual and cultural activists in the respective communities who have the courage to move out ahead of whatever the mainstream community is prepared to contribute. Political and financial support should be directed toward them, especially by forward-thinking third parties. But as this process progresses and as it becomes clear that it is bilateral, in that both communities witness respect for their dead coming from their enemies, the representatives of each community can become increasingly mainstream. Eventually there should be appropriate ceremonies for the highest political and religious representatives. It complicates matters if these leaders have personally shed the blood of the victims. It would be better if representatives are as high as possible on either side without offending the victims' families. This can only be ascertained inductively, case by case. Naturally, if representatives need to be slightly less powerful or famous in order to achieve this on one side, the same must be done in terms of parallel ceremonies for the other side.

None of this should attempt to co-opt or usurp private needs to mourn their dead alone. No one should be forced to participate in these processes, which should not be seen to supplant private gestures. But they could be a powerful adjunct to mourning that is already in place. Forced mourning by irresponsible authorities would be a disaster and should be defunded immediately.

A further and deeper step is not only acknowledgement and memorialization of the dead, but actual apologies. There are powerful rituals regarding this as well. I have addressed ceremonies of Jewish *teshuva*, "repentance," and Arab *sulha*. Here I just want to highlight one aspect of Jewish repentance involving going to the graves of the dead and asking forgiveness before witnesses. This would have a powerful impact on all cultures concerned. Monuments and the detailed historical acknowledgment of individual lives, families, and clans would not only enhance and complete the mourning process but also do great honor to the relatives of the victims.

There is more to mourning the results of war than mourning the dead, for more is lost than lives. Land is the principal point of conflict, but also a major subject of mourning. Whatever final status talks provide in terms of boundaries, if there is to be a two-state solution, one primarily Jewish state and one primarily Arab state, then there will have to be extensive mourning over land. There would have to be a commemoration of past ownership in both the land of Israel and Palestine. The mourning would be over past exclusive ownership. This may not be able to take place for those who do not accept final boundaries, but for those who could, a powerful cultural message would emerge. Jews will have to mourn areas of ancient Judea and Samaria that they cannot own, as Arabs must acknowledge what they can no longer own.

Alternatively, and wherever feasible, the process in question should be seen not as mourning, but acknowledgment of at least symbolic dual ownership and dual belonging. Or it could be mourning over past exclusive ownership (for Jews something in the distant past, although if settlers evacuate from certain places, they will feel the loss directly), but one that merges into a new relationship of dual belonging, if not exclusive sovereignty. For example, many villages and settlements, both inside and beyond the Green Line, could be acknowledged as having a dual heritage, albeit now one exclusive sovereignty.

As issues of acknowledgment work themselves out in terms of the status of Palestinian refugees, it is possible that cities, such as Haifa in Israel, or Hebron in the West Bank, or various Jewish settlements inside Israel proper, could acknowledge past residents. Perhaps there could be committees created, such as Palestinian Former Residents of Jaffa, or the Jewish Committee for the Cultural Preservation of Tekoa. Such people would be honored, and given some role in advising current residents, empowered to create ceremonies and memorials. Refugees would be entitled to join this organization even if they eventually resettle in other regions and receive restitution.

None of these efforts will remove the sting of disappointment completely for many people as the final and necessary compromises are reached. But, as opposed to the last disastrous fifty years of propped-up delusions that are callously foisted by politicians upon both these communities, it is time for third parties to set in motion a psychologically healthy and realistic path of embracing what will be gained by two states and mourning over what is lost. This may set in motion some important avenues of reconciliation for at least some people and also give due acknowledgement for wrongs done in the past, which is vital for the eventual normalization of ethical and political relations between these peoples.

If only a portion of these recommendations are acted upon, this may be sufficient to set in motion a spiral of prosocial gestures between enemies. That is what we are seeking, a mythic reversal of relations, a renewal of old constructs of friendship and even familial brotherhood, or cousinhood, that will create the necessary space and trust to make difficult political compromises.

A significant problem with these recommendations is that right beneath the surface of demands for acknowledgment of wrongs done are legal issues of culpability and financial responsibility. It may very well be that the backdrop of financial concerns retards the interpersonal and intercultural possibilities here. Thus it is incumbent upon us to build in a degree of elasticity into our models. For example, we may have to help combatants come up with formulas of acknowledgment that do not necessarily impinge upon future negotiations over reparations and restitution. Furthermore, it may be the case that individual citizens would be perfectly happy to acknowledge past wrongs, whereas official representatives may be more circumspect. But we should devise formulas that allow everyone to participate to the best of their ability. I raise this here as one of many complexities that need to be resolved inductively and experimentally.

Apologies, Repentance, and Forgiveness Possibilities

I want to build on some of the ideas of *teshuva* and *sulha*, previously mentioned, to conceive of practical gestures that could resonate culturally with all sides of the conflict. Let me begin with the concept of *teshuva gemurah*, "complete or absolute repentance," or the highest kind of repentance. As mentioned earlier, it involves a return to the same place and opportunity of crime, but a decision to reverse one's previous actions. This is a seamless way of uniting the psychodramatic interaction of combatants in conflict, with a psychodramatic healing process. It takes one through trauma, which is often recalled involuntarily and obsessively by victims, but this time with an eye to reversing its impact. It is proof positive of profound change in the enemy in a way that transcends words. This is a way to neutralize the compelling psychic fixation on the past. In effect, it is a psychological/moral method of reversing history. Rationally, one cannot bring back time, one cannot reverse history. But emotionally it is possible to attenuate the repetition compulsions of psychic traumas by bringing one to the same place and opportunity but with the crucial nonviolent or antiviolent shift in deed and in conscious memory.

Let me give some possible examples, although again I emphasize how important it is to elicit these from the victims themselves to see what they would devise. Ultimately, we should be able to say to combating groups, all of whom have suffered, "What will it take from your enemy to undo the past? What are you waiting to hear from him, to see him do?" I recommend going to locations, such as Deir Yassin for Arabs, and simultaneously to Ma'alot for Jews, recounting and acknowledging the loss of lives, honoring their memory, and then devising culturally appropriate ways to honor and nurture life on that spot. Perhaps there could be a commitment on that spot to support the victim community's hospitals, or adopt victim families' medical costs or pension costs. There could be blood donations, bone marrow drives, with the shedding of blood replaced by the donation of blood for life-saving activities, the blood of each community donated to save lives in the other community. Or participants could plant fruit trees and flowers. This must be decided by local actors sensitive to cultural needs: measures that are life enhancing and meaningful are the key.

Or let us take land destruction. The burning of Israeli forests and the uprooting of Palestinian olive trees could be reversed by the planting of both kinds of trees in symbolic ways and places.

The integrity of the home is a critical cultural/psychological phenomenon, crucial in Arab and Islamic culture. This needs to be actively restored. The invasion of homes by soldiers could be reversed by an honoring ceremony for homes, a new way to enter those homes with gifts, or with mortar and bricks to build more.

Public spaces, such as shopping districts, are a central feature of all cultures. Public spaces are particularly prized objects by Israelis, and ceremonies should be conceived to reverse the terrorist assault on them. This has been as deep a violation of Jewish cultural space, such as, for example, Ben Yehuda street in Jerusalem or Mahane Yehuda, as has been the invasions of Arab homes. Perhaps penance could be accomplished by plaques donated by the Arab community honoring the victims, or simply friendship plaques, or perhaps Arab-Israeli intercultural booths or centers, places where people could go to inquire about engaging the other community.

The same holy places that were defiled in violence could become objects of rebuilding, such as old mosques and ancient synagogues. This could include the consecration by the enemy of objects or books sacred to the other community. In place of the competition over sacred spaces comes alternating ceremonies of prayer and song led by sheikhs, rabbis, and priests, without artificially merging all into one but by a sequential honoring of each tradition. Sequences of gestures can work as effectively as simultaneous, bilateral gestures.

Detention camps, prisons, and scenes of destruction could become symbolically and literally replaced by centers where teams of Israeli and Palestinian psychologists and social workers give counseling to those who are traumatized by effects of the conflict. Specific centers can be named with plaques that memorialize large numbers of victims on both sides, thus providing families and friends with an honorable entry into its precincts, rather than just the stigma associated with desperately seeking emotional counseling.

Pregnancy counseling for the poor on both sides and counseling for poor families with children could replace or subvert the image and reality of children abused by and lost to this conflict. The inauguration of such activities could be accompanied by ceremonies and perhaps monuments that specifically bring this connection to public consciousness.

The borders of the two communities, objects of so much fear, hatred and disrespect, could become places of absolute honor and compassion. Thus, border guards and security personnel from both sides, subsequent to training in cultural conflict resolution, will participate in a revisitation of border crossings, but with an utterly different pattern of interaction. Civility and kindness at the borders between the peoples will take on the highest priority and will have to be combined carefully with security needs and good conflict management methods as frustrations occur. For example, one inaugurates, as part of a border ceremony, an ambulance that always awaits at the border, in case any one who must cross over needs to be taken to a hospital on the other side. Gifts, rather than just the sight of guns, await at the border for anyone going in each direction for the first time. There would be packets at the border that state explicitly the human rights that you have in going over to the other country, in addition to key phone numbers for safety and security, as well as information on sites to be visited that are relevant to the respective culture.

Some more literal recreations of *sulha* ceremonies and *teshuva* ceremonies must be attempted by bold religious actors on both sides as a paradigm for more modest actions by the majority. The key here is for the most forward-thinking religious or cultural actors on both sides to model all of the powerful symbolic subtleties that we studied earlier as a way of stimulating appropriations of these ceremonies by many others. For example, the fact that all the senses, such as the taste and smell of bitter coffee, are used in *sulha* ceremonies is extremely important. The importance of the handshake, the moment of touch between adversaries that is not violent but now a symbol of trust, is critical. The use of salt is important, as it is a deep symbol biblically as well as in all the Abrahamic traditions. Mourning foods and celebration foods are critical linkages here, as long as dietary rules and customs are respected at the intercultural moment.

Why is all this important? Just as victims of conflict feel a complete assault on their bodily person, so, too, must healing ceremonies address the whole person with all of his or her senses. Let us explore some more details in this regard, which are critical. The talmudic notion that someone can and should be asked for forgiveness three times before witnesses, that they have a right to ritualistically refuse at first is a critical detail. It means that we must build into this process the right of victims to express their rage—several times, to not be just "nice" or "forgiving." The fact that it should be before witnesses intimates that in very bad cases it is the victim's right that these ceremonies and acknowledgments be public. In others words, the victim has the right to put their adversaries through a little shame, if only a ritualized form of it. That too is critical.

Essentially, we are talking about two kinds of reversals, reversals of loss of life and injury and reversals of humiliation. These are replaced by intensive and bold moves of life giving and of honor. Needless to say, other emotions or moral and spiritual states such as compassion are a critical ingredient of these gestures. None of this should be attempted, in its literal form, by major political actors who may be seen to be abusing sacred cultural constructs. Furthermore, without proper sensitivities, they could easily perform it badly. But honestly, these kind of calculations of what will resonate and what will not with large numbers of people, and who are the best actors to engage in this, has to be carefully considered as time goes on and circumstances change.

Some might think that I am speaking of sheer fantasy, that "this will never happen." First of all, it has already happened. Such gestures happen all the time between *individual* Israelis and Arabs. But we have not devised ways to generalize it to large populations. We have not provided the ability to extend this model, slowly and carefully, into the public consciousness. This is what we must do so that eventually it overtakes, perforce, the psychology of political and cultural leaders. This requires funding, the support of courageous community leaders and activists, and some serious, indigenous brainstorming to think of ways to make this truly effective and revolutionary for larger populations.

I want to reiterate the cultural and psychological foundations of my proposals. As we studied earlier, both *sulha* ceremonies and concepts of *teshuva gemurah* have elements to their processes that involve a mirroring of and acknowledgment of crime that then reverses its devastating effect. This is what I seek. It is a set, any set, of external gestures that symbolically reverse injuries and thus are absorbed into internal processes of coping with the past, living with the present, and envisioning a future. The goal is to affect enough people on both sides to create a contagion or spiral of prosocial relations that eventually overwhelms the violent and proto-violent behaviors of others in each group.

A further thought on these gestures concerns higher and lower levels of ethical behavior. In many cultural and religious traditions there are very subtle ethical systems in which there is required behavior, preferred behavior, and heroic behavior, or very pious behavior. Much of the literature about conciliatory gestures in the Abrahamic traditions suggest levels of repentance or reconciliation that are not required but are laudable. But it turns out that many of the best gestures we have outlined are often found in this category. Furthermore, forgiveness in some traditions, such as in Islam, can sometimes be seen as not required but as an act of courage and/or generosity, as we have seen. Furthermore, we have seen that in Judaism unilateral forms of forgiveness are pious and laudable but not required. But we must access these higher levels of reconciliation by inducing *bilateral* actions. In other words, if we build these gestures into bilateral ceremonies, as a part of mutual trust-building measures, we can stimulate the best cultural resources on all sides.[3]

Shared Ground Rules and Conflict Anticipation

Often, as I have reflected on what went wrong in the Oslo peace process it occurs to me to examine also what went right but that ended up damaging the process anyway. What I mean by this is the excellent relationships that developed between some of the major negotiators. These people knew the names not only of each others' children but also the grandchildren. They told jokes to each other about their respective leaders. In other words, they developed trust and intimacy. But their major failing, at least in my assessment, is that they assumed that millions of people were prepared to make the same compromises that they were contemplating, paying a much higher price for such compromises, and yet without any of the relationship building that they had experienced!

A key element of that relationship building was the formal and informal creation of ground rules, almost treaty-style, in the relationship-building process. This is basic to many trainings in conflict resolution, and for good reason. Why did no one think to get the larger communities on both sides used to such ground rules? The answer veers between arrogant neglect, fear of the masses, and the deliberate use of the masses' rage for a bargaining chip.

One of the unspoken ground rules was that family is important in relationship building. This could and should translate into parallel intercultural peacemaking processes that require improved family contacts as part of the program of international peacemaking. This is already happening in terms of a few of the victims' families on both sides, but it is privately, poorly funded and not supported in a profound way by the "official" peacemakers or third parties like the United States. It affects maybe five hundred families. This is not enough to create cultural movement of any kind.

Another ground rule was patience, or the ability to persist in relationship even when some extremists were doing terrible things in their name. We must ask ourselves how to extend this ground rule to a much larger group of Israelis and Palestinians.

Among the best of these negotiators—not all—another ground rule was respect even in the midst of profound disagreement. This too must be the basis for intercultural ground rules.

As we extend the ground rules to broad populations, we should consider incorporating values that resonate with each culture. Some forward-thinking organizations should develop an intercultural treaty, not a complete treaty but at least an intercultural one that consists of ground rules that specify how to proceed in the conflict and in its possible resolution. The focus would be on the means, not the ends, on the style of interaction, not its outcome, on ethical guidelines of behavior that can be acted upon now. Many Israelis and Palestinians want this, as long as it addresses aspects of the others' behavior that cause them the most fear and injustice.

Joint Chanting and Prayer

Some important rituals that emerged in the last few years have involved some sheikhs, rabbis, and other activists engaging in various prayer services together. These have included Sufi dances, but also chanting that alternates Jewish and Muslim meditations on peace. These joint practices have been conducted in a way that, at least in principle, would not offend a large spectrum of practitioners on both sides. However, it should also be said that many others on both sides would never participate in such joint religious rituals, even those who may be sympathetic with the goals of the gesture. Furthermore, many others would be extremely threatened by the implied syncretism of such work.

A very wide spectrum of actors are at work here. I argue that many avenues to transformation of public consciousness can and should take place. This work has been powerful at key moments for many participants. For example, at the height of the Intifada of 2000–2001 there were Jews and Muslims chanting Shalom and Salaam, together, near the Temple Mount, right down the street sometimes from the violence! It is even more interesting to me that fundamentalists on both sides did not attack this group but merely ignored them. That is a pivotal accomplishment.

The pessimistic analysis would be that these chanters were not attacked because they were not a real threat to fundamentalist interests, and they could not fundamentally change the situation. The moment they could do so, they would have been attacked. Possibly. But this does not explain why the more delinquent among *haredi* youth who attacked Reform Jews at the Western Wall, or women at the Western Wall, would not have taken the opportunity to go against this group. Maybe this group of chanters tied into a symbolic process that did not immediately threaten or offend anyone. This suggests that there are ritualistic ways to seep into the cultural consciousness without immediately creating violent reactions.

The reaction of many people in Israel and Palestine, brutalized into toughness by this endless confrontation, is that such gestures of prayer actually display weakness and frailty. In many cultures, however, especially those influenced by Taoism and Buddhism, this way of stimulating individual and collective change is not perceived as weak or ineffectual but, on the contrary, as more effective and powerful. The reason is that it does not provoke a counter-response but rather seeps into the consciousness of enemies as part of the realm of possibility. Such a strategy of social change appears to me to be a vital and nonviolent alternative that is currently missing, almost entirely, from the Israeli and Palestinian cultural landscapes. It is not combative but it is challenging. It is filled with a sense of love and care but is not passive and quietistic. It is a response to violence and hatred that third parties need to foster and support much more, precisely because the effectiveness of this approach may not appear to be obvious currently to many peace activists on the ground. In this case, I am arguing for a method of cultural intervention that is not exactly inspirational when viewed from the perspective of the majority of the cultures in question, even the majority of the peacemaking subcultures. Nevertheless, it is supportive of indigenous processes that do exist and in this sense is still effective.

We need many more such efforts, but they must reach a broader spectrum of actors, especially religious actors. Local activists must creatively devise ceremonies that even fundamentalists may embrace or at least respect. The Interfaith Encounter Association does courageously engage in some of these activities, and they do in fact reach a broader range of religious actors on both sides. Yehuda Stolov's brilliant work with this group has been a quiet, shining light in the midst of many setbacks.

As of this writing, the situation is more violent than ever, which makes it difficult to contemplate such joint rituals. There are some people who join such rituals precisely when conflict seems much worse and more hopeless, as if, in desperation, they turn to ritual and nonrational transformation of conflict. Many others, however, cannot bring themselves to meet the enemy other ritually when that other is hurting their own group so badly. For this reason, such rituals can and should be most forcefully supported in the sociopolitical space and time between war and peace, such as the many wasted years of the Oslo process, when such ritual transformations should have been heavily supported by both sides officially, rather than being marginalized and scoffed at by the ruling liberal elites in strange consort with the rejectionists. It is in the space in between war and peace that such rituals can seep into the public consciousness and create new possibilities.

There always is a nucleus of actors when these joint rituals crop up. This nucleus, which cuts across religious lines, consists of people who often have long-standing and deep relationships of trust with each other, across enemy lines, that survive even when one group in the conflict engages in some horrible act of violence. Thus, relationship building is once again the critical underpinning of many other conflict-resolving activities. But the key is that relationship building occurs between people who then take that relationship into some creative mythic space of actions for peace, justice, and reconciliation. That is a critical way in which their relationship building results in effective influence on a larger population.

Third parties, such as donors and NGOs, must learn how to keep their ears to the ground, to learn to spy out every action that is being taken, and to seek out those who are acting boldly. People who engage in creative ritual exchanges may have insights, perceptions, and creative impulses that could change the face of a conflict if they were properly funded. But they are not necessarily the kind of people who are savvy at fund-raising and publicity. On the contrary, they are often nonconformists who have arrived at their creative ways by avoiding the "talents" necessary to fit into the status quo. For this reason, courageous funders and third parties who are engaging in self-examination about their failures in the Middle East must actively seek out such people and nurture their talents, and especially their ability to affect a much wider audience.

Sin and the Possibilities of a Truth and Reconciliation Commission

A carefully honed version of the Truth and Reconciliation Commission (TRC) that South Africa made famous, but that has also been instituted in varying forms in other conflicts, should be considered here when the time is right. It should be considered as a part of an interim or final settlement on the official diplomatic track of any renewed peace process. There are disenfranchised groups in this conflict, never represented at the official level, whose needs and interests constantly skew official conversations. Such a commission could channel their legitimate rage and need for acknowledgment. TRCs are also highly dramatic, ritualistic frameworks that could allow for a proxy mythic process of war and peace, conflict and reconciliation.

A Palestinian activist said to me recently that, more than anything else, there must be full acknowledgment by the world, and by Israelis, of the Nakbeh (the Catastrophe), as Palestinians refer to 1948. Of course, that acknowledgement includes acknowledgment of only her version of the history, which involves only Jewish sins and only Palestinian victimization. What will come out of good commissions, or joint efforts at historical investigation, however, is at least a partial recognition of victimization, a telling of many stories, and hopefully admissions of wrongs done. This will never satisfy those whose narcissism cannot allow for any wrongs in their own group. But it will go a long way to satisfy some of this need.

For many Palestinians, Nakbeh is tied together in complicated ways with the "right of return." Demands for the latter, of course, shut down the conversation with the vast majority of Israelis and Jews, who look upon an unconditional right of return as the final strategy in a Palestinian, Arab, and Muslim effort to get back the whole land, to have two states, not one, but this time through demographic victory. Demographic war is especially the stock and trade of fundamentalist methods in many parts of the world, which is why it is so tied to anti-abortion and anti-birth-control stances. Poverty and maximum fertility are the key ingredients of this process.

But this need on the part of Palestinians to hear acknowledged a right of return goes well beyond the fundamentalists. What their progressives say is that, at the same time, they recognize that the return will not happen completely. What they seek is *acknowledgment* of the right. But Israelis see this as a ploy to achieve international delegitimation of the entire concept of a two-state solution, with one state primarily Jewish, and one state primarily Palestinian. This is enormously complicated by the fact that there are regional divergences here between Palestinians. Israeli Arabs, or Israeli Palestinians, have as their major goal a non-Jewish state in which they could be equal citizens. Gazans tend to focus on the settlements in Gaza, West Bankers on the settlements there, and the prisonlike conditions. Refugees or foreign citizens focus on the right of return.

Trying to navigate the varying demands is complicated, and most liberal Jews have given up in response to the deaths and injuries of Jews in the latest Intifada. They feel intuitively that the most important thing that Jews are being requested to do is to disappear. There are serious efforts to come up with rational compromises on these issues. But I argue that we have here, especially in 2001, a number of maximalist positions being advocated for the first time in decades by moderate Palestinians, in addition to Israeli electoral "maximalist" positions being expressed by virtue of electing Sharon. This suggests to me that rational bargaining positions have become severely distorted by brutal injury on both sides, and deep existential fear and rage. One can certainly blame some of this on bad politicians and failed capacities to avoid violence. But the very processes were constitutionally flawed. The march of rational conflict resolution processes, in the absence of acknowledgment of deeper issues, has provoked this extremism even more than the individual failings of Barak and Arafat in 2000.

Full acknowledgment of the past may help neutralize the current drive to maximalist bargaining positions. I was told unofficially by Palestinians that this is precisely what happened to Arafat's bargaining position in the summer and fall of 2000. He seemed to be prepared to make a deal in which there would be only a modest right of return with no acknowledgment of responsibility in exchange for many other territorial compromises. The lobby and influence of refugees grew dramatically for a variety of reasons, however, and Arafat was told very clearly that he would not survive if he came back from Camp David without a right of return. If this is true, the official diplomatic processes suffered a severe blow because the refugees had not seen themselves represented in the process all along. Their plight was never acknowledged, their circumstances never really improved, and no one bothered to devise a way in which they could have seen immediate benefits of the peace process over the past twelve years. No peace process can survive or should be attempted unless it reforms these basic flaws.

When the time is ripe, a TRC will be a critical adjunct to material and concrete solutions to the refugee tragedy. Cultural processes must accompany the evolution of the status of the refugees at every juncture. And the past cannot and should not be buried. It should be acknowledged and mourned, with a promise for change. But this will have to happen on both sides, with all the atrocities of terrorism equally exposed and acknowledged.

As far as the legal ramifications, everyone has something to be feared here in terms of class-action law suits. The acknowledgments will have to carry with them immunity from civil as well as criminal courts if we are to receive the full cultural and psychological benefits of this process of open disclosure. Some individuals may come forth and apologize. Others may not. But there will be much more shared truth on the table than there is now, especially since there is none currently. This change in itself will stimulate very important cultural transformations in both groups. On a religious level, it will resonate deeply and disturbingly with the acknowledgment of sin and the force of repentance. It will cause many religious arguments. But I believe it could be one of the most important elements in helping Abrahamic monotheism to recover its moral integrity, something that has been severely distorted by this long and brutal war.

Care for Enemies

Caring for enemies is a principle and practice that, in its literal form, always attracts a few actors on both sides who then have a dramatic impact by virtue of their courage. This could include helping victims of violence, or working with children, visiting hospitals, and other creative interactions. Various sources in the Abrahamic traditions support such behavior, as we have discussed. I must emphasize that there is a fine line between expressing care for an enemy in trouble and appearing to your own group as a traitor. A few will *always* consider you a traitor by virtue of any prosocial gesture toward or even sentiment expressed about an enemy. But, for the majority, what seems necessary for acceptance is that one's prosocial gesture toward a suffering enemy be (1) clearly not a shifting of allegiance, an either/or position, and (2) expressed equally to suffering members of one's own group. The latter is where most progressives fail.

In its less literal form, the principle of caring for an enemy is often expressed by the better diplomats. They couch their criticisms of the other side in the context of praise for accomplishments and advancements. They focus their criticism on the violent actions of their adversary but not on a characterization of their enemies as such. This expresses a kind of care that is critical for the transformation of human relationships. In religious terms it involves Abrahamic notions such as "hating the sin and not the sinner," or seeing the image of God in all people that implies that even in the context of rebuke and anger there should be acknowledgment of the greatness of another human being. This is a powerful cultural reminder to avoid the either/or drive of conflict, aggression toward an enemy or passivity before him. Such a combination of care and criticism is neither passive nor aggressive. It points to engagement that is caring, but not the kind that capitulates before the sins of the other, a critical model for general populations.

Once again, the constructive ways in which this was actualized by certain diplomats during the Oslo process should have become the basis for a very broad-based inculcation of this approach in the general population. The two sides should have been engaged in a constant combined process of care and criticism which, at each stage, would have become a litmus test for the next stage of relationship building.

What I would have recommended as interim gestures of care and criticism, for example, would have been a broad-based bilateral exchange of care that would be subject to criticism. For example, I would have taken two or three issues and made them a litmus test. For Israelis, I would have offered a commitment to a completely different and utterly transformed relationship at the border, with soldiers, and with police in general, as outlined earlier. For Palestinians, I would have outlined a systematic set of adult and child, formal and informal, educational measures designed to expose their people to a completely different and humanized picture of Jews, Israelis, Judaism, and Jewish history.

Step by step, these gestures of care could have been tested against each other, encouraged and praised when successful, and criticized where they were failing. The evolution of the peace process would have been absolutely dependent on these successes. The mediation of bilateral actions would have become a principal, if not *the* principal role of major third parties, rather than endless mediated negotiations on final status issues. For example, incremental surrender of contested lands would have been offered in exchange for the

Arab care of Jewish holy spaces. In other words, the Jews would have offered land back that was misappropriated in various places and the Arabs would have demonstrated in those same regions a respect for the Jewish aspects of the region. The same could be done within the Green Line. Such bilateral gestures could have set the stage for increasingly difficult compromises in the final status arrangements. Indeed, they could be tailored incrementally to actions at the most controversial places, such as Jerusalem and the Temple Mount. There is no doubt in my mind that this will have to be a key to processes in the future that actually intend to be permanently successful.

Bereaved Parents as Ritual Means of Transformation

The Parents' Circle, which has brought together Jewish and Palestinian parents who have lost their children in the violence, is a powerful model of reconciliation. Furthermore, its directors filmed these amazing encounters and developing relationships. The film can form the basis for shifting attitudes about the possibilities in future Arab-Israeli relations. Some peacemaking efforts are flawed in principle, some in practice. But there are others, such as this one, in which their major flaw, and the reason they failed to have a greater impact is simply that they needed far more publicity and many more participant families.

These families are so important because they comprise the truly injured. Vamik Volkan, in personal comments made to me in 2001, distinguished between psychic danger and real danger. He stated that the problem with groups in conflict is the constant confusion between very real dangers that must be addressed, and psychic dangers that become reified in the mind and the emotions but that truly distort reality and thwart the realistic possibilities of human relations. I would add to this by distinguishing between true injury and psychic/vicarious injury. Many people are injured vicariously each time that someone from their group is violently murdered. Such vicarious injuries are often the true impediment to transforming relations between enemies. Actual victims, both the injured and the families of the dead, are really in a completely different psychological space vis-à-vis the experience of violence.

The same can be said for soldiers who have seen war and politicians who advocate it. I have often found myself preferring to work with soldiers and policemen rather than right-wing politicians. The actual experience of violence and loss does not necessarily turn people into either hawks or pacifists. It actually can create either. But it does nuance and deepen their understanding of this fundamental human experience, namely, of violence and its consequences. Correspondingly, this turns direct victims of violence, in some ways, culturally speaking, into a kind of resource, a moral source of authority. Giving voice to them could not be more important. From a moral point of view, they should have not the only voice but a much larger say in the future of peace and violence, wherever their voices lead. This is what is accomplished by the Parents' Circle. Here is the central point. Their bereavement should be the *real* bereavement, their injury should be the *true* injury, not the kind of injury that is conjured by demagogic politicians. Their injury, not the psychic injury, should gain prominence, because it will lead to authentic healing in the long run.

Monotheism has focused on victims of violence, particularly parents who lose their children, as a source of forgiveness. As mentioned earlier, the rabbinic notion that if someone is a good man and he buries a child, then all his sins are forgiven, points to a kind of moral authority and power that one must give over to these parents. Perhaps there could be a bilateral cultural agreement between these two peoples, Israelis and Palestinians, that in whatever fighting between them that ensues, that parents who have lost children are in a different category. Both sides treat them with magnified compassion and special respect, and treat them as if they have been forgiven as enemies. They would thus become a beachhead of reconciliation, a cultural icon that disallows by its very existence blanket condemnation of all peoples on both sides. And this would be operationalized independently of what those parents said about the killers of their children, because, after all, we allow many things, outrageous things, to people steeped in their grief. Moreover, they should have an honored place in any peace process of the future. Not only should their sacrifice be recognized, they should have some voice in the final decision-making processes. They become yet another vehicle of including the general population in the nonviolent struggle for peace and justice. But, more important, they become the real and authentic symbol of injury and the consequences of violence and thus suck the wind out of the psychic dangers and injuries conjured by demagogic rhetoric on all sides. This is key to peacebuilding and conflict transformation.

New Identity Issues

As mentioned in earlier chapters, one aspect of psychic and moral transformation in various Abrahamic traditions involves shifting one's name and identity. This is perhaps the most problematic method of personal transformation to extend to large groups. In some ways, both on a personal and collective level, if someone is prepared to shift their identity to some degree, to make peace with another, then the peace is already at hand. Furthermore, it is easier for a person to hit rock bottom alone, face himself, and then change than it is to do this before an adversary. Thus, people in intimate relationships will often leave or find some way to destroy that relationship, and only then, when alone, come face to face with the need to change in some fundamental way. It is extremely hard to change one's identity right in the face of an enemy who is trying, as far as you can tell, to obliterate your identity. This is as true in families as it is in the life of nations.

Thus, to some degree, the step that I recommend must take place within the safety and solitude of each people. They must face alone the consequences of almost a century of hatred and violence and its continuing impact on their children and their own mental health. They must come to terms with what their identity is but also what it can be in the future. There must be an authentic search by people from all sides of the political and cultural spectrum to ask together, in a positive sense, "What is a Palestinian?" and "What is an Israeli?" Can a Palestinian be only Muslim? Only religious? Only anti-Israel? Can a Palestinian also reside in Israel as a loyal citizen? Can a Jew be a Palestinian citizen and truly belong there? Is this a fantasy or a possibility? Can a non-Jew truly be an equal citizen in Israel, an Israeli, or not? Is Israel primarily a Jewish state, partly, completely, not at all? Does "Jewish" mean something cultural or something religious? Does a good Israeli or Palestinian share his land, or does that obliterate his identity? Can I have many positive identities at once? A Jew, an Israeli, a human being, an active citizen, a Palestinian, an Arab, a Muslim, a Christian, an activist committed to human rights, a child of Abraham, a child of Adam? It would be good to imagine the answers to these questions in two distinct environments, one violent, the current situation, and one nonviolent, in some distant future perhaps. How would the answers change, or would they? If they would, then why, and what does it say about one's identity?

The prevailing efforts to address these issues have been framed in negative terms, as a protest against the status quo, as a questioning, for example, of the very foundations of a state. As long as this remains a contest of competing negative identities, an effort to obliterate religious and cultural identities of one's adversaries, it will be a war forever. But if it can be framed in new symbolic ways, especially with multiple identities possible, and emerging from strong relationship-building and trust-building practices, then the chances are it will appeal to a much larger mass of people. And they will provide the political space for truly courageous political leaders.

There needs to be serious efforts to think about the multiple identities expressed through national institutions. There needs to be a bill of rights for both countries, and a set of national symbols, on both sides, such as anthems, that will embody multiple identities and a pluralistic culture. But these steps will be maximally threatening to cultural purists on both sides if they attempt to merge all identities into one. Ways must be devised to recognize multiple identities and a pluralistic community. This will have to be done in both countries in the future. For this reason, for the healthy identity of both communities, there should be a significant Palestinian population of Israel, recognized as such in terms of equal civil rights, and a parallel Jewish population of Palestine, recognized as such with equal civil rights. Both states will then begin to resemble the binational entity originally envisioned, diluting the cultural and psychological trauma of radical separation from and loss of ancestral lands.

The Calendar as Ritual Experience

A minority but mainstream group of people representing all the major religions should devise a way to demonstrate respect for the fasts and celebrations of other communities. This is already done by the Israel Interfaith Association, among others, but the practice should become much more widespread. It should include ways to support, where religiously possible and permissible, the celebrations or mourning of the other religious communities, which could have a powerful and positive impact. This must be done publicly by significant cultural figures on all sides, but they need not be the most powerful figures. It is much more important that whoever engages in such activities be perceived as sincere and authentic in his or her gestures. This activity, furthermore, does not need to be done by the majority and not by fundamentalists. But it does need to be done in a way that will not be offensive to cultural and religious purists.

This has also already occurred to some degree in the context of various seminars. Furthermore, forward-thinking people, already engaged in ritual processes of transformation, should think jointly and inter-religiously about special days on the calendar for joint mourning of tragic moments of inter-religious encounter, going very far back in history and right up to the present. Of course, I am thinking about the Crusades, pogroms, expulsions, but also the moments of tragedy in the Jewish-Arab encounter of the last hundred years.

In a parallel process, this group should conceive and devise joint days of positive memory and commemoration. This could include significant persons from the past who represent a shared cultural history of respect, such as Maimonides. Perhaps there could be Jewish-Jordanian commemorations of the life of King Hussein, or Jewish figures inspired by Arab poets, philosophers, and even spiritual masters. Certainly shared historical interest in Sufism would qualify in this regard. Joe Montville is investing extensive energy in analyzing the inter-monotheistic patterns of coexistence in Moorish Spain, for example. This must be accomplished in concert with historians who could give an accurate and unromantic view of the past, but also an honest sketch of good times and circumstances. Of course, such calendar celebrations can and should be built on any positive milestones that emerge in the Palestinian-Israeli relationship, if it begins to improve. I suggest a new calendar that supplements the life cycle of each community and that offers an identity to all that is overarching, that does not threaten the life cycle of each community, but that provides a multiple experience of spiritual and cultural life cycle, and thus a healthy, multiple identity. Thus, the rhythm of life and ritual merge into a new and internalized consciousness of coexistence, which transforms the future into a deepening and filling out of cultural identity, rather than threatening its continuation.

Land Attachments

I mentioned in earlier chapters that there is an old Jewish, rabbinic idea of voluntary exile as a way of overcoming sin. There is a way in which the experience of exile, of being a refugee, is exactly what makes the love of land so precious a gift. But it also is the basis, on a religious level, of making land into a kind of idolatry, a focus of ultimate value before which all other values must be sacrificed. This is an old Abrahamic theme, land as gift, but also as snare. On both a religious and psychological plane, the dream of land has become a goad to survival, but also a snare for both cultures.

I think it bears reflection on how, ritually and mythically speaking, people from both communities can begin to demonstrate some acknowledgment of ways in which the struggle over land has affected their ethical/spiritual condition. We cannot recommend as an antidote voluntary exile, nor even symbolic exile, however, since exile is the place of pain for both peoples. Yet, exile, travel, and life in many places are a habit of both Israelis and Palestinians. My suggestion is that the theme of exile, return, and the reality of refugee life, become a common area of inquiry and joint commemoration: a way to embrace the refugee but also an acknowledgment and appreciation of home as the deepest cultural need. The most powerful and obvious way to accomplish this is through a museum of the international refugee that would detail the lives of Jews and Palestinians as exiles, in the past and in the present. It would be dispassionate, but it would have a mission, an educational focus that aimed to teach people, especially the young generation, about the plight of refugees the world over. As such, it could escape the narcissistic focus on only Jews and Arabs, a key problem of many conflict resolution techniques. It would also acknowledge the pain and loss of each community, as well as their dreams.

The experience of massive and distant migration is one of the most pervasive of modern human experiences. If it can become a source of shared understanding, respect, and sympathy, it can become yet another important cultural/psychological bridge. It is a way to engage the past but also the present, to apologize and acknowledge by deed and symbol, and not by words. It would have to have museum branches accessible to both communities, and perhaps a central location on the border between them. If successful, it could be a proud model of a new kind of peacemaking that could help other groups in conflict. Even if the funds are initially unavailable for an entire museum, approximations to this joint venture could be devised, such as exhibits that travel between the communities, and internationally. I fully acknowledge that the status of the refugees and the right of return is one of the most vexing stumbling blocks to a full peace. But I do believe in interim gestures, such as this one, providing a kind of energy to the transformation of relationships. The latter sets the stage for more successful negotiations.

If, furthermore, such symbolic gestures are combined with presettlement, interim bilateral and global commitments to steadily improve the lives of the Palestinian refugees, something that justice demands of *both* sides here, then the combination will provide the intellectual engine for permanent solutions. It is only through this process that high-level negotiations will be allowed finally to succeed. The deed must come first, and then the word. Deeds must be done, and then the words we seek will be spoken.

The Poor

Aid to others as a form of peacemaking is something that I have advocated in earlier chapters. I therefore recommend that there be careful, bilateral consideration of how this could be done in a way that would be transformative to both communities. It clearly carries with it the risk of humiliation of poor people, in both communities. This problem is not limited to areas of conflict. It is the essential problem of global poverty relief and development programs.

A collaborative effort on both sides should include good psychologists, social workers, development experts, and knowledgeable, creative religious and cultural representatives. The Arab-Israeli and Jewish communities may be able to devise something effective in this regard, whereas the problems beyond the Green Line, in this regard, would be formidable. Needless to say, drawing upon the rich resources in each cultural tradition regarding social justice, charity, generosity, and respect for human beings, would be essential to the success of the effort. But the landmines in each religious tradition would have to be anticipated and circumvented.

Charitable generosity and aid in development, just like the ritual gestures mentioned in earlier sections, can be a nonverbal form of apology and acknowledgment. The more moral gestures and psychological means that we have at our disposal to act as apology and acknowledgment, the better will be our peacemaking processes. This avoids all the legal fears of verbal acknowledgment, and it also circumvents that perennial enemy of reconciliation, saving and losing face. That is not to say that very often there will be private moments, powerful moments, of exchanged words and apologies. We expect that and want it to happen. But we do not want anyone to feel shackled to verbal means only of reconciliation and, therefore, choose not to buy into the relationship-building processes that we seek.

Study as Peacebuilding

As mentioned previously, study as a mode of intermonotheistic relationship building has some very exciting possibilities, some of them already in evidence. The process of study is clearly oriented toward the educated elite, of course. Although teachers and educators emerging from such a process would be in an infinitely better position to create educational programming, for adults as well as children, it could truly be transformative for a much larger population.

The transformative results of such study, when done well, are many: (1) honor of adversarial communities by the act itself of shared study, (2) ripple effects in the masses by everyone hearing about this process of honoring, especially if media are wisely utilized and official actors decide to actually encourage such activity, (3) the participants themselves developing a much more nuanced understanding of their adversaries' moral assets and moral problems inside their tradition, and especially inside the lived reality of the other's religious world, thus undermining patterns of demonization, and (4) discovery of shared insights, symbols, and values that can become the basis for creative and new intercultural processes of moral relationship building and conflict resolution.

If this is done poorly, it can result in (1) Arrogant asymmetries in presentation of the materials, (2) a confirmation of the worst fears of adversaries about repressive elements in the other's tradition without corresponding prosocial values, (3) a pitting of two monotheisms against the third, and (4) an overly intellectual exercise that leaves no room for and is unprepared for the inevitable outbursts of injury and conflict, thus squandering the opportunity for increased understanding. In other words, all steps in this process must be performed with great care and expertise, and a heavy dose of ongoing self-examination.

Social Contract and Covenants

Contracts play a critical role in monotheistic history, beginning with the divine/Noachide covenant with humanity, and especially the Abrahamic covenant with God. But there are many biblical covenants, including many between erstwhile enemies, even family enemies, such as in the book of Genesis. In the lived reality of Jewish and Islamic life, honoring contracts and treaties is an entrenched and sacred experience in some ways. It is certainly acceptable as a cultural practice. The concept of New Covenant is central to Christianity as well. We must build on this.

All the best work in conflict resolution training workshops begins with the creation of shared principles, especially when the group is diverse and includes adversaries, as most of my trainings do. I purposely call these shared principles "treaties," "covenants," or "contracts," as I have learned from others in the Middle East. Contracts accomplish many things. They immediately give voice and power to everyone in the room, so that this is not done later by the participants themselves in destructive ways. They acknowledge difference and diversity but also evoke higher shared values where everyone doubted there were any. Examples of rules that my trainees devised include everyone listened to with respect, waiting to speak until others finish, voluntary time limits on speaking (e.g., no more than five minutes, but preferably two minutes), honoring of other people's religious traditions but permission to question and challenge, anger expressed by other than personal abuse. The rules emerge spontaneously from an extremely diverse population from around the world. I have heard these emerge from rooms containing twenty-five people from fifteen countries and all the major religions.

In a good encounter, these principles will occasionally be violated, due to the engaged passions. But the contract will bring everyone back to the center eventually, like a constitution or social contract, and often it will be accompanied by powerful apologies as mini-conflicts and dramas recreate the larger conflict. And it will become a model, conscious and unconscious, for building a new civilization across enemy lines.

But the contracts that I envision go much farther than providing the basis for group encounters and workshops. Along the lines of the Jerusalem treaty analyzed earlier, I would like to see efforts to generate literally dozens of treaties and contracts between forward thinking subgroups of the respective populations that will act as irrefutable symbols and beacons for everyone else. Let treaties and contracts, and debates over their violation, proliferate and diversify. Let them empower and engage and frustrate every subsector of the civilizations. Let the official treaties be one part only of a much larger, ultimately more powerful, revolution in the course and style of the conflict.

There should be covenants between Jewish and non-Jewish workers and employees about an honorable and trusting relationship, mutual rights, and responsibilities. Let mothers do the same, and teenagers, psychologists, doctors, police officers, rabbis and sheikhs, scientists and human rights activists. Let the courageous ones in both populations—and there I mean many whom I have met—say in cultural language what they will and will not do to each other and for each other in the future. Let them commit themselves as signators to new, interim social contracts, and let this proliferate until it filters up to the formal and official process of constructing lasting solutions to the coexistence of these two peoples.

We cannot underestimate the importance of interim treaty concepts, such as the Arab *hodna*, cease-fire, mentioned earlier, contracts that could be about bilateral nonbelligerency on the West Bank coupled with a commitment to abstain from theft and invasion of property by force. There should be honor contracts at the borders, about police behavior and civilian behavior. Civilians should agree to full disclosure and respect. Police agree to respect, compassion, no insults, no slurs, listening commitments, accommodation of special needs, especially medical ones, and the use of weapons as only a last resort.

There should be cultural contracts in business relations, above and beyond legal necessity, that each intergroup contact can cement a new way of life, one step at a time. This is what the Oslo process needed and failed to accomplish. It failed to mandate an incremental change in the way everyone was treated on both sides as human beings. This is what I seek now as the *essential* core of a new process of social change that opens the door to profound political change.

Trust Building

Trust building follows directly from the previous point. The fulfillment of contracts breeds trust. Partial fulfillment breeds partial trust but also partial disappointment and fear. But the latter is better than the disgraceful abandonment of the public space to callousness and belligerency during the Oslo years, while a very few were busy transforming their own relations.

We need an incremental set of steps, especially in conditions where de-escalation is necessary. I am thinking also of the first-track diplomats following in this route. Where possible, it should occur in local settings and regions, such as Jerusalem, where local first-track representatives (like mayors and city councils) agree to smaller bilateral promises that are fulfilled or not fulfilled within a week or month. This has been tried many times in de-escalation efforts, but it has never been broad-based enough and inclusive enough of the activities and behaviors of the general populations, which is vital for empowerment and the creation of a spiral of good will. First-track actors cannot accomplish this alone, but they do need to lead the effort where possible. We must work on ways to build and sustain trust in small ways that culturally resonate, that address basic human needs, and that are capable of being built up incrementally.

Self-Examination and the Move from Barrier to Bridge

To conclude the specific recommendations, I return to the original space of all peacemaking, and that is the individual and his or her heart. All the power of and failures of peacemaking originate inside the human heart or psyche. We all have much more power in peace and conflict than we realize, and we also possess many of its failures. Even the structural injustices of conflict, such as those involving police power, and land and asset distribution, originate in a series of bad decisions by individuals who often thought they were doing the right thing but who failed to examine honestly their attitudes and actions, and the consequences of their actions.

The most insidious and important practical element in the process of self-examination is for each individual and each subgroup on all sides of a conflict—including the third parties—to understand the powerful human need to have enemies and allies, as Vamik Volkan has taught us. Such a driving power of identity formation emerges from this process of differentiation. We cannot eliminate the need for individuation and differentiation, nor should we want to. What we can hope to accomplish is to enable ourselves and others not to demonize one person or group as we come to establish our own identity. We all tend to do this, but through regular processes of self-examination, we must learn not to transfer hatred as we seek to live, and as we seek to make peace.

On the contrary, we must train ourselves to achieve our identities through differentiation that is less violent, less destructive. Furthermore, we must always search for what we share with adversaries over and above the differences, and thus search for some higher common values and visions even as we hold to adversarial positions and identities in other matters. This is a constant challenge along the political spectrum of every group and subgroup. If people across cultures in Israel and Palestine learn how to differentiate and individuate with less hatred and rage, this will have a significant impact on the Palestinian-Israeli conflict. This must happen inside the two communities as well, both of which are currently riddled with demonized others. The purpose is not to make everyone the same, or even for everyone to love each other, but to discover identity without hatred and rage, and also overarching values and practices that provide bridges to all sides of conflicts.

None of this can happen until the third parties, the peacemakers, both within the Palestinian and Israeli communities, as well as outside third parties, subject themselves to regular self-examination regarding the issues of rage, demonization, and self-definition. I have concluded more and more that the failings and the answers to this conflict lie with the peacemakers, both official and unofficial actors. It is the peacemakers, due to our prejudices and need to have enemies and allies, who have lost opportunities to collaborate with each other with humility and vision, to help the parties evolve, to empathize at every moment with people on both sides, to help the principal parties see what they are doing to perpetuate the conflict, and what they can realistically do differently.

A corollary of this issue of the internal workings of the individual is the question of how to become a bridge between enemies, especially when you are a member of one of the enemy groups. This is one of the most difficult tasks that a human being is ever asked to do. Yet it is a crucial capacity for the future of human civilization. Balancing a relationship between one's own group and an enemy entails constant psychological work. One must balance ethics of care for one's group, compassion for victims, a commitment to multiple values such as loyalty, peace, and justice, which often compete with each other in wrenching ways. But this is important training, because the ethical/spiritual balancing act of competing commitments parallels strategic efforts to be an effective bridge in actual conflict resolution practices.

Recommendations to Officials

I have referred throughout this book to new approaches in official diplomacy that could fundamentally transform the Palestinian-Israeli conflict. I want to emphasize just a few at the end. There has to be far less emphasis in the future (in this conflict as well as numerous other intractable conflicts) on final-status negotiations and far more on the mediated means by which relationships between the ruling elites and their masses change vis-à-vis their enemies. Processes of relationship building must come into far greater balance with outcomes and goals. Therefore, the word, the use of the word for negotiation and dialogue, must share to a far greater degree the psychodramatic stage of violence de-escalation and peace processes. The word must share this stage with the deed, with action, with gestures, that can be seen as ethical or spiritual or even mythic, depending on who is interpreting them. But the deed must take on far greater importance.

This means that the third parties, from the grass roots third parties to the official third parties, must retrain themselves professionally and psychologically to understand the central significance of the human act, from the subtle civilities and incivilities inside the elite negotiating room all the way to the most crass behavior of callous policemen. They must come to believe and internalize that a signed agreement, a piece of paper—no matter how valued initially—means nothing next to the power, both destructive and redemptive, of the human deed in both its moral and symbolic manifestation. Third parties must come to believe that the elite are both more powerful and less powerful than they think they are. They are less powerful in that they find it difficult to believe just how constrained they are by the will of the majority. When most people hate and want their enemies dead, then there is nothing they can

sign to change that until they learn what it is truly needed to lessen that hatred. They must submit to the masses of their people and their rage, instead
of manipulating them and trying to outmaneuver their basic sensibilities. On
the other hand, leaders have far greater capacity to heal the masses, to truly
lead a civilization than they think. It is the third party's obligation to help
leaders see their true potential and also realistically assess what it will take
for the majority of their people to come to a political space of peace and justice. There is simply no other way to heal this Palestinian-Israeli conflict.

So much damage and so many violent actors with a fair degree of independence are involved in this conflict that unless officials move at every step
with the masses of people in mind and with an attention to how they can be
transformed, then this process will always be artificial, a veneer of peace for
the sake of petty political needs. And the rage will erupt again and again with
always more dangers elicited from this region's volatile mix of global interdependencies. The masses of people must become a principal part of the peace
process, and until they are ready to, then the process itself will be stalled.
Furthermore, all the courageous actors on the ground already must be given
national prominence in both communities by official actors. A peace process
must be a slow and steady cultural revolution in both enemy communities,
not a secretive gimmick. And there is no cultural revolution or evolution
without a very visible, incremental increase in two material concerns of the
human being and the human family: basic safety, fundamental dignity.

Finally, official diplomacy, without surrendering its basic control over the
state, must encourage and make room for cultures and religions to engage in
parallel peace processes. This must be considered an essential adjunct to official peace processes. Now, the key actors in these cultural and religious
processes need not be political party heads or heads of religious hierarchies.
They can be lower level actors with a commitment to shared values of conflict resolution and ethics. No one wants to suggest the hijacking of official
diplomacy by demagogic religious or cultural leaders who happen to be on
top. But some significant presence of culture and religion's representatives,
taken very seriously, is indispensable.

Had this measure been in place from the beginning of the Oslo process, it
is very clear to me, from an ongoing set of interviews with many representatives, that the Temple Mount would never have become the battleground that
it has become. Many things could have been different. This will take very
careful work by official actors as to how to do this well. But in some form
this is essential for the future of both communities.

The most promising form of inclusion requires the religious and cultural
communities to struggle over and come to some shared sets of ethical values
and acknowledgments of each other. These values will become a yardstick
of the relationship in which each group is no longer evaluated by an inherent
good in one and evil in the other, but rather by the degree to which each ad-
heres to the agreed-upon values, enshrined in treaty and covenant. Such a
process requires intensive relationship building over time, not just formal and
rather wasteful conferences and public forums. Finally, there should be a more

confidential inclusion of religious actors in the tough decision making that will be necessary to deal with the final status of holy sites and sacred lands. But the latter will only result in stalemate unless relationships, trust, and acknowledgment of past wrongs evolve over time.

Postscript on the Future

The process of entering deeply into other cultures can be very daunting to those who feel inadequate to the task and are also frustrated by the demands of time in deadly conflicts. There exists a reckless sense of urgency in both official and unofficial Western methods of intervention in deadly conflicts. As the best theoreticians and practitioners of conflict resolution in our generation, such as Volkan, Lederach, and Montville, have taught us all, indepth diagnosis and subsequent healing of destructiveness that has seeped into human experience on a cultural level takes time, a great deal of time. But the time is well spent because it is far less damaging than intervening, failing, withdrawing, and intervening recklessly again, which is the common pattern of absurdly repetitive Western interventions. It cannot continue this way.

The lived culture of peoples in conflict is constantly in flux and can change for the better or the worse. It exists and takes on a life of its own, at least it has for me in this conflict. I sense that it is waiting to deepen or destroy peace processes, official and unofficial. But it does resonate with the masses of people in ways that an elite negotiation process never will.

It behooves those who come to realize the simple but profound truth that there is no peace without people to insist that the masses of people be included inextricably in peace processes that occur in the context of any further interventions in this region. If either side refuses to do this, then I would recommend, especially to official third parties, to stay out, and explain their reason publicly. Principled nonintervention is also a form of intervention, or at least a significant way of affecting parties to a conflict. This is especially true when that third party is a very powerful actor, like the United States, which is valued and needed by both sides as a source of power and legitimacy.

The mediated inclusion of cultural values, symbols, and deeds in the peace process will, by their very nature, lead to a far more profound and just process of conflict resolution that will protect, benefit, and heal a very large number of people. It is only in this way that we can ever hope to bring this tragic and bitter conflict to some possibility of ending. This conflict holds several cultures hostage. Theft and murder on a large scale are the greatest cancers in the value system of these trapped and arrested cultures. Most cultural actors, even those who reject peace, know this in their hearts and search for a way out of this hell. But no way out has been presented to these rejectionist guardians of ethnic and religious culture. No way has been offered to address either their dreams or their nightmares, their needs or their disappointments, nor their unbearable rage and injury.

That is the fault of the third parties. It is our job to help people out of the hell that they are often implicated in creating. Some day many of them will be able to do the same for us, intervening in our conflicts. There is no sense of cultural and psychological superiority of the third party, least of all this writer. It is in the very nature of deadly injury and conflict that human beings, very gifted and courageous human beings, can be perceptive and brilliant about others while blinded by immersion in their own inextricable web of conflict. They do have many of the answers, but our job is to help them find these answers in ways that are far more creative and careful than anything attempted thus far. I have offered just a few suggestions to help them find those answers in their own cultures, and my suggestions are just a sample and a mere beginning.

It is our job to enter into the damaged and strange world of enemies and enemy systems, to suspend judgment, to see truths on all sides, to see justice and injustice on all sides, to engage in a level of empathy that is enormously demanding, all to help evoke peace processes that resonate at the most profound level of human consciousness and experience. If enough of us, on all levels of intervention, do this persistently and patiently, I do believe that we can stimulate a fundamentally new path to peace, which will resonate in a far more effective way with primal Abrahamic sensibilities that are at the core of this conflict. Our intervention will make the path to true peace and authentic justice slower—and more certain.

Notes

Chapter 1

1. See L. A. Coser, *Continuities in the Study of Social Conflict* (New York: Free Press, 1967); Morton Deutsch, "Constructive Conflict Resolution: Principles, Training, and Research," in *The Handbook of Interethnic Coexistence*, ed. Eugene Weiner (New York: Continuum, 1998), 199–216.

2. For example, there is a very interesting set of essays on cultural influences and conflict resolution in Kaj Bjorkqvist and Douglas P. Fry eds. *Cultural Variation in Conflict Resolution: Alternatives to Violence*, (Mahwah, N.J.: Erlbaum, 1997), 37–88. Articles cover conflict resolution among the Semai, Toraja, Margaite, and the people of Tonga. It is mentioned briefly that the Toraja are now mostly Christian, but still with adherents of the traditional religion, *alukta*. The article on the Semai clearly delineates religious beliefs and principles, such as the dichotomous division of the *nonmaterial* world into *gunik*, protective kin, and *mara'*, the malevolent spirits. This dichotomy impacts strongly, argues the author, on ways of coping with conflict. But, astonishingly, the word "religion" is never used in the article! In fact, it cannot be found in the index to the entire book! This is curious and calls out for interpretation, suggesting Western psychic cleavages and prejudices rather than indigenous ones. Clifford Geertz has done some interesting analysis of religion, culture, politics, and conflict, but not conflict resolution. See his *Interpretation of Cultures* (HarperCollins, 1973), 167ff., and generally part 4.

3. For a definition of conflict transformation, see J. P. Lederach, "Beyond Violence: Building Sustainable Peace," in *The Handbook of Interethnic Coexistence*, 242–45; Ron Kraybill, "Peacebuilders in Zimbabwe: An Anabaptist Paradigm for Conflict Transformation" (Ph.D. diss., University of Capetown, 1996).

4. See Marc Gopin, *Between Eden and Armageddon: The Future of World Religions, Violence, and Peacemaking* (New York: Oxford University Press, 2000).

Chapter 2

1. I use these last two terms separately because conflict resolution, while appropriate to certain circumstances, has a rather limited usefulness in cultural contexts. Many cultures, for example, may have poor precedents for resolution of a problem between enemies but may be more likely to have mythical constructs that maintain relationships in family and society, despite underlying differences. They also may be rich in common symbols and dreams that provide a nonviolent glue to the society, while at the same time not necessarily expressing this as a resolution of a conflict.

2. Based on a particular Christian interpretation of Genesis 15:6, Abraham is seen as the "knight of faith" who is "justified" by that act of faith. This becomes an important justification of the Pauline move to emphasize faith over works and cast Abraham as the first true follower of the Pauline Jesus. See Heb. 11:8–12, 17–19; Gal. 3:6–9, 15–18. But see James 2:20–24, which suggests a different perspective in which Abraham is justified by both faith and works, the latter being much closer to the original Jewish position on Abraham.

3. Gen. 17:5.

4. Esau is also called Edom (Gen. 25:30; 36). The enmity between the nation of Edom and Israel is apparent in many places in the Bible and parallels mythically the competition and struggle between Jacob and Esau. In later history, especially when Roman persecution of Jews became intense, Esau and Edom became identified with Rome (Talmud Yerushalmi Ta'anit 4:8, 68d; Gen. Rabbah 65:21, for example). When the Roman Empire became the Christian Roman Empire, and the persecutions took on religious zeal and significance in the church, Esau and Edom came to symbolize everything that is evil about the persecution and the persecutors. As far as isolated positive statements about Esau in rabbinic literature, some rabbis admired his capacity for honor of father, while others believed that he expressed authentic compassion and even repented of his cruelties (Gen. Rabbah 65: 16; 66:13). Furthermore, there is a sense from some rabbis that the Jewish people paid a price for the suffering incurred by Esau when his birthright was taken by Jacob, that his cries are paid for by Jewish cries in later history (Genesis Rabbah 67:4). We have here at least some hermeneutic basis for remorse over the past relationship, and a perception of some good in the ancient fraternal enemy. It is a minority view in the classical Jewish sources, but new historical contexts and new relationships often become the basis hermeneutically for turning something culturally minor into something major and vice versa. That is the whole assumption of my work. As far as Ishmael is concerned, his identification with Islam is confirmed by Islam's own stories that clearly have an effect on Jewish sources. See note 5.

5. Pirkei de Rabbi Eliezer 30; Midrahs ha-Gadol Gen.: 339–40. For a translation, see Hayim Bialik and Yehoshua Ravnitzky, eds., The Book of Legends, trans. William Braude (New York: Schocken, 1992), 39–43. Ishmael's two wives are identified in the rabbinic story as Ayesha and Fatima, who are Muhammad's two wives in the Qur'an! The influence of one on the other is obvious but not clearly understood causally. Furthermore, the rabbinic story of Abraham's instigation of Ishmael's divorce from his first wife also appears in Islamic sources, though I have been unable to verify this for certain in Islamic sources. See H. A. R. Gibb and J. H. Kramers, Shorter Encyclopedia of Islam (Leiden: Brill, 1991), s.v. "Ismail." Extra-Qur'anic sources are very hard to verify. Despite many negative evaluations, and support of Sarah's decision to banish Hagar and Ishmael, there are some positive evaluations of Ishmael by the rabbis. A man who sees Ishmael in a dream will be blessed (T. Berakhot 56b). Most important, Ishmael is seen to have repented completely at the end of his father's

lifetime (T. Baba Bathra 16b). Here too there is an interpretive basis for nuancing the complicated relationship between these brothers on a Jewish spiritual level. Of course, the notion is a common one in the Abrahamic monotheisms of seeing the alienated other as *good to the degree to which*, through story and allegory, the other repents of his ways. The potential and the peril of this theological move is, once again, made clear through hermeneutics. If, on the one hand, such repentance stories signify mainly the potential for change and for goodness even in enemies, then they are conducive to peacemaking and coexistence. If, on the other hand, the repentance stories about nonbelievers are meant to signify a conversion story, then they do not encourage peacemaking and coexistence. In this form they only signify the absorption of the enemy other into the self, not an acceptance of the other's existence, and certainly not a love of the other, in any normal sense of that term. Thus, repentance stories about Jews in Christian and Islamic literature that are interpreted to mean or literally say that the end result is conversion hardly can be included in the hermeneutics of reconciliation. Of course, in the Islamic case, it is somewhat easier because the definitions of the acceptance of Islam or the true worship of Allah are subjects of endless debate. Liberal Muslims could conceivably read such stories not as conversion stories—if they wish to—but rather stories in which Jews in the time of Muhammad purified their own practice and worship *as Jews* as a result of contact with Muhammad. It would be impossible for Christians to read or reread a story about a Jew who finds Jesus Christ as anything but a conversion story, although I should not preempt creative interpretation in any tradition.

6. In almost none of the literature of any of the faiths is the tragedy and mistreatment of Hagar truly confronted. The Bible clearly shows God's care for Hagar, but not a true confrontation with Abraham's actions regarding this maidservant. No one, in any faith, seems to take Abraham to task for his decision. I presume that part of the reason for this is God's instruction to Abraham, according to the Bible, to listen to Sarah and expel Hagar and Ishmael. I am convinced, however, that the Deuteronomy text (21:17), cited midrashically by Ishmael himself, concerning the proper and improper treatment of multiple wives and eldest sons, seems to me to be an inner biblical exegetical repudiation of Abraham's choice—and God's own command in the Genesis story! The later, and authoritative, Jewish legal source on inheritance actually sides with Ishmael! What does this mean? How is a traditional Jew supposed to integrate the Deuteronomic instruction on inheritance and God's support in Genesis for the opposite? It seems to beg interpretation, more hermeneutic development, and perhaps opens the door for a contemporary revisitation of the larger Abrahamic family as a religious entity.

7. Gen. Rabbah 53:11. For a translation, see Bialik and Ravnitzky, eds., *The Book of Legends*, 39–41.

8. Avivah Zornberg, *Genesis: The Beginning of Desire* (Philadelphia: Jewish Publication Society, 1995), 134–36.

9. Note the opposite Jewish modern hermeneutic trend about Arab-Jewish relations that can be found in Waskow's midrashic readings, as I have analyzed them in chapter 4.

10. Deut. 23:8.

11. Gen. 25:17. I thank Yaacov Travis for pointing out this text and its significance.

12. Just nine verses before Ishmael is "gathered unto his people," the Bible records this of Abraham in Gen. 25:8. On Isaac, Gen. 25:39; on Jacob, Gen. 49:33; on Aaron, Num. 20:24; on Moses, 32:50.

13. I use Gadamerian concepts throughout my work. See Hans Gadamer, *Truth and Method*, 2d rev. ed., trans. Joel Weinsheimer and Donald G. Marshall (New York: Crossroad, 1989).

14. *Tafsiru 'l-Baizawi*, p. 424.

15. See, for example, Thomas Hughes, *A Dictionary of Islam* (London: Allen: 1895), 216–20.

16. Cyril Glassé, *The Concise Encyclopedia of Islam* (San Francisco: Harper and Row, 1989), s.v. "Ishmael."

17. Qur'an, Surah 37:83ff.

18. Qur'an, Surah 2:125, 127; 19:54, 55

19. Qur'an, Surah 29:55.

20. See, for example, Surah 2:40–86; 7:161–71.

21. Abdullah Yusuf Ali, ed. and trans., *The Holy Qur'an: Text, Translation and Commentary* (Brentwood, Md.: Amana, 1989), 1150, n. 4101.

22. Ibid., n. 4102

23. See Mark Edwards et al., eds., *Apologetics in the Roman Empire: Pagans, Jews and Christians* (New York: Oxford University Press, 1999); Hans Conzelman, *Gentiles, Jews, Christians: Polemics and Apologetics in the Greco-Roman Era*, trans. by M. Eugene Boring (Minneapolis: Fortress, 1992); and Hanne Trautner-Kormann, *Shield and Sword: Jewish Polemics against Christianity and Christians in France and Spain from 1100 to 1500* (Tübingen: Mohr, 1993). For a contemporary example of Christian apologetics, see Norman Geisler, *Baker Encyclopedia of Christian Apologetics* (Grand Rapids, Mich.: Baker, 1999).

24. See John 14:6. John 8 is very revealing in this regard. The exchange between Jesus and the Pharisees, and later in the chapter, "the Jews," suggests a competition over who is the authentic father. The Pharisees claim that Abraham is their father, but Jesus questions that based on their actions. They then say, in verse 41, that they are not illegitimate children, and that God himself is the father of all of them. But Jesus says that they cannot be from God, because if that were true they would love Jesus who is from the Father. Finally, John has Jesus say in verse 41 that these Jews are actually from another father, the devil. And thus begins the earliest theological stage of the monotheistic violence of Europe, first and foremost against the Jews. There is a theological spiral of action/counter-reaction, typical of all conflict. Jesus' illegitimacy as son is proclaimed by the crowd, counterclaims of illegitimacy ensue, and finally John ups the ante, as it were, in a fateful way, by leaving behind completely the notion of one father for all and instead introducing a rival father, the devil. With this move we see the beginning of theological justifications for literal dehumanization of the adversary other. Dehumanization is almost a necessary adjunct of all integroup violence. The theological overlay of dehumanization in the attribution of family origins to the devil, however, gives this drive great strength and prevents natural, humanistic guilt feelings from swaying the believer away from compassion. This was as true of the psychosocial dynamics of anti-Semitism and the Crusades as it was in the Salem witch trials.

25. Traditional Jewish prayer entails elaborate attempts to propitiate a God capable of strict justice as well as infinite mercy, and an elaborate set of needs that clearly reflect the painful realities of national disappointments. But after all the tough internal dynamics of Jewish traditional prayer have been exhausted, all the prayers end with peace, and, to some extent (reflected in the blessing *ve'hol ha'hayyim*, as well as *aleinu*), a vision of future unity of humanity (of course, on monotheistic terms). (On peace as the culmination of Jewish prayers and blessings, see Lev. Rabbah 9:9.)

Ultimate visions of peace and brotherhood in monotheistic consciousness, all the way from formal Jewish prayers to informal Middle East conversations, appear to be a kind of prayer, in and of themselves, a hope to escape the tangled web of conflicting human realities and identities. It is hopeful in its ubiquitous character, but frustrating in its poverty of skill in achieving anything resembling peace inside the reality of human diversity.

26. See John Paul Lederach, *Preparing for Peace: Conflict Transformation across Cultures* (Syracuse, N.Y.: Syracuse University Press, 1995).

27. See Pope John Paul's Christmas message of December 24, 1997. One source for this is www.cnn.com/world/9712/24/vatican/index.html.

28. Personal correspondence 5/6/98.

29. Marc Gopin, *Between Eden and Armageddon: The Future of World Religions, Violence and Peacemaking* (New York: Oxford University Press, 2000).

30. Personal interview, October 15, 2000.

31. Gen. 23:4; 18:1–8.

32. Gen. 15:13; Exod. 12:48; Lev. 19:33.

33. Note the self-definition of the Israelite tribe in Egypt as strangers (Exod. 22:20), and the ubiquitous moral law and moral remonstration about abuse and love of the stranger (Exod. 23:9; Deut. 10:19; 24:17; 27:19). The stranger laws are among the most ubiquitous in all of Hebrew biblical literature. I have listed a small sampling.

34. Lev. 19:16.

35. The ancient myths and their influence are self-evident. But contemporary myths of the United States are relevant here as well. The myth of the foundation of the United States seems to be a vital belief for millions of Americans. It has only been with repeated assaults by injured minorities that history books have made some space for the dark side of American foundations. And even this is vigorously opposed to this day by irredentists in many states and regions. It seems vital to not acknowledge the brutal destruction of Native American life, for example. In general, countries founded on the ruins of a prior civilization find it essential to create founding myths that demonize earlier history and sanctify what came with the establishment of the new order. This is a constant myth in history up to our own day, and it is universal. The belief that democracy is a fully functioning real entity in the United States—a fundamental part of most political rhetoric and electioneering—is a myth. It is a construct that we like to believe exists, even though in practice very few people actually get to participate actively in democracy, nor could many, given their economic and educational limitations in a political system dependent on fund-raising by educated and politically connected people. I am not saying that democracy is a fabrication, but it is an ideal construct, only pieces of which actually function in reality. A plutocracy in which some have the power to garner popular votes by advertising seems closer to the reality of most contemporary democracies. I would always prefer Western government to other systems, but its reality is only a shell of its myth. Its strongest contribution is probably not democracy but the infusion of civil and human rights into the consciousness of the modern world. Even though these rights can be secured more easily by those who can pay the most expensive attorneys, the fact is that universal civil rights is a revolutionary contribution to the quality of human life, historically speaking. Another Western myth today that motivates millions is that endless consumption is a good thing, despite the fact that millions have been made miserable by family life in which "things" are abundant, but where time is absent. The benefits of perpetuating this myth for the contemporary interpretation of market economics is obvious. But from Confucius to Aristotle many ancient peoples oper-

ated with a different mythic construct of the Golden Mean, in which moderation was the key to happiness. That education will make you a better person is another contemporary myth, despite the obvious evidence that the most highly educated people have played critical roles in the twentieth century in the conceptualization and orchestration of genocide, the most barbarous of all human crimes, from Germany and Austria to Cambodia and the Balkans. Of course, the psychological capacity to live by religious or secular ethical values has always made people "better" or good, throughout time and space. It is a universal constant, and they do not need a scintilla of education in science to have those values. I have spent my life devoted to education, but the naiveté of this particular myth has allowed educational systems, from kindergarten to graduate school, to fall down in their task of building the good human community. For it is only when educational systems infuse their teaching with values that they create a decent human community. They simply gave up the task, due to a variety of complicated reasons, for which both progressives and conservatives are responsible in their inability to coalesce on shared values. This failure puts all of us at risk, even in the best of modern civilizations. Ask any educated Sarajevan if they could have dreamed in the 1970s of a genocide orchestrated by a psychiatrist and a published poet, and I will show you people fooled by the myth of modern, scientifically centered education.

36. This is a strong theme in Jeremiah. See ch. 30 generally. It is so pervasive that it even applies to exile and return in certain gentile nations. See Jer. 49: 3, 39. On the theme that exile actually atones for sins, see Talmud Bavli (henceforth T.B.) Berakhot 56a, T.B. Sanhedrin 37b. For the related concept that moving one's place in the world can bring a positive change of fate, see T.B. Ta'anit 24b.

37. Gen. 49:5–7.

38. Regina Schwartz, *The Curse of Cain: The Violent Legacy of Monotheism* (Chicago: University of Chicago Press, 1997). This seeps into much Western reflection on the origins of European violence. See, for example, Michael Ignatieff, *The Warrior's Honor: Ethnic War and the Modern Conscience* (New York: Metropolitan, 1998).

39. Gen. 12:3.

40. Gen. 18:19.

41. For background on midrashic ways of thinking and framing the world, see Michael Fishbane, *The Exegetical Imagination: On Jewish Thought and Theology* (Cambridge, Mass.: Harvard University Press, 1998).

42. Note the repeating theme of chosenness that is always tied, at least ideally, to service in some way to humanity as a whole.

43. The first two times that the adjective, "hated," *senu'ah*, is used in the Five Books of Moses, it refers to the tragic state of the unloved matriarchs, in Gen. 29:31 and 29:33. The only other time that the same adjective is used in the entire Five Books is in Deut. 21:15, where the law specifically prohibits any kind of prejudice against the children of the rejected wife! This cannot be a coincidence. To my mind, it is an intrabiblical hermeneutic of atonement for ancient wrongs done in family and intertribal relations, an evolution of Jewish moral consciousness regarding polygamy's devastations that seeks to right the wrongs of history. This is deeply authentic, embedded in the oldest strata of Jewish spiritual traditions, and it suggests a precedent for evolution in other intrafamilial attitudes.

44. There is a fascinating verse in Mic. 7:20, which states, "You will give truth (*emet*) to Jacob, and compassion (*hesed*) to Abraham, as you promised to our fathers in the old days." It is the culminating promise of Micah and the last verse. The

penultimate verse speaks of God covering over the sins of the people, forgiving them. In later rabbinic literature, there is a fairly universal assumption that Jacob's essential attribute was truth, and Abraham's was compassion. This is fairly ironic, considering the fact that Jacob had to survive or chose to survive by first deceiving his brother and then his father-in-law. He payed a heavy price for this his whole life. Abraham did show a great deal of compassion to guests and to the people of Sodom, in his defense of them before God. But his principal acts of faith involved listening to a voice of God to send out of his house Hagar and his son Ishmael (they would have died without divine intervention) and then offering his son as a sacrifice. I cannot help but at least speculate that the rabbis were responding polemically to contemporary detractors accusing these two Patriarchs of lacking exactly these two moral traits that the rabbis assigned to them. The double irony, however, is that the Jewish prophets would later attack the children of these Patriarchs for lacking these very traits. Thus, when Micah predicts the bestowal of these traits on the people as a final promise, one wonders what he may mean. A friend of mine made a daring suggestion that the messianic hope expressed by Micah is to give to people exactly what they have lacked, or what they need to complete history and to atone for past wrongs. This has interesting implications for us. The ability of adversaries to acknowledge past wrongs is critical to peacemaking. Here, in mythic terms, we have the possible prophetic precedent for acknowledging what went wrong in these patriarchal families, what drove the original wedge between Ishmael and Isaac, their mothers, and what drove the wedge between Jacob and Esau. This is the first critical step toward healing. There is ample record in rabbinic sources for what was wrong with Ishmael and Esau, what made them dangerous, but little recognition on the whole of what may have been done wrong to them. Such a balanced analysis, however, is a critical prelude to the mythically based conflict resolution that is necessary here for the religious adherents of these traditions. More on mythic healing and mythic conflict resolution is found later in the book.

Chapter 3

1. It is always hard to sell this one to parents of murdered children.

2. On the influence of the emotions on perception, see Daniel Goleman, *Emotional Intelligence* (New York: Bantam, 1994).

3. See Oscar Nudler, "On Conflicts and Metaphors: Toward an Extended Rationality," in *Conflict: Human Needs Theory*, ed. John Burton (New York: St. Martin's 1990), 177–204; Jayne Docherty, "When the Parties Bring Their Gods to the Table: Learning Lessons from Waco" (Ph.D. diss., George Mason University, 1998). Related to my subject is the important work by Lisa Schirch, "Ritual Peacebuilding: Creating Contexts Conducive to Conflict Transformation" (Ph.D. diss., George Mason University, 1999).

4. See Kevin Avruch's most recent work, *Culture and Conflict Resolution* (Washington, D.C.: U.S. Institute of Peace, 1998).

5. See, for example, Demetrios Julius, Joseph Montville, and Vamik Volkan eds. *The Psychodynamics of International Relationships* (Lexington, Mass.: Lexington Books, 1991). For the foundations of my methodology, see Gopin, *Between Eden and Armageddon: The Future of World Religions, Violence, and Peacemaking* (New York: Oxford University Press, 2000).

6. This was one of the main drawbacks to the influence of the Palestinian Au-

thority leadership on the masses of Palestine. The perception and reality of that relationship prevented there from being an authentic role model of new relationship to Israelis and Jews, even where this was authentically being expressed by representatives of the PA. Clearly, one must add that the repressive facts on the ground contributed to the failure of peace with Israelis to become embedded in the popular consciousness. The blame rests with both elites.

7. Jewish ritual coming of age is 13 for boys and is commemorated by engaging in a series of challenging intellectual rituals followed by various celebrations. I grew up as an Orthodox Jew, and this experience was intense and important.

8. In an essay entitled "Concerning the Conflict of Beliefs and Opinions," Rabbi Kook the Elder had said, "The concept of tolerance is aware that there is a spark of divine light in all things, that the inner spark of divine light shines in all the different religions, as so many pedagogics for the culture of humanity, to improve the spiritual and material existence, the present and the future of the individual and of society." See Abraham Isaac Kook, *Abraham Isaac Kook: The Lights of Penitence, the Moral Principles, Lights of Holiness, Essays, Letters and Poems*, compiled and translated by Ben Zion Bokser (New York: Paulist Press, 1978), 273.

9. Frohman enjoyed telling me that when he met with Shimon Peres about peace with Arabs, he said to Peres, "You know, here we are, two 'poylishe yidden' [two Polish Jews]!" And then Frohman said to me, "You know what I mean by that, Reb Moshe [he would only call me by my Hebrew name]? Do you know what I am saying?" And I am not sure what he meant to this day. But I think he meant that, for all of their visions of the future and courageous views of Jewish-Arab relations, he and Peres should "know the score," that they know how little a Jewish life has been worth in the past to non-Jews, that they know what it is to deal with what you have and to make the best of it to survive. But I am still not sure what he meant. That is the way it is with his oblique messages in subtle combination with sharp humor.

10. See Rabbi Menachem Froman, "A Modest Proposal," Jerusalem Report, October 25, 1999.

11. I will critically examine later the tendency of some peacemaking Jews in Israel to seek out Muslim partners and avoid or dismiss the Christian Palestinian minority. There are many reasons for this, and later, in the section dealing with pragmatic strategies, I will weigh the costs and benefits of separate relationship building between the three Abrahamic faith communities.

12. This, by the way, is one of the great weaknesses of second-track diplomacy, namely, the poverty of intervenors who actively and aggressively connect and coordinate their own efforts with the ongoing negotiations of first-track actors. Frohman is one of the few actively pursuing this linkage.

13. I have touched on this in my previous book, *Between Eden and Armageddon*, ch. 2.

14. I have deleted several paragraphs of the letter involving strategic processes of getting everyone to the peace table, to avoid jeopardizing ongoing relationship building and delicate positions of some of the parties.

15. In deleted parts of the letter, I indicated that excluding certain religious forces that are antistatist from the peace process guarantees that they will oppose future visions of the state. It is only by including them that one can commit everyone to a vision of the future states of the region as stable and in which everyone, even the most religious, will have a stake. Now some would call this naive, in the sense that religious antistatists have no intention of altering their view of the future. Perhaps this may turn out to be true, but one will lose nothing in at least exploring many

possibilities and building relationships. Keep in mind that this same argument was made ad nauseum for excluding groups like the ANC, IRA, and the PLO, a strategy that led nowhere for decades. We must believe that if diplomacy and relationship building has a transformative effect on erstwhile guerilla groups, then it can also have an impact on fundamentalist groups opposed to the state. I never cease to be amazed at how the rhetoric, hermeneutics, and self-definition of rejectionists groups can change almost overnight—upon acceptance of their right to exist and be normalized or mainstreamed into a part of the envisioned future. There are no guarantees here, but intelligent gambling is in the very nature of secular peace processes and diplomacy. I only argue for its extension to religious parties to conflicts.

16. Note that in the previous paragraph the president uses vital words such as "understanding," "cultural dimensions," and "distorted perceptions" to describe conflict and its solutions. But the next paragraph reduces all of these processes to "religious dialogue." This is a typical response to conflict today in that most people, especially nonspecialists, tend to conflate all conflict resolution into "dialogue." I will explore in a later chapter the value of dialogue, specifically the use of verbal exchanges between enemies in public settings. But, in the course of examining alternatives, I will also highlight the limits of verbal exchange in addressing those aspects of conflict that are most relevant to the experience of the masses of people—especially poor people—in conflict.

17. Personal correspondence, 7/15/99.

Chapter 4

1. One way to look at the massive success of fascism across European culture in the early part of the twentieth century is that its racial symbols and nationalist flags, parades, dogmas, and practices constituted a desperate attempt on the part of millions of people to recapture the old traditional world of clear inclusions and exclusions, replete with institutionalized, ancient symbols of who was saved and who was damned, who was good and who was evil, who was superior and who was inferior. Being superior to someone seems to be a sad but universally practiced human method of identity affirmation and worth confirmation that is hardly limited to elites. It is practiced by the poor as well as the rich, by Europeans as well as Indians and Africans. The markers can be economic symbols, such as clothing and cars or other valuables, but it is also often the degree of lightness and darkness of skin (not just black and white) and, of course, the old reliable marker, gender. The optimists of liberalism, while successfully promoting vital social and legal changes in Western society, have not sufficiently understood that with which they are tinkering when they have attempted to eliminate old, encrusted systems of privilege and identity. This writer hardly laments their effort, but I do suggest that as one attempts to improve civilization it is vital to understand the old psychological and social constructs with which we are tampering. The twentieth century has proved, if nothing else, that, whether it be the environment or human social organization, as we attempt to change for the better as a species we must do so delicately, with a keen eye to everyone's needs and proclivities, whether it be those of different classes, ethnicities, and religious identities of humanity, or the intricate web of species whose lives are interdependent with ours.

2. For example, there is frequent emphasis in Christian/Islamic dialogue on the honor of Jesus who is considered a prophet and honored by Islam, mentioned fre-

quently in the Qur'an. Christians I know who are more pro-Islamic often mention this honoring of Jesus with great pride. There is by definition no such bond between Judaism and Christianity concerning Jesus since the essential break between the original Jewish followers of Jesus and the other Jews was over Jesus. What may be possible now in Jewish/Christian dialogue about Jesus, from a hermeneutic point of view, is another matter.

3. By "shared," I mean that although the Hebrew Bible is not a sacred book of Islam, Islam acknowledges Jewish prophecy as legitimate, albeit imperfect. Clearly, there is enough theological room here for both sides to share this metaphor of human value.

4. Of course, they would never refer to "ugliness" in a religious tradition, but rather use other, softer characterizations, such as "texts that are difficult to comprehend," or "traditions that require careful interpretation," or "mysteries beyond human understanding."

5. A cursory look at Exod. 23, the Ten Commandments, and the Sermon on the Mount would suffice. As far as the prohibition of selling weapons to people suspected of using them immorally, see T.B. Avodah Zarah 15b; T.B. Makkot 10a; Tosefta Avodah Zarah 2; Tractate Cuthim 1; Maimonides, *Mishneh Torah*, Laws of Murder and Protection of Life, 12:12. Of course, we are all guilty of this today. Anyone who pays taxes has a portion of it go to national defense, which involves an industry that "must" produce more than required for defense to be economically viable due to "economies of scale." Therefore, we are all part of an arms bazaar that has made millions of people very rich and killed millions of others, especially in poor countries.

6. Of course, intergroup rape deserves a separate category of legitimate moral outrage. But it is clear from countless examples in history that the moral outrage is often overshadowed by the male sense of violation of the body of the group that, at least at the moment of rape, becomes identified with the body of the victim. The earliest biblical example, for which Jacob severly rebukes his sons, is the former's murder of an entire town due to the rape of their sister Dinah (assuming even that the correct biblical translation is that she was raped). See Gen. 34; 49:5-7.

7. Marc Gopin, *Between Eden and Armageddon: The Future of World Religions, Violence, and Peacemaking* (New York: Oxford University Press, 2000).

8. See Aaron Samuel Tamaret, "Herut," in *Pacifism and Torah: Works by Aaron Samuel Tamaret* (Hebrew), ed. by Ehud Luz (Jerusalem: Dinur Center, 1992), 125-42.

9. See Joseph Soloveitchik, "Kol Dodi Dofek," in *In Aloneness, in Togetherness: A Selection of Hebrew Writings*, ed. with an introduction by Pinchas Peli (Jerusalem: Orot, 1976), 359-62.

10. Rabbi Judah Loewe, *Tiferet Yisroel* (Jerusalem: Mekhon Yerushalayim, 1999), ch. 25, ch. 30. This has ancient rabbinic roots in the prayer of the Talmudic Amora, Rabbi Alexandri, who lists the "yeast in the dough" and "the empire" as the things that prevent us from doing God's will (T.B. Berakhot 17a). By mentioning "the empire," the rabbi is connecting thematically inner struggles with evil and outer struggles with social and political evil.

11. Philip Birnbaum, *The Birnbaum Haggadah* (New York: Hebrew Publishing Company, 1976), 60, s.v. *ho lahmoh anyah*.

12. This is an old theme of biblical and rabbinic Judaism, stemming back as early as Psalms (e.g., 147:10), but it is especially important today to understanding the struggle between Ultra-Orthodox, *haredi* Jewish life, which still centers the *mitsvot* in the achievement of empowerment versus those Jews, in Israel and the Diaspora, who locate empowerment completely in the sphere of military and political might. This is a basic struggle in Jewish life today. Of course, there are no hard and fast categories

here, and one should approach conflict with a knowledge of stated positions but also awareness of how often groups cannot be understood by their own self-definition. Thousands of *haredim* today put large amounts of their trust in political might, while thousands of children of the Kibbutzniks—the classic Zionists who placed their trust in power, not God—are at the forefront of peacemaking with Arabs, tired and sickened by generations of war. It seems that many—not all, to be sure—*haredim* are "entering history," despite themselves, dirtying their hands with power and money in the Israeli political process, at the same time that, in the thousands, the children of the Kibbutz get on the first plane to India to find themselves and some spiritual truth, as soon as they are able. Ironically, the latter group of young people, in some ways, are opting out of Jewish history and certainly out of military Jewish history, at least the ones who never come back. A strange reversal is going on, at least among some in both camps, secular and religious.

13. See Daniel Boyarin, *Unheroic Conduct: The Rise of Heterosexuality and the Invention of the Jewish Man* (Berkeley: University of California Press, 1997).

14. See also the traditional text of the ancient Passover Haggadah wherein several key passages emphasize the movement from a lowly state of idolatry or exile to an elevated *spiritual* state. See, for example, Birnbaum, *Birnbaum Haggadah*, p. 74, s.v. *mi-tehila ovde avodah zarah.* . . .

15. See, for example, Yalkut Shimoni, Emor, #654, on the lack of mention of the *mitsvah* of happiness on Passover due to the death of the Egyptians. This rabbinic trend emphasized that victory over the Egyptians and their violent deaths actually detracted from the other joys of the holiday. Many centuries later, Levi Yitshak of Berditchev focused on the centrality of supernatural miracles in the Exodus story as the heart of the message, namely that God created the world out of nothing and, therefore, has the power to alter its natural course. See Norman Lamm, *The Religious Thought of Hasidism: Text and Commentary* (New York: Yeshiva University Press, 1999), 567–68. Again the focus was removed from political or military celebration.

16. For a history of the perception of the Jew in European lands, see, for example, Frank Manuel, *The Broken Staff: Judaism through Christian Eyes* (Cambridge, Mass: Harvard University Press, 1992).

17. On the critical role of this wood in the biblical description of the Tabernacle, the precursor of the Temple, see generally Exod. 35–37.

18. "When the King Messiah comes, he will begin only with peace, as it states, 'How welcome on the mountain are the footsteps of the herald announcing peace' . . . (Isa. 52:7)" (Lev. Rabbah 9:9). On Elijah, the once-angry prophet, as a transformed reconciler of hearts in the end of time, see Mal. 3:23–24.

19. See Arthur Waskow, *Seasons of Our Joy* (Toronto: Bantam, 1982), 216–18. For an overview of the use of midrashic thinking to rework old Jewish myths, see also Phyllis Ocean Berman and Arthur Ocean Waskow, *Tales of Tikkun: New Jewish Stories to Heal the Wounded World* (Northvale, N.J.: Jason Aronson, 1996).

20. See *Yalkut Shimoni* 2:944; T.B. Rosh Hashanah 19b. See also Lamm, *The Religious Thought of Hasidism*, 566, n. 233.

21. Waskow is referring midrashically here to Deut. 30:19, "I call heaven and earth to witness against you this day. I have put before you life and death, blessing and curse. Choose life, if you and your children would live."

22. Waskow, *Seasons of Our Joy*, 218.

23. See Benamozegh, *Israel and Humanity*, trans. Maxwell Luria (New York: Paulist Press, 1994). For a contemporary critique of his universal paradigm, see Marc Gopin, *Between Eden and Armageddon*, ch. 5.

24. Deut. 7:7.

25. Gen. 22:17, 26:4; Deut. 1:10, 10:22.

Chapter 5

1. I prefer the term "perpetuated mourning" to "unresolved mourning." The latter implies that mourning is a problem to be resolved, or merely a psychological condition. But it is not just a psychological condition. It is a moral and spiritual act, a deed of communal commitment and engagement that links the world of the living and the world of the dead, the past, present, and future. It is not just a problem or pathology. Thus a mourning that is perpetuated is also an act of devotion. It may also be pathological, and, more important for my purposes, it may need to be outweighed or overwhelmed by competing moral and spiritual priorities, such as ending a cycle of needless death of innocents, both one's own as well as those of the enemy. But mourning must be honored as a moral act, a path of devotion. If, after the massive death of innocents, it is excessive, then perhaps that is what is called for morally. Who are we to judge this? But, in the face of war, we do need to be able to articulate countervailing religious and moral principles that can help this kind of mourning move in a less deadly direction that does not perpetuate itself.

2. This can be stated boldly by a polytheistic system but be right beneath the surface in ethnonationalist monotheistic systems that occur in various forms in all the monotheisms. Note this citation from Hindutva fusion of religion and people and land: "[T]he Hindu people . . . is the Almighty manifesting Himself. . . . [T]he Hindu people is our God" (M. S. Golwalker, *Bunch of Thoughts* [Bangalore: Vikram Prakshan, 1966], 25). I thank Rajmohan Gandhi for pointing out this in his essay "Hinduism and Peacebuilding" in *Religion and Peacebuilding*, ed. Harold Coward and Gordon Smith (New York: SUNY, 2002), chapter on Hinduism.

3. The language of the Jewish liturgy on the Ten Days of Repentance, and, in particular, on the Day of Atonement, emphasizes that when standing before God the believers must admit that they have all sinned repeatedly. The text says that one must resist thinking that we are all righteous and have not sinned. "We are not so brazen and obstinate as to say before You, God, our God and the God of our forefathers, that we are righteous and have not sinned—rather, we and are forefathers have sinned." This precedes the detailed confession of sins. See R. Nosson Scherman, ed. and trans., *The Complete Artscroll Machzor Yom Kippur* (Brooklyn, N.Y.: Mesorah, 1986), 18, 92, 358, 418, 494, 598. This is in contrast to other times or "moods" in the Jewish people's religious consciousness. For example, at the beginning of every chapter of the Chapters of the Fathers, it is traditional to say a rabbinic refrain in which the following biblical verse is central: "Your people are all righteous; they shall possess the land forever; they are a plant of my own, the work of my hands, wherein I may glory" (Isa. 60:21). This is cited in order to demonstrate that all of Israel will inherit the World to Come, a future rabbinic vision of paradise. See Philip Birnbaum, trans. and annotator, *Daily Prayer Book: Ha-Siddur Ha-Shalem* (New York: Hebrew Publishing Company, 1977), 477–78. There is clearly a struggle in the literature on how easily one admits to human failure versus the compassionate or loving act of declaring everyone worthy of fruits of righteousness. Furthermore, the text says that there is no one on earth who does not sin (1 Kings 8:46). This text stood in important contrast for traditional Jews to the theology of the sinless Jesus, as well as the infallible papacy, and explained for them the sins of the church. But to be fair, doctrines or assump-

tions of human infallibility plague and are a perpetual trap of most organized religions, including Judaism *in its lived reality* of rabbis past and present who cannot be challenged on key issues. Infallibility assumptions are, in turn, the breeding ground of elite manipulation of the masses of religious believers in the service of ethnonationalized religious bigotry and persecution. One of my students recently concluded research on religion's role in the Holocaust in Slovakia. What emerged was not any implication of a Vatican and a pope that ignored the plight of Jews; there were many private urgings from the Vatican regarding the fascist policies. Rather, there was a failure of a strong, public moral voice from the Vatican which, *by its absence*, allowed Slovakia's Catholic leadership to synthesize ethnonationalism, Catholicism, and a policy of persecution and expulsion. More important to my point here, there were many decent Catholics in this country, and perhaps all over Europe, who wanted to do the right and courageous thing but felt leaderless and confused. Thus, the centralization of moral authority in the Vatican and the pope and the doctrines of infallibility left many decent people in a position of failing to do the right thing, only because of presumptions that "the pope must know better." This is a passive way in which the overvaluation of and overdependence upon religious leadership can stifle moral courage and independence in the face of deadly conflict. On the disappointment with the silence of the pope of a Slovakian Holocaust survivor and eye witness, see Joseph Kalina, *A Holocaust Odyssey* (Lanham, Md.: University Press of America, 1995), 42. On pleas to the Vatican and its quiet efforts and failures to stop the deportations in Slovakia, see generally Vilem Pre'an and Stanislav Kovr'nok, eds., *Vatik'n a Slovensk' Republika, Dokumenty* (Bratislava: Slovak Academic Press, 1992), especially 46–117. I thank my student Simona Gould for these sources, their translation, and her excellent work on this subject.

4. I daresay that this is part of the brutal calculus that has left the basic human needs of Palestinians refugees unattended and neglected in every Middle Eastern country, with one possible exception being Jordan to a certain degree. Who is responsible? Many power groups, including but by no means limited to the Israelis.

5. See Louise Branson and Dusko Doder, *Milosevic: Portrait of a Tyrant* (New York: Free Press, 1999), and Charles Simic, "Anatomy of a Murderer," *New York Review of Books,* January 20, 2000, 26–29. I was particularly impressed with details on the miserable lives of Milosevic and his wife, both abandoned by parents, Milosevic's parents having committed suicide. More needs to be investigated in this regard.

6. See generally, on apocalyptic religion, Richard Landes and Arthur P. Mandel, *Vision and Violence* (Ann Arbor: University of Michigan Press, 1992).

7. See Isa. 11:6 on a utopian vision of the future. *Masekhet Derekh Erets Zuta,* Chapter on Peace, reports, in the name of Rabbi Jose the Gallilean, that Messiah's very name is peace, citing as support Isa. 9:5, where a future leader is referred to as *sar shalom,* "prince of peace." The same Rabbi Jose declares in the same rabbinic source that, based on Isa. 52:7, when Messiah reveals himself to the Jewish people, he will begin the revelation only with peace.

8. On the struggle of modern and medieval definitions of the two realms in Islam, see Sohail Hashmi, "Interpreting the Islamic Ethics of War and Peace," in *The Ethics of War and Peace,* ed. Terry Nardin (Princeton, NJ: Princeton University Press, 1996), 146–166, but especially 155ff. My own work has brought me in contact with many sheikhs. One in particular indicated to me that, in a recent national meeting of sheikhs, there had been a quiet agreement to stop teaching the principles of *dar al-Islam* and *dar al-harb* because "they do not reflect an authentic teaching of classical Islam," presumably meaning that their origin is medieval. This amazed me. I was also im-

pressed that a national body had to agree to do this very quietly. It made me realize the pressure on sheikhs to not openly confront the more militant expressions of Islam today. Thus, the possibility for hermeneutic evolution is clear, and the obstacles to it are clear also. More work needs to be done on when and how the moral parameters of these two realms have changed. Other promising realms to be studied include *dar al-sulh* (realm of peace or reconciliation) and *dar al-'ahd* (realm of covenant). I used the latter concept as part of an editorial/proposal on how to view the Old City in Jerusalem as part of a peace deal between Israel and Palestine. See Marc Gopin, "Share Jerusalem or Battle Forever," *Boston Globe*, September 24, 2000, Focus section. This was published a few days before the beginning of the Intifada of 2000. More on this in chapter 9.

Chapter 6

1. Beginning with Freud and Marx, but continuing with the work of Girard, as well as other writers such as Mark Jeurgensmeyer and Sudhir Kakar, we have been treated to an understanding of the foundations of religious violence. But no parallel school of investigation exists that focuses scientifically on prosocial religious systems of interaction that have implications on a social/political level. There is a subtle assumption that the violence caused by religion far outweighs any prosocial contribution in the construction or reconstruction of civil society. The spasms of religious violence and persecution in history outweigh in many scientific minds the contribution of religion to the day-to-day commitment of billions of religious people in history to coexistence with difficult family members and community members.

2. The Turkish Consul in France, Yolga Namik, repeatedly challenged the Nazis, and defended and saved four hundred Jews during World War II. He was a Muslim. When asked about this, he said, "Yes, thanks be to Allah, as you say, I am a Muslim. But that does not at all signify that I feel differently from you French, or Jews, or whoever. That didn't hinder me from saving Jews, on the contrary! It is the humane qualities in a person that are important. If a man is good, kind, God—be it the God of Allah, of Jews, of Christians, of other religions—God, then, will take you into His Paradise. . . . it goes better for you if you begin at once to show love, to help one's fellow man" (Marek Halter, *Stories of Deliverance: Speaking with Men and Women Who Rescued Jews from the Holocaust*, trans. M. Bernard [Chicago: Open Court, Carus, 1998], 194). This book quoted herein is quite relevant to issues of healing old wounds, an issue that we shall address later on. Notice here Yolga Namik's intuitive hermeneutic of Islam. His Islamic concept of paradise is a place for all good, kind people, and the effort to help fellow human beings on earth is the principal vehicle to heaven. The only ones not going to paradise in his context were the Nazis and those who helped them. Now scholars will instinctively react that this man does not really know Islamic doctrine, that this is not authentic Islam. But the very nature of my thesis questions who should determine what is and what is not authentic religion. The accumulated practices and intuitions of people does determine and has determined, since the dawn of humankind, what is "authentic," despite the best efforts of guardians of organized religions. Over time, what is bold and even insane in one generation, such as the actions of this Turkish man, becomes the norm in another generation. To take another example, no one could convince the broad spectrum of my Islamic students back at George Mason University that the expression of *jihad* was violent. It was critical in their self-image as young American Muslims that *jihad*

is a holy principle of struggle for justice at a nonviolent level, this despite what they clearly knew was being touted by many Middle Eastern organizations. Now, this is a complicated subject, but, simply put, one can find both interpretations of *jihad* in the classical sources. But what we see among these students is a living, evolving herme-neutic that very much depends for its future on how it is viewed and nurtured.

3. Nazi culture had this element to it, often overlooked as researchers and the rest of us sought to distance ourselves from them, a deep need of post–World War II Western culture. But the fact is that the same SS men who took pleasure in throwing Jewish babies in the air and catching them with their bayonets, were also instructed to and did distribute fresh bread to poor Aryan women and children. I was horrified when I first saw the photographs of the distribution. Numbed by pictures of atroci-ties, I was more horrified by the complication of their mindset and culture, but it taught me a permanent lesson that the gravest danger to human psychology is not sadism but selective sadism, not unqualified hate, but hate beyond the boundaries of one's moral universe. After all, many human cultures on earth easily recognize and im-prison, or execute, indiscriminate sadists, but they often pin medals on those whose sadism is circumscribed by some physical, racial, or ethnic boundary in wartime, as long as the atrocity has been covered up in some way. Covering up and simultaneously winking at outer-directed atrocity by the group seems to be a deeply ingrained human collective method of protecting the group. We can suppress this drive with interna-tional law, but I argue that we can only conquer it by unmasking and healing the existential fear that leads groups to passively support such selective barbarity.

4. These are Jews originating in Arab or North African lands, as opposed to Ashkenazim from European lands.

5. This level of tolerance in Islam for Judaism did not hold true for those deemed to be idolaters, such as African animists or Hindus. However, the principal mode of Islamic interaction with such cultures has been political and military domination, not elimination. Where does the eliminationist drive come from in European religious theology? Is it the obsession with the devil? This also requires further study. Islamic history requires further study in terms of the theological arguments that justify the behavior of Islam toward idolaters in places such as Africa and India, and how toler-ance and intolerance have waxed and waned over time and in different locations. It also must be acknowledged that there are eliminationist and genocidal Islamic fanta-sies that have become embedded in al-Qaida and its sympathizers. This is plainly evident since September 11, 2001.

6. See the articulation of this by Frank Griswold, the Presiding Bishop and Pri-mate of the Episcopal Church of the United States, "Listening with the Ear of the Heart," in *Crosscurrents* 49:1 (1999), 16–18. On compromise as a commandment in Judaism, see T.B. Sanhedrin 6b: Rabbi Joshua the son of Korha says, "It is a *mitsvah* to compromise (*livtso'ah*), as it states, 'Truth and the justice of peace (*mishpat sha-lom*) execute within your gates [Zech. 8].' But is it not the case that where there is justice there is no peace, and where there is peace there is no justice? But where then *is* there justice with peace? Thus say that it is with compromise."

7. See Michael Henderson, *The Forgiveness Factor* (London: Grosvenor, 1996).

8. "What the law could never do . . . God has done: by sending his own Son in a form like that of our own sinful nature, and as a sacrifice for sin, he has passed judg-ment against sin. . . ." (Rom. 8:3). Of course, this is not just a Christian notion. It has old Jewish roots, though it is certainly not as dogmatically central to Jewish belief and practice, as is the death of Jesus for the sake of forgiveness. There is an ancient idea that the death of the righteous atones for the sins of a generation. See *Midrash*

Tanhuma ed. (Buber) *ahre mot* 10. As far as collective versus individual responsibility, this is a complex issue. On the one hand, Exodus states that God visits the sins of the fathers on the sons (20:5; 34:7), whereas Deut. 24:16 (as well as II Kings 14:6) explicitly states that the sons should never die for the sins of the fathers. One harmonizing hermeneutic of this paradox may be that the latter texts may address human forms of punishment while the former refers to divine retribution. But it may reflect countervailing biblical trends. The Hebrew Bible tends to hold accountable as well as to punish whole groups for the sins of the majority of that group, such as the Sodomites, Egyptians, Edomites, Moabites, Amonites, Canaanites, and so on. Sometimes the punishment is permanent, and sometimes for a few generations, but it is definitely a collective punishment.

9. See Everett L. Worthington, ed., *Dimensions of Forgiveness: Psychological Research and Theological Perspectives*, (Templeton Foundation Press, 1998). This has become a popular subject as well. See Ellen Michaud, "Add Years to Your Life: Learn to Forgive," *Prevention* (January 1999), who cites the work of Enright, among others, one of the principal proponents of forgiveness.

10. Catherine T. Coyle and Robert D. Enright, "Researching the Process Model of Forgiveness within Psychological Interventions," in Worthington, ed., *Dimensions of Forgiveness*, 142.

11. J. S. Albright, M. R. McMinn, and K. R. Meek, "Religious Orientation, Guilt, Confession, and Forgiveness," *Journal of Psychology and Theology* 23 (1995): 190–97, as cited in Worthington, ed., *Dimensions of Forgiveness*, 264–66.

12. See, for example, *The Psychodynamics of International Relationships*, Demetrias Julios, Joseph Montville, and Vamik Volkan, eds. (Lexington, Mass.: Lexington Books, 1990).

13. See, for example, the range of projects and interests of the Preventive Diplomacy program at CSIS, which Joe Montville heads. http: www.csis.org.prevdipl/, visited 12/22/00.

14. Exod. 34:7. This verse is said countless times on the holiest day of the Jewish year, the Day of Atonement and is emphasized as the most important characteristic of God.

15. There are numerous sources in the Torah (I use the term interchangeably with the Hebrew Bible). See, e.g., Mic. 7:18–20. For Allah as merciful, see in the Qur'an, Surahs 6:26; 5:74; 15:49; 16:119. For Allah as forgiving, see 4:25; 5:74; 85:14. See, for Christianity, Heb. 10:11–18. See also the perceptive comments on Christian forgiveness by Miroslav Wolf, *Exclusiveness and Embrace* (Nashville: Abingdon Press, 1996), 119–25.

16. Talmud Bavli (henceforth T.B.) 133b.

17. The last phrase is a translation of *zekhuyot* in this context only.

18. T.B. Yoma 86b.

19. Ibid.

20. See, for example, Mal. 3.7; Zech. 1:7, and the important discussion in Ezekiel 18. See also the rabbinic text of the Standing Prayer, the *Amidah* of Yom Kippur in R. Nosson Scherman, ed. and trans., *The Complete Artscroll Machzor Yom Kippur* (Brooklyn, N.Y.: Mesorah, 1986), 86–88, s.v. *Elokenu, ve'eloke avotenu, mehal*. This prayer is said every year on the Day of Atonement, many times. It reflects the notion of continuous forgiveness in response to the need *every year* to "wipe away" the sins of the people, thus acknowledging and etching into stone, so to speak, an eternal drama of human behavior, sin, repentance, and divine forgiveness.

21. *Tanakh: The Holy Scriptures* (Philadelphia: Jewish Publication Society, 1985), 1266.

22. This nuance is captured by the verb *maha*. See Ps. 51:3. It is also often associated with the washing away of sin.

23. Many texts, including Mic. 7: 18–20, emphasize the divine quality of infinite patience, *erekh apayim*. The daily standing prayer, the *Amidah*, refers to God as a *mohel ve'soleakh*, a Being whose essential quality or name is Forgiver and Pardoner. See Philip Birnbaum, trans. and annotator *Daily Prayer Book: Ha-Siddur Ha-Shalem*, (New York: Hebrew Publishing Company, 1977), 85. This emphasizes that forgiveness is built into a permanent relationship between God, the individual, and the community. Clement of Rome appeals similarly for a Christian perception of God that becomes a role model for the human being. "Let us turn our eyes to the Father and Creator of the universe, and when we consider how precious and peerless are His gifts of peace, let us embrace them eagerly for ourselves. Let us contemplate Him with understanding, noting with the eyes of the spirit the patient forbearance that is everywhere willed by Him, and the total absence of any friction that marks the ordering of His whole creation." Clement of Rome, "Harmony and Cooperation," in *Early Christian Writings*, trans. by Maxwell Staniforth (New York: Penguin, 1978), 33.

24. See Mic. 7:18; Prov.19:11.

25. T.B. Hagigah 5a; T.B. Berachot 12b.

26. Avot of Rabbi Nathan 40:5, statement of Rabbi Elazar ben Rabbi Yossi.

27. T.B. Shabbat 105b.

28. T.B. Berachot 5b.

29. T.B. Yoma 86b; *Otzar Midrashim*, Gadol u'Gedulah 6.

30. There seems to be a parallel structure of the moral human trait of *ma'aver al middotav*, occuring in early rabbinic literature (T.B. Ta'anit 25b), and the divine quality of *ma'aver al pesha*, the "wiping away of sin." In both cases, divine and human, it involves a kind of surrender of justifiable indignation to achieve a higher moral goal of compassion and, above all, patience. See *Orhot Tzadikim* (n.d.; rpt. Jerusalem: Eshkol, 1946), chs. 4, 8, and 12.

31. Ibid.

32. Rabbi Moshe Cordovero, *Tomer Devorah* (Venice, 1588; rpt. New York: Feldheim, 1993), ch. 1, 7–11. Cordovero continues (1, 17–19) to describe the effectiveness of never perpetuating one's anger. Citing Exod. 23:5 on the biblical commandment to help one's enemy, he quotes T.B. Pesachim 113b, which suggests that the anger that one party feels to the other in this text is due to the fact that A witnessed B committing a crime but does not have a second witness and thus cannot bring B to justice, according to Jewish law. This makes A hate B. But the Bible instructs the believer to help this criminal with his burden anyway, as a gesture of love, in order to help B literally leave behind (a midrashic rereading of the phrase *azov ta'azov* in the biblical verse) his sin. Thus, Cordovero applies this process of reconciliation even to those whom one sees as violators of the norms of society or the norms of the Torah.

33. It would be interesting to do a study measuring what we usually refer to as "unconditional love," namely, the tendency to express strong levels of care for loved ones even when they do things with which we profoundly disagree. Do those who have a tendency to be peacemakers have a strong quotient of unconditional love for loved ones relative to the larger population? Or, perhaps, is there an inverse proportionality, wherein those who have greater tolerance for enemy groups have less tolerance for their own immediate love relationships? What evokes in some the human capacity to care, even in the context of extreme disappointment, is relevant to the study of conflict resolution.

34. We will speak later about other religious values that involve the temporary suspension of judgment of others until one comes to truly understand them. This opens a vital space in the relationship for open-minded listening, the avoidance of rash judgments, while holding to one's valuation of justice. Ultimately, maintaining a sense of justice requires judging the actions of others, but if it is coupled with a temporary suspension, training in listening and empathy, then one's sense of justice is likely to become more nuanced and subject to compromise with the enemy's perspective on justice.

35. See, for example, Jonah Gerondi (d. 1263), *The Gates of Repentance* (Jerusalem: Feldheim, 1976). For a contemporary set of essays on repentance, see Pinchas Peli, *Soloveitchik on Repentance: The Thought and Oral Discourses of Rabbi Joseph B. Soloveitchik* (New York: Paulist Press, 1984).

36. Maimonides' Laws of Repentance are to be found in his *Mishneh Torah*, the Book of Knowledge. For an English translation and commentary, see *Maimonides, Mishneh Torah, Hilchot Teshuvah: A New Translation and Commentary*, by Rabbi Eliyahu Touger (New York: Maznaim: 1987).

37. Maimonides, *Mishneh Torah*, Laws of Repentance, 1:1.

38. Ibid., 2:1ff.

39. T.B. Yoma 87a.

40. T.B. Yoma 86a.

41. Personal Letter from Alan Canton, Sacramento, Calif., June 29, 1999, circulated by Leah Green and the Compassionate Listening Project.

42. Gen. 17:5.

43. See Lev. 26:34–35, where the land finally gets its "rest," its Sabbath, when its inhabitants are removed by God. They will be removed if they fail to give the land the kind of rest that leads to justice. The land resting was an important part of the just distribution of resources, according to biblical ethics, wherein the poor could receive the benefits of the land during those resting years.

44. See Marek Mejor, "Suffering, Buddhist Views of Origination of," in *Routledge Encyclopedia of Philosophy*.

45. *Orhot Tzadikim*, ch. 4. But Cordovero explicitly avoids this rather bifurcated, even schizophrenic approach to the complex world of human failings, which keeps prosocial values reserved only for those who have been deemed righteous by some human power structure. The problem with his approach, however, is the implied limitation of many of these methods of interaction to fellow Jews. See Cordovero, *Tomer Devorah*, 13–17. This is an old crux in Jewish tradition, and parallels exist in the other monotheistic faiths. In all of them, traditional ethical language usually circumscribes many of the most important ethical principles to fellow believers, "those who accept Allah," or who call themselves Muslims, or those who are "brothers and sisters in the body of Christ," and so forth. It certainly affects the ethical values that today would be vital in establishing universal human rights, the essential problem of a group that has a "special" relationship to God. And yet, I have argued elsewhere that we cannot escape the need of ethnic groups, and the need of religious groups, to feel special, unique. Ethical values for most people cannot be simple Kantian categorical propositions. There must be special categories of care for those to whom one feels closer. The problem is that in many traditional structures the result is serious prejudice and double standards. Thus, we suggest study of the prosocial side of these traditions in the areas of forgiveness and peacemaking and evaluation of its effectiveness, and argue, if appropriate, for extending the application of these values to nonbelievers. Many believers today would welcome the study, while others will fiercely reject reaching

out to nonbelievers. But this is a much larger problem that I have begun to address elsewhere. See Marc Gopin, *Between Eden and Armageddon: The Future of World Religions, Violence, and Peacemaking* (New York: Oxford University Press, 2000).

46. See Abdullah Yusuf Ali, ed. and trans., *The Holy Qur'an, Text, Translation and Commentary* (Brentwood, Md.: Amana, 1989), Surah 2:109, n. 110. Scholars should investigate the connection between this last notion of divine forgiveness as a covering and the biblical and rabbinic notion of *over al pesha*, or *moheh pesha*, mentioned earlier.

47. Technically there are two different sins here. One is straight idolatry, that is, believing in many deities. But there is also sin in henotheism, believing in a pantheon, even if Allah or God would be the head of that pantheon. The Christian trinity would also be included here, as another example of joining Allah to other gods. The Jewish perspective is similar.

48. See Rabia Terri Harris, "Nonviolence in Islam: The Alternative Community Tradition," in *Subverting Hatred: The Challenge of Nonviolence in Religious Traditions*, ed. D. Smith-Christopher (Boston: Boston Research Center for the Twenty-first Century, 1998), 95–114.

49. Bawa Muhaiyaden, *Islam and World Peace: Explanations of a Sufi* (Philadelphia: Fellowship Press, 1987), 34, as cited in Harris, "Nonviolence in Islam," 111. Muhaiyadeen is a Sri Lankan, a minority caught in the middle of larger Hindu-Buddhist violence. This is striking and confirms for me, as do other cases, that ideal peacemakers emerge as minorities in situations where larger forces battle each other, often providing the sensitive religious observer a unique perspective from which to interpret his/her own tradition.

50. Of course, this is to be distinguished from a historian's efforts to understand a text in its *sitz im leben*, a task entirely different from the one facing the believer when he/she has to decide what to really believe when it comes to matters of life and death, what is at the heart of the tradition and what is at the periphery, and where the will of God really lies, all questions of interpretation in the context of the most fundamental faith decisions. Despite the fact that the Abrahamic traditions appear to pre-arrange these decisions for the believer, this is far from the case when it comes to life's very hard questions about violence and peace. Centuries-old traditions, in their sheer size, can circumscribe the range of interpretation, but they cannot prevent individual interpretation about the hard choices. There are just too many voices in these traditions. Of course, part of our challenge is the many combatants who live within fundamentalist *social* expressions of these religions, wherein every effort is made to prevent individual interpretation. But even here the diversity of the responses to basic questions of peace and violence is impressive.

51. I have included this sub-section in the larger discussion of Islam, but the results apply equally to intervention in other religious communities.

52. On the importance of empowerment in conflict resolution, or specifically in conflict transformation, see B. Bush and J. Folger, *The Promise of Mediation* (San Francisco: Jossey-Bass, 1994).

53. *Avot of Rabbi Nathan* 23:1.

54. See also Gopin, *Between Eden and Armaggedon*, 191–192, on the role of gender and peacemaking. I have to mention here just how remarkable was the frequency with which Chairman Arafat used the phrase "peace of the brave" in almost every speech and commentary that he made during the past few years. One tired reporter said to me, "If he says 'peace of the brave' one more time I'm gonna punch him." Now, the political language of speech writers is often dull and nauseatingly repeti-

tive. Some cynics argued that Arafat has limited English and has few phrases at his disposal to describe the process whenever asked by reporters. But I believe differently. I think he is a very smart man, who knows his culture well, whatever other criticisms we have of him and his actions. He knows that diverting a community from war to peace requires a perpetual hermeneutic reworking of what it means to be brave. Bravery is the essence of a fight for "justice," a *jihad*, which must be translated into a new emotion for peacetime. And the quote from the Qu'ran was one small part of his effort to accomplish this cultural shift. Here we see, from the textual evidence, that both Jewish and Islamic sources have done the same thing at various times. Of course, Arafat has failed to adhere to his own advocacy of nonviolent bravery, which is at least one part of the current challenge.

55. On suspension of judgment, see, for example, Matt. 7:1–5 and the Jewish source, Pirkei Avot 2:4, the statement of Hillel, "Do not judge your fellow until (or unless) you have been in his place (or life circumstances)." Both sources refer to figures from the same period of Jewish history, the beginning of the first millennium.

56. "Yahya related to me from Malik that Yahya ibn Said said that he heard Said ibn al-Musayyab say, 'Shall I tell you what is better than much prayer and *sadaqa*?' They said, 'Yes.' He said, 'Mending discord. And beware of hatred—it strips you (of your *deen*)'" (*Malik's Muwatta* 47.1.17).

57. *Hallal* is also a word referring to Islamic food that is considered acceptable for eating. Once again the parallels of the lived religion of Judaism and Islam are extraordinary. *Kosher* is the proper word regarding Jewish food that can be legally eaten. But it also is used both rabbinically, and in today's lived Judaism, as a moral descriptor. A *koshere yid* in Yiddish is a Jew who is a good, God-fearing person.

58. George Irani, "Rituals of Reconciliation: Arab-Islamic Persectives," delivered at the United States of Peace (unpublished), p. 3. For an updated version, see Irani, "Rituals of Reconciliation: Arab-Islamic Persectives," *Mind and Human Interaction*, vol. 2, no. 4 (2001); 226–45. See also Nathan Funk and George Irani, "Rituals of Reconciliation: Arab-Islamic Perspectives," *Kroc Institute Occasional Paper* no. 19 (August, 2000); and Elias Jabbour, *Sulha: Palestinian Traditional Peacemaking Process* (Montreal, N.C.: House of Hope, 1996).

59. Irani, "Rituals of Reconciliation," p. 27.

60. In my consultation with Rabbi Menahem Froman, he said he spoke with certain radical Islamic leaders about peace, and they responded with the possibility of declaring a *hodna* between Jews and Arabs on the West Bank. Now skeptics, and those in the Jewish community who do not trust the Arab and Islamic community, immediately see in this a trick, not authentic peace, a legal gimmick but no real acceptance. But Froman, understanding the subtlety of religious legal categories, hermeneutics, and trust-building, was eager to embrace a stage-by-stage process of religious treaties. He did not see it as a trick, but as a first step that naturally could be legally reneged—as all first steps can be—but a step that would significantly advance the drive toward trust with even the most militant rejectionists. The stage of *hodna* could lead to more intimate relations and more just living arrangements, which could in turn translate into other legal categories of Islam involving open-ended treaties that would postpone the militant dream of an all-embracing domination of the non-Muslim other to a distant future. Personal Interview, Menahem Froman, Tekoa, West Bank, April 1998.

61. In my training of Islamic students in 1999, we had occasion to compare different forms of *diya*, and it turned out that in at least one country the *diya* involved a number of women going from the clan of the perpetrator to be taken as wives by the clan

of the victims, as compensation for murder. Now I raised in class, on this basis, one of the classic dilemmas of intercultural conflict resolution. How far do you go in submitting or adhering to cultural practices of reconciliation, if those practices violate the basic standards of individual human rights, which the intervenor may believe to be the non-negotiable basis for any civil society? How much weight should one put on the opinions of the people whose rights are being violated, such as the women in this case? Or is it a matter of principle, whether or not these women submit to their own transfer to another tribe? To put it more simply, what if your peacemaking methods are a gross violation of justice to certain individuals? This question is barely being addressed currently, with dogmatism as the only solution on all sides of the debate, and very little subtle analysis of how we as human beings should confront fundamental moral dilemmas. My personal answer, for the record, is that I could never support such a *diya*, no matter how much I wanted to respect a local culture. On the other hand, if the compromise prevented a massive outbreak of hostilities involving many deaths of men, women and children, I would have to think long and hard, with deep knowledge of all possibilities in the situation, before I would decide what to support. I come with my own "prejudice," that the violent loss of innocent lives should be avoided at all costs and may be more significant morally than the suppression of some people's freedom of choice. Imagining such "impossible" choices would be a healthy— if aggravating—conflict resolution training device. For this devolves into dilemmas involving noninterference duties of third parties and no-win "lifeboat" ethics questions to which there are no clear answers. Conflict resolution theory and practice would advance further if we all started facing these questions rather than hiding from them.

62. Mohammed Abu-Nimer regularly conducts conflict resolution training in which he has the members of the group sign a contract to enforce whatever principles that they agree as a group will govern their training class. This is a fascinating hermeneutic reworking of a traditional context. But it is also a very modern enactment of John Locke's notion of social contract as the basis for society's existence and moral integrity. The traditional context of culture takes for granted rules of cultural engagement that have always been assumed by everyone, and the process of *sulh* ritualizes it. When Abu-Nimer conducts his training with people who may or may not be traditional, who may or may not share any cultural principles, he effectively recreates or creates anew a culture of the classroom, based upon his contractual model of human social integrity. When we have trained together, as many as fifteen cultures from around the world have been represented in the classroom, which thus serves as a fascinating laboratory of global community and social contract in a self-consciously multireligious context (observations based on co-teaching with Abu-Nimer, May 1997). Abu-Nimer has struggled with this question of contract. See his "Conflict Resolution in an Islamic Context," *Peace and Change* 21, no. 1 (January 1996): 22–40.

63. Non-Arab cultures of the Middle East merit much deeper investigation in this regard. One of my students, Neamatollah Nojumi, has alerted me, through some fine research, to a traditional elite body called the Loya Jirgah, which played a critical role in nonviolent conflict resolution in the past in Afghanistan. The war in Afghanistan of 2001 has now made this institution quite well known. This should be investigated for future possibilities and even for some insights into the current conflict within the country and between it and other countries. See Afghanistan Loyah Jirgah, *Loyah Jirgah (Grand Assembly): Documents* (Kabul: Afghanistan Today, 1987).

64. See http://www.planet.edu/~alaslah. They claim to have mediated over a thousand disputes, resolving 87 percent of them. *Sulh* figures prominently in their literature, and they seem to have a good reputation. Not surprisingly, the larger conflict

between Israelis and Palestinians, or Jews and Christians and Muslims, is addressed less successfully in their literature. The Israelis were referred to on their website collectively as "the Oppressor" and Palestinians as "the oppressed." The use of the singular to describe both sides eliminates effectively the possibilities of distinguishing members of the groups, and acknowledging rights and wrongs committed by individuals. Singular language for large groups of people, in general, is the tool of stereotype and is thus inherently conflict generating. The Israeli soldiers are referred to as "toy soldiers" of the Oppressor. Of course, the dehumanized language depicting the enemy hardly reflects the subtle attention to conflict resolution psychology that characterizes the rest of their literature. This is unfortunate, reflecting the general failure thus far of the international conflict resolution community to intervene in any effective way that humanizes both sides of the Arab/Israeli conflict. Such dehumanized language is understandable and even expected from victims of oppression, no matter what their conflict resolution training may be. But it is less forgivable from the outside community of religious peacemakers who, with a paltry few, unfunded exceptions, have truly failed to become an effective bridge of peacemaking, unlike their role among warring Christians in Ireland, for example. Their presence could help steer mediation methods in a better direction. Western conflict resolvers, culturally Christian, have natural tendencies to build bridges to both sides in Europe, Latin America, and Africa. But this does not hold in the case of Israel, curiously. I believe it has roots in old, unacknowledged Christian fear of and antagonism toward Jews and their problems, and this has served poorly the needs of peacemaking in the Arab/Israeli conflict. Western, Christian progressives do not like to admit that they carry around old cultural problems, but we all do. In general, peacemakers who are religious have trouble extending their wisdom beyond their own religious/tribal/cultural affiliations. This is one of our principal challenges and ongoing failings in terms of conflict resolution practice. Just as an interesting technical exercise, one will find, in tracing the "hits" on Infoseek, that as of 1999, the Mennonite Central Committee cites enthusiastically the religious work of *sulha*, and the work of Wi'am as a Christian Palestinian organization. I will be glad to be proved wrong, but I have found no links between MCC and Rabbis for Human Rights, or Oz ve-Shalom, or the Open House in Ramle, in other words, with Jewish religious peacemakers. There is actually some good Jewish-Christian peace work taking place in Israel, with the Catholic Church and other bodies. Oddly, the historic Peace Churches are largely absent from this crucial bridge building to the Jewish community. Israelis note this well and, therefore, often tell me that they do not see them as peace churches at all. That is a sad, wasteful, and useless division of religious peacemakers.

65. Report e-mailed by Christian Peacemaker Teams, Hebron, 3/7/97.

66. Rabbi Froman has remarked to me that, more than signed agreements between rabbis and sheikhs, he is interested in securing the lasting image of rabbis and sheikhs embracing each other in a public ceremony. He believes—rightly I think—that the psychological impact of such an event on believers would be far more important than the written treaty. He is looking to transform the psychological/spiritual construct of our religious worlds, opening up millions of believers on both sides to a new spiritual understanding of the enemy "other."

67. I refer here to the periodic forced disputations and forced sermons inflicted upon a large number of Jewish communities in European history. Jews, to keep their synagogues open, would be forced to listen to church emissaries go on in rich detail, in the Jewish synagogues themselves and during services, about how Jews were going to hell if they did not accept Jesus. Even my parents and many others of their generation have reported to me that they were forced in U.S. public schools in the 1930s to

sing Christian songs and were threatened with punishment for failing to comply. It was at this time that public schools made prayer compulsory and could espouse religion, both of which the Christian Right would like to reinstitute.

Chapter 7

1. See fuller discussion of this in ch. 1.

2. Let me emphasize that "success" for me does not mean a happy encounter in which there is no fighting. I think fighting is necessary and important for conflict resolution processes. But these processes require careful guidance and skilled mediation. My disappointment with the large group encounter is that it disempowers many decent intermediaries. There are certainly a range of skills in the field, and some manage large groups better than others. But it is an inescapable fact of both dialogic encounter between enemies, and the educational encounter as such, that large numbers detract from the quality of the encounter. Worse still, I have seen too many people, especially in the Arab/Israeli conflict, leave a large dialogue convinced—where they were not before—that peace is impossible. Something is wrong, then, with the obsession with dialogue as the equivalent of peacemaking—certainly in the Middle East.

3. See Marc Gopin, "Forward," in Shireen Hunter, *The Future of Islam and the West* (Westport, Conn.: Praeger, 1998), vi–xi.

4. See Robert Chazan, "Jewish Suffering: The Interplay of Medieval Christian and Jewish Perspectives," *Occasional Papers II*, Trinity College (1998). On the general attitude of the church right up to the nineteenth century, in which forced sermons continued though less frequently, see David Kertzer, *The Kidnapping of Edgardo Mortara* (Newbury Park, Calif.: Vintage, 1998).

5. Abraham Sperling, *Sefer Ta'ame ha-Minhagim u-Mekore ha-Dinnim* (Jerusalem: Eshkol, n.d.), 498.

6. Ibid., 495, 502, 507, 544.

Chapter 8

1. Gen. 6:8, 34:11; Exod. 11:3; Esther 2:17. On charisma or grace as the most valued human asset, see Prov. 22:1. It is a difficult word to translate but includes the meanings of grace, benevolence and favor, but with a special attachment to the facial metaphor. On the relationship of *hen* (favor) with pity or compassion, *tahanunim*, see Zech. 12:10. Zechariah has a vision of God who brings destruction on other peoples who are near Jerusalem, but who, at the same time, fills the House of David and the inhabitants of Jerusalem with a spirit of *hen ve'tahanunim*, "grace and compassion," as they lament over the dead of the *other* peoples, as if the dead were their own children, their own favored son or firstborn. This suggests a powerful prophetic precedent for the extension of *hen* to enemies, especially in the context of Jerusalem.

2. See Stuart Altmann, "The Structure of Primate Communication," in *Social Communication Among Primates*, ed. Stuart Altmann (Chicago: University of Chicago Press, 1967), 325–62; N. G. Blurton Jones, "An Ethological Study of Some Aspects of Social Behaviour of Children in Nursery School," in *Primate Ethology*, ed. Desmond Morris (Chicago: Aldine, 1967), 347–68. See generally David B. Givens, "Eye Contact," in *The Nonverbal Dictionary of Gestures, Signs, and Body Language Cues* (2000), at http://members.aol.com/nonverbal3/refs.htm, visited 11/17/00.

3. Lev. 19:32; 19:15; Exod. 23:3.

4. See Deut. 28:50 and Dan. 8:23, on evil empires and rulers in terms of this characteristic; T.B. Ta'anit 7b; Otsar Midrashim Messiah 3.

5. See Ps. 34:17 on the face of God and the destruction of the wicked, but Ps. 42:3 on the desire to see the face of God. On beseeching the face of God and prayer, see I Kings 13:6; II Kings 13:4. On the face of God and destruction, see also Jer. 3:12; Ezek. 15:17. Ps. 27:8 suggests a powerful reconciliation through the metaphor of the face. "On Your behalf has my heart said, 'Seek My face'; Your Face will I seek."

6. Deut. 7:2.

7. See in general Majid Fakhry, *Ethical Theories in Islam* (Leiden: Brill, 1994). Being honored is a coveted experience but depends, according to the Qur'an, on righteousness, Surah 49:13; 95:4. Entering into another's home is a particular point of interaction that is either respectful or not. It is vital in Islamic ethics that this be done with honor and respect (see Surah 24:27–29), since it relates strongly in context to sexual morality, but also, clear from the text, it involves the basic dignity of the home. Note also *Malik's Muwatta*, Book 49, Number 49.3.4:

Yahya related to me from Malik from Yahya ibn Said that Said ibn al-Musayyub said, "Ibrahim, may Allah bless him and grant him peace, was the first to give hospitality to the guest and the first person to be circumcised and the first person to trim the moustache and the first person to see grey hair. He said, "O Lord! What is this?" Allah the Blessed, the Exalted, said, "It is dignity, Ibrahim." He said, 'Lord, increase me in dignity!'

On honor as an Arab value predating Islam, see Reuven Firestone, *Jihad: The Origin of Holy War in Islam* (New York: Oxford University Press, 1999), 30–31.

8. The most famous quote is "Ben Zoma said, 'Who is honored? He who honors all God's creatures" (M. Avot 4:1). Note also, for example, Midrash Shohar Tov 17, "Rabbi Joshua ben Levi said, 'When a human being walks down the street a coterie of angels go before him, proclaiming and announcing: Make way for the image of God' (based on Gen. 5:1)!"

9. See, for example, Yair Sheleg, "From Yiddishkeit to Yeshivashram," *Ha'aretz*, September 29, 2000; idem, "Faith Healers," *Ha'aretz*, April 21, 2000.

10. *Tractate Derekh Eretz Zuta* 1; *Avot of Rabbi Nathan* 15; For a representative collection of rabbinic approaches to humility, see Moshe Chayim Luzzatto, *The Path of the Just*, trans. Shraga Silverstein (Jerusalem: Feldheim, 1969), ch. 22. There are numerous sources on silence and its relationship to understanding. See Midrash Rabbah (ed. Margoliot) Lev. 16:5; Midrash Tanhuma (ed. Warsaw) *Va'ye'tseh* 6; Otsar Midrashim Alpha Beta d'Ben Sira, paragraph 19; Tractate Derekh Erets Zuta 7; T.B. Pesahim 99a.

11. See, for example, Qur'an 7:161; 57:16.

12. See Midrash Rabbah Deut. 7:12; Midrash Tanhuma (ed. Warsaw), Bereshit 4, Vay'erah 8, Ki Tisah 15.

13. Numbers 12:3.

14. See Marc Gopin, "The Religious Component of Mennonite Peacemaking and Its Global Implications," in *From the Ground Up: Mennonite Contributions to International Peacebuilding*, ed. Cynthia Sampson and John Paul Lederach (New York: Oxford University Press, 2000), 233–55.

15. See the Mideast Citizen Diplomacy website: http://www.mideastdiplomacy.org.

16. See, for example, Iris Kraus, "Shot Palestinian boy's organs donated," *Ha'aretz*, Monday, November 17, 1997, on the family of Ali Jawarish, a seven year-old boy shot

by an Israeli soldier, who donated his organs to save lives. These gestures are rare events, but instead of being a blip on the news such gestures should be become centerpieces of change. The people who make these gestures should be the heroes of the peacebuilding community, and supported by the international community. Most importantly, their radical gestures can become the paradigm for more moderate, easy to replicate, moral and symbolic gestures for others embroiled in the conflict.

17. See http://www.openhouse.org.il/holart.htm, visited 1/02/01. Dahlia's original letter to the son of the owner of the house, who was in prison for an act of terrorism, created a sensation when it first was published. See Dahlia Landau, "A Letter to a Deportee," *Jerusalem Post*, January 15, 1988.

18. The Caux center is organized by work teams, with the specific intention of creating relationships through shared work. This is cost-effective, equalizing of relationships, and a powerful, non-dialogic way of developing relationships.

19. See Job 1:21. On the text of the Jewish ceremony for the death of loved ones, referred to as Tsiduk ha-Din, or "acknowledgment of divine justice," see Phillip Birnbaum, *The Daily Prayer Book:Ha-Siddur Ha-Shalem* (New York: Hebrew Publishing Company, 1977), 735–40. On the laws governing recitation of the blessing of acknowledgment of a just God in the face of death, see Aaron Felder, *Yesodei Semachos* (New York: Felder, 1974), 1–2.

20. Gen. 27:1.

21. Gen. Rabbah 65:10. The simple meaning of the biblical text is that Isaac lost vision in old age, but the legend takes the biblical message in a different direction.

22. "When others harm us, it gives us the chance to practice patience. . . . Since it is our enemies who give us this great opportunity, in reality they are helping us." Tenzin Gyatso, *A Flash of Lightening in the Dark of Night: A Guide to the Bodhisattva's Way of Life* (Boston: Shambhala, 1994), 64.

23. On Gandhi's experiments with getting each religious group to facilitate the ritual observances of the other groups, see Mohandas Gandhi, *An Autobiography: The Story of My Experiments with Truth* (1927, 1929; rpt. Boston: Beacon Press, 1957), 331.

24. Deut. 16:14.

25. It should be noted that the acceptance in the 1950s of German reparations by the Israeli Knesset caused one of the most serious threats to Jewish Israel's internal stability in the entire history of the state. None other than Menahem Begin led the charge and struck a deep chord with the Israeli public. See Ehud Sprinzak, *Brother against Brother: Violence and Extremism in Israeli Politics from Altalena to the Rabin Assasination* (New York: Free Press, 1999), ch. 2.

Chapter 9

1. See Lamia Lahood, "PA Minister: Intifada Was Planned since July," *Jerusalem Post*, March 4, 2001, p. 2.

2. See generally Kevin Avruch, *Culture and Conflict Resolution* (Washington, D.C.: U.S. Institute of Peace, 1998).

3. I use the terms "reconciliation," "rapprochement," and "relationship restoration" interchangeably and only as examples. Each cultural approach to this subject contains nuances that veer it in the direction of one or more linguistic descriptors. I use several here not to be imprecise but to model an openness to varied cultural descriptions and methods of peacemaking.

Chapter 10

1. Kevin Avruch, *Culture and Conflict Resolution* (Washington, D.C.: U.S. Institute of Peace Press, 1998), 5–21.

2. Ibid., 18–19.

3. I should mention here also that, based on my observations of numerous enemy encounters, in addition to interviews, it seems to me that sometimes a sequential approach to gestures works better than simultaneous gestures. One provokes the other. The problem with sequential gestures is that the one who goes first risks the shame brought on if the other does not reciprocate. I leave this as an interesting challenge that should be thought through and decided upon based on particular contexts.

Bibliography

Abu-Nimer, Mohammed. "Conflict Resolution in an Islamic Context." *Peace and Change* 21, no. 1 (January 1996), 22–40.

Albright, J. S., M. R. McMinn, and K. R. Meek. "Religious Orientation, Guilt, Confession, and Forgiveness." *Journal of Psychology and Theology* 23 (1995): 190–197. As cited in *Dimensions of Forgiveness Psychological Research and Theological Perspectives*, edited by Everett L. Worthington. Philadelphia: Templeton Foundation Press, 1998, 264–66.

Ali, Abdullah Yusuf, ed. and trans. *The Holy Qur'an: Text, Translation and Commentary*. Brentwood, Md.: Amana, 1989.

Altmann, Stuart. "The Structure of Primate Communication." In *Social Communication among Primates*, ed. Stuart Altmann. Chicago: University of Chicago Press, 1967, 325–62.

Avruch, Kevin. *Culture and Conflict Resolution*. Washington, D.C.: U.S. Institute of Peace, 1998.

Benamozegh, Elijah. *Israel and Humanity*. Trans. Maxwell Luria. New York: Paulist Press, 1994.

Berman, Phyllis Ocean, and Arthur Ocean Waskow. *Tales of Tikkun: New Jewish Stories to Heal the Wounded World*. Northvale, N.J.: Jason Aronson, 1996.

Bialik, Hayim, and Yehoshua Ravnitzky, eds. *The Book of Legends*. Trans. by William Braude. New York: Schocken, 1992.

Birnbaum, Philip. *The Birnbaum Haggadah*. New York: Hebrew Publishing Company, 1976.

Birnbaum, Philip, trans. and annotator. *Daily Prayer Book: Ha-Siddur Ha-Shalem*. New York: Hebrew Publishing Company, 1977.

Bjorkqvist, Kaj, and Douglas P. Fry, eds. *Cultural Variation in Conflict Resolution: Alternatives to Violence*. Mahwah, N.J.: Erlbaum, 1997.

Blurton Jones, N. G. "An Ethological Study of Some Aspects of Social Behaviour of Children in Nursery School." In *Primate Ethology*, ed. Desmond Morris. Chicago: Aldine, 1967, 347–68.

Boyarin, Daniel. *Unheroic Conduct: The Rise of Heterosexuality and the Invention of the Jewish Man*. Berkeley: University of California Press, 1997.

Branson, Louise, and Dusko Doder. *Milosevic: Portrait of a Tyrant*. New York: Free Press, 1999.

Bush, B., and J. Folger. *The Promise of Mediation*. San Francisco: Jossey-Bass, 1994.

Chazan, Robert. "Jewish Suffering: The Interplay of Medieval Christian and Jewish Perspectives." *Occasional Papers II*, Trinity College, 1998.

Clement of Rome. "Harmony and Cooperation." In *Early Christian Writings*, trans. Maxwell Staniforth. New York: Penguin, 1978, 33–35.

Conzelman, Hans. *Gentiles, Jews, Christians: Polemics and Apologetics in the Greco-Roman Era*. Trans. M. Eugene Boring. Minneapolis: Fortress, 1992.

Cordovero, Rabbi Moshe. *Tomer Devorah*. Venice, 1588; repr. New York: Feldheim, 1993.

Coser, L. A. *Continuities in the Study of Social Conflict*. New York: Free Press, 1967.

Coyle, Catherine T., and Robert D. Enright. "Researching the Process Model of Forgiveness within Psychological Interventions." In *Dimensions of Forgiveness: Psychological Research and Theological Perspectives*, ed. Everett L. Worthington. Philadelphia: Templeton Foundation Press, 1998, 139–61.

Demetrios, Julius, Joseph Montvill, and Vamik Volkan, eds. *The Psychodynamics of International Relationships*. Lexington, MA: Lexington Mass.: 1991.

Deutsch, Morton. "Constructive Conflict Resolution: Principles, Training, and Research." In *The Handbook of Interethnic Coexistence*, ed. by Eugene Weiner. New York: Continuum, 1998, 199–216.

Docherty, Jayne. "When the Parties Bring Their Gods to the Table: Learning Lessons from Waco." Ph.D. diss., George Mason University, 1998.

Edwards, Mark et al., eds. *Apologetics in the Roman Empire: Pagans, Jews and Christians*. New York: Oxford University Press, 1999.

Fakhry, Majid. *Ethical Theories in Islam*. Leiden: Brill, 1994.

Felder, Aaron. *Yesodei Semachos*. New York: Felder, 1974.

Firestone, Reuven. *Jihad: The Origin of Holy War in Islam*. New York: Oxford University Press, 1999.

Fishbane, Michael. *The Exegetical Imagination: On Jewish Thought and Theology*. Cambridge, Mass.: Harvard University Press, 1998.

Froman, Rabbi Menachem. "A Modest Proposal." *Jerusalem Report*, October 25, 1999, p. 55; also appears at http://www.capitaloftheworld.org/essays/00/09/14/0843231.shtml

Funk, Nathan, and George Irani. "Rituals of Reconciliation: Arab-Islamic Perspectives." *Kroc Institute Occasional Paper*, no. 19 (August 2000).

Gadamer, Hans. *Truth and Method*. 2nd rev. ed. Trans. by Joel Weinsheimer and Donald G. Marshall. New York: Crossroad, 1989.

Gandhi, Mohandas. *An Autobiography: The Story of My Experiments with Truth*. 1927, 1929; Repr. Boston: Beacon Press, 1957.

Gandhi, Rajmohan. "Hinduism and Peacebuilding." In *Religion and Peacebuilding*. ed. Harold Coward and Gordon Smith, New York: SUNY Press, 2002.

Geertz, Clifford. *The Interpretation of Cultures*. HarperCollins, 1973.

Geisler, Norman. *Baker Encyclopedia of Christian Apologetics*. Grand Rapids, Mich.: Baker, 1999.

Gerondi, Jonah. *The Gates of Repentance*. Jerusalem: Feldheim, 1976.

Gibb, H. A. R., and J. H. Kramers. *Shorter Encyclopedia of Islam*. Leiden: Brill, 1991.

Girard, René. *Violence and the Sacred*. Trans. by Patrick Gregory. Baltimore: Johns Hopkins University Press, 1979.

Givens, David B. *The Nonverbal Dictionary of Gestures, Signs, and Body Language Cues*. At http: //members.aol.com/nonverbal2/diction1.htm, visited 11/17/00.

Glassé, Cyril. *The Concise Encyclopedia of Islam*. San Francisco: Harper and Row, 1989.

Goleman, Daniel. *Emotional Intelligence*. New York: Bantam, 1994.

Golwalker, M. S. *Bunch of Thoughts*. Bangalore: Vikram Prakshan, 1966

Gopin, Marc. *Between Eden and Armageddon: The Future of World Religions, Violence, and Peacemaking*. New York: Oxford University Press, 2000.

————. "Forward." In Shireen Hunter, *The Future of Islam and the West*. Westport, Conn.: Praeger, 1998, vii–xi.

————. "The Religious Component of Mennonite Peacemaking and Its Global Implications." In *From the Ground Up: Mennonite Contributions to International Peacebuilding*, ed. Cynthia Sampson and John Paul Lederach. New York: Oxford University Press, 2000, 233–55.

————. "Share Jerusalem or Battle Forever." *Boston Globe*. September 24, 2000, "Focus" section, 2.

Griswold, Frank. "Listening with the Ear of the Heart." *Crosscurrents* 49:1 (1999), 16–18.

Gyatso, Tenzin. *A Flash of Lightening in the Dark of Night: A Guide to the Bodhisattva's Way of Life*. Boston: Shambhala, 1994.

Halter, Marek. *Stories of Deliverance: Speaking with Men and Women Who Rescued Jews from the Holocaust*. Trans. by M. Bernard. Chicago: Open Court, Carus, 1998.

Harris, Rabia Terri. "Nonviolence in Islam: The Alternative Community Tradition." In *Subverting Hatred: The Challenge of Nonviolence in Religious Tradtions*. ed. by D. Smith-Christopher. Boston: Boston Research Center for the Twenty-first Century, 1998, 95–114.

Hashmi, Sohail. "Interpreting the Islamic Ethics of War and Peace." In *The Ethics of War and Peace*, ed. Terry Nardin, Princeton, N.J.: Princeton University Press, 1996, 146–66.

Henderson, Michael. *The Forgiveness Factor*. London: Grosvenor, 1996.

Hughes, Thomas. *A Dictionary of Islam*. London, Allen: 1895.

Ignatieff, Michael. *The Warrior's Honor: Ethnic War and the Modern Conscience*. New York: Metropolitan, 1998.

Irani, George. "Rituals of Reconciliation: Arab-Islamic Perspectives." *Mind and Human Interaction*, vol. 2, no. 4 (2001): 226–245

Jabbour, Elias. *Sulha: Palestinian Traditional Peacemaking Process*. Montreat, N.C.: House of Hope, 1996.

Jirgah, Loyah Afghanistan. *Loyah Jirgah (Grand Assembly): Documents*. Kabul: Afghanistan Today, 1987.

Julius, Demetrios, Joseph Montville, and Vamik Volkan, eds. *The Psychodynamics of International Relationships*. Lexington, Mass.: Lexington Books, 1990.

Kakar, Sudhir. *The Colors of Violence: Cultural Identities, Religion, and Conflict*. Chicago: University of Chcago Press, 1996.

Kalina, Joseph. *A Holocaust Odyssey*. Lanham, Md.: University Press of America, 1995.

Kertzer, David. *The Kidnapping of Edgardo Mortara*. Newbury Park, Calif.: Vintage, 1998.

Kook, Abraham Isaac. *Abraham Isaac Kook: The Lights of Penitence, the Moral Principles, Lights of Holiness, Essays, Letters and Poems*. Compiled and translated by Ben Zion Bokser. New York: Paulist Press, 1978.

Kraus, Iris. "Shot Palestinian boy's organs donated." *Ha'aretz*, November 17, 1997. A7.

Kraybill, Ron. "Peacebuilders in Zimbabwe: An Anabaptist Paradigm for Conflict Transformation." Ph.D. diss., University of Capetown, 1996.

Lahood, Lamia. "PA Minister: Intifada Was Planned since July." *Jerusalem Post*, March 4, 2001.

Lamm, Norman. *The Religious Thought of Hasidism: Text and Commentary*. New York: Yeshiva University Press, 1999.

Landau, Dahlia. "A Letter to a Deportee." *Jerusalem Post*, January 15, 1988.

Landes, Richard, and Arthur P. Mandel. *Vision and Violence*. Ann Arbor: University of Michigan Press, 1992.

Lederach, J. P. "Beyond Violence: Building Sustainable Peace." In *The Handbook of Interethnic Coexistence*, ed. by Eugene Weiner. New York: Continuum, 1998, 242–45.

———. *Preparing for Peace: Conflict Transformation across Cultures*. Syracuse, N.Y.: Syracuse University Press, 1995.

Loewe, Rabbi Judah. *Tiferet Yisroel*. Jerusalem: Mekhon Yerushalayim, 1999.

Luzzatto, Moshe Chayim. *The Path of the Just*. Trans. Shraga Silverstein. Jerusalem: Feldheim, 1969.

Maimonides, Mishneh Torah, Hilchot Teshuvah: A New Translation and Commentary. Trans. Rabbi Eliyahu Touger. New York: Maznaim, 1987.

Manuel, Frank. *The Broken Staff: Judaism through Christian Eyes*. Cambridge, Mass.: Harvard University Press, 1992.

Mejor, Marek. "Suffering, Buddhist Views of Origination of." In *Routledge Encyclopedia of Philosophy*, ed. Edward Craig. London: Routledge, 1998.

Michaud, Ellen. "Add Years to Your Life: Learn to Forgive." *Prevention* (January 1999).

Muhaiyaden, Bawa. *Islam and World Peace: Explanations of a Sufi*. Philadelphia: Fellowship Press, 1987.

Nudler, Oscar. "On Conflicts and Metaphors: Toward an Extended Rationality." In *Conflict: Human Needs Theory*, ed. by John Burton. New York: St. Martin's, 1990, 177–204.

Orhot Tzadikim. Jerusalem: Eshkol, 1946.

Peli, Pinchas. *Soloveitchik on Repentance: The Thought and Oral Discourses of Rabbi Joseph B. Soloveitchik*. New York: Paulist Press, 1984.

Pre'an, Vilem, and Stanislav Kovr'nok, eds. *Vatik'n a Slovensk' Republika, Dokumenty*. Bratislava: Slovak Academic Press, 1992.

Scherman, Nosson R., ed. and trans. *The Complete Artscroll Machzor Yom Kippur*. Brooklyn, N.Y.: Mesorah, 1986.

Schirch, Lisa. "Ritual Peacebuilding: Creating Contexts Conducive to Conflict Transformation." Ph.D. diss., George Mason University, 1999.

Schwartz, Regina. *The Curse of Cain: The Violent Legacy of Monotheism*. Chicago: University of Chicago Press, 1997.

Sheleg, Yair. "Faith Healers." *Ha'aretz*, April 21, 2000.

———. "From Yiddishkeit to Yeshivashram." *Ha'aretz*. September 29, 2000.

Simic, Charles. "Anatomy of a Murderer." *New York Review of Books*. January 20, 2000, B2.

Soloveitchik, Joseph. "Kol Dodi Dofek." In *In Aloneness, in Togetherness: A Selection of Hebrew Writings*. Ed. with an introduction by Pinchas Peli. Jerusalem: Orot, 1976, 359–62.

Sperling, Abraham. *Sefer Ta'ame ha-Minhagim u-Mekore ha-Dinnim*. Jerusalem: Eshkol, n.d.

Sprinzak, Ehud. *Brother against Brother: Violence and Extremism in Israeli Politics from Altalena to the Rabin Assassination*. New York: Free Press, 1999.

Tamaret, Aaron Samuel. "Herut." In *Pacifism and Torah: Works by Aaron Samuel Tamaret* (Hebrew). Ed. Ehud Luz. Jerusalem: Dinur Center, 1992, 125–42.

Tanakh: The Holy Scriptures. Philadelphia: Jewish Publication Society, 1985.

Trautner-Kormann, Hanne. *Shield and Sword: Jewish Polemics Against Christianity and Christians in France and Spain from 1100 to 1500*. Tübingen: Mohr, 1993.

Waskow, Arthur. *Seasons of Our Joy*. Toronto: Bantam, 1982.

Wolf, Miroslav. *Exclusiveness and Embrace*. Nashville: Abingdon Press, 1996.

Worthington, Everett L., ed. *Dimensions of Forgiveness: Psychological Research and Theological Perspectives*. Philadelphia: Templeton Foundation Press, 1998.

Yusuf Ali, Abdullah, trans. *The Holy Qur'an: Text, Translation and Commentary*. Brentwood, Md.: Amana Corporation, 1989.

Zornberg, Avivah. *Genesis: The Beginning of Desire*. Philadelphia: Jewish Publication Society, 1995.

Index